SENNACHERIB, KING OF ASSYRIA

ARCHAEOLOGY AND BIBLICAL STUDIES

Brian B. Schmidt, General Editor

Editorial Board:
Aaron Brody
Annie Caubet
Billie Jean Collins
Israel Finkelstein
André Lemaire
Amihai Mazar
Herbert Niehr
Christoph Uehlinger

Number 24

SENNACHERIB, KING OF ASSYRIA

Josette Elayi

SBL PRESS

Atlanta

Copyright © 2018 by Josette Elayi

All rights reserved. No part of this work may be reproduced or transmitted in any form or by any means, electronic or mechanical, including photocopying and recording, or by means of any information storage or retrieval system, except as may be expressly permitted by the 1976 Copyright Act or in writing from the publisher. Requests for permission should be addressed in writing to the Rights and Permissions Office, SBL Press, 825 Houston Mill Road, Atlanta, GA 30329 USA.

Library of Congress Cataloging-in-Publication Data

Names: Elayi, Josette, author.
Title: Sennacherib, King of Assyria / by Josette Elayi.
Description: Atlanta : SBL Press, [2018] | Series: Archaeology and biblical studies ; number 24 | Includes bibliographical references and index.
Identifiers: LCCN 2018020287 (print) | LCCN 2018031643 (ebook) | ISBN 9780884143185 (ebk.) | ISBN 9781628372175 (pbk. : alk. paper) | ISBN 9780884143178 (hbk. : alk. paper)
Subjects: LCSH: Sennacherib, King of Assyria, -681 B.C. | Assyria—Kings and rulers—Biography. | Assyria—History.
Classification: LCC DS73.83 (ebook) | LCC DS73.83 .E43 2018 (print) | DDC 935/.03092 [B] —dc23
LC record available at https://lccn.loc.gov/2018020287

Printed on acid-free paper.

Contents

Abbreviations vii
Chronology of Sennacherib's Reign xv

Introduction 1

1. Portrait of Sennacherib 11
   1.1. Physical Portrait   11
   1.2. Name and Family   12
   1.3. Childhood   18
   1.4. Personality   19

2. Sennacherib, the Crown Prince 29
   2.1. Designation as Crown Prince and Functions   29
   2.2. Sennacherib's Correspondence as Crown Prince   32
   2.3. Relationship between the Crown Prince and His Father   40

3. Accession and Priority Campaigns (705–701) 43
   3.1. Accession to the Throne   43
   3.2. Campaign against the Kulummeans   44
   3.3. First Babylonian Campaign   44
   3.4. Zagros Campaign   48
   3.5. Third Campaign to the West   52

4. Consolidating the Empire (700–695) 89
   4.1. Second Babylonian Campaign   90
   4.2. Fifth Campaign to the North   94
   4.3. Campaign against Cilicia   100

	4.4. Campaign against Tabal	104

5. Focusing on Babylonia and Its Allies (694–689) 107
    - 5.1. First Phase of the Campaign against Elam — 107
    - 5.2. Second Phase of the Campaign against Elam — 112
    - 5.3. Third Phase of the Campaign against Elam — 113
    - 5.4. First Two Phases of the Eighth Campaign — 116
    - 5.5. Expedition against the Arabs — 123
    - 5.6. Siege and Destruction of Babylon — 125

6. End of Reign (688–681) 133
    - 6.1. Babylon after Its Destruction — 133
    - 6.2. Problem of Succession — 138
    - 6.3. Sennacherib's Murder — 145

7. Traditions and Reforms 153
    - 7.1. Main Reforms — 154
    - 7.2. Religious Reform — 166

8. Building and Innovation 173
    - 8.1. Building Activities — 173
    - 8.2. Innovations — 190

9. Conclusion: Assessment of Sennacherib's Reign 203

Selected Bibliography 211
Index of Ancient Sources 221
Index of Modern Authors 222
Index of Personal Names 229

Abbreviations

ÄAT	Ägypten und Altes Testament
ABS	Archaeology and Biblical Studies
AfOB	Archiv für Orientforschung Beiheft
AHw	Von Soden, Wolfram. *Akkadisches Handwörterbuch*. 3 vols. Wiesbaden, 1965–1981.
A.J.	*Antiquitates judaicae*
Anab.	Xenophon, *Anabasis*
AnOr	Analecta Orientalia
AnSt	*Anatolian Studies*
AOAT	Alter Orient und Altes Testament
AoF	Altorientalische Forsuchungen
AOTU	*Altorientalische Texte und Untersuchungen*
ARAB	Luckenbill, Daniel David. *Ancient Records of Assyria and Babylonia*. 2 vols. Chicago: University of Chicago Press, 1926–1927. Repr., New York: Greenwood, 1968.
ARMT	Archives Royales de Mari, transcrite et traduite
ArOr	*Archív Orientální*
ARRIM	*Annual Review of the Royal Inscriptions of Mesopotamian Project*
AS	Assyriological Studies
AUSS	*Andrews University Seminary Studies*
BA	*Biblical Archaeologist*
BaF	Baghdader Forschungen
BaghM	*Baghdader Mitteilungen*
BAR	*Biblical Archaeology Review*
BASOR	*Bulletin of the American Schools of Oriental Research*
Bib	*Biblica*
Bib. hist.	Diodorus Siculus, *Bibliotheca historica*
BIN	Babylonian Inscriptions in the Collection of James B. Nies
BiOr	*Bibliotheca Orientalis*

BM	tablets in the collections of the British Museum
BN	*Biblische Notizen*
BZAW	*Beihefte zur Zeitschrift für die alttestamentliche Wissenschaft*
CAH	*Cambridge Ancient History*
CdE	*Chronique d'Égypte*
CDOG	*Colloquien der Deutschen Orient-Gesellschaft*
chr.	chronicle
COHP	*Contributions to Oriental History and Philology of Columbia University*
col.	column
CT	*Cuneiform Texts from Babylonian Tablets in the British Museum*
Demetr.	Plutarch, *Demetrius*
Descr.	Avienus, *Descriptio orbis terrae*
DoArch	*Dossiers d'Archéologie*
Ébib	*Études bibliques*
ErIsr	*Eretz-Israel*
Fam.	Cicero, *Epistulae ad familiares*
HIMA	*Revue Internationale d'Histoire Militaire Ancienne*
Hist.	Herodotus, *Historiae*
HS	*Hebrew Studies*
HSAO	*Heidelberger Studien zum Alten Orient*
IEJ	*Israel Exploration Journal*
IOS	*Israel Oriental Studies*
ISIMU	*ISIMU: Revista sobre Oriente Próximo y Egipto en la antigüedad*
IrAnt	*Iranica Antiqua*
JAEI	*Journal of Ancient Egyptian Interconnections*
JANES	*Journal of Ancient Near Eastern Studies*
JAOS	*Journal of the American Oriental Society*
JARCE	*Journal of the American Research Center in Egypt*
JBL	*Journal of Biblical Literature*
JBQ	*Jewish Bible Quarterly*
JCS	*Journal of Cuneiform Studies*
JdI	*Jahrbuch des deutschen archäologischen Instituts*
JEgH	*Journal of Egyptian History*
JEOL	*Jaarbericht van het Voorazitisch-Egyptisch Gezelschap (Genootschap) Ex oriente lux*

JESHO	*Journal for the Study of the Economic and Social History of the Orient*
JNES	*Journal of Near Eastern Studies*
JSOT	*Journal for the Study of the Old Testament*
JSOTSup	Journal for the Study of the Old Testament Supplement Series
KAI	Donner, Herbert, and Wolfgang Röllig. *Kanaanäische und Aramäische Inschriften.* 2nd ed. Wiesbaden: Harrassowitz, 1966–1969.
KASKAL	*KASKAL: Rivista di storia, ambiente e culture del vicino oriente antico*
l(l).	line(s)
LBAT	Sachs, A. J. *Late Babylonian Astronomical and Related Texts Copied by T. G. Pinches and J. N. Strassmeier.* Providence: Brown University Press, 1955.
1 Macc	1 Maccabees
2 Macc	2 Maccabees
MC	Mesopotamian Civilizations
Mes	*Mesopotamia*
NABU	*Nouvelles Assyriologiques Brèves et Utilitaires*
ND	field numbers of tablets excavated at Nimrud (Kalḫu)
NEAEHL	Stern, Ephraim, ed. *The New Encyclopedia of Archaeological Excavations in the Holy Land.* 4 vols. Jerusalem: Israel Exploration Society & Carta; New York: Simon & Schuster, 1993.
NeHeT	*Revue numérique d'Égyptologie*
NJB	New Jerusalem Bible
NumC	*Numismatic Chronicle*
o.	obverse (front) of a tablet
OAC	Orientis Antiqui Collectio
OBO	Orbis Biblicus et Orientalis
OIP	Oriental Institute Publications
OLA	Orientalia Lovaniensia Analecta
OLZ	*Orientalistische Literaturzeitung*
Or	*Orientalia* (NS)
OrAnt	*Oriens Antiquus*
OTE	Old Testament Essays
OTS	Old Testament Studies
PALMA	Papers on Archaeology of the Leiden Museum of Antiquities
PaP	*Past & Present*

PIASH	Proceedings of the Israel Academy of Science and Humanities
PNA	Baker, Heather, and Karen Radner, eds. *The Prosopography of the Neo-Assyrian Empire*. Helsinki: Neo-Assyrian Text Corpus Project, 1998–.
r.	reverse (back) of a tablet
RA	*Revue d'assyriologie et d'archéologie orientale*
RAI	Rencontres assyriologiques Internationales
RB	*Revue biblique*
RGTC	Répertoire Géographique des Textes Cunéiformes
RIMB	Royal Inscriptions of Mesopotamia, Babylonian Period
RINAP	Royal Inscriptions of the Neo-Assyrian Period
RINAP 1	Tadmor, Hayim, and Shigeo Yamada, eds. *The Royal Inscriptions of Tiglath-Pileser III (744–727 BC) and Shalmaneser V (726–722 BC), Kings of Assyria*. Winona Lake, IN: Eisenbrauns, 2011.
RINAP 3	Grayson, Albert Kirk, and Jamie Novotny. *The Royal Inscriptions of Sennacherib, King of Assyria (704–681 BC)*. 2 vols. Winona Lake, IN: Eisenbrauns, 2012–2014.
RINAP 4	Leichty, Erle. *The Royal Inscriptions of Esarhaddon, King of Assyria (680–669 BC)*. Winona Lake, IN: Eisenbrauns, 2011.
RlA	*Reallexikon der Assyriologie*. Edited by Erich Ebeling et al. Berlin: de Gruyter, 1928–.
ROMOP	Royal Ontario Museum Occasional Papers
SAA	State Archives of Assyria
SAA 1	Parpola, Simo. *The Correspondence of Sargon II, Part I*. SAA 1. Helsinki: Helsinki University Press, 1987.
SAA 2	Parpola, Simo, and Kazuko Watanabe. *Neo-Assyrian Treaties and Loyalty Oaths*. SAA 2. Helsinki: Helsinki University Press, 1998.
SAA 3	Livingstone, Alasdair. *Court Poetry and Literary Miscellanea*. SAA 3. Helsinki: Helsinki University Press, 1989.
SAA 5	Lanfranchi, Giovanni Battista, and Simo Parpola. *The Correspondence of Sargon II, Part II*. SAA 5. Helsinki: Helsinki University Press, 1990.
SAA 6	Kwasman, Theodore, and Simo Parpola. *Legal Transactions of the Royal Court of Nineveh, Part I, Tiglath-Pileser III through Esarhaddon*. SAA 6. Helsinki: Helsinki University Press, 1991.

SAA 7	Fales, Frederick Mario, and John Nicholas Postgate. *Imperial Administrative Records, Part I*. SAA 7. Helsinki: Helsinki University Press, 1992.
SAA 10	Parpola, Simo. *Letters from Assyrian and Babylonian Scholars*. SAA 10. Helsinki: Helsinki University Press, 1993.
SAA 11	Fales, Frederick Mario, and John Nicholas Postgate. *Imperial Administrative Records, Part II*. SAA 11. Helsinki: Helsinki University Press, 1995.
SAA 12	Kataja, Laura, and Robert Whiting. *Grants, Decrees and Gifts of the Neo-Assyrian Period*. SAA 12. Helsinki: Helsinki University Press, 1995.
SAA 15	Fuchs, Andreas, and Simo Parpola. *The Neo-Babylonian Correspondence of Sargon II, Part III: Letters from Babylonia and the Eastern Provinces*. SAA 15. Helsinki: Helsinki University Press, 2001.
SAA 16	Luukko, Mikko, and Greta Van Buylaere. *The Political Correspondence of Esarhaddon*. SAA 16. Helsinki: Helsinki University Press, 2002.
SAA 17	Dietrich, Manfred. *The Neo-Babylonian Correspondence of Sargon and Sennacherib*. SAA 17. Helsinki: Helsinki University Press, 2003.
SAA 18	Reynolds, Frances. *The Babylonian Correspondence of Esarhaddon*. SAA 18. Helsinki: Helsinki University Press, 2003.
SAA 19	Luukko, Mikko. *The Correspondence of Tiglath-Pileser III and Sargon II from Calah/Nimrud*. SAA 19. Helsinki: Helsinki University Press, 2012.
SAA 20	Parpola, Simo. *Assyrian Royal Rituals and Cultic Texts*. SAA 20. Helsinki: Helsinki University Press, 2017.
SAAB	*State Archives of Assyria Bulletin*
SAAS	State Archives of Assyria Studies
SAAS 2	Millard, Alan. *The Eponyms of the Assyrian Empire: 910–612 BC*. SAAS 2. Helsinki: Neo-Assyrian Text Corpus Project, 1994.
SAAS 3	De Odorico, Marco. *The Use of Numbers and Quantifications in the Assyrian Royal Inscriptions*. SAAS 3. Helsinki: Neo-Assyrian Text Corpus Project, 1995.
SAAS 9	Melville, Sarah Chamberlain. *The Role of Naqia/Zakutu in Sargonid Politics*. SAAS 9. Helsinki: Neo-Assyrian Text Corpus Project, 1999.

SAAS 11	Mattila, Raija. *The King's Magnates: A Study of the Highest Officials in the Neo-Assyrian Empire*. SAAS 11. Helsinki: Neo-Assyrian Text Corpus Project, 2000.
SAAS 12	Waters, Matthew William. *A Survey of Neo-Elamite History*. SAAS 12. Helsinki: Neo-Assyrian Text Corpus Project, 2000.
SAAS 20	Adali, Selim. *The Scourge of God*. SAAS 20. Helsinki: Neo-Assyrian Text Corpus Project, 2011.
SAAS 23	Svärd, Saana. *Women and Power in the Neo-Assyrian Palaces*. SAAS 23. Helsinki: Neo-Assyrian Text Corpus Project, 2015.
SANE	Sources of the Ancient Near East
SBTh	Studia Biblica Theologica
Sem	*Semitica*
SHCANE	Studies in the History and Culture of the Ancient Near East
Sir	Sirach/Ecclesiasticus
TA	Tel Aviv
TCS	Texts from Cuneiform Sources
Tob	Tobit
Transeu	*Transeuphratène*
VAB	Vorderasiatische Bibliothek
VeEc	*Verbum et Ecclesia*
VT	*Vetus Testamentum*
VTSup	Supplements to Vetus Testamentum
WAWSup	Writings from the Ancient World Supplement Series
WBJb	*Jahrbuch: Wissenschaftskolleg zu Berlin*
WVDOG	Wissenschaftliche Veröffentlichungen der deutschen Orient-Gesellschaft
YBC	Yale Babylonian Collection
ZA	*Zeitschrift für Assyriologie*
ZTK	*Zeitschrift für Theologie und Kirche*

Key to Transliterated Words

kibrāt	Akkadian words are indicated by italics.
DINGIR	Sumerian word signs are indicated by capital letters

Explanation of Symbols

[ ]	single brackets enclose restorations.
⌈ ⌉	raised brackets indicate partially visible signs.

( )   parentheses enclose additions in the English translation.
...   a row of dots indicates gaps in the text or untranslatable words.

Chronology of Sennacherib's Reign

Dates (BCE)	Year of Reign	Campaigns and Activities
705	Accession year	Accession to the throne on the twelfth day of Abu (August).
704	Year 1	Expedition against the Kulummeans (by Sennacherib's officer). Campaign against Babylonia (first campaign). Ashur-nâdin-shumi possibly crown prince. Beginning of the construction of the southwest palace.
703	Year 2	Campaign against Babylonia (continued). Bêl-ibni appointed king of Babylon.
702	Year 3	Campaign in the Zagros (second campaign). Against the Kassites and Yasubigallians, and Ashpa-bara of Ellipi. Annexation of the Bît-Barrû district. Rebuilding of the Nergal temple at Tarbisu.
701	Year 4	Campaign to the west (third campaign). Against Lulî of Tyre. Pacification of the Philistine cities, buffer states between Assyria and Egypt. Against Hezekiah of Judah, who retained his throne.
700	Year 5	Campaign against Babylonia and Bît-Yakin (fourth campaign). His son Ashur-nâdin-shumi appointed king of Babylon. Urdu-Mullissu possibly crown prince.
699	Year 6	
698	Year 7	
697	Year 8	Campaign against rebellious cities on Mount Nipur and Maniye of Ukku (fifth campaign).
696	Year 9	Against Kirûa of Cilicia (by Sennacherib's officer: governor of Que?).

CHRONOLOGY OF SENNACHERIB'S REIGN

695	Year 10	Against Gurdî, Tabalian ruler of Til-Garimmu (by Sennacherib's officer).
694	Year 11	Maritime expedition against Elam (sixth campaign). Capture of his son Ashur-nâdin-shumi, delivered to the Elamites.
693	Year 12	Campaign against Elam (seventh campaign).
692	Year 13	Campaign against Elam (continued).
691	Year 14	Campaign against the Elamite-Babylonian coalition (eighth campaign). Battle of Halulê. End of the construction of the southwest palace.
690	Year 15	Expedition against the Arabs (by Sennacherib's officer). Possibly limited expedition against Elam. Siege of Babylon.
689	Year 16	Capture and destruction of Babylon.
688	Year 17	Babylon officially left rulerless.
687	Year 18	
686	Year 19	
685	Year 20	
684	Year 21	
683	Year 22	Esarhaddon crown prince. Succession treaty. Building of the *akītu* house in Assur.
682	Year 23	
681	Year 24	Departure of Esarhaddon to escape the conspiracy of his brothers in Nisannu (April). Murder of Sennacherib on the twentieth of Tebêtu (January).

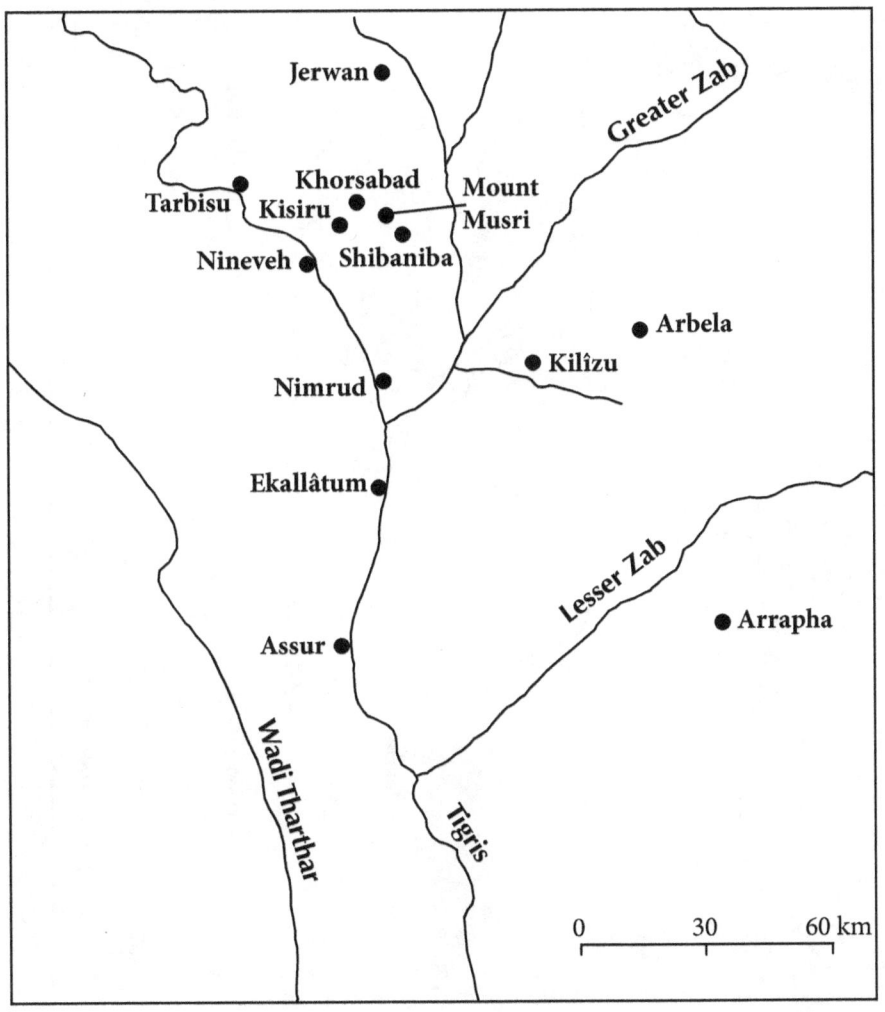

Fig. 1. The Assur-Nineveh-Arbela triangle

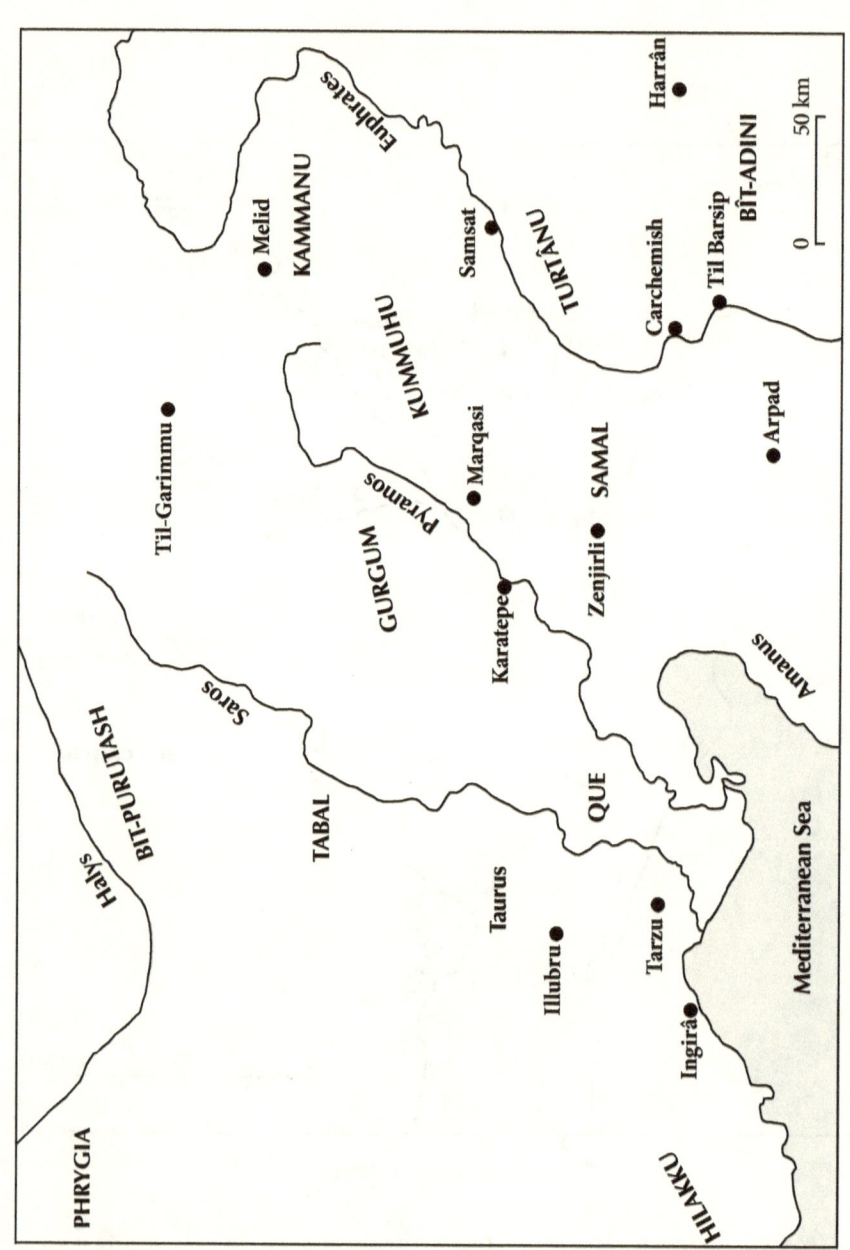

Fig. 2. The northwest of the empire

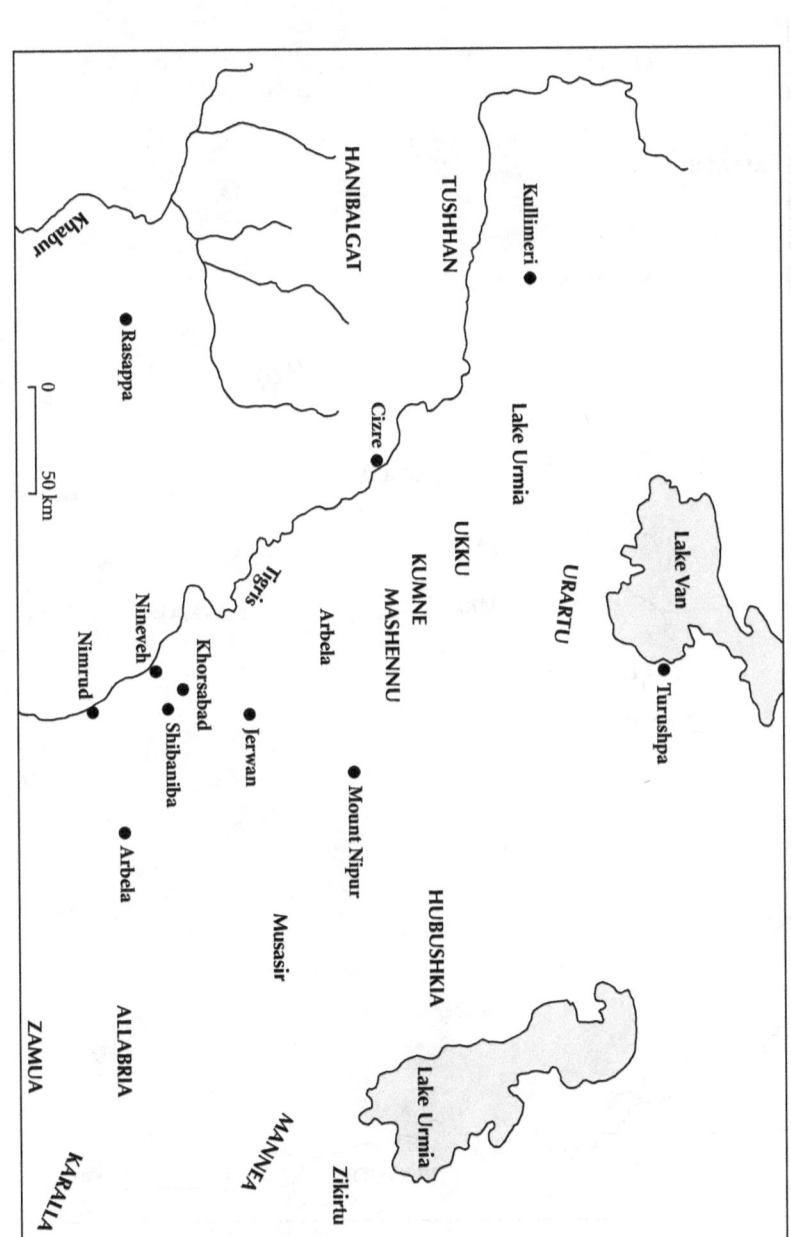

Fig. 3. The north of the empire

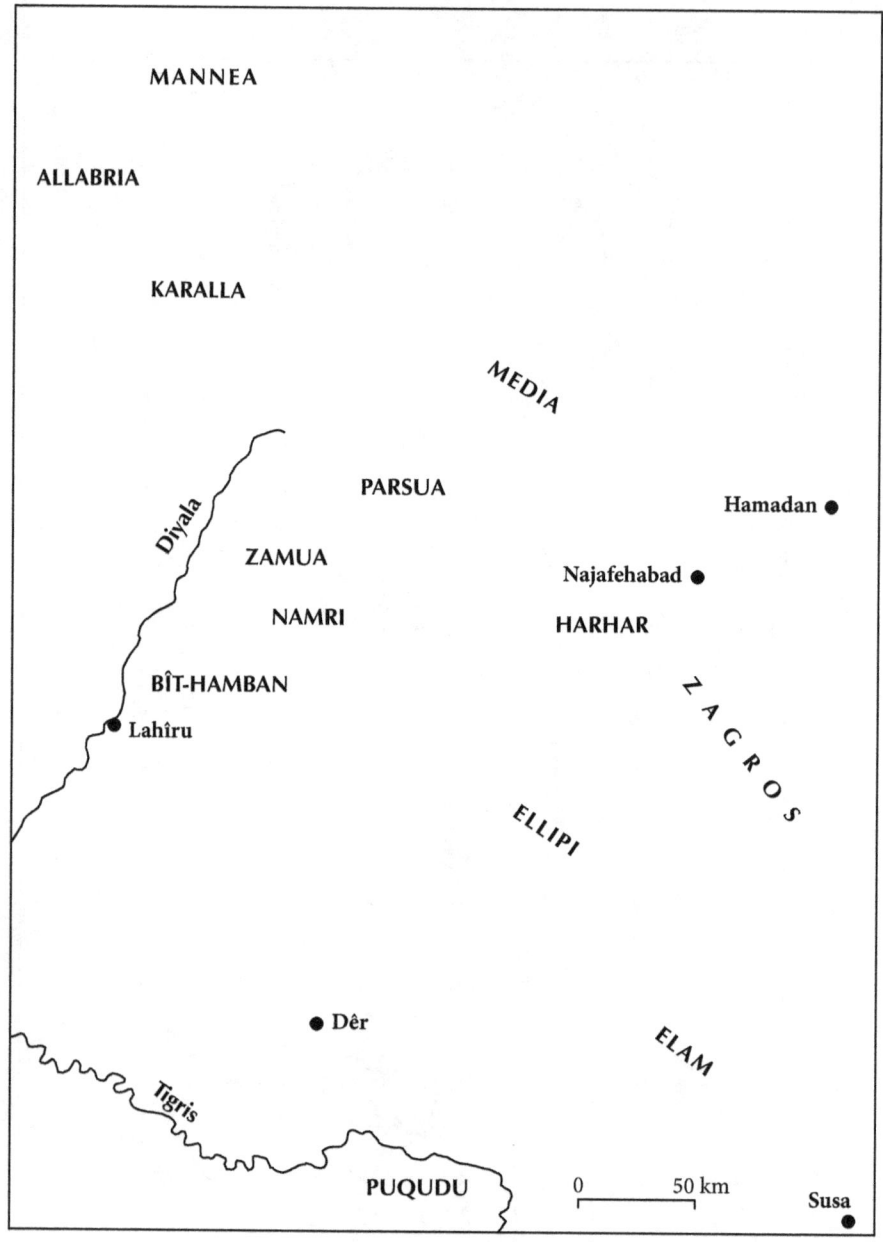

Fig. 4. The eastern states

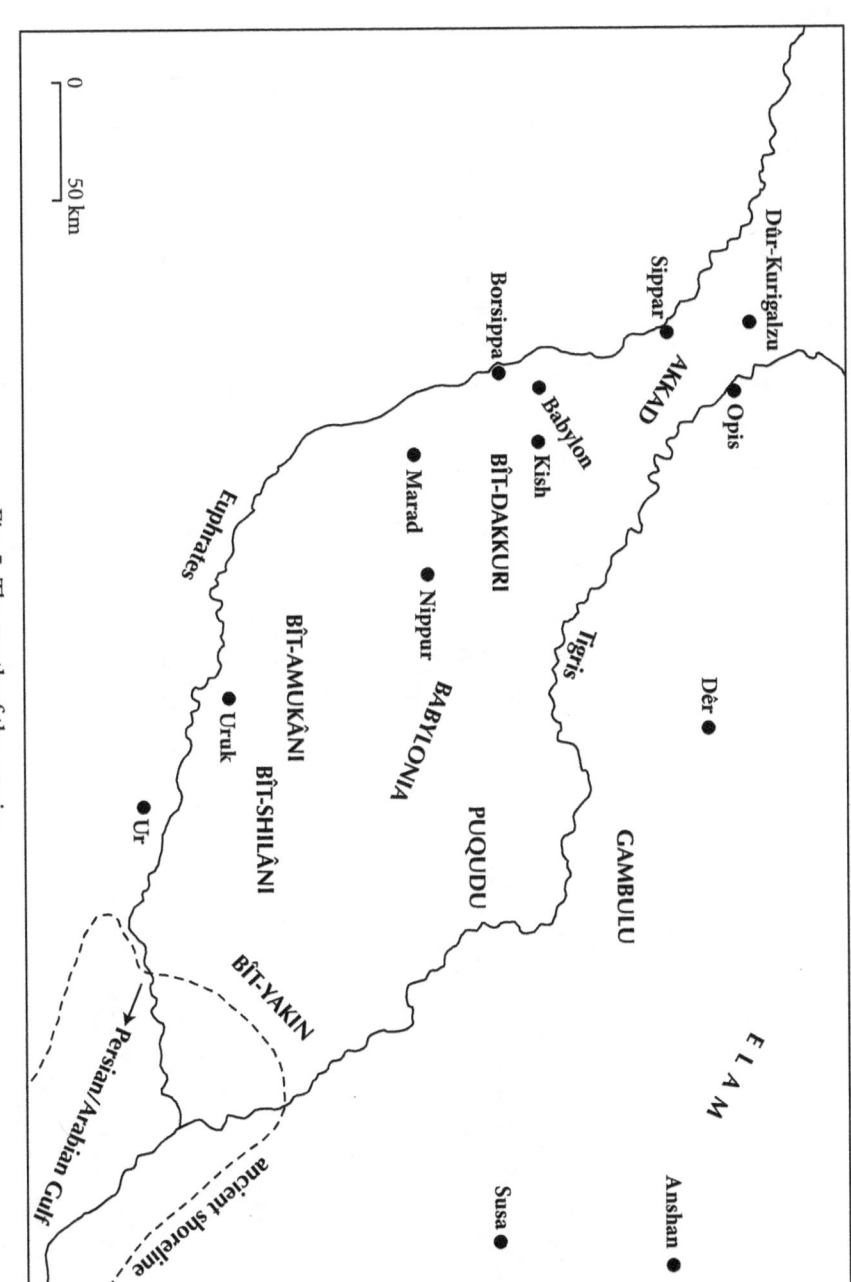

Fig. 5. The south of the empire

Introduction

Sennacherib, successor of his father, Sargon II, reigned over Assyria from 705 to 681 BCE. He was one of the main Neo-Assyrian kings, particularly famous for his expert knowledge. The history of his reign is well known from abundant Akkadian sources, most of them dominated by an apologetic view. However, the image of Sennacherib conveyed to us through the centuries is chiefly negative. This negative image has two origins: the first is its presentation in the Bible as that of the bad king who attacked Judah and besieged Jerusalem and Lachish. The second origin is his responsibility in the Babylonian tragedy through his contemptuous and destructive actions against this city. The literature from later periods gives narrative amplifications of the biblical and unfavorable classical material, as in Greek accounts of Sennacherib's reign. For example, in 1815 Lord Byron presented the Assyrian king as a merciless predator in a famous poem:

> The Assyrian came down like the wolf on the fold,
> And his cohorts were gleaming in purple and gold;
> And the sheen of their spears was like stars on the sea,
> When the blue wave rolls nightly on deep Galilee.[1]

The reputation of Assyrian kings' ferocity was further amplified by the discovery of archaeological remains in Iraq during the nineteenth century that included representations and descriptions of their cruelty. For exam-

---

1. Lord Byron, *The Complete Poetical Works*, ed. J. J. McGann (Oxford: Oxford University Press, 1981), 3:309–10; Eckart Frahm, *Einleitung in die Sanherib-Inschriften*, AfOB 26 (Vienna: Institut für Orientalistik, 1997), 21–28. See also Lytton Strachey, "Sennacherib and Rupert Brooke," in *The Really Interesting Question and Other Papers*, ed. Paul Levy (London: Weidenfeld & Nicolson, 1972), 42–44; Joseph Verheyden, "The Devil in Person, the Devil in Disguise: Looking for King Sennacherib in Early Christian Literature," in *Sennacherib at the Gates of Jerusalem: Story, History and Historiography*, ed. Isaac Kalimi and Seth Richardson (Leiden: Brill, 2014), 389–431.

ple, Sennacherib boasted of having slit the throats of his Elamite enemies like sheep: "I filled the plain with the corpses of their warriors like [grass]. I cut off (their) lips and (thus) destroyed their pride. I cut off their hands like the *stems* of cucumbers in season."[2]

On his ascent to the throne, Sennacherib inherited the Assyrian Empire, the true founder of which was his grandfather Tiglath-pileser III, who reigned from 744 to 727,[3] because he created a truly imperialist-dependent system, a strong and effective source of considerable wealth. This system was characterized by the ongoing mechanism of conquest to annex "the four regions (of the world)" (*kibrāt arba'i*) and the growing weight of the Assyrian administration, which oppressed the conquered states. Sennacherib's father, Sargon, who ruled from 722 to 705, played an important and prestigious role in the history of the Neo-Assyrian Empire, providing its driving force at the peak of its renown.[4] Sennacherib belonged to the so-called Sargonids group, a term that did not designate a new dynasty but rather the sequence of Sargon's successors. Sennacherib, Esarhaddon, and Ashurbanipal increased the power and wealth of the Assyrian Empire still further.

The Akkadian inscriptions related to the history of Sennacherib's reign are numerous and even overabundant. Most of them are housed in museum collections, such as the British Museum in London and the Vorderasiatisches Museum in Berlin. Others are scattered around the world in private collections. Several large inscribed objects were reburied and left in the site, such as at Nineveh. These inscriptions can be divided into two categories: royal and nonroyal.[5]

---

2. RINAP 3.1:183, 22.vi.10–12.

3. Paul Garelli, "The Achievement of Tiglath-pileser III: Novelty or Continuity?," in *Ah Assyria ... Mélanges H. Tadmor*, ed. Mordechai Cogan and Israel Eph'al (Jerusalem: Magnes, 1991), 46–51. However, John Nicholas Postgate considered that there was continuity between the Medio-Assyrian and Neo-Assyrian periods. See *The Land of Assur and the Yoke of Assur: Studies on Assyria: 1971–2005* (Oxford: Oxbow, 2007).

4. See Josette Elayi, *Sargon II, King of Assyria*, ABS 22 (Atlanta: SBL Press, 2017). It is not necessary to be precise all the time in saying "Sargon II" because there cannot be any confusion in this book with Sargon of Agade.

5. Bruno Meissner and Paul Rost, *Die Bauinschriften Sanheribs* (Leipzig: Pfeiffer, 1893); Daniel David Luckenbill, *The Annals of Sennacherib*, OIP 2 (Chicago: University of Chicago Press, 1924); G. L. Russell, "Sennacherib's Annals: A Foundational Text Study" (PhD diss., Dropsie College, 1967); Frahm, *Einleitung in die Sanherib-Inschriften*; RINAP 3.1–2; Eckart Frahm, "Sanherib," *RlA* 12:12–22; *PNA* 3.1:1124–27

Some royal inscriptions can be very long (over five hundred lines). Several duplicated exemplars of the well-known Nineveh texts were preserved in Assur and Nimrud (Kalhu). Until Sennacherib's sixth year of reign (699), royal inscriptions were written on clay cylinders. From his seventh year (698), clay cylinders were abandoned in favor of clay prisms with more surface area (three- to ten-sided). All these texts generally give detailed accounts of his military campaigns presented in chronological order and of his building operations, and they are frequently called annals. They are complemented by clay tablets and cones, stone stelae, slabs and blocks, bull and lion colossi, rock reliefs, and smaller clay and metal objects. In the royal inscriptions of Sennacherib's successors, allusions can also be found to his reign.[6]

Two problems are associated with royal inscriptions: dating and propaganda. The so-called double dating by regnal year and eponymate sporadically occurred in some colophons, fixing Sennacherib's first regnal year to 705, 704, or 703. However, there are no grounds for accepting these inconsistencies: he ascended the Assyrian throne on the twelfth day of Abu (August) 705.[7] In the annals, his military campaigns are numbered with figures that differ from the regnal years. The number of campaigns and the precise years of some of them are difficult to establish because they are merely numbered as first, second, and so on, up to eight. Even if this official numbering is only supposed to include the campaigns led by the Assyrian king, the Assyrian army no longer undertook annual marches targeting new conquests. In total, between his accession year (705) and his sixteenth year (689), twelve campaigns are recorded in all the inscriptions, four of them probably led by his officials.[8] By combining the different sources, it will be possible to propose a plausible chronology. The second difficulty for the historian when using the royal inscriptions is to decipher

---

(with bibliography); Jamie Novotny, "The Royal Inscriptions of Sennacherib: An At-a-Glance Akkadian Glossary of the RINAP 3 Corpus," *SAAB* 20 (2017): 79–129.

6. *PNA* 3.1:1126–27 (with bibliography).
7. *PNA* 3.1:1117; SAAS 2:48 and 70–71.
8. RINAP 3.1:10, table 1; Hayim Tadmor, "World Dominion: The Expanding Horizon of the Assyrian Empire," in *Landscapes: Territories, Frontiers and Horizons in the Ancient Near East*, ed. Lucio Milano, Stefano De Martino, Frederick Mario Fales, and Giovanni Battista Lanfranchi, RAI 44.1 (Padova: Sargon, 1999), 61; Bradley J. Parker, *The Mechanics of Empire: The Northern Frontier of Assyria as a Case Study of Imperial Dynamics* (Helsinki: Neo-Assyrian Text Corpus Project, 2001), 97.

them through the filter of propaganda by consulting the different sources and identifying the distorted information.⁹

The nonroyal inscriptions are often undated, but they are much less distorted by propaganda. They belong to several categories, starting with the chronographic one: king lists, eponym lists, and chronicles such as the Babylonian Chronicles and the Assyrian Eponym Chronicle for the beginning of Sennacherib's reign,¹⁰ useful for dating the events. The category of letters is disappointing because they are much less numerous than Sargon's and Esarhaddon's letters. Moreover, almost all of them belong to the period when Sennacherib was crown prince. The theory that the epistolary archive of his reign was destroyed after his murder does not seem to be valid because many letters in the archives may remain unidentified.¹¹ A few letters written after his death allude to events from his reign.¹² The number of economic documents on clay tablets positively identified as dating from Sennacherib's reign is relatively large, and they are probably still more numerous, but the attribution to his reign is uncertain for several documents. This is especially the case for the fragments not physically joined, which makes it difficult to confidently attribute them to the same tablet.¹³ When they can be so identified, they make it possible to gain further insight into Assyria's economic situation under Sennacherib.

There are also external sources written in Aramaic, Hebrew, and Greek, such as the story of Ahiqar, the Bible, the histories of Herodotus, and later texts such as those of Berossus and possibly Menander.¹⁴ The

---

9. Antii Laato, "Assyrian Propaganda and the Falsification of History in the Royal Inscriptions of Sennacherib," *VT* 45 (1995): 198–226; Katsuji Sano, "Die Repräsentation der Königsherrschaft in neuassyriascher Zeit: Ideologie, Propaganda und Adressaten der Königsinschriften," *Studia Mesopotamica* 3 (2016): 215–36.

10. Frahm, "Sanherib," *RlA* 12:12–22; *PNA* 3.1:1117; SAAS 2; Albert Kirk Grayson, *Assyrian and Babylonian Chronicles*, TCS 5 (Winona Lake, IN: Eisenbrauns, 2000).

11. SAA 1; SAA 5; SAA 17. See Simo Parpola, "A Letter to Sennacherib Referring to the Conquest of Bit-Ha'iri and Other Events of the Year 693," in *Ex Mesopotamia et Syria Lux: Festschrift für Manfred Dietrich*, ed. Oswald Loretz, Kai A. Metzler, and Hanspeter Schaudig (Münster: Ugarit-Verlag, 2002), 576.

12. *PNA* 3.1:1126–27 (with bibliography).

13. SAA 6:38–159, nos. 34–200.

14. *PNA* 3.1:1117; Frederick Mario Fales, "Multilingualism on Multiple Media in the Neo-Assyrian Period: A Review of the Evidence," *SAAB* 16 (2007): 95–122; Frahm, *Einleitung in die Sanherib-Inschriften*, 24–28; James Miller Lindenberger, *The Aramaic*

late literature is mainly based on the biblical and classical accounts of Sennacherib's reign. All the external sources must be used carefully for a reconstruction of Sennacherib's reign, with a precise assessment of their more or less important distortions.

Nonwritten documentation dating from Sennacherib's reign is also historically important. The main information is provided by the reliefs from his palace in Nineveh (Mosul), which he called "Palace without Rival" (*ekallu ša šānina la išû*).[15] They are partly representations of the Assyrian king's conquests, focusing on spectacular actions, sometimes accompanied by an epigraph, similar to our modern comics. These reliefs are complementary to the texts, but some of them provide information that is not mentioned in the written sources. In 1847 the so-called Southwest Palace was discovered and excavated between 1847 and 1851 by Austen Henry Layard.[16] The main interest focused on the discovery of a small inner chamber (Room XXXVI) with wall reliefs depicting Sennacherib's siege of the Judean walled city of Lachish that was identified by the epigraph and recorded in the Bible (2 Kgs 18:13–14).[17] It was the first archaeological confirmation of an event known from the Bible. The Southwest Palace was then excavated by Hormuzd Rassam and Henry Creswicke Rawlinson (1852–1854), then incidentally by William Kennett Loftus (1854–1855). George Smith's discovery, in his campaigns of 1873 and 1874, of a fragmentary account of the deluge generated a wave of

---

Proverbs of Ahiqar (Baltimore: Johns Hopkins University Press, 1983), 3–4; Tawny L. Holm, "Memories of Sennacherib in Aramaic Tradition," in Kalimi and Richardson, *Sennacherib at the Gates of Jerusalem*, 295–323; Gerbern S. Oegema, "Sennacherib's Campaign and Its Reception in the Time of the Second Temple," in Kalimi and Richardson, *Sennacherib at the Gates of Jerusalem*, 325–45; Rivka Ulmer, "Sennacherib in Midrashic and Related Literature: Inscribing History in Midrash," in Kalimi and Richardson, *Sennacherib at the Gates of Jerusalem*, 347–87; Verheyden, "Devil in Person," 389–431; Herodotus, *Hist.* 2.141 (Σαναχάριβος); Josephus, *A.J.* 10.1–23; 2 Kgs 18:13–37, 19; 2 Chr 32:1–23; Isa 29:5–9, 30:27–33, 31:5–8, 36:13–22, 37:1–38; Mic 1:8–16; Tob 1:18–22; Sir 48:18–22; 1 Macc 7:41–42; 2 Macc 8:19, 15:22–24.

15. RINAP 3.2:38, 39.74.

16. Austen Henry Layard, *Nineveh and Its Remains I–II* (London: Murray, 1849); Layard, *Discoveries in the Ruins of Nineveh and Babylon* (London: Murray, 1853); Layard, *A Second Series of the Monuments of Nineveh* (London: Murray, 1853); Paul-Émile Botta, *Monuments de Ninive III–IV* (Paris: Imprimerie Nationale, 1849).

17. John Malcolm Russell, *Sennacherib's Palace without Rival at Nineveh* (Chicago: University of Chicago Press, 1991), 40.

excitement among both scholars and educated public. Several excavation campaigns were episodically led in the palace: again by Hormuzd Rassam (1878–1882), E. A. Wallis Budge (1889–1891), L. W. King (1903–1904), and Reginald Campbell Thompson (1905, 1931–1932).[18] The most recent excavations were sponsored by the Iraqi Department of Antiquities and directed by T. Madhloom (1965–1968). Some reliefs from Sennacherib's palace are now mainly housed in the Iraq Museum (Baghdad), British Museum (London), Musée du Louvre (Paris), Vorderasiatisches Museum (Berlin), and Metropolitan Museum of Art (New York).[19] They also survive in drawing formats made during the excavations.[20]

Numerous works, large and small, mention Sennacherib.[21] Every general history of Assyria or Mesopotamia includes short studies on this king; the most useful ones are those compiled by Albert Kirk Grayson and Eckart Frahm.[22] All these books, although titled *History of Sennacherib*, were devoted to his inscriptions, sometimes accompanied by some historical comments. The first one was George Smith's *History of Sennacherib* published in London in 1878; in fact, the book, focused on inscriptions, was unfinished and completed by Archibald Henry Sayce.[23] The main books were those written by Bruno Meissner and Paul Rost in 1893, Daniel David Luckenbill in 1924, G. L. Russell in 1967, Eckart Frahm in 1997, and finally

---

18. George Smith, *Assyrian Discoveries* (London: Bagster & Sons, 1875), 94–144; Hormuzd Rassam, *Asshur and the Land of Nimrod* (New York: Eston & Mains, 1897), 3–7, 39; E. A. Wallis Budge, *By Nile and Tigris II* (London: Murray, 1920), 22, 67–83; Reginald Campbell Thompson and Richard Wyatt Hutchinson, *A Century of Exploration at Nineveh* (London: Luzac, 1929), 59–69; Cyril John Gadd, *The Stones of Assyria* (London: Chatto & Windus, 1936), 83–85; T. Madhloom, "Nineveh, 1968–69 Campaign," *Sumer* 25 (1969): 44–49; Russell, *Sennacherib's Palace without Rival at Nineveh*, 4, 40–44.

19. Russell, *Sennacherib's Palace without Rival at Nineveh*, xi, 269–88.

20. Austen Henry Layard, *Monuments of Nineveh from Drawings Made on the Spot* (London: Murray, 1849); Botta, *Monuments de Ninive III–IV*.

21. RINAP 3.1:6–9 (bibliography); Eckart Frahm, ed., *A Companion to Assyria* (Malden, MA: Wiley-Blackwell, 2017), 183–86; Mario Liverani, *The Imperial Mission* (Winona Lake, IN: Eisenbrauns, 2017).

22. Albert Kirk Grayson, "Assyria: Sennacherib and Esarhaddon (704–669 B.C.)," in *The Assyrian and Babylonian Empires and Other States of the Near East, from the Eighth to the Sixth Centuries B.C.*, ed. John Boardman et al., 2nd ed., CAH 3.2 (Cambridge: Cambridge University Press, 1991), 103–41; Frahm, "Sanherib," *RlA* 12:12–22; *PNA* 3.1:1113–27.

23. See RINAP 3.1:7.

Albert Kirk Grayson and Jamie Novotny in 2012.²⁴ Some other books are devoted to a specific historical feature of Sennacherib's reign. For example, those of Leo L. Honor, David Ussishkin, William R. Gallagher, Lester L. Grabbe, Paul S. Evans, Isaac Kalimi and Seth Richardson, Nazek Khalid Matty, and Claudio Saporetti particularly focus on his third campaign.²⁵ Those of Archibald Paterson and Richard D. Barnett focus on his palace in Nineveh.²⁶ Works by Thorkild Jacobsen, Seton Lloyd, Frederick Mario Fales, and Roswitha Del Fabbro focus on the aqueducts of Jerwan.²⁷

The purpose of this book is to study, for the first time, the history of Sennacherib's reign in all its aspects: political, military, economic, social, ideological, religious, technical, and artistic. Modern historians used to consider history as a process essentially governed by structural or systemic causes. Putting too much emphasis on the impact of the "great men" has become relatively unfashionable.²⁸ However, the biographical approach is not dead and continues to flourish in the popular branches of history, with

---

24. Meissner and Rost, *Die Bauinschriften Sanheribs*; Luckenbill, *Annals of Sennacherib*; Russell, "Sennacherib's Annals"; Frahm, *Einleitung in die Sanherib-Inschriften*; RINAP 3.1:1–2.

25. Leo L. Honor, *Sennacherib's Invasion of Palestine: A Critical Source Study*, COHP 12 (New York: Columbia University Press, 1926); David Ussishkin, *The Conquest of Lachish by Sennacherib*, PIASH 6 (Tel Aviv: Tel Aviv University Press, 1982); Francolino C. Gonçalves, *L'expédition de Sennachérib en Palestine dans la littérature hébraïque ancienne*, Ébib 7 (Paris: Gabalda, 1986); William R. Gallagher, *Sennacherib's Campaign to Judah: New Studies*, SHCANE 18 (Leiden: Brill, 1999); Lester L. Grabbe, ed., *"Like a Bird in a Cage": The Invasion of Sennacherib in 701 BCE*, JSOTSup 363 (Sheffield: Sheffield Academic, 2003); Paul S. Evans, *The Invasion of Sennacherib in the Book of Kings: A Source-Critical and Rhetorical Study of 2 Kings 18–19*, VTSup 125 (Leiden: Brill, 2009); Kalimi and Richardson, *Sennacherib at the Gates of Jerusalem*; Nazek Khalid Matty, *Sennacherib's Campaign against Judah and Jerusalem in 701 B.C.: A Historical Reconstruction*, BZAW 487 (Berlin: de Gruyter, 2016); Claudio Saporetti, *Sennacherib e la Bibbia*, Teletè 3 (Acireale, Italy: Bonanno, 2017).

26. Archibald Paterson, *Assyrian Sculptures: Palace of Sennacherib* (The Hague: Nijhoff, 1915); Russell, *Sennacherib's Palace without Rival at Nineveh*; Richard D. Barnett, Erika Bleibtreu, and Geoffrey Turner, *Sculptures from the Southwest Palace of Sennacherib at Nineveh* (London: British Museum, 1998).

27. Thorkild Jacobsen and Seton Lloyd, *Sennacherib's Aqueduct at Jerwan*, OIP 24 (Chicago: Oriental Institute of the University of Chicago, 1935); Frederick Mario Fales and Roswitha Del Fabbro, "Back to Sennacherib's Aqueduct at Jerwan: Reassessment of the Textual Evidence," *Iraq* 76 (2014): 65–98.

28. Marc Van De Mieroop, *Cuneiform Texts and the Writing of History* (London: Routledge, 1999), 39–85; Eckart Frahm, "Family Matters: Psychohistorical Reflections

an endless production of new biographies of Alexander, Cleopatra, and Nero, for example. The present book downplays neither the structural factors nor the biographical approach. In contrast to the history of Sargon's reign,[29] that of Sennacherib's reign is well documented concerning his family background, his childhood and youth, and the long period when he was crown prince before he ascended the throne. The abundance and variety of sources enable the proposal of a comprehensive assessment of the psychological factors that shaped his character and how, in turn, it influenced his approach to politics. Eckart Frahm has attempted a psycho-historical investigation of Sennacherib and his time, and some of his interpretations can be accepted.[30]

Several issues are raised and, wherever possible, answered: What were Sennacherib's qualities and skills? What were his shortcomings? What was his relationship with his father? How did he react to Sargon's violent and inauspicious death on the battlefield? Why did he not officially commemorate his father's memory? Did he avenge him? Did he have a clear plan or program at the beginning of his reign, or did he simply respond to various challenges in different areas as and when they arose? What did he attempt to achieve, and how did he go about fulfilling his objectives? How did he manage to consolidate the Assyrian Empire and to drive it at the peak of its ascent? Were military campaigns as important to him as prestigious building projects, or did he think it was more important to expand or to embellish the empire? What can be said of his personal evolution during his reign? Was he more a reformer or a conservative? In what areas can it be said that he succeeded or, conversely, failed?

My methodology consists in adapting to the specific topic of the book and to the available sources.[31] My approach is always multidisciplinary: political, strategic, economic, geographic, ethnographic, along with text studies, onomastic analyses, and so on. For me, history is primarily down to earth, implying that I stay closely in line with the documents. Only then is it possible to move on to a historical synthesis, with a partial summary at the end of each chapter. The limited framework of a book has forced me

---

on Sennacherib and His Times," in Kalimi and Richardson, *Sennacherib at the Gates of Jerusalem*, 163–222.

29. Elayi, *Sargon II, King of Assyria*, 13–15.
30. Frahm, "Family Matters," 163–222.
31. On my conception of history, see Josette Elayi, "Être historienne de la Phénicie ici et maintenant," *Transeu* 31 (2006): 41–54.

to make choices in selecting from a mass of overabundant data, accompanied by a consistent series of comments, that appeared to me fundamental and relevant for the topic of this book. Some facts and minor features had to be omitted through necessity. The letters written by Sennacherib as crown prince are related to events of Sargon's reign, already analyzed in my previous book,[32] and are therefore less developed here. The format and progression of the present book are built around decisive events and determining facts. I have selected the interpretations that seemed to me the most plausible. Different interpretations that have been put forward are discussed or presented in notes. Sometimes I reached the conclusion that, given the current state of research, it is impossible to choose between various hypotheses.

It is usual to start a biography with a portrait, and chapter 1 ("A Portrait of Sennacherib") strives to encompass the king's personality through his inscriptions before seeing him in action: his name, his family, his childhood, his youth, and his character. Now, Sennacherib presented an attractive image of himself, but to what extent is this image true or distorted by propaganda? Chapter 2 ("Sennacherib, the Crown Prince") investigates the long period during which the king was crown prince in order to determine the date of his selection to succeed Sargon, his functions and his actions, and his relationship with his father. In chapters 3–6, the book follows a chronological order, mainly based on the various texts of the annals. Chapter 3 ("Accession and Priority Campaigns [705–701]") explains the basis on which Sennacherib managed to succeed Sargon to the throne and analyzes his priority campaigns. Chapter 4 ("Consolidating the Empire [700–695]") analyzes the subsequent campaigns that he conducted in order to solve militarily the problems encountered in other parts of the empire. Chapter 5 ("Focusing on Babylonia and Its Allies [694–689]") is related to all the military operations that were necessary to completely overcome Assyria's archenemy: Babylon. Chapter 6 ("End of Reign [688–681]") focuses on the last years of Sennacherib's reign, when external military campaigns were replaced by internal political struggles, ending in the king's murder. Chapter 7 ("Traditions and Reforms") explains how the Assyrian Empire was administered under Sennacherib's reign and what reforms he had inaugurated. Chapter 8 ("Building and Innovation") examines all the building projects initiated by Sennacherib and presents his innovations in different

---

32. Elayi, *Sargon II, King of Assyria*, 115–52.

domains. Finally, the book concludes with an assessment of his contributions to the evolution of the Assyrian Empire as compared with the state it was in at the beginning of his reign, as well as the positive and negative consequences of his decisions and actions ("Conclusion: Assessment of Sennacherib's Reign"). At the end of the book, readers will find research aids, in line with the publisher's requirements: a selected bibliography for each chapter; an index of ancient texts used; an index of the personal names cited, followed by brief comments and dates for situating them both in a diachronic and synchronic perspective; and an index of modern authors cited. Eight maps locating all the geographical terms mentioned in the book are also provided.

1
Portrait of Sennacherib

1.1. Physical Portrait

There exist so many representations of Sennacherib, mainly in the Southwest Palace of Nineveh, that we ought to have a good idea of his physical portrait.[1] The king was represented in various attitudes and contexts, for example, receiving booty, supervising the transport of the bull colossi, on campaign in Babylonia, or shooting at lions from a Phoenician galley on the Tigris (?).[2] Most of the time he is depicted in his chariot, more rarely standing or sitting on his throne, with fly whisks from behind.[3] He is raising his hand in salutation, shooting with a bow, or holding a sword. It is a long sword in its scabbard, kept at the waist, the lower end extending behind him. His costume consists of a long dress reaching down to the ankles, ornamented with motifs such as rosettes. Over this dress he wears a large mantle, with the outer edge embroidered and fringed. He wears sandals on his feet. The features of his face are modeled with precision: thick, raised eyebrows, heavy lids and delineated iris, full lips topped with a small mustache. The styling of his hair and his beard are sophisticated, combining ringlets and curls. He wears fine jewelry: earrings, bracelets, and arm-bangles. His headdress consists of a tall, conical cap, flat at the top and surmounted by a small pointed tip, decorated with bands of rosettes and long ribbons. He is rarely represented without a headdress, and even when he was hunting or when he was still crown prince, his diadem, with

---

1. Barnett, Bleibtreu, and Turner, *Sculptures from the Southwest Palace of Sennacherib at Nineveh I–II*.
2. Russell, *Sennacherib's Palace without Rival at Nineveh*, 72, fig. 40; 110, fig. 57; 144, fig. 75; 206, fig. 112.
3. SAA 7:29, fig. 7 (BM 10904).

two pendant ribbons, makes him recognizable.[4] His tall headdress, making him appear taller, no doubt emphasized his status to the onlooker.

The representations of the king were manipulated so as to convey his godlike semblance by using different devices: the progressive removal of protective deities indicates that he was granted their roles; he is shown enthroned facing to the left, as were the major Mesopotamian deities, or he is depicted close to a major god in anthropomorphic shape.[5] Sennacherib's representation was not a realistic portrait but the conventional image of an Assyrian king, which looked like those of Ashurnasirpal II or Sargon, for example. How could the Assyrians recognize him? The key was the location where he was represented: his Southwest Palace in Nineveh.[6] All things considered, the numerous representations of Sennacherib still do not provide us with information about his complete physical portrait. They were intended to show an idealized image of how he wanted to be seen and how he possibly saw himself, but not of how he appeared exactly in reality, which we shall never know.

1.2. Name and Family

The name of Sennacherib in Akkadian was *Sīn-aḫḫē-erība*, with some variants and scribal errors in the writing.[7] It meant "Sin has replaced the brothers," probably because he was not the firstborn son, but his elder brothers had all died by the time he was born. The name was translated *snḥryb* in Hebrew, *šnḥ'ryb* in Aramaic, Σαναχάριβος in some Greek writings, and Σεν(ν)αχηριμ in the Septuagint. The Bible artificially linked this name to the Hebrew *ḥrb*, "destroy," and *ḥrp*, "shame."[8] In Assyria it was forbidden to give the name "Sennacherib" to a commoner, according to a

---

4. SAA 1:26, fig. 10.

5. Tallay Ornan, "The Godlike Semblance of a King: The Case of Sennacherib's Rock Reliefs," in *Ancient Near Eastern Art in Context: Studies in Honor of Irene J. Winter by Her Students*, ed. Jack Cheng and Marian H. Feldman (Leiden: Brill, 2007), 161–78.

6. Today it is sometimes difficult to distinguish between sculptures of Sennacherib and Ashurbanipal because Sennacherib's palace was restored by his grandson (Barnett, Bleibtreu, and Turner, *Sculptures from the Southwest Palace of Sennacherib at Nineveh I–II*, xii).

7. PNA 3.1:1113.

8. Moshe Garsiel, *Biblical Names: A Literary Study of Midrashic Derivations and Puns* (Ramat Gan, Israel: Bar-Ilan University Press, 1991), 46–48.

1. PORTRAIT OF SENNACHERIB

document from Nineveh dated from about 670 BCE: it would have been considered a taboo and a sacrilege.⁹

Sennacherib was a legitimate king, as he was the son of Sargon, king of Assyria (722–705) and of Babylonia (710–705). This relationship is not mentioned in his inscriptions,¹⁰ but it is referenced in those of his successors Esarhaddon, Ashurbanipal, Shamash-shumu-ukîn, and Sin-sharru-ishkun, all of whom mention their ancestry.¹¹ Moreover, for many years he had been designated crown prince of Sargon.¹² The identity of Sennacherib's mother is still debated. The hypothesis of Atalia, wife of Sargon, is contradicted by several factors.¹³ Among others, if she were Sennacherib's mother, she was born around 760 and lived at least until 692, but the body found in the royal Nimrud royal grave was only between thirty and thirty-five years old.¹⁴ The most recent hypothesis, proposed by Eckart Frahm and E. Weissert, seems to be plausible; they provide a new reading of a stela from Assur known from 1913 and apparently intentionally mutilated: "Stela of Ra'īmâ, mother of Sennacherib, king of the world, king of Assyria."¹⁵ Ra'īmâ, "beloved," is interpreted as a variant of Raḫīmâ, a

---

9. Laura Kataja, "A Neo-Assyrian Document on Two Cases of River Ordeal," *SAAB* 1 (1987): 65–68.

10. Except for one text, possibly to be attributed to Sennacherib: SAA 3:77, 33.10'.

11. See references in *PNA* 3.1:1113.

12. Hermann Hunger, *Babylonische und assyrische Kolophone*, AOAT 2 (Neukirchen-Vluyn: Neukirchener Verlag, 1968), 138, no. 512, l. 5.

13. For the different hypotheses, see Stephanie Dalley, "Yabâ, Atalyā and the Foreign Policy of the Late Assyrian Kings," *SAAB* 12 (1998): 83–98; Dalley, "Recent Evidence from Assyrian Sources for Judaean History from Uzziah to Manasseh," *JSOT* 28 (2004): 387–401; Dalley, "The Identity of the Princesses in Tomb II and a New Analysis of Events in 701 BC," in *New Light on Nimrud: Proceedings of the Nimrud Conference Eleventh–Thirteenth March 2002*, ed. John Curtis, Henrietta McCall, Dominique Collon, and Lamia al-Gailani Werr (London: British Institute for the Study of Iraq, 2008), 171; Farouk N. H. Al-Rawi, "Inscriptions from the Tombs of the Queens of Assyria," in Curtis, McCall, Collon, and al-Gailani Werr, *New Light on Nimrud*, 119–38; *PNA* 3.1:1113; Sarah C. Melville, "Neo-Assyrian Royal Women and Male Identity: Status as a Social Tool," *JAOS* 124 (2004): 44–46; David Kertai, "The Queens of the Neo-Assyrian Empire," *AoF* 40 (2013): 114–15; SAAS 23:186, nos. 40–41.

14. Ahmed Kamil, "Inscriptions on Objects from Yaba's Tomb in Nimrud," in *Gräber assyrischer Königinnen aus Nimrud*, ed. Muayad Damerji and Ahmed Kamil (Mainz: Verlag des Romisch-Germanischen Zentralmuseums, 1999), 13–18.

15. Frahm, "Family Matters," 179–81. For the first publication, see Walter Andrae, *Die Stelenreihen in Assur*, WVDOG 24 (Leipzig: Hinrichs, 1913), 9–10, no. 4.

West Semitic and probably Aramaic name. Harrân as the origin of Raimâ is presented as a speculative but tempting hypothesis.[16]

Sennacherib's paternal grandparents are known. His grandfather was Tiglath-pileser III, who reigned from 745 to 727, as is attested by two of Sargon's inscriptions.[17] His paternal grandmother could have been Iabâ, who was the queen and wife of Tiglath-pileser III. Iabâ and Banîtu were possibly the same person, which would explain the mention of three names and there being only two bodies in the Nimrud grave.[18] As for Sennacherib's maternal grandparents, they have not yet been identified because the origin of his mother Raimâ has not been clearly established. Based on Atalia being the alleged mother of Sennacherib and on the name Iabâ, it has been argued that Sennacherib's grandparents were members of the royal family of Judah.[19] Hence the claim of the Judean king Ahaz to be a "servant" and "son" of Tiglath-pileser III (2 Kgs 16:7) and Sennacherib's policies toward Judah would be explained by the particularly close relations with this country's ruling family. This hypothesis remains unproved, all the more so as Atalia was not Sennacherib's mother and the relation of Iabâ with *yph*, "beautiful," is not evident. However, the fact that Atalia, queen of Sargon, had a name similar to the Hebrew name Atalyâh(u) could mean that she originated from Judah at the very most. An affiliation given to Sennacherib remains unexplained: he is said to belong to the "dynasty of Habigal," while Shalmaneser V belonged to the "dynasty of Baltil (Assur)."[20] Relating "Habigal" either with "Habiru" or with "Hanibalgat" is speculative in the present state of documentation.[21]

Sennacherib had several brothers and at least one sister. His name implies that he had elder brothers who all died before his birth.[22] As stated in a letter written to Sargon by his teacher Hunnî, he had several younger

---

16. Frahm, "Family Matters," 180–81.

17. Felix Thomas, "Sargon II, der Sohn Tiglat-pilesers III," in *Mesopotamia-Ugaritica-Biblica: Festschrift für Kurt Bergerhof zur Vollendung seines 70; Lebensjahres am 7. Mai 1992*, AOAT 232 (Kevelaer, Germany: Butzon & Bercker, 1993), 465–70.

18. Dalley, "Identity of the Princesses in Tomb II," 171; Melville, "Neo-Assyrian Royal Women and Male Identity," 44–46; SAAS 23:186, nos. 40–41.

19. Dalley, "Yabâ, Atalyā and the Foreign Policy of the Late Assyrian Kings," 83–98.

20. Albert Kirk Grayson, "Königslisten und Chroniken B. Akkadisch," *RlA* 6:93; *PNA* 3.1:1114.

21. *PNA* 3.1:1114.

22. See p. 12.

brothers (*mārē šarri gabbu*), all unnamed.²³ The reference made by Berossus to a brother of Sennacherib ruling Babylon seems to be erroneous.²⁴ Some brothers are mentioned later, in a letter dated around 670, stating that they were protecting Esarhaddon.²⁵ A sister called Ahat-abisha is known from Sargon's annals and from a letter of crown prince Sennacherib, who reported to his father a letter sent by his sister's majordomo.²⁶ Sargon gave her in marriage to Ambaris, king of Tabal/Bit-Purutash. When Ambaris was removed to Assyria with his family after his revolt, there is no reason to think that Ahat-abisha stayed in Tabal as Assyrian administrator.²⁷

According to the tradition of polygamy practiced by Assyrian kings, Sennacherib had a harem.²⁸ Two of his wives are known by name: Tashmêtu-sharrat and Naqi'a. The third possible identified wife is inferred from the damaged Assur stela that is better read as Raimâ, mother of Sennacherib.²⁹ It is not clear whether the two known wives held the position of "queen" (*sēgallu*, MÍ.É.GAL, literally "woman of the palace") simultaneously or successively. In other words, were they primary or secondary consorts?³⁰ It seems more likely that the title of *sēgallu* was a position for one woman only, at least until the death of her husband the king and sometimes afterwards.³¹ Tashmêtu-sharrat, whose name in Akkadian meant "Tashmêtu is queen," bore this title for most of Sennacherib's reign. Naqi'a inherited the title at the end of the reign, possibly because Tashmêtu-sharrat was deposed or died or because she was retrospectively given this title during the reign of Esarhaddon, attested on a bead, but now lost: "Naqi'a, queen of Senna[cherib]." When mentioning Tashmêtu-sharrat, Sennacherib was enthusiastic. In the Nineveh Southwest Palace,

---

23. See p. 18; SAA 1:110, 133.11.

24. Stanley Meyer Burstein, *The Babyloniaca of Berossus*, SANE 1.5 (Malibu, CA: Undena, 1978), 23.

25. Simo Parpola, *Letters from Assyrian Scholars to the Kings Esarhaddon and Assurbanipal*, part 2, *Commentaries and Appendixes*, AOAT 5.2 (Kevelaer: Butzon & Bercker, 1983), 239, 464 (also in Leroy Waterman, *Royal Correspondence of the Assyrian Empire* [Ann Arbor: University of Michigan Press, 1930–1936], letter 1217 + CT 53.118).

26. *ARAB* 2.25, 55; SAA 1:32, 31.r.27.

27. *PNA* 1.1:59; Elayi, *Sargon II, King of Assyria*, 102.

28. SAA 6.1:72–87, nos. 81–99.

29. See p. 13; Frahm, "Family Matters," 179–81.

30. As stated by Melville, "Neo-Assyrian Royal Women and Male Identity," 37–57.

31. SAAS 23:186–87, nos. 39–48; SAAS 9:16–29.

an inscription for her was written on the lions flanking the door of Room LXV, probably the entrance to her quarters: "Moreover, for Tashmêtu-sharrat, the palace lady, my beloved spouse, whose form the goddess Bêlet-ilî made more perfect than (that of) all (other) women: I had a palatial hall for lovemaking, happiness, and exultation built, and (then) I stationed sphinxes of white limestone in its gates"; this was followed by blessings for her.[32] There is no reason to attribute his enthusiasm to a "late conquest";[33] it is possible that he met her before Naqi'a.

Naqi'a was better known than his other wives because of her important role during the reigns of her son Esarhaddon and grandson Ashurbanipal. Her Aramaic name meant "pure," and her Akkadian name was Zakûtu. Her bilingual name makes it possible that she came from outside Assyria proper, but there is no proof of a Syro-Palestinian or a Babylonian origin in the present state of documentation.[34] She probably plotted in urging Sennacherib to appoint her son Esarhaddon as crown prince against the claims of his half-brother Urdu-Mullissu, in Nisannu (April) 683 at the latest.[35] If she married Sennacherib in the decade 720–710 BCE,[36] her son Esarhaddon would have been around thirty years old in 683. Before 683, did she start playing a political role during Sennacherib's reign? Military units for the queen appeared in the reign of Sargon and/or Sennacherib, but a precise relation with Naqi'a's influence has not been proven.[37] We do not know when she died, but apparently she did not long outlive her son

---

32. RINAP 3.2:42, 40.44″b–46″; *PNA* 3.1:1320; Frahm, *Einleitung in die Sanherib-Inschriften*, 121; Karen Radner, "The Seal of Tašmetum-šarrat, Sennacherib's Queen, and Its Impressions," in *Leggo! Studies Presented to Frederik Mario Fales on the Occasion of His Sixty-Fifth Birthday*, ed. Giovanni Battista Lanfranchi, Daniele Morandi Bonacossi, Cinzia Pappi, and Simonetta Ponchia, Leipziger Altorientalische Studien 2 (Wiesbaden: Harrassowitz, 2012), 687–98.

33. Rykle Borger, "König Sanheribs Eheglück," *ARRIM* 6 (1998): 5–11.

34. SAAS 9:13–16; Melville, "Neo-Assyrian Royal Women and Male Identity," 44–46; Melville, "Royal Women and the Exercise of Power in the Ancient Near East," in *Companion to the Ancient Near East*, ed. Daniel C. Snell (Oxford: Blackwell, 2005), 219–28; Kertai, "Queens of the Neo-Assyrian Empire," 114–15; SAAS 23:39–49, 52–61, 64–65, 71–85, 189–209, 213–16, 222–23.

35. See p. 151. PNA 1.1:189; 3.1:1114–15.

36. Frahm, *Einleitung in die Sanherib-Inschriften*, 4; SAAS 9:91.

37. See p. 156. Saana Svärd, "Changes in Neo-Assyrian Queenship," *SAAB* 21 (2015): 162–69.

Esarhaddon, who died in 669, or in any case she retired from court life at that time.[38]

Sennacherib had at least seven sons, whose names are attested, some of them listed together with mythological heroes.[39] His eldest son was Ashur-nâdin-shumi, whom he installed as king of Babylon in 700 and who was probably killed in 694.[40] His second-eldest son was Ashur-ilî-muballissu, called *māru tardennu*, "second son."[41] Both of them were given a house in Assur by Sennacherib, as was his third son, Ashur-shumu-ushabshi. Urdu-Mullissu (possibly ʾ*drmlk* in the Bible) was another son, who became the murderer of his father.[42] The names of other sons are more uncertain, such as Nergal-shumu-ibni (restored name) and Nabû-sharru-usur (*śrʾṣr* in the Bible; 2 Kgs 19:37; Isa 37:38).[43] It is not clear who was the mother of all these sons, but probably Tashmêtu-sharrat was mother of at least some of them. Conversely, we know for certain that Naqiʾa was the mother of Esarhaddon, her eldest son, who was also the youngest of Sennacherib's sons, as he admitted himself: "I was the younger brother of my elder brothers."[44]

Only one of Sennacherib's daughters is known by name: Shadditu. In a land-sale document she is referred to as "daughter of Sennacherib and sister (or half-sister) of Esarhaddon, king of Assyria," and protective rituals were performed on her behalf.[45] Her mother was probably Naqiʾa, because she is the only known sister of Esarhaddon and has been considered part of the royal family as late as 672; Shadditu or another daughter was married to the Egyptian Shusanqu.[46]

---

38. SAAS 9:90.

39. Borger, "König Sanheribs Eheglück," 8–11; Frahm, *Einleitung in die Sanherib-Inschriften*, 4, 140 (not his youngest son); PNA 3.1:1114–15; SAAS 9:17 and n. 30.

40. See p. 93.

41. However, this term is discussed (PNA 1.1:162–63). See also PNA 1.1:189; 3.1:1114–15; C. B. F. Walker, "Some Mesopotamian Inscribed Vessels," *Iraq* 42 (1980): 85.

42. See p. 148.

43. PNA 3.1:1115.

44. Rykle Borger, *Die Inschriften Asarhadons, Königs von Assyrien*, AfOB 9 (Graz: self-pub., 1956), Nin, Ai, l. 8; RINAP 4:45, 5.i.1.

45. SAA 6:200–201, no. 251; SAAS 23:88–91, 134, 163, 226–27, 229; PNA 3.2:1181.

46. SAAS 9:17–18; SAA 6:125–26, no. 142. See PNA 3.1:1115 and, for a different interpretation, Hans-Ulrich Onasch, *Die assyrischen Eroberungen Ägyptens*, ÄAT 27.1 (Wiesbaden: Harrassowitz, 1994), 15.

1.3. Childhood

The date proposed for Sennacherib's birth is around 745.[47] The following arguments have been put forward in support: his eldest son, Ashur-nâdin-shumi, was named king of Babylon in 700, meaning that he was at least twenty years old. Therefore, he was born at the earliest in 720, which means that his father Sennacherib was then at least twenty years old. I have proposed dating his father Sargon's birth to around 770 or at least 760.[48] Assyrian men used to marry when they were between twenty-six and thirty-two years old, but members of the royal family possibly married earlier.[49] Therefore, circa 745 would be a plausible date for Sennacherib's birth. Information on his childhood is scanty. As his grandfather Tiglath-pileser III and his father, Sargon, were living in the royal residence in Nimrud, Sennacherib was probably born there and spent his childhood and youth there. Sargon stayed in Nimrud until 710, but Sennacherib moved to Nineveh at some point after his designation as crown prince, and he also had a residence in the city of Tarbisu (modern Sharif Khan), a few kilometers to the north of Nineveh. His education was not necessarily that of a future crown prince because he was not destined to become a king. According to protocol, his father, Sargon, should not have had access to the throne. His brother (or half-brother) Shalmaneser V was the expected heir to the throne, and it was he who succeeded Tiglath-pileser III on his death. Sennacherib was educated, together with the other royal children, by Hunnî, who was their teacher and supervisor. He wrote a report on the well-being of the royal children to their father.[50] Sennacherib probably received the usual Assyrian education, that is, the education of a scribe, learning languages (Sumerian and Babylonian) and some elements of arithmetic. It is uncertain whether he followed the "second cycle" of studies, including the art of divination and literature. It was through a combination of circumstances that his father, Sargon, acceded to the throne. First,

---

47. Parpola, *Letters from Assyrian Scholars to the Kings Esarhaddon and Assurbanipal*, 239 n. 390; *PNA* 3.1:1116.

48. Elayi, *Sargon II, King of Assyria*, 28–29.

49. Martha T. Roth, "Age at Marriage and the Household: A Study of Neo-Babylonian and Neo-Assyrian Forms," *Comparative Studies in Society and History* 29 (1987): 737.

50. SAA 1:110, 133.7–13. However, at the date of this letter, Sennacherib was already crown prince.

Shalmaneser V had died after only five years of reign; second, his father, Sargon, succeeded in overcoming massive opposition to become king of Assyria.[51] Third, he was chosen by his father as crown prince shortly after 722, forbidding any kind of contestation. It was at that moment that he probably started to complete his education as a future king.

1.4. Personality

The personality of Sennacherib ought normally to be deduced from his numerous inscriptions. However, these inscriptions were not written by the king himself but by royal scribes, as a matter of practice under the king's inspiration. Their method of composition was typically based on the reutilization of preexisting textual materials and on the transfer of several passages from text to text, using stereotypical formulae. All the royal inscriptions are dominated by propaganda, the objective being to present Sennacherib as surpassing all other kings, due to his exceptional qualities. Nevertheless, by examining them with a critical eye and by comparing them with nonroyal inscriptions, it is possible to identify some characteristic features of Sennacherib's personality. Just like his predecessors, he displayed excessive pride and had a high opinion of himself: "[The god Ash]ur, father of the gods, looked steadfastly upon me among all the rulers [and he made my weapons greater than (those of) all who sit on (royal) daises]."[52] He detailed with pleasure the qualities associated with his intelligence: "The god Ninshiku gave me wide understanding equal to (that of) the sage Adapu (and) endowed me with broad knowledge."[53] He considered himself a "perfect man" (*eṭlu gitmālu*), "foremost of all rulers" (*ašared kal malkī*).[54] The cult of his image prompted him to be represented at different places throughout his empire. He had carved stelae made, bearing his image as a majestic and all-powerful king during his campaigns, in conspicuous places and along a passageway: for example, on the face of Judi Dagh, in eastern Anatolia; in Jerwan, north of Nineveh; at the Nahr el-Kelb, north of Beirut; or along the royal route that he had widened in Nineveh. These stelae are sometimes mentioned in the annals: "I had a stele made, had all the victorious conquests that

---

51. See p. 29.
52. RINAP 3.2:48, 42.2b–3a.
53. RINAP 3.2:57, 43.4a; 3.2:92, 49.4.
54. RINAP 3.1:128, 17.i.8–9.

I achieved over them written on it, and I erected (it) in (that) city (Bît-Kilamzah)."[55] He also had himself represented on the reliefs of the Southwest Palace of Nineveh.[56]

Sennacherib was an experienced man when he ascended the throne because, for more than fifteen years, he had been crown prince and was mentored by his father, Sargon, on the affairs of the Assyrian Empire. This means that he was well acquainted with all the related issues. Unlike his father and predecessors, he was not a conqueror who dreamed of conquering the world, as is shown by the fact that several of his inscriptions were not mainly devoted to his conquests but to his building projects.[57] However, he did attribute himself with the traditional titles signifying that he ruled over the whole world: "king of the world" (*šar kiššati*), "king of the four quarters" (*šar kibrat arba'i*), putting forward his greatness and power: "the great king" (*šarru rabû*), "the strong king" (*šarru dannu*).[58] Most of his campaigns were aimed at maintaining order in the empire by suppressing revolts and reconquering lost territories; he also needed to bring back an abundant booty to help finance his building projects. He already had plenty to do to achieve these aims. He described himself as a "virile warrior" (*zikaru qardu*), a "fierce wild bull" (*rīmu ekdu*): "I raged up like a lion, then put on armor (and) placed a helmet suitable for combat on my head. In my anger, I rode quickly in my exalted battle chariot, which lays enemies low. I took in my hand the mighty bow that the god Assur had granted to me (and) I grasped in my hand an arrow that cuts off life."[59] He presented all his campaigns as being victorious, as was the tradition, for unsuccessful military campaigns would have been regarded by his people as strong indications that he was no longer favored by the gods.[60] Sennacherib boasted of his formidable resistance in the

---

55. RINAP 3.2:310, no. 223; 3.2:317–26, nos. 224–28; 3.1:237, no. 38; 3.1:174, 22.ii.5–9; Anne-Marie Maïla-Afeiche, *Le site de Nahr el-Kalb*, Bulletin d'Archéologie et d'Architecture Hors-Série V (Beirut: Minstère de la culture, Direction Générale des Antiquités, 2009), 42, no. VII (15), 243 (possible identification).

56. Russell, *Sennacherib's Palace without Rival at Nineveh*.

57. Elayi, *Sargon II, King of Assyria*, 16–17. Sennacherib was not "an expansionist" (Hayim Tadmor, "World Dominion," 61).

58. RINAP 3.1:172, 22.i.2–3.

59. RINAP 3.1:128, 17.i.8.

60. Bustenay Oded, *War, Peace, and Empire: Justification for War in Assyrian Royal Inscriptions* (Wiesbaden: Reichert, 1992); Laato, "Assyrian Propaganda and the Falsification of History," 200.

most difficult terrains: "Where it was too difficult for (my) chair, I kept forward on my (own) feet like a mountain goat. I ascended the highest peaks against them (enemies)."[61] However, he was not as invested in his campaigns as his predecessors had been, sometimes delegating the command of an expedition to one of his generals. He was convinced, just like other Assyrian kings, that his gods approved his policies, and he fought "with the strength of the god Assur."[62]

As he was "the guardian of truth who loves justice" (*na-ṣir kit-ti ra-'i-im mi-šá-ri e-piš*), his wars, supported by the national god Assur, were deemed as just, and he was entitled to punish and mistreat his enemies and to spare those who were not guilty. For example, in one inscription he declares: in the city of Ekron "I killed the governors (and) nobles who had committed crime(s) and hung their corpses on towers around the city; I counted the citizens who had committed the criminal acts as booty; (and) I commanded that the rest of them, (those) who were not guilty of crimes or wrong doing, (to) whom no penalty was due, be allowed to go free."[63] Sennacherib's descriptions of atrocities do not appear to express acts of sadism, as is the case in Ashurnasirpal II's inscriptions, but they are traditional descriptions. The severed head was a topic that had always attracted attention, and it was an indispensable element in Assyrian warfare. Sennacherib filled the plain with the corpses of his enemies and made their blood flow over the earth. He hung the enemy corpses on poles and placed them around the city in order to frighten and demoralize its inhabitants.[64] Besides using traditional metaphors of massacre, Sennacherib describes the effects of their fear in a new, realistic manner: "Their hearts throbbed like the pursued young of pigeons; they passed their urine hotly, (and) released their excrement inside their chariots."[65]

Now, to what degree such depictions of atrocities reflect reality remains an open question due to the one-sided nature of our primary

---

61. RINAP 3.1:178, 22.iii.81–iv.9a.

62. RINAP 3.1:129, 17.i.41; Galo W. Vera Chamaza, *Die Omnipotenz Aššurs* (Münster: Ugarit-Verlag, 2006); Frederick Mario Fales, *Guerre et paix en Assyrie: Religion et impérialisme* (Paris: Cerf, 2010), 69–88.

63. RINAP 3.2:293, 213.2; RINAP 3.1:132, 17.iii.24–32. See Hayim Tadmor, "Sennacherib, King of Justice," in *The Moshe Weinfeld Jubilee Volume*, ed. Chaim Cohen, Avi Hurvitz, and Shalom M. Paul (Winona Lake, IN: Eisenbrauns, 2004), 385–90.

64. RINAP 3.1:173, 22.i.60–62; 183.vi.2, 4–5, 10–12.

65. Marc Van De Mieroop, "Metaphors of Massacre in Assyrian Royal Inscriptions," *KASKAL* 12 (2015): 299–309; RINAP 3.1:184, 22.vi.29b–33.

sources. For example, the account of the battle of Halulê (campaign eight) was presented as an eloquent glorification of Sennacherib's victory over his Babylonian and Elamite opponents, while the Babylonian Chronicles claim that the Assyrian army was forced to retreat: the emphasis put on this battle in the annals may have been overcompensation for what must have been a loss of face.[66] In any case, Sennacherib used a rhetoric and tactics of intimidation, a kind of psychological warfare in the modern sense of the term; he had inherited it from Sargon, who himself followed the example of Tiglath-pileser III, a master in this art.[67] Even though Sennacherib used psychological warfare, he primarily used classic warfare, just like his predecessors. He had an efficient spy system, and when he was crown prince, he summarized the intelligence reports for his father. What kind of relations did he have with his troops? Except for the core of the "royal contingent," an elite unit led by members of the royal family, the Assyrian army was a heterogeneous, colorful, and multiethnic entity. It was made up of provincial troops, armies of vassal kings, prisoners of war, and various auxiliaries.[68] According to the principle of divide and rule, the constituent parts of the Assyrian army could not plot and form an alliance against Sennacherib but probably competed to obtain his favor. In return for their services, most soldiers were likely to receive a piece of land; mercenaries and auxiliaries possibly received some form of payment. However, the main incentive to fight must have been the share of expected war spoils. For example, after having devastated the city of Til-Garimmu, the Assyrian king shared the booty: "I divided up the rest of the substantial enemy booty like sheep and goats among my entire camp and my governors, (and) the people of my great cult centers." In Chaldea, he let his

---

66. Van De Mieroop, "Metaphors of Massacre in Assyrian Royal Inscriptions," 299.

67. Theodore J. Lewis, "You Have Heard What the Kings of Assyria Have Done," in *Swords into Plowshares: Isaiah's Vison of Peace in Biblical and Modern International Relations*, ed. Raymond Cohen and Raymond Westbrook (Basingstoke, UK: Macmillan, 2008), 79–80; Ariel M. Bagg, "Where Is the Public? A New Look at the Brutality Scenes in Neo-Assyrian Royal Inscriptions and Art," in Cohen and Westbrook, *Swords into Plowshares*, 45–56.

68. John Nicholas Postgate, "The Invisible Hierarchy: Assyrian Military and Civilian Administration in the Eighth and Seventh Centuries BC," in Postgate, *Land of Assur and the Yoke of Assur*, 331–60; Robin Archer, "Chariotry to Cavalry: Developments in the Early First Millennium," in *New Perspectives on Ancient Warfare*, ed. G. Garrett Fagan and Matthew Trundle, History of Warfare 59 (Leiden: Brill, 2010), 57–80.

troops do the plundering: "I let (my) troops eat the grain (and) dates in their gardens (and) their crops in the countryside."[69]

One of Sennacherib's qualities as a warlord was to concede his failures; his return from Elam in 693, caused by bad weather conditions, was freely acknowledged in the annals: "I was afraid of the rain and snow in the gorges, the outflows of the mountains."[70] One major defect was his irascible, vindictive, and impatient character; when he was dominated by his feelings and when things did not go smoothly, his "rage" (*uggatu*) pushed him to reach irrational decisions. Thus the murder of his son was one of the reasons that caused him to order the radical annihilation of Babylon in 689: "I roared loudly like a storm (and) thundered like the god Adad against all the troops of the wicked enemies.... I blew like the onset of a severe storm against the enemy on (their) flanks and front lines."[71]

Sennacherib was more interested in building projects than in military campaigns: the latter he conducted through necessity, the former for pleasure because he was a passionate builder. No other Assyrian king left such a vast quantity of inscriptions regarding building activities, and no one else described his technical details with such care and knowledge. He was probably influenced by his father's personal involvement in building the new capital, Khorsabad (Dûr-Sharrukîn). Sennacherib's building projects were so important for him that several prisms from Nineveh and Assur are inscribed with a relatively short text describing his first four campaigns and a much longer building report on Nineveh.[72] He presented himself as "expert in every type of work," in contrast to his ancestors, who "had had constructed [a palace] for their lordly dwelling, but whose construction they had carried out inexpertly."[73] He was conscious of his abilities as "the builder of Assyria," skills that were given to him by the gods: "With the extensive wisdom that the god Ea had given me, with the perspicacity that (the god) Assur had granted to me, I took counsel with myself and made up my mind to open the gate of Ehursaggalkurkurra towards the rising sun, facing east."[74]

---

69. RINAP 3.1:136, 17.v.15–22; 3.2:297, 213.50.
70. RINAP 3.1:181, 22.v.6–11a.
71. RINAP 3.1:183, 22.v.74–78. See Lionel Marti, "Sennacherib, la rage du prince," *DoArch* 348 (2011): 54–59.
72. RINAP 3.1:89–146, nos. 15–17.
73. RINAP 3.2:50, 42.22'–23'; 3.2:58, 43.7b–9a.
74. RINAP 3.2:243, 166.10–12; 3.2:247, 168.9b.

Sennacherib was a highly innovative ruler, fond of experiments. He boasted having personally introduced a number of architectural, metallurgical, and horticultural innovations.[75] He was aware of being gifted, in contrast to his ancestors, who "gave thought on the matter through ignorance (and) failure.... (But) as for me, ... with the ingenious mind that the prince, the god Ninshiku, had granted to me (and) taking counsel with myself, I intensively pondered how to perform this work ... with my (own) ideas and knowledge."[76] He presented himself as the inventor of a new technique of metalwork casting: "So that it will be known to *future generations*: I increased therein the amount of tin. Know through this that I myself had this metal-work cast."[77] We may suppose that he himself knew how to read and write because of all the reports he had to deal with when he was crown prince and because he was able to acquire his outstanding technical knowledge. He probably participated in the enrichment of the royal libraries of Nineveh, Nimrud, and Khorsabad, which had been constituted on Assyrian kings' initiatives.[78] He was also an aesthete with a very good artistic and eclectic taste for several branches of the arts, as illustrated in all his building designs, which benefited from his innovations. He was also a reformer, particularly in religious and military domains (see pp. 169, 177).

We lack elements of personal information to enable us to interpret Sennacherib's religious beliefs. However, through all his inscriptions, he followed the Assyrian tradition by extolling the role played by his gods. Several inscriptions mention them at the beginning: mainly Assur, of whom he was the favorite, then Anu, Enlil, Sîn, Shamash, Adad, Marduk, Nabû, Nergal, Ishtar, the Sebetti, "the great gods."[79] Many other gods are mentioned, such as Bêlet-ilî, Ninshiku, and Ea, who gave him his skills and wisdom.[80] Sennacherib had a special relationship with Assur; as depicted in the Tablet of Destinies, he humbled himself before him and prayed to him for blessings, most of all for the continuation of his dynasty: "Let the

---

75. See p. 190.
76. RINAP 311:140–41, 17.vi.85–vii.8.
77. RINAP 3.2:225, 160.23–25.
78. Jeremy Black, "The Libraries of Kalhu," in Curtis, McCall, Collon, and al-Gailani Werr, *New Light on Nimrud*, 261–65; Dominique Charpin, *La vie méconnue des temples mésopotamiens*, Docet omnia 1 (Paris: Les Belles Lettres, 2017), 118–34.
79. RINAP 3.2:313, 223.1–2.
80. RINAP 3.2:57, 43.3–4a.

base of my throne be secure as a mountain for long days to come."[81] He started his campaigns at the command of Assur, who gave him power and strength, helped and encouraged him.[82] As he was conscious of the importance of the gods at war, they were permanently present in all his campaigns, through rituals and sacrifices in order to please them and to obtain victories. Standards showing images of the gods, probably mounted on chariots, accompanied the soldiers during their march and were visible to all during the battles. No doubt the religious rituals calmed fears, convinced the soldiers that they were fighting for a just cause, and helped them in the most desperate situations.

Sennacherib also consulted the gods for his building projects, such as the *akītu* house in Assur: "In a favorable month, on a propitious day, through the craft of the purification priest (and) the wisdom of the exorcist, I laid its foundation."[83] As another example, for the opening up of a canal sluice gate, he offered them several precious gifts: "carnelian, lapis lazuli], ... [precious] stone[s, turtles (and) tortoises *whose likeness(es) are cast in* silver (and) gold, aromatics], (and) fine oil"; and sacrifices: "I offered pure] sacrifices [of fattened oxen (and) an abun]dance [of sheep to the great gods, who march at my side (and) who make my reign secure."[84] He did not forget to pray to them in order to be supported efficiently, by offering gifts and sacrifices: "[I prayed to the great gods; they heeded my supplications and ma]de [my] han[diwork] prosper."[85] When he prayed to them for obtaining victory over his enemies, they immediately heeded his prayer and came to his aid. He prayed that he might attain a very old age and secure his throne for himself and his offspring. He recorded all that he did for the gods, as evidenced by his commitment to bring cult centers to completion; he fashioned images of the gods and represented and depicted an epic battle between Assur and Tiâmat with her horde of monsters on the temple's bronze gate of the *akītu* house. Having made

---

81. A. R. George, "Sennacherib and the Tablet of Destinies," *Iraq* 48 (1986): 133–46, l. 20.
82. RINAP 3.1:32, 1.4; 3.1:97, 15.iv.15′–16′; 3.1:194, 23.iii.43–44; 3.1:198, 23.v.4.
83. RINAP 3.2:248, 168.30b–33.
84. RINAP 3.2:215, 155.r.6′–8′; 3.2:213, 154.r.4′–5′.
85. RINAP 3.2:215, 155.r.9–10a.

an image of himself in front of the representation of the god Assur, he expressed humility in the Tablet of Destinies.[86]

Another characteristic of Sennacherib's personality, when he was not blinded by his feelings, was his realism. He had a comparatively realistic worldview, as shown by several indications. For example, for the reliefs of his Southwest Palace he created a bird's-eye perspective, more true to reality. In the monumental bull colossi, he decided to suppress the fifth leg to give these sculptures a more naturalistic appearance. He had a great ability of adaptation and did not hesitate to revise his decisions; for example, he entertained different successive ways of dealing with the problem of Babylon. He presented himself as a wise and benevolent king who "renders assistance," "goes to the aid of the weak," and is, in other words, the "shepherd of the people."[87] He is said to have been affectionate and thoughtful, which seems true if we consider his relationship with his wife Tashmêtu-sharrat, as shown in the inscription written for her on the lions flanking the door of Room LXV.[88] He has even been considered as possibly feminist, which is absurd regarding somebody who had a harem.[89] However, the apparent evolution of the status of royal women during Sennacherib's reign could be due to his acknowledgment, to some extent, of the role of women or to the result of manipulation of the king by his wives. Both explanations seem to be correct, as is shown, on the one hand, by the representation of god Assur for the first time with a prominent female companion, and, on the other hand, by the change of crown prince imposed by Naqi'a.[90]

In short, Sennacherib wanted to project an image of intelligence, ability, justice, piety, benevolence, and energy. This image was differentiated because it had to be associated with a diversity of audiences, such as the palace circle in Nineveh and the temple circle in Assur. Accordingly, in Nineveh there was a prevalence of royal titles related to the military-territorial superiority of the Assyrian Empire and to benevolence and justice toward the subjects. Conversely, in Assur the titulary was completely

---

86. RINAP 3.2:220, 158B.14′–18′; 3.2:239–44, no. 166; George, "Sennacherib and the Tablet of Destinies," 133–46.

87. RINAP 3.1:128, 17.i.5–6; 3.2:57, 43.2.

88. See p. 181; Marti, "Sennacherib, la rage du prince," 54–59.

89. Julian E. Reade, "Was Sennacherib a Feminist?," in *La femme dans le Proche-Orient antique*, ed. Jean-Marie Durand, RAI 33 (Paris: Éditions Recherche sur les Civilisations, 1986), 139–45. On his harem, see SAA 6:71–97, nos. 81–108.

90. See p. 151.

demilitarized, and the relationship with the gods came to the fore, with no link to political activity.[91]

---

91. Mario Liverani, "Critique of Variants and the Titulary of Sennacherib," in *Assyrian Royal Inscriptions: New Horizons in Literary, Ideological, and Historical Analysis*, ed. Frederick Mario Fales, OAC 17 (Rome: Istituto per l'Oriente, 1981), 225–57.

2
SENNACHERIB, THE CROWN PRINCE

2.1. Designation as Crown Prince and Functions

Sennacherib was designated as crown prince by his father, Sargon. We know his exact title from the colophon of a text dated to Sargon's reign: "great (crown) prince (literally: eldest royal son) of Sargon" (*mār šarri rabû ša šarru-kīn*).[1] In the letters he wrote to Sargon when he was crown prince, he called himself the king's "servant" (*urdu*), and he called the king "my lord" (*bēlía*),[2] in accordance with the formal address used in letters to the ruler. The appointment of a crown prince was inaugurated by Tiglath-pileser III: he had designated Shalmaneser V as his heir, and this habit was systematized by his successors, except for Shalmaneser V, who probably did not have the time for that during his short reign. When did Sargon designate Sennacherib as crown prince? The exact date is unknown, but several dates have been proposed, such as 715 or at the very beginning of Sargon's reign.[3] A date at the beginning of Sargon's reign is the most plausible, possibly before his first military campaign of 720, for several reasons. First, he had seen that Shalmaneser V had not had enough time to designate his heir. Second, even though Sargon was not a usurper because he was a son of Tiglath-pileser III and a brother (or half-brother) of Shalmaneser V, he may not have been the only member of the royal household

---

1. Hunger, *Babylonische und Assyrische Kolophone*, 138, no. 512.4–5; *PNA* 3.1:1113.
2. SAA 1:31, 31.1–2.
3. Simo Parpola, "The Royal Archives of Nineveh," in *Cuneiform Archives and Libraries*, ed. Klaas R. Veenhof (Leiden: Nederlands Historisch-Archaeologisch Instituut te Istanbul, 1986), 233; Francis Joannès, *Dictionnaire de la civilisation mésopotamienne* (Paris: Laffont, 2001), 767.

to lay claim to the throne.⁴ Third, and for unknown reasons, he had to face massive opposition in Assyria. Therefore, it was vital for him to secure his throne during his accession year (722 BCE) and his first year (721 BCE). Another means to secure his throne was to designate as his successor and crown prince Sennacherib, who was at that time beyond dispute his eldest son, already around twenty-five years old and hence totally legitimate, to succeed him. It seems plausible to date this designation to 721, after the first internal struggle of 722 and before starting his military campaigns in 720. This arrangement was probably decided and set up in Nimrud, where both of them were living at this time.

Afterward, Sennacherib was obliged to reside, at least partly, in Nineveh, where the house of succession (*bīt redûte*) was located, just as Esarhaddon and Ashurbanipal, who mention that this place was devoted to crown princes,⁵ did subsequently. It was situated on the site of the later north palace of Ashurbanipal, still called *bīt redûte*.⁶ In this house of succession, Sennacherib, like later Assyrian crown princes, exercised royal power in collaboration with his father or in his absence. This house of succession functioned as the seat of the Assyrian government, in any case, during the absences of Sargon, when he was away on campaign and during his long sojourn in Babylonia from 710 to 707. However, after the inauguration of Khorsabad, from 706 to 705, Sennacherib probably had his official residence there as crown prince. After his father's death, he moved his residence to Nineveh, taking with him his father's voluminous correspondence; all the letters and documents from Sargon's lifetime in the so-called Kuyunjik collection were probably filed in this palace.⁷

What were the functions of Sennacherib as crown prince, from around 721 to 705? Did they evolve significantly during this long period of more than fifteen years? His functions were probably not exactly the same during his father's absences, when he seems to have taken on some of the most important royal duties: major political and administrative responsibilities. He kept his father continually informed about matters of state

---

4. Elayi, *Sargon II, King of Assyria*, 27–28.

5. *ARAB* 2.761; *PNA* 3.1:1116; Ali Yaseen Ahmad and Albert Kirk Grayson, "Sennacherib in the Akitu House," *Iraq* 61 (1999): 187–89.

6. Frahm, *Einleitung in die Sanherib-Inschriften*, 3.

7. See p. 164; Frahm, *Einleitung in die Sanherib-Inschriften*, 8; SAA 17:xix–xx. On the difficult problems concerning the royal archives of Nineveh, see Parpola, "Royal Archives of Nineveh," 232–34.

that were of significance; for example, concerning the emissaries of Kummuhu bringing tribute, he wrote to his father: "The king, my lord, should write me to whom they are supposed to give it."[8] However, in situations of emergency, Sennacherib was necessarily obliged to make decisions alone. Therefore, when Sargon was not able to rule during his absences, even indirectly, as he could not be consulted due to the difficulty of communication, Sennacherib replaced him and acted as a kind of regent. This position supposed a relationship of confidence between father and son, and a degree of equality between them. A relief from Sargon's palace in Khorsabad represents Sargon with his son, the crown prince Sennacherib, who is recognizable from his diadem with two ribbons pended from behind, the same as that of the king.[9] Both are quite similar except for the headdress, scepter, and mantle of the king, and they appear to be in discussion with each other as equals.

Sennacherib was mainly in charge of military intelligence and of relations with Assyrian governors and local rulers. He also granted audiences to messengers and emissaries. He received tribute and gifts and distributed them. He had to deal with domestic affairs and to inform Sargon about the progression of his building projects. Finally, he probably had to solve any kind of administrative problems. The information on all these subjects is provided by only a dozen letters written by the crown prince to Sargon, and one letter written to the crown prince by Nabû-riba-ahhe, one of his subordinates.[10] Some of these letters are dated by month and day, but unfortunately not by year: sometimes the mention of an event known from other sources provides a date. Royal messages, especially from the crown prince to the king, were considered so important that they were carried and delivered by members of the royal guard (*ša-qurbūti*), an elite corps largely if not exclusively composed of eunuchs, who played a major role during Sargon's reign. The royal mail was considered so important that it was only entrusted to the eunuchs, who were considered as the most reliable and trustworthy men imaginable.

---

8. SAA 1:33–35, 33.r.1–3.

9. Paul-Émile Botta and Eugène Flandin, *Monuments de Ninive I* (Paris: Imprimerie Nationale, 1849) 12; SAA 1:26–27, fig. 10.

10. SAA 1:27–41, nos. 29–40; SAA 5:198–99, no. 281; Peter Dubóvský, *Hezekiah and the Assyrian Spies: Reconstruction of the Neo-Assyrian Intelligence Services and Its Significance for 2 Kings 18–19* (Rome: Pontifical Biblical Institute, 2006), 266.

2.2. Sennacherib's Correspondence as Crown Prince

In my previous book I considered the problems of western, northwestern, and northern states where our available sources testify to Sennacherib's interventions, as seen from the point of view of Sargon the conqueror.[11] Here I consider them from the point of view of Sennacherib, the crown prince, referring to the previous book for detailed analyzes of Sargon's campaigns. In the west, one letter from the crown prince (no. 29) relates to Ashdod: "The tribute of the Ashdodites was brought to Kalhu; I have received it, sealed it and deposited it in the … palace."[12] The mention of the Ashdodites instead of the king of Ashdod means that the sending of tribute occurred after 711 (year eleven of Sargon), when he suppressed Ashdod's second revolt and turned it into an Assyrian province, ruled by an Assyrian governor.[13] This revolt had started when King Azuri withheld his tribute: Sargon himself conducted his first campaign against him in 713 (year nine) and replaced him with his brother Ahî-Mîti. After a short while, the Ashdodites expelled him from the throne and elevated Yamani to reign over them, a man who had no claim to the throne and who started a new revolt. According to Isaiah (20:1), Sargon sent his commander-in-chief, who forced Yamani to flee to Egypt; he captured the city, spoiled it, deported its population, and settled people from the mountains of the east in the city. Therefore, letter 29 from the crown prince is dated from between 711 and 705; it is helpful in dating the other events mentioned in this letter.[14]

Another letter (no. 32) mentions "Judah" (KUR]-*ia-ú-da-a-a*). Its ending is badly damaged, and it is impossible to determine the context. The letter was written after the defeat of the Urartians by the Cimmerians, which occurred in 715 or spring 714, anyway before Sargon's eighth campaign, in June 714.[15] The governors of Rasappa and Til Barsip (Tell Ahmar), south of Carchemish on the Upper Euphrates, are also men-

---

11. Elayi, *Sargon II, King of Assyria*, 122–23, 131, 138.
12. SAA 1:29, 29.r.22–25.
13. *ARAB* 2.30, 62, 79. See Elayi, *Sargon II, King of Assyria*, 57–58.
14. See p. 34.
15. Askold I. Ivantchik, *Les Cimmériens au Proche-Orient*, OBO 127 (Göttingen: Vandenhoeck & Ruprecht, 1993), 47; Mirjo Salvini, "Sargon et l'Urartu," in *Khorsabad, le palais de Sargon II, roi d'Assyrie*, ed. Annie Caubet (Paris: La Documentation française, 1995), 143; Elayi, *Sargon II, King of Assyria*, 138–39.

2. SENNACHERIB, THE CROWN PRINCE

tioned in the damaged passage, but the letter provides no information, as these regions had already been Assyrian provinces since the beginning of the first millennium.[16] A fragment of a Sargon inscription was found at Til Barsip, possibly belonging to a bull colossus, not to a stela.[17] It is impossible to know during which campaign this inscription was engraved, but it must date from after the conquest of Babylonia in 710. A last toponym is also mentioned in the damaged passage of letter 29: Adia, which was a town in central Assyria, possibly modern Sheikh Adi.[18]

Letter 33 from the crown prince refers to Kummuhu in the northwest of the empire.[19] He asks his father whether he has to send him the tribute brought by emissaries from Kummuhu to Babylon or to receive it himself. In the meantime, "the tribute and the mules are entrusted in the Commagenean embassy, and the emissaries too are there, eating their own bread."[20] This letter means that Sargon was then in Babylon, where he stayed between 710 and 707. A more precise date can be provided for this letter. Kummuhu (classical Commagene) was a Neo-Hittite kingdom, located in the region between Carchemish and Melid. After a long period of good relations between Assyria and Kummuhu, King Mutallu withheld tribute from Assyria and allied with Argishti II, king of Urartu. This occurred in 709 (year thirteen) according to the annals, while according to the eponym lists it was in 708.[21] Sargon besieged and captured the capital city of Mutallu (classical Samosata, modern Samsat).[22] He annexed Kummuhu to Assyria and placed it under the control of the "commander-in-chief of the left" (*turtānu šumēlu*). Therefore, Kummuhu was again paying tribute in 708 or 707: it is the date of letter 33.

Letter 31 mentions that Sennacherib had received a letter from Tabal, written by Nabû-lêʾi, the majordomo of Ahat-abisha, Sargon's daughter, married to Ambaris, king of Tabal. The contents of the letter are not given: "I am herewith forwarding it to the king, my lord."[23] Sargon had restored

---

16. Joannès, *Dictionnaire de la civilisation mésopotamienne*, 702, 852–54.
17. Walter Farber and Karlheinz Kessler, "Eine Inschrift Sargons II. aus Til Barsib," *RA* 67 (1973): 163–64; *ARAB* 2.28; Karen Radner, "Aššur-dūr-pānīya, Statthalter von Til-Barsip unter Sargon II. von Assyrien," *BaghM* 37 (2006): 185–95.
18. SAA 1:33, 32.r.15.
19. SAA 1:33–35, no. 33.
20. SAA 1:33, 33.11–14.
21. *ARAB* 2.64; SAAS 2:48.
22. For details on this campaign, see Elayi, *Sargon II, King of Assyria*, 107–9.
23. SAA 1:32, 31.26–29.

Hullî on the throne of Tabal proper/Bit-Purutash; then, shortly later, he replaced him by his son Ambaris, without providing any reason. He gave him his daughter Ahat-abisha, together with the land of Hilakku, because he wanted to raise him above his other vassals in this area.[24] However, in 713 (year nine), Ambaris plotted with Rusâ I of Urartu, Midas of Phrygia, and other kings of Tabal to drive the Assyrians from the region. Sargon responded vigorously to Ambaris's treason, as he had forgotten the favors received, and annexed Tabal as an Assyrian province. Therefore, letter 31 is to be dated from around 713, after Ambaris's marriage with Ahat-abisha and before his treason.

Letter 29 is an important letter, devoted to the north of the empire, except for the mention of the tribute from the Ashdodites.[25] Sennacherib starts by giving information about the fort of Kumme, which was being built by the Assyrians and was making good progress. This preliminary information is necessary for understanding the following messages from Ariye, ruler of Kumme, brought by his messenger. It was a very complex situation. Kumme was one of the small states to the north of Assyria that enjoyed the leadership of a local ruler and was an ally of the Assyrians until Sargon's reign.[26] It was ruled by Ariye and Ariazâ, who were either king and crown prince or corulers.[27] However, Ariye was the superior, named the "city lord" (*bēl āli*) of Kumme.[28] This title was used for recently subjugated Assyrian vassals. However, it is contradicted by the fact that Argishti II, the new king of Urartu, complained about not having received any greetings from Kumme since his accession: it means that, in Urartian eyes, Kumme was considered as an autonomous state. As a matter of fact, Ariye of Kumme had certain obligations toward Sargon, guaranteed by a treaty: to supply manpower, horses, and timber, and mainly to provide intelligence reports on the neighboring states. Kumme was in an excellent strategic position, on the direct mountain route leading from Assyria's heartland to the center of Urartu. At the same time, Ariye entertained close relations with Argishti II and also provided him with men and information.[29] He was in fact a double agent, as he was encouraged by Assyria

---

24. *ARAB* 2.25, 55; see Elayi, *Sargon II, King of Assyria*, 102–3.
25. See p. 32.
26. See Elayi, *Sargon II, King of Assyria*, 124–25.
27. SAA 5:91, no. 116; Parker, *Mechanics of Empire*, 90; *PNA* 1.1:130–31.
28. SAA 1:44, no. 41.
29. SAA 5:76–77, no. 95; 5:82–83, no. 105.

to be a spy working for Urartu because this was seen as a good way of gaining access to Urartu and gathering intelligence about it. The Assyrian system of espionage controlled by Sennacherib was highly efficient. He received the message from Ariye that Ariye had sent to the Urartian king (the Assyrian governors were building a fort in Kumme) and Argishti II's answer (an order to capture the Assyrian governors alive and to bring them to Urartu). Ariye thus ends his message to Sennacherib as follows: "I do not have the full details yet; as soon as I have heard more, I shall write by express to the crown prince that they should rush troops to me."[30]

Sennacherib provided Sargon with a second complementary report, sent to him by Ashur-rêsûwa, a permanent Assyrian ambassador (*qēpu*, "trustworthy man") at Ariye's court. He was a high-ranking intelligence agent reporting on Urartian activities. He provided information on military operations and on the king of Urartu's plans: he failed in an operation in Zikirtu, an operation that was not described because the facts were supposed to be known; he left troops in Waisi (Urmia?); he entered Mannea with a few troops: "I have not heard about the invasion yet, but I shall write you as soon as I have heard more." Mannea was a sensitive region because the earlier united kingdom was actually divided into two states: the independent state of Zikirtu, allied with Urartu, with its capital city Parda; and the Assyrian vassal state of Mannea, having Izirti as its capital.[31] Sennacherib was also responsible for maintaining good relations with Assyrian vassals, as is stated at the end of the letter: "A messenger of the Mannean (king) has come to me bringing a horse as the audience gift and giving me the regards of the Mannean.... I dressed him (in purple) and put a silver bracelet on his arm."[32] The second point in Ashur-rêsûwa's report concerns his observation of the governor in the Urartian province border area, his travels, and the improvement in roads and the construction of bridges, which could represent a threat for Kumme. It ends in this way: "as soon as I have heard what it is all about, whether he is coming with troops or whether he is clean (*zakû*). I shall immediately write to the crown prince."[33]

The third report provided by Sennacherib to Sargon was that of the ruler of Arzabia, although it is far from clear to us. Arzabia was a town near Kumme and Ukku. This ruler had some kind of problem with the

---

30. SAA 1:28, 29.18–21.
31. See Elayi, *Sargon II, King of Assyria*, 129–36.
32. SAA 1:29, 29.r.18–21.
33. SAA 1:29, 29.r.7–10.

ruler of Ukku. Ukku was a small buffer state between Kumme, the Assyrian loyal vassal, and the frontier of Urartu.[34] The name of its king is not written in the sixteen letters mentioning Ukku, only being referred to as "the Ukkean."[35] Just like Kumme, Ukku was forced to send spies to gather information for the Assyrians and also for the Urartians. According to another letter, the king of Ukku had been sent by the Urartians to meet with the king of Kumme in order to persuade him to throw off the Assyrian yoke.[36] The two kings met in Elizki, a neutral town located in a mountain pass between Ukku and Kumme. It is uncertain whether this meeting concerned the arbitration of the ruler of Arzabia.

Letter 30, whose beginning is broken off, is attributed to the crown prince and is also concerned with Urartian affairs. The first report sent by Sennacherib to his father comes from Ashur-rêsûwa: from the remaining sentence, it seems to be related to Ariye's court.[37] The second report was brought to the crown prince by Shulmu-bêli, deputy of the palace herald Gabbu-ana-Ashur.[38] This high official was stationed in Kurbail (modern Gir-e-pan?) and operated on the Urartian border. Therefore Shulmu-bêli was presumably based somewhere in the province of his official and was in charge of surveillance of the Urartian border and of the small independent states in this region. He informed Sennacherib about a letter that Urzana, king of Musasir, had written to him. The news was that the troops of the Urartian king had been defeated on his expedition against the Cimmerians and that the governor of the Urartian city of Waisi had been killed. The battle between Urartians and Cimmerians occurred in 715 or spring 714.[39] Urzana's letter ends as follows: "We do not have detailed information yet, but as soon as we have it, we will send you a full report."[40] Then letter 30 probably continued the report of Shulmu-bêli: the cavalryman under the command of Sharru-lû-dâri, a military official active on the Urartian border, had disappeared and was on the run in Urartu.[41] The passage is

---

34. See Elayi, *Sargon II, King of Assyria*, 122–24; Josette Elayi, "The Buffer States in the Neo-Assyrian Empire," in *Festschrift G. Garbini* (forthcoming).
35. SAA 5:136, no. 190; Parker, *Mechanics of Empire*, 95 and n. 437.
36. SAA 1:44, no. 41.
37. SAA 1:29, 30.1′–2′.
38. SAA 1:29–31, 30.3′–10′ and r.1–11; *PNA* 3.1:1272–74; 1.2:412–13.
39. See p. 32.
40. SAA 1:31, 30.r.1–2.
41. SAA 1:31, 30.4.3–5; *PNA* 3.2:1248–50.

too damaged to be able to understand other news in connection with "the scouts of the household of the palace herald operating in the territory of Hubushkia," located somewhere north of Musasir.[42]

Letter 31 is well preserved and provides complementary information about the defeat of Rusâ, king of Urartu, by the Cimmerians. The first report sent by Sennacherib to his father was that of the unnamed king of Ukku. It provided detailed but incomplete information regarding the Urartian defeat: "Eleven of his governors have been eliminated [with] their troops; his commander-in-chief and two of his governors [have been taken prisoners]. He (himself) came to take [the road to …]."[43] The second report, coming from Ashur-rêsûwa, was presented as following on from his first report on the defeat and dealt with the situation in Urartu after the defeat of Rusâ: "Now his country is quiet again and each of his magnates has gone to his province. Kaqqadanu, his commander-in-chief, has been taken prisoner; the Urartian king is in the province of Wazaun."[44] Kaqqadanu was possibly related to the Urartian royal family and, before his capture by the Cimmerians, conquered Musasir.[45] The third report came from Nabû-lê'i, governor of the province of Birtu, situated on the Lesser Khabur, north of modern Dohuk.[46] He must not be confused with the other Nabû-lê'i quoted at the end of this letter, who was the majordomo of Ahat-abisha. He has obtained his information from the guards of the forts along the border separating Assyria and Urartu, and who enjoyed an excellent observation position. The number of magnates killed by the Cimmerians differed from the report of the Ukkean king: three instead of eleven. The report recounted that Rusâ himself had escaped and returned to his country, but as yet not his army. Sennacherib had received similar reports directly from the guards of the forts along the border. He gives another piece of information that he had probably obtained from them: "The (king) of Musasir and his brother have gone to greet the Urartian king, and the messenger of the (king) of Hubushkia has also gone to greet him."[47] In what circumstances did they go to greet the Urartian king? It

---

42. SAA 1:31, 30.r.6–11; Elayi, *Sargon II, King of Assyria*, 143–44.
43. SAA 1:31, 31.9–18. See Elayi, *Sargon II, King of Assyria*, 138–39.
44. SAA 1:31–32, 31.21–29; Ali Çifçi, *The Socio-economic Organization of the Urartian Kingdom* (Leiden: Brill, 2017).
45. *PNA* 2.1:605–6; SAA 5:xix.
46. SAA 1:32, 31.r.4–15.
47. SAA 1:32, 31.r.17–22.

could be after the sack of Musasir by Sargon in 714, when Rusâ possibly retook this city.[48]

Letter 32 is badly damaged, mainly in the last passage concerning Judah, Rasappa, and Til Barsip.[49] The first part of the letter is about the events in the north. The first report was provided by somebody whose name is in the broken part of the tablet. Sennacherib asked him about the Urartians, and he gave an account completing the other reports: "The Urartian [and his magnates were *defeated*] on their expedition [against] the Cimmerians, and they are very much afraid of the king, my lord. They tremble and keep silent like women, and nobody [...] the forts of the king, my lord."[50] The comparison with women for expressing cowardice is also used for Rusâ, who behaved "like a woman in labor."[51] The conclusion of the first report is that "the situation was very good," obviously for the Assyrians. The following passage concerning "the emissary of the Mannean king," probably sent to Urartu, is too damaged to be understood.

Besides Sennacherib's main function consisting of controlling military intelligence, he was also in charge of domestic and various other affairs. He was assigned to the reception and distribution of the tribute and audience gifts. He was conforming to the orders of Sargon, all the time or only occasionally, as in the case of the Kummuhu tribute referred to in letter 33.[52] Anyway, after the distribution, he informed his father, as evidenced in letter 34, which is a precise and detailed account of a distribution, although complete information is lacking, probably mentioned in the broken end of the tablet.[53] All the items attributed are described with their nature, quantity, origin, and beneficiary of the attribution. The beneficiaries were the palace, the queen, the crown prince (that is to say, himself), the great vizier, the commander-in-chief, the high official (*sartinnu*), the second vizier, the chief eunuch, the palace superintendent, the overseer of the domestic quarters, the scribe of the palace, the chariot driver, and the "third man." The goods attributed were adapted in nature and quantities: the palace received the greatest number, the magnates received a

---

48. SAA 5:xvii, xx; Kathryn F. Kravitz, "A Last-Minute Revision to Sargon's Letter," *JNES* 62 (2003): 94 (with bibliography).
49. See p. 32.
50. SAA 1:32–33, 32.11–16.
51. *ARAB* 2.155.
52. See p. 32.
53. SAA 1:35–36, no. 34; SAAS 11:145.

number of goods according to their rank. The nature of the goods attributed depended on the identity of the beneficiary: for example, the queen received many tunics and togas; the scribe received two scrolls of papyrus.

Letter 35 is badly damaged but concerns an order given by Sargon for investigating and solving an affair related to Nabû-etir-napshati, his associate, and their men in Nimrud, possibly a quarrel between officials or a commercial affair.[54] Letter 37 concerns demands made to him by the charioteers of the palace guard. Sennacherib asks his father to specify what he wants: "What does the king, my lord, order?"[55] It means that he was anxious to obey Sargon's orders to the letter.

Some letters are related in some way to the building of Sargon's new capital of Khorsabad. The badly preserved letter 36 is about floods, which had "advanced very considerably [in the province] of Nineveh, [in] Dûr-Sharrukîn and in the province of Kurbail."[56] These floods probably disrupted the building of Khorsabad. Letter 39, also damaged, attributed to Sennacherib, informs Sargon about the work going on in Khorsabad.[57] It mentions the problems concerning Gidgiddânu, an individual working in Khorsabad with his brothers and another person in charge of Ashur-of-Lions, probably a statue of Assur, and Sennacherib impresses on them the need to do their work. He did not allow the domestics to light fires in Khorsabad. The building of Khorsabad was entrusted to Tab-shar-Ashur.[58] However, letter 39 proves that the crown prince also played a leading role in the building of Sargon's capital. It is not surprising that, after such an experience, he was fond of architectural projects when he became king. Another letter, badly damaged, sent by Sennacherib to Sargon, could also be related to the building of Khorsabad.[59] It deals with trees for the royal orchards: medlar trees, cypresses, and vines are the words that can be read, and also the name of an individual named Tûâiu.[60] It is interesting to stress that Sennacherib was very much committed to the laying out of parks and gardens when he was king. All the letters related to the building of Khors-

---

54. SAA 1:36–37, no. 35; *PNA* 2.2:831–32; 3.1:1116.
55. SAA 1:37–38, 37.r.12–13.
56. SAA 1:37, 36.r.2′–5′.
57. SAA 1:38–41, no. 39; K. Watanabe, review of SAA 1, *BiOr* 48 (1991): 188; *PNA* 1.2:422–23; 2.2:720–21; 3.1:1116.
58. Elayi, *Sargon II, King of Assyria*, 127–29, 132, 203.
59. SAA 5:198, no. 281.
60. *PNA* 3.2:1327.

abad are dated between 717, date of the beginning of his project, and 707, date of the inauguration of Sargon's new capital. Other letters sent by the crown prince to his father are too badly preserved to be understood.[61]

2.3. Relationship between the Crown Prince and His Father

This correspondence provides some insight into the long period of more than fifteen years during which Sennacherib was crown prince. The question of the relationship between the crown prince Sennacherib and his father, Sargon, is complex and has to be investigated because the functioning of the Assyrian Empire during this long period was based on it. All his letters written to Sargon give the impression that Sennacherib was respectful but friendly. He uses the accepted manner for a subject to address his king: "To the king, my lord, your servant Sennacherib. Good health to the king, my lord."[62] This first official formula is followed with a sentence specific to Sennacherib: "Assyria is well, the temples are well, all the king's forts are well. The king, my lord, can be glad indeed."[63] The intention was that he wanted to please his father, and it seems that he was at ease with somebody that he knew quite well. He never discusses the royal orders but obeys Sargon scrupulously and consults him as often as possible. Sennacherib's attitude toward his father implies that Sargon had total trust in his son.

One question arises: Was Sennacherib frustrated because he was never associated with the royal campaigns or entrusted with military operations? Even if he was not a warrior, he could have been interested by the glory attached to war feats. He could have been ambitious enough to initiate a coup in order to seize power. He was mature enough to become a king himself: he was around twenty-five years old in 721 and forty in 705; he was married; he had children; and he had the same style of life as his father, with a palace and a harem. Either he was loyal to Sargon and did not want to seize power illegitimately, or he was not very interested in reigning. Maybe both explanations are correct. Another question arises: Why did Sargon never associate his son with his military campaigns? First, there was no need to legitimate the crown prince, who was, in any event,

---

61. SAA 1:38, no. 38; 1:41, no. 40.
62. SAA 1:28, 29.1–3; 1:31, 31.1–3; 1:32, 32.1–2; 1:33, 33.1–3; 1:35, 34.1–3; 1:36, 35.1–3; 1:37, 36.1–3 and 37.1–3; 1:38, 38.1–3.
63. SAA 1:28, 29.4–6.

unquestionably his legitimate heir. Second, he possibly dreaded that Sennacherib would become too powerful and ambitious as a warlord.

In spite of the apparent good relationship between father and son, some contradictory elements indicate that Sennacherib preferred to keep his distance from Sargon. First, he did not reside in the same place as his father, except for his short sojourn in Khorsabad, the royal capital built by his father, from 706 to 705. Even though he probably attended the official inauguration of Khorsabad in 706, he is not mentioned by name in Sargon's inscriptions related to this event: "Sitting down in my palace together with rulers from the four quarters (of the world), with the governors of my land, with the princes, the eunuchs, and the elders of Assyria, I celebrated a feast."[64] As a matter of fact, Sargon was convinced at that time that he was still going to reign for a long time: "The gods who dwell in heaven and earth, and also in this city, were pleased with my command and therefore granted me for all times the privilege of building this city and growing old in it."[65] After his father's death, Sennacherib abandoned Khorsabad as a royal residence.

He is not mentioned in Sargon's royal inscriptions and, in turn, as seen above, Sargon is not mentioned in his son's royal inscriptions. Sennacherib did not set out his genealogy, as his successors did, for example, his son Esarhaddon, who had inscribed: "I am Esarhaddon, king of the universe, king of Assyria, mighty warrior, first among all princes, son of Sennacherib, king of Assyria; (grand) son of Sargon, king of the universe, king of Assyria."[66] Moreover, he never celebrated the memory of his father. How can this be understood? First, as Sargon's legitimate heir, he was not obliged to legitimate himself as king, in contrast with Esarhaddon, who encountered difficult successional issues. Second, Sargon's ignominious death, with his body not being retrieved for burial and his camp falling prey to the enemy, left the crown prince shocked, and he had to ponder what were the sin(s) his father had committed to deserve such an infamous death.[67]

It is important to distinguish between what was his official position and the reality of his feelings. He had to preserve appearances and to

---

64. *ARAB* 2.74.
65. *ARAB* 2.122.
66. *ARAB* 2.507. For Ashurbanipal, see *ARAB* 2.767.
67. See p. 44; Hayim Tadmor, Benno Landsberger, and Simo Parpola, "The Sin of Sargon and Sennacherib's Last Will," *SAAB* 3 (1989): 3–51.

maintain his rank, which was not difficult because he seems to have been devoted, loyal, and not ambitious. However, he possibly felt overshadowed by his father and was relieved, after this long period of more than fifteen years, to be able to exist by himself, with his own individual personality, different from that of Sargon. As seen above, Sennacherib was not primarily a warlord. He was an expert and even a scholar, an aesthete and somebody who was interested in a very wide range of subjects and who seemed to be happy with life. He asked the gods "for the lengthening of his days, the happiness of his heart, the stability of his reign," in other words to live to be old and happy, with a prosperous offspring.[68]

---

68. *ARAB* 2.461, 441.

3
Accession and Priority Campaigns (705–701)

3.1. Accession to the Throne

After Sargon's death, Sennacherib ascended the throne of Assyria: "I solemnly took my seat on the throne and took command of the population of Assyria amid obedience and peace."[1] Normally he ought to have come to power without meeting any resistance from other possible pretenders to the throne, as he had been the undisputed crown prince for more than fifteen years. However, the circumstances of his accession were not favorable. His father had been killed on the battlefield far away, probably in Tabal, in an unclear context.[2] Sennacherib's duty was to bury his deceased predecessor in the city of Assur, but this was impossible because Sargon's body had not been recovered by the Assyrians. The absence of a funeral for the deceased king, as prescribed by tradition, was clearly considered highly inauspicious and undoubtedly made an impression on Assyrian court circles. A later text reported that Sennacherib was so dismayed by this event that he investigated the nature of Sargon's sin (or sins), which was considered to have been the cause of his unhappy end.[3] Another consequence of this event was the transfer of the royal court from Khorsabad to Nineveh, immediately after Sennacherib had become king. He probably considered Sargon's new capital as cursed because of his infamous death, and it was reduced to a ghost town, with only a military garrison until the end of the Assyrian Empire. Other consequences could have been the sudden

---

1. *ARAB* 2.257.
2. SAAS 2:48; Elayi, *Sargon II, King of Assyria*.
3. Tadmor, Landsberger, and Parpola, "Sin of Sargon and Sennacherib's Last Will," 3–51; Elayi, *Sargon II, King of Assyria*, 210–17; Frederick Mario Fales, "The Road to Judah: 701 B.C.E. in the Context of Sennacherib's Political-Military Strategy," in Kalimi and Richardson, *Sennacherib at the Gates of Jerusalem*, 225–32.

interruption of Sargon's architectural ameliorations in the cultic capital of Assur, and Sennacherib's building project in Tarbisu: the reconstruction of the temple of Nergal, the netherworld god.[4] Although not explicitly stated, this reconstruction, commemorated in two cylinder inscriptions possibly dating from 702, may have been inspired by his father's fate.[5]

3.2. Campaign against the Kulummeans

After Sennacherib's accession to the throne, on the twelfth day of Abu (August) 705, almost immediately revolts occurred throughout the Assyrian Empire. A campaign against the Kulummeans is mentioned in an eponym chronicle for year 704, under the eponymate of Nabû-dênî-epush. This text is badly damaged but can be partly restored: GAL.MEŠ *ina* UGU ⌈*lú*ku-lum-ma-a-a*⌉ […], "The magnates against the Kulummeans […]."[6] What is clear is that Sennacherib did not participate in this campaign but sent his magnates in his stead, possibly so as not to take any risks himself at the very beginning of his reign, given also that it was in a dangerous area, or because he was campaigning at the same time against Merodach-baladan.[7] His probable intention was to take revenge for the killing of his father. Another campaign was conducted against the Kulummeans in 695.[8] The 704 campaign was probably unsuccessful, as it is never mentioned in Sennacherib's inscriptions. Nevertheless, it had been absolutely essential to undertake it because of public opinion: the Assyrian king had to be seen to be trying to avenge his father's death.

3.3. First Babylonian Campaign

There was another priority at the beginning of Sennacherib's reign: the instability of the political situation in Babylonia (Kâr-Duniash) repre-

---

4. See pp. 188–89.

5. Frahm, *Einleitung in die Sanherib-Inschriften*, 188–90 (T162, T163, T164, T164a); *PNA* 3.1:1120, 1123.

6. Israel L. Finkel and Julian E. Reade, "Assyrian Eponyms, 873–649 BC," *Or* 67 (1998): 252; Eckart Frahm, "704 v. Chr.," *NABU* 4 (1998): 106; Frahm, "Nabû-zuqup-kēnu, das Gilgameš-epos und der Tod Sargons II," *JCS* 51 (1999): 83–84; Fales, "Road to Judah," 228–33; *PNA* 3.1:1118.

7. SAA 15:li–lii, no. 41; Fales, "Road to Judah," 232 and n. 30.

8. See p. 105.

3. ACCESSION AND PRIORITY CAMPAIGNS (705–701)

sented a danger for the Assyrian Empire. He chose to follow closely his father's operational footsteps. The contradictions between the documents show that there was some confusion about who was king in Babylonia during this period. The Babylonian King List A attributes a reign of two years to Sennacherib after Sargon's reign: the Ptolemaic Canon describes this period as "kingless" (ἀβασίλευτα), possibly because he was hated by the Babylonians for having destroyed their capital.[9] According to a document from Nippur dated posthumously to the nineteenth year of Sargon, after a one-month reign of Marduk-zâkir-shumi II, Marduk-apla-iddina II, known as Merodach-baladan in the Bible, again usurped the kingship over Babylonia, for a nine-month reign, more probably at the beginning of 704 than in 703.[10] What happened exactly? On Sargon's death, by virtue of the succession, Sennacherib inherited the double kingdom of Assyria and Babylonia, but the usurper Marduk-zâkir-shumi II took the throne for a short period, followed by the usurper Merodach-baladan.[11] Who was Merodach-baladan? In the Assyrian royal inscriptions, he is also named "king of the land of Chaldea, who dwelled on the shore of the sea."[12] He claimed to be the grandson of Erîba-Marduk, a Chaldean chief who seized the throne of Babylon from 769 to 761.[13] He was also referred to as the "son of Yakin," that is, a member or the head of the Chaldean tribe of Bît-Yakin. He was sometimes named "son of Zerî," that is, a member or the head of a tribe called Bît-Zerî. For the year 710 the eponym lists mention "To Bît-Zerî."[14] The conglomerate of tribes and cities headed by Bît-Yakin

---

9. *PNA* 3.1:1118; Grayson, "Königslisten und Chroniken B. Akkadisch," 6:93 iv.12′, 101; Grant Frame, *Babylonia 689–627 B.C.: A Political History* (Leiden: Nederlands Instituut voor het Nabije Oosten, 1992), 53–54.

10. As proposed by John A. Brinkman and D. A. Kennedy, "Documentary Evidence for the Economic Base of Early Neo-Babylonian Society: A Survey of Dated Babylonian Economic Texts, 721–626 B.C.," *JCS* 35 (1983): 13–14.

11. Louis D. Levine, "Sennacherib's Southern Front: 704–689 B.C.," *JCS* 34 (1982): 29–40.

12. Grant Frame, "The Inscription of Sargon II at Tang-i Var," *Or* 68 (1999): 31–57, 37, 40, l. 25.

13. John A. Brinkman, "Merodach-baladan," in *Studies Presented to A. Oppenheim* (Chicago: Oriental Institute of the University of Chicago, 1964), 6–53; Joannès, *Dictionnaire de la civilisation mésopotamienne*, 523–25; SAA 19:xlvii–xlviii; *PNA* 2.2:705–11.

14. SAAS 2:47 and 60.

was probably called Bît-Zerî: therefore the "son of Yakin" and the "son of Zerî" would have been identical.[15]

As a matter of fact, relations between Assyria and Babylonia had always been fluctuating: for example, in the ninth century, Marduk-zâkir-shumi I called for help from Shalmaneser III, then gave help to King Shamshi-Adad V, following which Shamshi-Adad V captured the Babylonian King Marduk-balâssu-iqbi.[16] After this last Assyrian attack against Babylonia, there was a period of political confusion between 811 and 769, with the seizure of power by several Chaldean chiefs of Bît-Yakin, Bît-Dakkûri, and Bît-Amukâni. When the Babylonian King Nabû-nâsir called on Tiglath-pileser III for help in order to neutralize the Chaldean tribes, Babylonia passed under Assyrian control, except for a few short periods when some Chaldean tribal chiefs seized power. Nabû-mukîn-zêri, Chaldean chief of the tribal political unit of Bît-Amukâni, after removing another rebellious candidate, Nabû-shuma-ukîn II, from the throne, became king of Babylon in 732. The people of Babylon, deeply distrustful of the Assyrians and terrified of the Chaldeans, fell prey to raids and other acts of violence. Tiglath-pileser III decided to intervene in Babylonian affairs: he marched against Nabû-mukîn-zêri and, in 728, he integrated Babylonia into the Assyrian Empire, becoming king of Babylonia, under the name of Pulû in order to spare the susceptibility of Babylonians. In fact, through the expedient of the double throne of Assyria and Babylonia, he gave the impression of an autonomous Babylonian state in the face of the Assyrian Empire. However, Tiglath-pileser III died one year later, in 727. His successor, Shalmaneser V, continued to occupy the throne of Babylon under the name Ulûlâyu, but his reign was short (726–722). Merodach-baladan had rallied all the Chaldean tribes and taken advantage of the troubles surrounding the royal succession in Assyria to recapture all the Babylonian territories occupied by Tiglath-pileser III and to proclaim himself king of Babylon in the same year that Sargon ascended the Assyrian throne.[17]

---

15. SAA 15:xv.

16. John A. Brinkman, *A Political History of Post-Kassite Babylonia 1158–722 B.C.*, AnOr 43 (Rome: Biblical Institute Press, 1968), 265–85; Peter Machinist, "The Assyrians and Their Babylonian Problem: Some Reflections," *Wissenschaftskollege zu Berlin Jahrbuch* (1984–1985): 353–64; Francis Joannès, *La Mésopotamie au Ier millénaire avant J.-C.* (Paris: Colin, 2000), 81–87.

17. Grayson, *Assyrian and Babylonian Chronicles*, 76, chr. 1, ii.31–32.

3. ACCESSION AND PRIORITY CAMPAIGNS (705–701) 47

He remained on the throne of Babylonia from 721 to 710, before being expelled by Sargon in 710, and again usurped the throne in 704.[18]

Sennacherib decided that it was necessary to conduct a campaign against Babylonia. This campaign, which occurred "at the beginning of (his) kingship," "on the twentieth day of the month Shabatu (February)," is dated to 704 both in the Assyrian Eponym Chronicles and in the Babylonian Chronicles.[19] It is described as Sennacherib's first campaign in several inscriptions, with some variation, the most detailed inscription being the so-called First Campaign Cylinder, duplicated on several clay cylinders from Nineveh and Assur.[20] An astrological report from Assur dated from 703 (year two), dealing with omens regarding Elam and Babylonia, could also be related to this campaign.[21]

Sennacherib first mentions the motive of the campaign: Merodach-baladan had convinced Shutruk-nahhunte II, the Elamite king, to ally with him "by presenting him with gold, silver, (and) precious stones."[22] He received assistance from Imbappa, the Elamite field marshal, together with an important body of troops. He also gathered together in Cutha the Chaldean and Aramean tribes and prepared for battle. Elam was a powerful state at that time, not in itself dangerous for Assyria but through its alliance with Babylonia. When Sennacherib received reports about the Elamite-Babylonian connection and Merodach-baladan's preparations, he "raged up like a lion and ordered the march into Babylon to confront him." In a first phase of military actions, he sent his magnates to confront Merodach-baladan in Kish. The magnates sent messengers to the Assyrian king asking for help. He first conquered the city of Cutha and then came to the aid of the Assyrian contingent attacked in Kish: "In my rage, I unleashed a fierce assault on Cutha, then I slaughtered the warriors surrounding its wall like sheep and took possession of the city." He defeated the enemy troops, put Merodach-baladan to flight to Guzummânu, and

---

18. Grayson, "Königslisten und Chroniken B. Akkadisch," 93; Stanley Mayer Burstein, *Babyloniaca of Berossus*, 23; Elayi, *Sargon II, King of Assyria*, 182–90.

19. RINAP 3.1:32, 1.5; SAAS 2:49; Grayson, *Assyrian and Babylonian Chronicles*, 76–77, chr. 1, ii.9–23.

20. RINAP 3.1:29–40. For other inscriptions, see *PNA* 3.1:1118; Luckenbill, *Annals of Sennacherib*, 48–60.

21. *PNA* 3.1:1118 (to be published by J. Finck).

22. RINAP 3.1:29–40. On Elam, see Elayi, *Sargon II, King of Assyria*, 171–75. On the historical context, see Parpola, "Letter to Sennacherib Referring to the Conquest of Bit-Ha'iri and Other Events of the Year 693," 571–72.

took booty in the two cities, people and animals. He captured Adinu, his nephew, together with Basqânu, a brother of Iatie, queen of the Arabs. In a second phase of military actions, Sennacherib entered Babylon, where he plundered the royal palace, treasure, people, and goods. He pursued the fugitive king into the midst of swamps and marshes but could not find him. However, in the course of his campaign, over the following months, he vanquished a great number of tribes of south Mesopotamia, a total of eighty-eight fortified cities and 820 smaller settlements. He ordered mass deportations of the "guilty" people who had supported Merodach-baladan and let his troops plunder and devastate the whole country. In Babylon, he appointed Bêl-ibni, a local aristocrat who had grown up in the Assyrian court, as a puppet king. According to some letters written to him, Bêl-ibni explained that he had fallen into disfavor at Sargon's court because of hostile accusations sent from Elam.[23] In a third phase of military actions, on his return home, Sennacherib received the tribute of Nabû-bêl-shumâti, the official in charge of the city of Hararatu, and he destroyed the city of Hirimmu, in the vicinity of Baghdad. He boasted having returned to Assyria with 208,000 captives, 7,200 horses and mules, 11,073 donkeys, 5,230 camels, 80,050 oxen, and 800,100 sheep and goats, without counting the booty carried off by his troops.

To summarize, the first Babylonian campaign spread over 704 and 703. Babylonia was again under Assyrian rule. However, Merodach-baladan had not been captured and still threatened the Assyrian king. The first campaign had not solved the Babylonian problem, as Babylonia was not yet completely pacified. Even if Sennacherib behaved as a true warlord, as demonstrated in lines 1 to 62 of the First Campaign Cylinder, the following part of the inscription (lines 63–95) shows that his main interest was his building project, for which he employed the people he had just conquered and deported to Assyria.

3.4. Zagros Campaign

Sennacherib's second campaign against the Zagros region took place in 702. It was another priority: Assyrian rule had been loosened in the eastern revolts, which also threatened the Assyrian Empire. In fact, the Zagros

---

23. Waterman, *Royal Correspondence of the Assyrian Empire*, 793. See John A. Brinkman, "Bêl-ibni's Letters in the Time of Sargon and Sennacherib," *RA* 77 (1983): 175–76; SAA 17:xx, 48–53, nos. 52–58.

dwellers did not threaten it directly, only if they provided military support to the enemies of Assyria, such as Elam. However, after the end of the main conflict against Urartu, even though the Urartian problem had not been completely solved, they probably had a somewhat marginal position, functioning mainly as a reserve, sourcing warriors and horses.[24] Moreover, Sennacherib wanted to present this campaign as a conquest of new territories. He marched to the land of the Kassites and of the Yasubigallians, east of Namri, "who since time immemorial had not submitted to the kings, my ancestors."[25] Their territories were located in high mountains, in a difficult terrain, where he was obliged to leave his personal chariot and to ride on horseback or to clamber up on foot. Central Zagros was inhabited by mountain dwellers, often considered as plunderers and rebellious people. Among their polities, there were some vassals of Assyria and five Assyrian provinces: Zamua/Mazamua/Lullumî, created by Ashurnasirpal II; Bît-Hamban and Parsua/Parsuash, created by Tiglath-pileser III; Kishesim and Harhar/Kâr-sharrukîn, created by Sargon.[26] The majority of the toponyms of the Zagros and of western Iran mentioned in the inscriptions cannot be localized with certainty.[27] The Zagros polities, having a tribal or familial organization, did not have kings but rulers designated as "city lord" (*bēl āli*) in Sargon's inscriptions who are not even mentioned in Sennacherib's inscriptions.

The second campaign is mentioned in several inscriptions, but not so detailed as the first campaign.[28] However, the summaries sometimes combine the events of the first and second campaigns; in particular, they

---

24. Giovanni Battista Lanfranchi, "The Assyrian Expansion in the Zagros and the Local Ruling Elites," in *Continuity of Empire: Assyria, Media, Persia*, ed. Giovanni Battista Lanfranchi, Michael Roaf, and Robert Rollinger (Padova: Sargon, 2003), 114–15.

25. RINAP 3.1:173, 22.i.65–71.

26. Elayi, *Sargon II, King of Assyria*, 160–61; Lanfranchi, "Assyrian Expansion in the Zagros and the Local Ruling Elites," 79–118.

27. Louis D. Levine, "Geographical Studies in the Neo-Assyrian Zagros I," *Iran* 11 (1973): 14–27; Levine, "Geographical Studies in the Neo-Assyrian Zagros II," *Iran* 12 (1974): 99–105; Julian E. Reade, "Kassites and Iranians in Iran," *Iran* 16 (1978): 137–43; Reade, "Iran in the Neo-Assyrian Period Geography," in *Neo-Assyrian Geography*, ed. Mario Liverani (Rome: Università di Roma La Sapienza, 1995), 31 (with bibliography); SAA 15:xxiv.

28. *PNA* 3.1:1118 (second campaign); Luckenbill, *Annals of Sennacherib*, 26–29 (second campaign). See *ARAB* 2.270–76 (first campaign), 277–82 (second campaign).

mention the attack on Hirimmu and the Zagros campaign, grouping them together.[29] According to Louis D. Levine, this would mean that, after the first campaign, Sennacherib did not return to Assyria.[30] After the capture of Hirimmu, he would have followed the route of the Diyala, directly to Namri, the area of the second campaign. His aim would have been to pacify this region in order to keep the communications corridor between Assyria and Babylonia open. This hypothesis fails to explain the last summarized inscriptions, which had somewhat confused the events, because in the Bellino Cylinder, which is dated in the eponymy of Nabû-lê'i (702 BCE), just after the first two campaigns, they were clearly separate events. First, Sennacherib defeated the people of the lands of the Kassites and of the Yasubigallians by besieging and capturing their fortified cities of Bît-Kilamza, Hardishpi, and Bît-Kubatti and destroying their small cities, some of them in the steppe being constituted by simple tents.[31] He reinforced the defenses of the fortress of Bît-Kilamza and deported populations from the mountains into cities, using a deportation policy, previously avoided by Sargon, who treated these populations differently.[32] Sennacherib placed the area under the authority of the governor of Arrapha and had a stela relating his conquest set up "in the middle of the city."[33] This stela has not been retrieved, and it is unclear whether this city was Hardishpi, Bît-Kubatti, or Bît-Kilamza.

The conquest of the city of Alammu, adorning the walls of Room XIV in the Southwest Palace of Sennacherib in Nineveh, is possibly related to the second campaign.[34] The epigraph inscribed above the walls of the city is unfortunately fragmentary: "[The city of] Alammu I besieged, [I conquered, I] carried off its spoil."[35] The localization of this city, represented on a mound, is not clear. A letter from the time of Sargon mentions

---

29. *ARAB* 2.325, 346; Levine, "Sennacherib's Southern Front," 37–39.

30. Levine, "Sennacherib's Southern Front," 37–39.

31. *ARAB* 2.236.

32. Elayi, *Sargon II, King of Assyria*, 155–58.

33. *ARAB* 2.236, 278. For the stelae found in Iran, see Sajjad Alibaigi, Abdol-Malek Shanbehzadeh, and Hossain Alibaigi, "The Discovery of a Neo-Assyrian Rock Relief at Mishkhas, Ilam Province (Iran)," *IrAnt* 47 (2012): 29–40.

34. Davide Nadali, "Sennacherib's Siege, Assault, and Conquest of Alammu," *SAAB* 14 (2002–2005): 113–32.

35. Russell, *Sennacherib's Palace without Rival at Nineveh*, 275; Russell, *Writing on the Wall: Studies in the Architectural Context of Late Assyrian Palace Inscriptions* (Winona Lake, IN: Eisenbrauns, 1999), 287.

3. ACCESSION AND PRIORITY CAMPAIGNS (705–701) 51

Alammu as the city where King Urzana of Musasir took refuge,[36] probably an eastern city near Musasir in Urartian-controlled territory. According to Davide Nadali, Alammu may have been captured during the second campaign.[37] However, this would mean that Sennacherib went to the north after having fought east of Namri and before going down southward to Ellipi. It is also surprising that the Alammu conquest, emphasized by its representation on the reliefs, is not mentioned in the royal inscriptions. However, there exist similar cases, such as that of Lachish.[38]

In a second set of military actions, Sennacherib moved against Ellipi, southeastward. Ellipi was an independent kingdom, located between Media and Elam, ruled by a king, Taltâ/Daltâ, who was a loyal vassal of Assyria from the reign of Tiglath-pileser III. In 707, he died, and a war of succession for the throne of Ellipi took place between Nibê and Ashpa-bara, sons of Taltâ's sisters, the former supported by Sargon and the latter by Shutruk-nahhunte II, king of Elam. Sargon had defeated Nibê and the Elamite army, and placed on the throne Ashpa-bara, who was in fact an intriguer and who revolted against Assyria in 702.[39] Before the Assyrian army's arrival, Ashpa-bara fled to distant parts. Sennacherib besieged, captured, and destroyed Marubishti and Akkudu, his royal residence cities, together with thirty-four small towns of their environs. He carried off a great amount of booty, people, and animals. The Ellipean district of Bît-Barrû was annexed, with Elenzash as capital city, and renamed Kâr-sin-ahê-eriba, "Sennacherib-burg." It was entrusted to the governor of the Assyrian province of Harhar.[40] Sennacherib boasted of his expansionist action: "And I added (this area) to the territory of Assyria,"[41] but it was only a part of the territory of Ellipi.

After the account of his military action in Ellipi, the account relating to the Medes is completely distorted by propaganda: "the distant Medes, whose name no one among the kings, my fathers, had (ever) heard."[42] In reality, the Medes were well attested in Assyrian sources from the late

---

36. SAA 5:105, 136.5.
37. Nadali, "Sennacherib's Siege, Assault, and Conquest of Alammu," 115.
38. See p. 74.
39. SAA 15:45–47, 67–69, 69.100–101; Elayi, *Sargon II, King of Assyria*, 69–70. On Elam, see Elayi, *Sargon II, King of Assyria*, 171–75 (with bibliography).
40. *ARAB* 2.237, 279–80, 307, 325, 346.
41. RINAP 3.2:79, 46.15.
42. *ARAB* 2.238.

ninth century onwards, even though the geographical location of their settlements is not easy to identify: in 835, for example, Shalmaneser III had already received tribute from Median rulers.[43] The names of various Median cities and of their city lords are listed in Sargon's Najafehabad stela.[44] Sargon had captured and integrated four Median cities (Nartu, Sikris, Shaparda, and Uriakku) into the province of Harhar, and other Median cities were submitted to tribute.[45] Sennacherib says that he received the tribute of the Medes, which is credible at least from some of them, but he adds another statement that seems to be unlikely: "To the yoke of my rule I made them submit," "[I destr]oyed their settlements."[46]

3.5. Third Campaign to the West

Sennacherib's third campaign, following on immediately from the Zagros campaign in 701, was the campaign to the west. The date of 701 is confirmed by comparing the Bellino Cylinder, dated from the eponymate of Nabû-lê'i (702), which does not mention this campaign, and the Rassam Cylinder, dated from the eponymate of Metunu (700), which does mention it. As a matter of fact, this campaign comprised three phases: against Phoenicia, against Philistia, and against Judah. However, the military operations against Judah, also recorded in the Bible, are the best known and the most discussed. Even though the publications related to Judah are overabundant and those related to Phoenicia and Philistia rather scarce, a serious historical approach must be adopted, hence giving equal consideration to the three phases of the third campaign, especially as they are partly interrelated. For Sennacherib, the third campaign was probably not very different from the two previous campaigns of his reign, and he did not distinguish between the three Levantine regions, all of them being in the Hatti: "In my third campaign, I went against the Hatti."[47] The campaign

---

43. Karen Radner, "An Assyrian View on the Medes," in Lanfranchi, *Continuity of Empires*, 38–40, 58.

44. Louis D. Levine, "Two Neo-Assyrian Stelae from Iran," *ROMOP* 23 (1972): 38–39, col. ii, ll. 46–70.

45. *ARAB* 2.11, 15; Radner, "Assyrian View on the Medes," 54, table 5; Elayi, *Sargon II, King of Assyria*, 163–69.

46. *ARAB* 2.238, 282, 308; RINAP 3.1:210, 26.i.9′.

47. *ARAB* 2.239. See K. Lawson Younger, "Assyrian Involvement in Southern Levant at the End of the Eighth Century B.C.E.," in *Jerusalem in Bible and Archaeol-*

3. ACCESSION AND PRIORITY CAMPAIGNS (705–701)

of 701 is generally interpreted as an Assyrian reaction to the withholding of the tribute imposed on the rebellious Phoenician, Philistian, and Palestinian cities. Coming from the north, Sennacherib followed a logical geographical route, and successively proceeded to Phoenicia, to Philistia southward, and to Judah eastward.

Against Phoenicia

Sennacherib did not give the reason for his intervention against Lulî, king of Sidon, as he did for Sidqâ, king of Ashkelon, for the people of Ekron, or for Hezekiah, king of Judah. What was the explanation, if this king only withheld the payment of tribute? It was probably because the reason was disreputable, as it pointed to his father's failure. As I have shown,[48] Sargon had besieged Tyre over a period of five years from 709 to 705, but he was unable to seize the island. However, he boasted falsely of having conquered Tyre in four duplicated cylinders dated from 706.[49] This lie can be understood because the unsuccessful siege of Tyre was the only failure that he encountered at the end of his reign (except for the campaign in which he was killed). Sennacherib could not accept this failure, but first he had to deal with the priorities: an expedition against the Kulummeans, a first campaign against the usurpation of Merodach-baladan in Babylon, and a second campaign to pacify the east. Then he went to the west to suppress the revolts there, the priority for him very likely being the defeat of Lulî and the conquest of Tyre. Why was Lulî, probably corresponding to Ελουλαίος of Josephus, named "king of the city of Sidon" (*šar* URU *ṣi-du-un-ni*)[50] in Sennacherib's inscriptions? In the ninth and eighth centuries

---

ogy: The First Temple Period, ed. Andrew G. Vaughn and Ann E. Killebrew (Atlanta: Society of Biblical Literature, 2003), 246–48; Fales, "Road to Judah," 223–48.

48. Elayi, *Sargon II, King of Assyria*, 67–72. Other reasons (not to pay a heavy tribute, same interests as Hezekiah) are less likely: Wallace Bruce Fleming, *The History of Tyre* (New York: Columbia University Press, 1915), 35; H. Jacob Katzenstein, *The History of Tyre* (Jerusalem: Schocken Institute for Jewish Research, 1973), 222, 226, 245–59; Walter Mayer, "Sennacherib's Campaign of 701 BCE: The Assyrian View," in *"Like a Bird in a Cage": The Invasion of Sennacherib in 701 BCE*, ed. Lester L. Grabbe (Sheffield: Sheffield Academic, 2003), 175.

49. *ARAB* 2.118.

50. RINAP 3.1:63, 4.32; 3.1:95, 15.iii.2; 3.1:114, 16.ii.78; 3.1:131, 17.ii.59; 3.1:175, 22.ii.38; 3.1:192, 23.ii.36; 3.1:210, 26.i.9'; 3.1:222, 34.13; RINAP 3.2:48, 42.7; 3.2:69, 44.17; 3.2:74, 45.1'; 3.2:79, 46.18; 3.2:183, 140.o.15'; Josephus, *A.J.* 9.283.

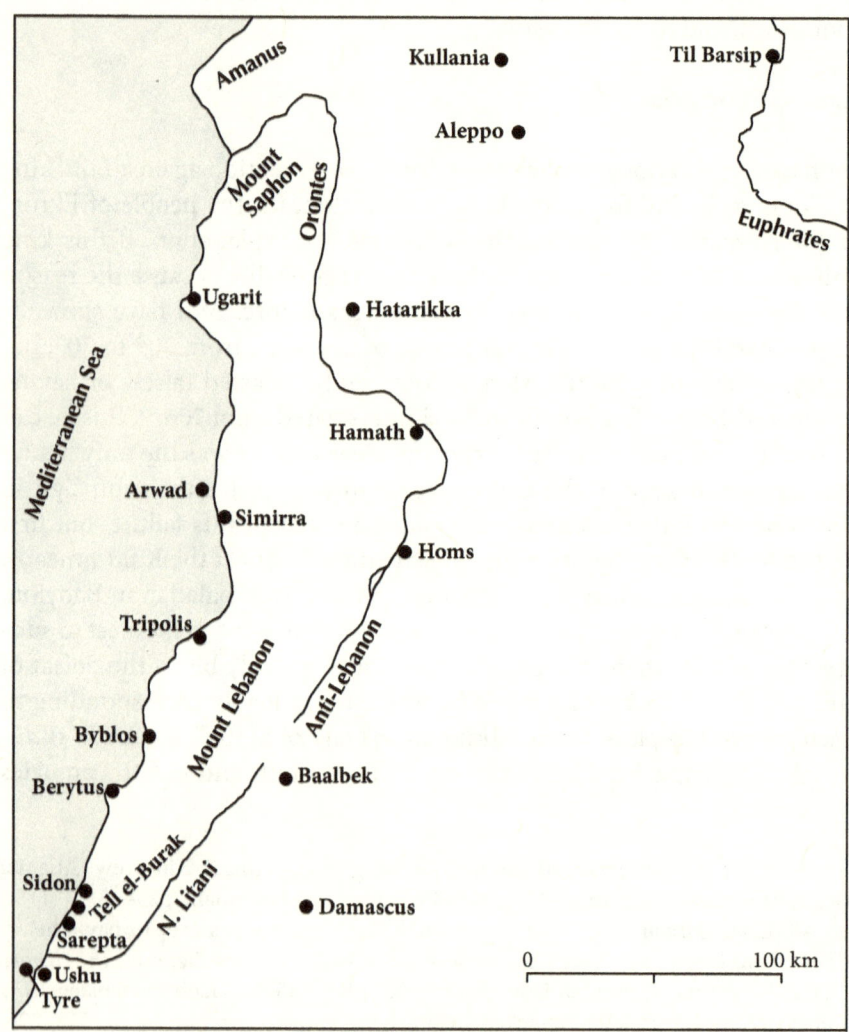

Fig. 6. Syria and Phoenicia

BCE, Ithobaal I and Hiram II, kings of Tyre, bore the title "king of the Sidonians" in a Phoenician inscription and in the Bible (1 Kgs 16:31).[51] The first interpretation proposed is that "Sidonians" meant "Phoenicians," which in some cases was exact.[52] The second interpretation proposed is that the king of Tyre had established his domination over Sidon and reigned over the double kingdom of Tyre and Sidon. Thus, Ithobaal I would have reigned over Tyre and Sidon, just as David and Solomon after him reigned over Israel and Judah.[53] This double kingdom would have existed until the end of Sennacherib's third campaign in 701, but possibly not continuously. In the list of the tributary kings to Tiglath-pileser III, the mention of Hiram (king) of Tyre and the absence of Sidon would mean that Hiram reigned over the two cities.[54] As is shown in the letters sent by the official Qurdi-ashur-lâmur to an unnamed Assyrian king, more likely Tiglath-pileser III than Sargon, he controlled the tax collectors of Tyrians and Sidonians, apparently both dependent on one single kingdom.[55] Finally, the enumeration of Lulî's towns in Sennacherib's inscriptions clearly showed that, in 701, he was king of Tyre and Sidon because these towns belonged to the two cities.[56] Lulî was probably residing in his palace on the island of Tyre because he had fled from it.[57] This was quite understandable because it was the most prestigious and the most secure place in his kingdom, as no conqueror had ever succeeded in capturing it.

During Sargon's five-year siege of Tyre, Sidon took advantage of the situation by freeing itself from the tutelage of Tyre, as stated by Josephus: "Sidon … and many other cities also revolted from Tyre and surrendered to the king of Assyria."[58] Yet, after Sargon's death, during the period from 705 to 701, Lulî undoubtedly tried to recover his territory: the enumeration of

---

51. *KAI* 49, no. 31.

52. Josette Elayi, "Les relations entre les cités phéniciennes et l'Empire assyrien sous le règne de Sennachérib," *Sem* 35 (1985): 20–21 (with bibliography).

53. Josette Elayi, *Histoire de la Phénicie* (Paris: Perrin, 2013), 143–44, 177.

54. *ARAB* 2.772; RINAP 1:46, 14.11; 1:70, 27.3; 1:77, 32.2; 1:122, 47.r.7′; 1:131, 49.r.5; 1:134, 50.r.5.

55. Henry William Frederick Saggs, "The Nimrud Letters 1952: Part II," *Iraq* 17 (1955): 127 (= ND 2715), col. xii, ll. 11, 15, 21; John Nicholas Postgate, *Taxation and Conscription in the Assyrian Empire* (Rome: Biblical Institute Press, 1974), 390; *PNA* 3.1:1021–22; Elayi, *Histoire de la Phénicie*, 163–65.

56. RINAP 3.1:63, no. 33; 3.1:95, 15.iii.8.

57. RINAP 3.2:46, no. 18.

58. Josephus, *A.J.* 9.285.

his towns in the Rassam Cylinder, for example,[59] shows that he had retaken the territory of Sidon. According to the Assyrian inscriptions, Sennacherib's expedition against Lulî was terrifying but without military confrontation: "Fear of my brilliance overwhelmed Lulî, the king of the city of Sidon, and he fled from the city of Tyre to Iadnana, which is in the midst of the sea"; "he became frightened of doing battle with me."[60] Sennacherib intended to present Lulî as a coward, but the Phoenician king had probably taken a realistic decision: for five years he had been besieged his impregnable island, and he had understood that being deprived of a continental territory for providing supplies was difficult to endure. Moreover, he was probably old, because he had been on the throne since around 728 BCE, after having succeeded Mattan II, who paid a heavy tribute to Tiglath-pileser III in 729.[61] The discussions on Lulî's reign are sometimes distorted by Na'aman's incorrect reading of "Shilta" in a lacunary inscription of Sargon, interpreted erroneously as a new king of Tyre.[62] If the chronology of events has been respected by the scribes, the surrender of Lulî's towns was not a reason for his flight because it occurred later. Did he flee to Cyprus in order to keep it in his possession?[63] In any case, it did not involve the whole island, only his colonies. He probably retired to his colony of Kition, where he could quietly continue to control Tyrian affairs, at least the island of Tyre. A variant of the Chicago Prism gives, instead of *in-na-bit*, "he fled," *in-na-kir*, "he moved his house,"[64] which is significant. It is uncertain whether the Cyprian kings continued to pay tribute to Assyria because they are never mentioned in Sennacherib's inscriptions. They were probably not disturbed by the Assyrian king, who had more urgent problems to solve. Therefore, Lulî could live quietly on an island that was again almost independent.

Sennacherib was probably proud because he had succeeded in expelling King Lulî from Tyre. That is why he might have illustrated this feat on a

---

59. RINAP 3.1:63, no. 33.

60. RINAP 3.2:79, 46.18; 3.2:69, 44.17.

61. According to Josephus (*A.J.* 9.284), Lulî reigned thirty-six years, but his reign was shorter.

62. Nadav Na'aman, "Sargon II and the Rebellion of the Cypriote Kings against Shilṭa of Tyre," *Or* 67 (1998): 239–47; *PNA* 2.2:669 (with bibliography). See Elayi, *Histoire de la Phénicie*, 173; Elayi, *Sargon II, King of Assyria*, 75.

63. Gallagher, *Sennacherib's Campaign to Judah*, 100–104.

64. Luckenbill, *Annals of Sennacherib*, 29, col. ii, l. 40 and n. 13; Elayi, "Les relations entre les cités phéniciennes et l'Empire assyrien sous le règne de Sennachérib," 22: *nakāru* is here the equivalent of *nābutu*.

3. ACCESSION AND PRIORITY CAMPAIGNS (705–701)

relief in his palace in Nineveh.⁶⁵ Part of a fortified island city is represented on a slab, with rows of round shields placed defensively on the crenellations. Inside the city is a beautiful three-story building, possibly the royal palace. From a gate opening onto the quay, a man is placing a child in a ship. Twelve warships and merchant ships are represented alongside, filled with warriors and ordinary people. Two other adjoining slabs represented the besieging Assyrian army. The man on the quay would have been Lulî, fleeing from Tyre with other Tyrians, on their ships. This representation of the Tyrian fleet could be significant: even if it had prevented Sargon and Sennacherib from seizing the island of Tyre, at least Sennacherib had succeeded in expelling Lulî and his family.⁶⁶

How long did Lulî live in Cyprus? The exact date of his death is difficult to pinpoint. The formula used for mentioning his death is *šadašu ēmid*, "he disappeared."⁶⁷ What does that mean? There is evidence that it implied that "he died" in the annals of Ashurbanipal, where it is used for King Yakinlu of Arwad in a later text mentioning *illiku ana šīmti*, "he died."⁶⁸ The bull inscription 2 and 3 explains the cause of his death as being his fear of Sennacherib: "In the same land (Iadnana), he disappeared on account of the awesome terror of the weapon of the god Assur, my lord."⁶⁹ The Assyrian king still tried to show that Lulî was a coward; but he probably died of a natural death. His death occurred after 700, the date of the Rassam Cylinder, where it is not mentioned, and before 697, the date of Cylinder C,⁷⁰

---

65. Layard, *Nineveh and Its Remains*, 2:128–29; Russell, *Sennacherib's Palace without Rival at Nineveh*, 165, fig. 85; John Malcolm Russell, "Layard's Description of Rooms in the Southwest Palace at Nineveh," *Iraq* 57 (1995): 73; SAA 2:23, fig. 8.

66. This interpretation is not accepted by Gallagher, who suggests, as "a conjecture," to identify Jaffa: "Room I, Slabs 14–18 of Sennacherib's Palace: Not a Depiction of Tyre," *NABU* (1997): 52–53, 56. He argues that Jaffa was the only coastal city taken by force in this campaign and that it was situated at the foot of a promontory. However, the place of the scene looks like an island, the numerous galleys probably represent the Tyrian fleet, and the fleeing family might represent Lulî's family, expelled by Sennacherib.

67. RINAP 3.1:95, 15.iii.2; *PNA* 2.2:668; Frahm, *Einleitung in die Sanherib-Inschriften*, 66; Gallagher, *Sennacherib's Campaign to Judah*, 94.

68. Gallagher, *Sennacherib's Campaign to Judah*, 94 (with bibliography).

69. RINAP 3.2:69, 44.18–19. This passage is misunderstood by Gallagher, *Sennacherib's Campaign to Judah*, 98–99 ("year" instead of "land"); Rykle Borger, *Babylonisch-Assyrische Lesestücke*, AnOr 54 (Rome: Pontifical Biblical Institute, 1979), 76.

70. RINAP 3.1:63, 4.32–34; 3.1:95, 15.iii.2.

the first subsequent inscription where it is mentioned. Therefore, Lulî fled to Cyprus in 701 and died at some moment between 699 and 697.

After Lulî's flight, Sennacherib did not take reprisals against his other cities, which immediately submitted: "The awesome terror of the weapon of the god Assur, my lord, overwhelmed the cities of Great Sidon, Lesser Sidon, Bît-Zitti, Sarepta, Mahalliba, Ushu, Akzibu, (and) Akko, his fortified cities (and) fortresses, an area of pasture(s) and water-place(s), resources upon which he relied, and they bowed down at my feet."[71] Lulî's cities, presented in geographical order from north to south, have all been identified; it is worth noting that no town north of Sidon is mentioned, hence this territory possibly terminated before Nahr ed-Damour at that time.[72] Sennacherib offered this territory to Ittobaal: "I placed Tu-ba-lu (Ittobaal) on his royal throne over them and imposed upon him tribute (and) payment (in recognition) of my overlordship (to be delivered) yearly (and) without interruption."[73] His policy was clear and was followed by his successors: to take advantage of the rivalry between the two neighboring cities of Tyre and Sidon as a way of weakening the rebellious city and favoring the other city.[74] Who was Ittobaal? He was "Sidonian" (URU *ṣi-du-un-na-a-a*).[75] He was undoubtedly loyal to the Assyrian king; therefore he could not belong to Lulî's family. He probably belonged to the royal Sidonian family that had been deprived of power by the royal Tyrian family. Sidon had rapidly recovered its prosperity at the beginning of Esarhaddon's reign. However, Ittobaal was strictly controlled by the Assyrian power: he was submitted to an "annual" (*šattišam*) tribute, with a particular insistence on it: "I imposed it on him without interruption" (*la ba-aṭ-lu ú-kin ṣe-ru-uš-šú*).[76]

What became of the island of Tyre after Lulî's flight? Its name is no longer mentioned in Sennacherib's inscriptions, only the name of Ushu, an

---

71. RINAP 3.1:63, 4.32.

72. Elayi, "Les relations entre les cités phéniciennes et l'Empire assyrien sous le règne de Sennachérib," 23; Elayi, *Histoire de la Phénicie*, 23–24. According to Hélène Sader, Sidon would also have possessed earlier a territory from north of Byblos to Enfe: "Les territoires des villes phéniciennes entre continuité et changement," in *La Phénicie hellénistique*, ed. Julien Aliqot and Corinne Bonnet, Topoi Supplement 13 (Lyon: Société des Amis de la Bibliothèque Salomon-Reinach, 2015), 116–17.

73. RINAP 3.1:64, no. 35.

74. Josette Elayi, "Tyr et Sidon, deux cités phéniciennes rivales," *Transeu* 49 (2017): 91–101.

75. Luckenbill, *Annals of Sennacherib*, 30, col. ii, l. 51.

76. Luckenbill, *Annals of Sennacherib*, 30, col. ii, l. 49.

3. ACCESSION AND PRIORITY CAMPAIGNS (705–701)

ancient Tyrian town located opposite the island; in fact, the Assyrian king denied its existence, as he could not take it. The result of his expedition against Lulî was the juxtaposition of two very differently sized territories: on one side a powerful city extending at least from Sidon to Akko, ruled by Ittobaal, a pro-Assyrian king; on the other side the independent city of Tyre, whose territory was reduced to the island, ruled from Cyprus by Lulî, then possibly after his death by another king of his family. The evolution of these two neighboring territories is not documented before the beginning of Esarhaddon's reign in 677, when Sidon was ruled by the powerful King Abdimilkuti/Abdimilkot, and Tyre by a weak king named Baal. However, the process of evolution can be understood: after having received the territory and the wealth of Tyre, Sidon benefited from the protection of Sennacherib, who encouraged its development, hence causing the ruin of Tyre. This would be one of the reasons why Tyre lost its leading status and why Sidon progressively became the leading Phoenician city. The island of Tyre encountered serious difficulties even though it still had possessions in southern Phoenicia and some colonies such as Kition in Cyprus: these possessions were located far away and, without supplies from the near-continental coastland, it probably began to be asphyxiated. Archaeological discoveries have confirmed this hypothesis. In Stratum I of the previously insular part of Tyre, dated from circa 700, Patricia Bikai was surprised to find pottery manufacture: "That pottery was being manufactured on the island at all is a surprise, as it undoubtedly meant that clay had to be brought from the mainland in ships; one would have expected that pottery would be made on the mainland and the finished pieces shipped out to the island."[77] If Stratum I was correctly dated, this is proof that, after 701, Tyre had such difficulties that it was obliged to bring clay to the island for pottery making. The clay probably did not come from the neighboring continental territory, which belonged to the rival city of Sidon, with whom relations were no doubt strained. It had to be brought from another part of the coast not belonging to Sidon, which was far from the island of Tyre. One may well ask whether the Tyrian difficulties at that time could also explain the decline in the quality of red-burnished ware in Stratum I and the absence of imported pottery in this single stratum.[78]

---

77. Patricia M. Bikai, *The Pottery of Tyre* (Warminster, UK: Aris & Phillips, 1978), 14, 67–68. This discovery would contradict the hypothesis of Katzenstein (*History of Tyre*, 53–54, 57–59), who supposed that Tyre and Sidon made later arrangement of territories.

78. Bikai, *Pottery of Tyre*, 53–54, 57–59.

In summary, Sennacherib's campaign against Lulî was officially presented as successful, even though the island of Tyre was not captured, a fact that was carefully concealed in the Assyrian royal inscriptions, and unfortunately the annals of Tyre have not been preserved.

During his expedition against Lulî, Sennacherib settled in "the plain of the city of Ushu," opposite the inaccessible island of Tyre, where eight western kings came and brought him gifts: "As for Minuhimmu the Samsimurunite, Tuba'lu the Sidonian, Abdi-liti the Aradian, Uru-milki the Giblite, Mitinti the Ashdodite, Bûdi-il the Beth-amonite, Kammûsu-nadbi the Moabite, Aya-râmu the Edomite, all the kings of the land of Amurru, they brought numerous presents for the fourth time, as their heavy audience gift before me and kissed my feet."[79] This episode is mentioned several times in Sennacherib's inscriptions, probably because he wanted to compensate for his inability to capture the island of Tyre. When did this episode take place? After the installation of Ittobaal of Sidon on the throne, because he was cited among the tributary kings, and before the second phase of Sennacherib's first campaign against Philistia, because the rebellious King Sidqa of Ashkelon, the prisoner King Padî of Ekron, and King Hezekiah of Judah are absent from the list of tributaries. All the kings mentioned are identified, except for Menahem (Minuhimmu) of Samsimuruna, whose location is still debated: possibly Baalbek, as it was named Heliopolis, "city of the sun," by the Greeks and as the Phoenician toponym could mean "setting sun."[80]

According to Sennacherib's inscriptions, the eight western kings paid tribute to him for the fourth time in 701, which meant that they had already paid it in 704, 703, and 702 BCE, sending it to Nineveh, but this time they paid it directly to the Assyrian king campaigning in the west. There are two difficulties: first, Ittobaal could not have paid for the fourth time, as he had only been installed on the throne of Sidon in 701; second, instead of the usual term *mandattu*, "tribute," other terms are used here: *tāmartu*, "audience gift," *igisû*, "present," and *biltu*, "payment." Therefore, the following hypothesis has been proposed: the western kings did not pay tribute for the fourth time but a "quadruple" payment (4-*šú*) because they had

---

79. RINAP 3.1:64, 4.36; 3.1:114, 16.iii.15; 3.1:131, 17.ii.75; 3.1:175, 22.ii.50; 3.1:192, 23.ii.47; RINAP 3.2:79, 46.19; 3.2:183, 140.o.19′.

80. Elayi, *Histoire de la Phénicie*, 175. Other hypotheses were proposed, such as in the vicinity of the estuary of the Nahr el-Kalb, or north of Arwad: RGTC 7.1:211–12 (with bibliography).

revolted against Sennacherib, and it was the heavy price they had to pay in order to be forgiven.[81] However, if they had revolted against Sennacherib, it is likely that it would have been mentioned in his inscriptions, as are the revolts of Sidqâ of Ashkelon, of the people of Ekron, and of Hezekiah of Judah. Therefore, the presence of Ittobaal in the list was either an error on the part of scribes or a simplification to avoid explaining that, contrary to the other kings, he was paying for the first time. Different terms for designating the payment were probably used because presents and gifts frequently accompanied the tribute, which had a broad meaning.[82]

Against Philistia

The next phase of Sennacherib's third campaign was his action against the rebellious cities of Philistia, not Ashdod, because its King Mitinti was a loyal vassal who paid tribute. It is unknown whether he had kinship with the pro-Assyrian King Ahî-Mîti, expelled by Yamani, then defeated in turn by Sargon in 711, and why he was allowed to keep the throne of Ashdod although Ashdod had been turned into an Assyrian province by Sargon.[83] The Bible reports that Hezekiah "beat the Philistines back to Gaza, laying their territory waste from watchtower to fortified town" (2 Kgs 18:7–8).[84] According to Caroline Van Der Brugge, Gaza would have been conquered by Hezekiah in order to take control of the northern entrance of the *via maris* to Egypt: for this interpretation she relies on the so-called Azekah inscription, but its dating from Sennacherib's reign is uncertain, and the name "Gaza" is restored in a lacuna of the text.[85] It is more likely that Silli-Bêl of Gaza remained loyal to the Assyrian king and was left autonomous because it was useful for reasons of economic profit (maritime or desert

---

81. Gallagher, *Sennacherib's Campaign to Judah*, 105–12; *PNA* 2.2:757–58.
82. Dalley, "Recent Evidence from Assyrian Sources," 388.
83. Elayi, *Sargon II, King of Assyria*, 57–61; Hayim Tadmor, "Philistia under Assyrian Rule," *BA* 29 (1966): 95; Nadav Na'aman, "The Brook of Egypt and Assyrian Policy on the Border of Egypt," *TA* 6 (1979): 71–72.
84. Unless otherwise stated, all biblical translations follow the New Jerusalem Bible.
85. Caroline Van Der Brugge, "Of Production, Trade, Profit and Destruction: An Economic Interpretation of Sennacherib's Third Campaign," *JESHO* 60 (2017): 306–7, 317–19. On the Azekah inscription, see RINAP 3.2:350–52, 1015 (with bibliography). According to Mordechai Cogan, a date during Sargon's reign seems most likely: "Restoring the Empire: Sargon's Campaign to the West in 720/19 BCE," *IEJ* 67 (2017): 162–63.

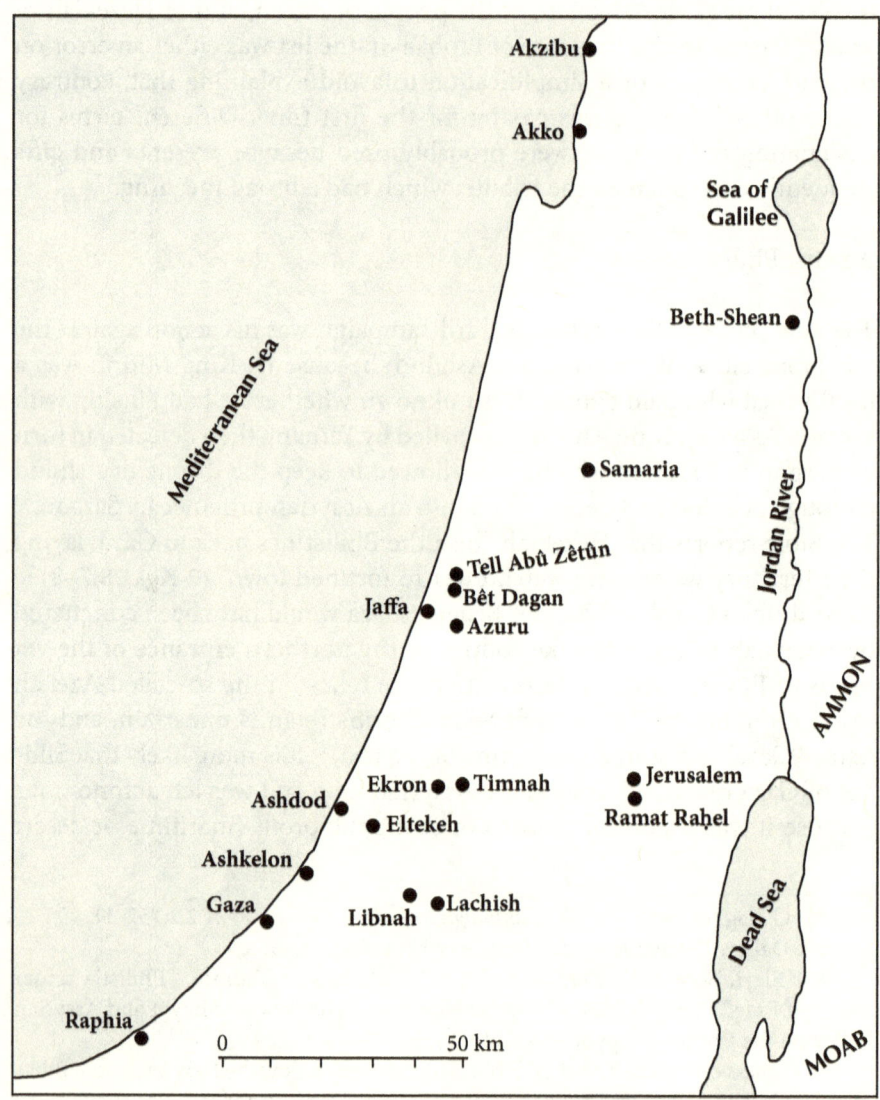

Fig. 7. Palestine

3. ACCESSION AND PRIORITY CAMPAIGNS (705–701)   63

trade) and Assyrian strategy, as a buffer state adjoining Egypt.[86] The same reason could possibly explain why the kingship was retained in the Assyrian province of Ashdod. Two cities of Philistia were rebellious: Ashkelon and Ekron. Sennacherib's action against Ashkelon is first mentioned: "Sidqâ, the king of the city of Ashkelon who had not bowed down to my yoke, I forcibly removed the gods of his father's house, himself, his wife, his sons, his daughters, his brothers, (and other) offspring of his father's house and took him to Assyria."[87] The filiation of Sidqâ is unknown, and one could think that he was a usurper because Sennacherib, after having taken him prisoner to Assyria, reestablished a member of the previous dynasty on the throne: "I set Sharru-lû-dâri, son of Rûkibtu, their former king, over the people of the city of Ashkelon and imposed upon him the payment of the tribute (and) gifts (in recognition) of my overlordship so that he (now) pulls my yoke."[88] However, his royal status and legitimacy were later confirmed when Mitinti II, son of Sidqâ, became king of Ashkelon.[89] Rûkibtu was probably the "former king," not Sharu-lû-dâri; his Assyrian name indicates a pro-Assyrian orientation of Rûkibtu, his father. Logically, Sennacherib himself led this expedition against Sidqâ of Ashkelon: after having received the tributes of the eight western kings in Ushu, he could have directed his army southward toward Ashkelon, along the *via maris*. He first had to cross an area around Jaffa belonging to Ashkelon, even though it was a long way away.[90] Hence, on his way he conquered this area before reaching Ashkelon: "In the course of my campaign, I surrounded, conquered, (and) plundered the cities of Bît-Daganna, Joppa, Banayarbarqa, (and) Azuru, the cities of Sidqâ that had not submitted

---

86. Gallagher, *Sennacherib's Campaign to Judah*, 110; PNA 3.1:1172; Elayi, *Sargon II, King of Assyria*, 55–56.

87. RINAP 3.1:64, 4.39; 3.1:96, 15.iii.5′; 3.1:114, 16.iii.26; 3.1:131, 17.ii.87; 3.1:150, 18.ii.0′′; 3.1:175, 22.ii.60; 3.1:192, 23.ii.57; 3.1:215, 29.i′; RINAP 3.2:80, 46.20; 3.2:184, 140.r.3; 3.2:188, 142.o.4′; 3.2:238, 165.iii.7.

88. RINAP 3.1:64, 4.40; PNA 3.1:1169, 1053–54; RINAP 3.2:1248.

89. *PNA* 2.2:757–58; D. Marcus, "Sharruludari, Son of Rubiktu, Their Former King: A Detail of Phoenician Chronology," *JANES* 9 (1977): 29–30; Tadmor, "Philistia under Assyrian Rule," 99; Gallagher, *Sennacherib's Campaign to Judah*, 117–19 (with bibliography).

90. The inclusion of the area of Jaffa in the city of Ashkelon looks strange and has been interpreted in different manners: Gallagher, *Sennacherib's Campaign to Judah*, 119 and nn. 32–34.

to me quickly."⁹¹ Bît-Daganna is identified with Bêt Dagan (biblical Bêt-dâgôn), about 9 kilometers southeast of Jaffa; Banayarbarqa was probably Ibn-Ibraq or Tell Abû Zêtûn (biblical Benê beraq), about 9 kilometers northeast of Jaffa; Azuru is identified with Têl Azor (biblical Âzôr), about 6 kilometers southeast of Jaffa.⁹² However, in all the inscriptions, this passage was mistakenly placed after the conquest of Ashkelon. Yet no action against Ashkelon is mentioned, and it is unclear how Sidqâ was captured. Either the pro-Assyrian party of Ashkelon handed him over to Sennacherib, or Sidqâ himself took the decision to surrender to save his life and those of his family.⁹³ Anyhow, it does not mean that Sennacherib did not go to Ashkelon, and there is no reason to place Sidqâ's captivity after the battle of Eltekeh, where the Assyrians defeated the Egyptians.⁹⁴

The next phase of Sennacherib's expedition to Philistia involved Ekron. The sequence of events seems to be logical in the Assyrian account, even if it has been questioned by some authors, with unconvincing arguments:⁹⁵ Sennacherib, after having suppressed the revolt of Ashkelon, whether he had stayed in the area of Jaffa or had come back from Ashkelon, was close to the next area of fighting: Eltekeh, Timnah, and Ekron. The Philistine city of Ekron is identified with Tel Miqne, near Kibbutz Revadim; Eltekeh, a Danite city, was possibly Tell esh-Shallaf, about 3 kilometers west of Rehoboth; Timnah was a Judean border town, identified with Tel Batash, about 7 kilometers northwest of Beth-shemesh.⁹⁶ The first step of the Ekron rebellion was the arrest of King Padî

---

91. RINAP 3.1:64, 4.41.

92. RGTC 7.1:38, 42, 48; Mordechai Cogan, *The Raging Torrent: Historical Inscriptions from Assyria and Babylonia Relating to Ancient Israel* (Jerusalem: Carta, 2008), 113, 118: Ashkelon is absent from the map, and the itinerary Jaffa-Ashkelon is not indicated.

93. Tadmor, "Philistia under Assyrian Rule," 96–97; Gallagher, *Sennacherib's Campaign to Judah*, 118.

94. See p. 67. Gallagher, *Sennacherib's Campaign to Judah*, 117, 123–25.

95. For example, Van Der Brugge, "Of Production, Trade, Profit and Destruction," 317–20, 326–27, suggested that Egypt was willing to negotiate a new trade agreement with Assyria instead of defending Judah. However, the suggestion that there was not a battle near Eltekeh but a negotiation is not based on any document.

96. Trude Dothan and Seymour Gitin, "Miqne, Tel (Ekron)," *NEAEHL* 3:1051–59; Seymour Gitin, "Tel Miqne-Ekron in the 7th Century B.C.E.: The Impact of Economic Innovation and Foreign Cultural Influences on a Neo-Assyrian Vassal City-State," in *Recent Excavation in Israel: A View to the West*, ed. Seymour Gitin (Dubuque, IA:

3. ACCESSION AND PRIORITY CAMPAIGNS (705–701) 65

by the city's anti-Assyrian party, with him being sent to King Hezekiah: "(As for) the governors, the nobles, and the people of the city of Ekron who had thrown Padî, their king who was bound by treaty and oaths to Assyria, into iron fetters and who had handed him over to Hezekiah of the land of Judah in a hostile manner, they became frightened on account of the villainous acts they had committed."[97] There is an opposition in the Assyrian text between the "treaty/covenant" (*adê*) and "oath" (*māmītu*) that bound Padî to Sennacherib, and the "abomination" (*anzillu*) committed by the Ekronites in disregarding the oath and treating their king "as an enemy" (*nakišu*).[98] Violating an oath was a sacrilegious offense, provoking a divine sanction, together with a punishment inflicted by the Assyrian king betrayed by his vassal.

The Assyrian account was placed on an ethical level to reinforce the image of a king of justice: those who respected their oaths and those who betrayed them. As a matter of fact, there were in reality two political attitudes toward Assyria: the pro-Assyrian attitude, such as that of King Padî, and the anti-Assyrian attitude, such as that of the Ekronites and Hezekiah of Judah, who joined forces against Sennacherib. Being conscious that it would be difficult to resist the Assyrian army, the Ekronites looked for powerful allies: "They formed a confederation with the kings of Egypt (and) the archers, chariots, (and) horses of the king of the land of Meluhha, forces without number, and they came to their aid."[99]

The Ekronite-Egyptian alliance was a *kitru* alliance, unholy and based on selfish motives, unlike the *adê*.[100] Sennacherib was the protector of the

---

Archaeological Institute of America, 1995), 61–79; David Ussishkin, "Sennacherib's Campaign to Philistia and Judah: Ekron, Lachish, and Jerusalem," in *Essays on Ancient Israel in Its Near Eastern Context: A Tribute to Nadav Na'aman*, ed. Yairah Amit, Ehud Ben Zvi, Israel Finkelstein, and Oded Lipschits (Winona Lake, IN: Eisenbrauns, 2006), 339–57; Cogan, *Raging Torrent*, 118–19. Gallagher doubts the location of Eltekeh at Tell ash-Shallaf (*Sennacherib's Campaign to Judah*, 123–24).

97. RINAP 3.1:64, 4.42; 3.1:96, 15.iii.8′; 3.1:114, 16.iii.41; 3.1:132, 17.iii.6; 3.1:150, 18.ii.15″; 3.1:175, 22.ii.73; 3.1:193, 23.ii.69; 3.1:218, 32.ii.6′; RINAP 3.2:8, 46.22; 3.2:184, 140.r.6; 3.2:189, 142.o.10′; 3.2:238, 165.iii.23. On Padî, see Seymour Gitin, Trude Dothan, and Joseph Naveh, "A Royal Dedicatory Inscription from Ekron," *IEJ* 47 (1997): 1–16; Seymour Gitin and Mordechai Cogan, "A New Type of Dedicatory Inscription from Ekron," *IEJ* 49 (1999): 193–202; *PNA* 3.4:978.

98. Gallagher, *Sennacherib's Campaign to Judah*, 120–21.

99. RINAP 3.1:64, no. 43.

100. Mario Liverani, "Kitru, Katāru," *Mes* 17 (1982): 43–66.

adê and had the support of the god Assur, so he could defeat his enemies, linked by a *kitru* alliance. The presentation of the Egyptian allies in this passage of the Assyrian inscriptions is difficult to interpret; it reflects Egypt's situation in 701 because it was recorded in 700 BCE (date of the Rassam Cylinder), and this passage was then transcribed verbatim in later editions compiled in 697, 696, 694, and 691. Who were the "kings of Egypt" (*šarrāni* KUR *mu-ṣu-ri*) and the "king of Meluhha" (*šar* KUR *me-luḫ-ḫa*)? And who were the "Egyptian princes" (literally "the sons of the Egyptian kings," DUMU.MEŠ LUGAL.MEŠ KUR *mu-ṣu-ra-a-a*) who were captured? From the Assyrian point of view, these Egyptian rulers were probably powerful enough to be described as kings. This period of the Twenty-Fifty Dynasty was chaotic and politically fragmented, the reigns of the pharaohs Shabaka and Shabatka in particular are still in debate. Three main hypotheses have been proposed: a coregency between the two pharaohs; a division of the kingdoms of Kush and Egypt ruled by Shabaka and Shabatka respectively; or an inversion of their reigns, Shabaka preceding Shabatka.[101] Dan'el Kahn's interpretation seems the most plausible: Shabatka succeeded Shabaka around 707/706, then was succeeded by Taharqa around 690.[102] The "kings of Egypt" mentioned in Sennacherib's inscriptions should probably be connected to the "princes of Egypt"; they were probably rulers from the Delta region who were theoretically loyal to the "king of Meluhha," that is, the Kushite king.[103] Tiglath-pileser III and Sargon already had contacts with Musri and Kush. According to the Bible, Shabatka summoned his brother Taharqa to fight against Sennacherib: he was named "king" although he only ascended the throne of Egypt and Kush eleven years

---

101. See, e.g., Anthony Spalinger, "The Year 712 BC and Its Implications for Egyptian History," *JARCE* 10 (1973): 95–101; Frank J. Yurco, "Sennacherib's Third Campaign and the Coregency of Shabaka and Shebitku," *Serapis* 6 (1980): 221–40 (first hypothesis). Donald B. Redford, "A Note on the Chronology of Dynasty 25 and the Inscription of Sargon II at Tang-i Var," *Or* 68 (1999): 58–60 (second hypothesis). Michael Bányai, "Ein Vorschlag zur Chronologie der 25. Dynastie in Ägypten," *JEgH* 6 (2013): 46–129; Frédéric Payraudeau, "Retour sur la succession Shabaqo-Shabataqo," *NeHeT* 1 (2014): 115–27 (third hypothesis). Dan'el Kahn, "The Inscription of Sargon II at Tang-i Var and the Chronology of Dynasty 25," *Or* 70 (2001): 1–18; Erik Hornung, Rolf Kraus, and David A. Warburton, *Ancient Egyptian Chronology*, Handbook of Oriental Studies 3 (Leiden: Brill, 2006), 494; Elayi, *Sargon II, King of Assyria*, 82.

102. Gallagher, *Sennacherib's Campaign to Judah*, 122–23 (with bibliography).

103. Stephanie Dalley, "Foreign Chariotry and Cavalry in the Armies of Tiglath-pileser III and Sargon II," *Iraq* 47 (1985): 43–45.

later, in 690 BCE (2 Kgs 19:8).[104] However, as demonstrated by Kahn and Wiliam R. Gallagher,[105] there is no reason to place the battle of Eltekeh later, after Sennacherib's invasion of Judah, and Taharqa may have led the Kushite forces as a commander.

The Assyrian army confronted Egyptian troops, partly Kushite, for the first time since the battle of Qarqar in 853 BCE in western Syria. The Assyrian victory over the Egyptians is described briefly compared to other accounts of Sennacherib's battles: "In the plain of Eltekeh, they sharpened their weapons while drawing up in battle-line before me. With the support of (the god) Assur, my lord, I fought with them and defeated them. In the heat of the battle, I captured alive the Egyptian charioteers (and) princes, together with the charioteers of the king of the land of Meluhha."[106] According to Karen Radner, the Egyptians mentioned in a house-sale document from Nineveh dated to 692 BCE were nobles hostages captured at the battle of Eltekeh in 701, Shoshenq possibly being among them.[107] The two Egyptian ship captains would also have been captured during the campaign of 701, which took place along the coast: however, Eltekeh was not on the coast, and there is no mention of Egyptian ships in the text. Another result of the Assyrian victory at Eltekeh was the capture of two minor towns: "I surrounded, conquered, (and) plundered the cities of Eltekeh (and) Tamnâ (Timnah)."[108] It is almost unanimously accepted that the battle of Eltekeh took place, except for Caroline Van Der Brugge, who considers that Sennacherib met the Egyptian delegation near Eltekeh,

---

104. Payraudeau doubts the presence of Taharqa related by the Bible: "Retour sur la succession Shabaqo-Shabataqo," 123.

105. Dan'el Kahn, "Tirhaka, King of Kush and Sennacherib," *JAEI* 6 (2014): 29–41; Gallagher, *Sennacherib's Campaign to Judah*, 123–25; see also Jeremy Pope, "Beyond the Broken Reed: Kushite Intervention and the Limits of *L'histoire événementielle*," in Kalimi and Richarson, *Sennacherib at the Gates of Jerusalem*, 105–60.

106. RINAP 3.1, 64–65, 4.44–45. For a survey of the relations between Assyria, Egypt and Kush before 671 BCE, see Silvie Zamazalová, "Before the Assyrian Conquest in 671 B.C.E.: Relations between Egypt, Kush and Assyria," in *Egypt and the Near East: The Crossroads*, ed. Jana Mynářová (Prague: Czech University, Czech Institute of Egyptology, 2011), 297–328.

107. SAA 6:125, no. 142 (K.294); Onasch, *Die assyrischen Eroberungen Ägyptens*, 15; Karen Radner, "After Eltekeh: Royal Hostages from Egypt at the Assyrian Court," in *Stories of Long Ago: Festschrift für Michael D. Roaf*, ed. Heather D. Baker, Kai Kaniuth, and Adelheid Otto, AOAT 397 (Münster: Ugarit-Verlag, 2012), 473–79.

108. RINAP 3.1:65, 4.46.

accompanied by swift-moving army units, to negotiate a new trading agreement with Assyria after Egypt's trade with Hezekiah had come to an end.[109] Replacing the accounts of diplomatic moves by those of military actions in the royal inscriptions would have been intended to glorify the Assyrian king: it is not a convincing argument. Debate persists as to the precise nature of the outcome of the battle of Eltekeh, and some authors doubt whether it was a decisive victory for the Assyrians.[110]

Sennacherib's objective was to suppress the Ekronite rebellion, not to capture, plunder, and destroy Ekron. After the defeat of Eltekeh, the rebellious Ekronites had no hope of resisting the Assyrians: either they decided to capitulate, or there was a popular uprising against them that enabled Sennacherib to take the city without resistance. The Assyrian king wanted to show himself as a just king, judging the Ekronites fairly and according to their deeds. He treated the rulers who had committed a "criminal act" (*ḫīṭu*) with harshness, hanging their corpses on towers around the city, not through cruelty or sadism but in the name of justice. A less severe punishment was applied to the citizens who had followed their rebellious rulers: he counted them as "booty" (*šallatu*), which meant that he could do anything he wanted with them. He set free the rest of the citizens, "who were not guilty of crimes or wrongdoing."[111] Thus, he wanted to teach subject peoples the deadly consequences of rebelling against him and the ensured well-being for remaining loyal to him. Egyptian forces did not apparently go to Ekron after Eltekeh to help the rebels. The last step in suppressing the revolt of the Ekronites was to restore the kingship and to reestablish Ekron as an Assyrian vassal city: "I brought out Padî, their king, from the city of Jerusalem and placed (him) on the royal throne over them and imposed upon him tribute (in recognition) of my overlordship."[112] If the Ekronite episode occurred before the attack of Judah, as it seems, how did Sennacherib manage to repatriate King Padî from Jerusalem? Probably not through negotiations with Hezekiah but by ruse or a commando operation, for example. The well-planned structure of the account of the first two phases of the third campaign,

---

109. Van Der Brugge, "Of Production, Trade, Profit and Destruction," 319–21.

110. Mordechai Cogan has summarized this discussion and referred to earlier literature: "Cross-Examining the Assyrian Witnesses to Sennacherib's Third Campaign," in Kalimi and Richardson, *Sennacherib at the Gates of Jerusalem*, 64–65.

111. RINAP 3.1:65, 4.47.

112. RINAP 3.1:65, 4.48.

against Phoenicia and against Philistia, shows that the military and political goals of Sennacherib had been achieved, with the exception of the failure regarding the small island of Tyre, which remained independent.

Against Judah

The Judean phase of the third campaign appears as being the most complicated to analyze because of the difficulties of interpretation and the contradictions of the different sources, due to the overabundant commentaries published, and because of the different approaches of the authors on this controversial subject. In no way is it my aim to reconstruct the complete history, which we cannot know in the present state of documentation, but merely to provide some insights so as to facilitate a better understanding of this highly complex episode. There are a remarkable variety of sources: Sennacherib's inscriptions recording the episode several times with a number of variants, biblical accounts (2 Kgs 18:13-19; Isa 36-37; 2 Chr 32), representations on Assyrian reliefs, archaeological discoveries, Egyptian and Greek sources, and problematic sources.[113] The main difficulty for the historian is the fact that several contradictions exist between these sources and that none of them is entirely reliable. However, some authors seem to believe that the sources related to their field of research are the best; others, studying the history of Israel and Judah, consider the Assyrian royal inscriptions as reliable sources of historical information

---

113. For Sennacherib's inscriptions, see RINAP 3.1:65-66, 4.42, 49, 52-60; 3.1:96-97, 15.iv.6-25; 3.1:115-16, 16.iii.74-iv.37; 3.1:132-33, 17.iii.38-81; 3.1:151, 18.iii.15-31; 3.1:176-77, 22.iii.18-49; 3.1:193-94, 23.iii.24-42; 3.1:210, 26.i.13; 3.1:222, 34.15; RINAP 3.2:48, 42.11; 3.2:69, 44.21; 3.2:80-81, 46.27b-33; 3.2:185, 140.r.16-21; 3.2:189, 142.r.5-8; 3.2:192, 143.i.1'. For representations on Assyrian reliefs, see Russell, *Sennacherib's Palace without Rival at Nineveh*, 160-63; Matty, *Sennacherib's Campaign against Judah and Jerusalem*, 67-89. For archaeological discoveries, see Lester L. Grabbe, "Introduction," in Grabbe, *"Like a Bird in a Cage,"* 3-20 (with bibliography). For problematic sources, see Herodotus, *Hist.* 2.41; Josephus, *A.J.* 10.1; J. H. Breasted, *Ancient Records of Egypt* (London: Luzac, 1906), 4:455; Tormod Eide, Tomas Hägg, Richard Holton Pierce, and László Török, eds., *Fontes Historiae Nubiorum: Textual Sources for the History of the Middle Nile Region between the Eighth Century BC and the Sixth Century AD*, vol. 1, *From the Eighth to the Mid-Fifth Century BC* (Bergen: University of Bergen Press, 1994), 145-58; M. F. L. Macadam, *The Temples of Kawa* (London: Oxford University Press, 1949), 1:115-16; see Gallagher, *Sennacherib's Campaign to Judah*, 12-20 (with bibliography).

concerning the events of this region. As is well known, the Assyrian royal inscriptions are characterized by ideological and propagandistic intentions, which have to be detected using a critical approach.[114] The biblical accounts are still more problematic because the text has gone through an elaborate history of writing and editing.[115] The Assyrian sources were intended to enhance the honor of Sennacherib, while the biblical accounts seek to enhance the honor of Yahweh.[116] The best method would be to consider each of the sources with an adapted critical approach and to combine them all in order to reach the best possible understanding of the Judean phase of Sennacherib's third campaign, even if some authors have written that reconciling all the sources is unacceptable or impossible.[117] The number of monographs and articles dedicated to this subject from the nineteenth century up to the present is so large that they cannot all be considered and analyzed. The main useful surveys of this bibliography are those of Brevard S. Childs, Lester L. Grabbe, William R. Gallagher, and Nazek Khalid Matty.[118]

The royal inscriptions do not indicate why Sennacherib attacked Judah, as they do for the previous revolts of King Sidqâ of Ashkelon and of the Ekronites, except in the bull inscriptions: "I ruined the wide district of Judah, (and) the recalcitrant (*šepṣu*) and strong (*mitru*) Hezekiah, its king, I made bow down at my feet." *Šepṣu* and *mitru* are related to Hezekiah, not

---

114. Laato, "Assyrian Propaganda and the Falsification of History," 198–226; Frederick Mario Fales, "Assyrian Royal Inscriptions: Newer Horizons," *SAAB* 13 (1999–2001): 119–20; Hayim Tadmor, "History and Ideology in the Assyrian Royal Inscriptions," in *"With My Many Chariots I Have Gone Up the Heights of Mountains": Historical and Literary Studies on Ancient Mesopotamia and Israel*, ed. Mordechai Cogan (Jerusalem: Israel Exploration Society, 2011), 25–46.

115. Jens Bruun Kofoed, *Text and Historiography and the Biblical Text* (Winona Lake, IN: Eisenbrauns, 2005), 164–70; David Bostock, *A Portrayal of Trust: The Theme of Faith in the Hezekiah Narratives* (Milton Keynes, UK: Paternoster, 2006).

116. Gert T. M. Prinsloo, "Sennacherib, Lachish and Jerusalem: Honour and Shame," *OTE* 13 (2000): 348–63.

117. See, e.g., Anthony Spalinger, "The Foreign Policy of Egypt Preceding the Assyrian Conquest," *CdE* 53 (1978): 36–38; Rüdiger Liwak, "Die Rettung Jerusalems im Jahr 701 v. Chr.," *ZTK* 83 (1986): 137–66.

118. Brevard S. Childs, *Isaiah and the Assyrian Crisis*, SBTh 3 (London: SCM, 1967), 11–18; Gallagher, *Sennacherib's Campaign to Judah*, 2–7; Grabbe, *"Like a Bird in a Cage,"* 20–34; Matty, *Sennacherib's Campaign against Judah and Jerusalem in 701 B.C.*, 3–11.

to Judah.[119] During the reign of Sargon, Judah, and probably already Hezekiah, was tributary to Assyria, and this Assyrian king called himself "subduer of Judah," although not reporting any military action against Judah, and neither does the Bible. A letter sent to Sargon by Marduk-rêmânni informed him that Judah, the Philistine and Transjordanian states, and Egypt were jointly delivering horses to the Assyrian capital as tribute.[120] Hezekiah revolted against Assyria, probably by withdrawing tribute and by forming an anti-Assyrian coalition. Sennacherib did not want to do without the Judean tribute, which was substantial, or to accept a troublemaker in the western part of his empire, especially if he wished to increase Judah's wealth through trade with Egypt. He possibly safeguarded routes for transporting surpluses of agrarian products such as olive oil and wine produced in the Shephelah and Negev regions to Egypt, either via Elath or via Gaza.[121]

What were the reasons for Hezekiah's revolt, and why was he so optimistic about his chances of success in front of the Assyrian army, which was unsurpassed in the Near East?[122] The burdens of vassaldom were heavy. He had to pay tribute, gifts, and all kinds of taxes. There were also trade restrictions, forced labor for Assyrian building projects, and the obligation to supply men for Assyrian military operations. The permanent demands placed on vassals were so restricting that they were constantly on the lookout for an opportunity to rebel. The epidemic that struck Assyria in 707 would have weakened the Assyrian army:[123] however, nothing is known about the nature of this epidemic, and it occurred six years before 701. Conversely, the shocking death of Sargon in 705, accompanied by the abandonment of the new capital of Khorsabad and followed by the loss of the throne of Babylon, probably influenced the revolts in the Assyrian Empire. According to the biblical accounts, an alliance would have been

---

119. RINAP 3.2:48, 42.10b–11a; 3.2:69, 44.20b–22a (incorrect translation). The translation of Luckenbill, *Annals of Sennacherib*, 77, l. 21, is better, except for *be-ru*, which has to be read *mit-ru*: see Novotny, "Royal Inscriptions of Sennacherib," 102 (*mit-ru*).

120. *ARAB* 2.137, 195; SAA 1:92, 110.r.4–13; see Elayi, *Sargon II, King of Assyria*, 52–54.

121. Van Der Brugge, "Of Production, Trade, Profit and Destruction," 306–8.

122. Gallagher, *Sennacherib's Campaign to Judah*, 263–74.

123. Grayson, *Assyrian and Babylonian Chronicles*, 76, chr. 1, ii.5; Wolfram von Soden, "Sanherib vor Jerusalem 701 v. Chr.," in *Bibel und alter Orient*, BZAW 162 (Berlin: de Gruyter, 1985), 149–57.

concluded between Babylonia and Judah in 705/704, with a visit of a Babylonian embassy to Hezekiah (2 Kgs 20:12-19; Isa 39:1-8; 2 Chr 32:31).[124] According to the hypothesis of an anti-Assyrian coalition, Hezekiah had been committed to cooperating with Merodach-baladan and to leading the rebellion in the west; other countries joined the rebellion, and Hezekiah forced the pro-Assyrian Philistine cities to cooperate by bringing parts of Philistia under his control; whether or not Egypt encouraged Judah and Philistia to rebel against Assyria is unknown. If this hypothesis is plausible, Lulî king of Tyre was intent on continuing his rebellion initiated at the end of Sargon's reign,[125] before possibly participating in the coalition. Anyway, when Hezekiah heard about the failure of the Chaldean coalition during the first campaign of Sennacherib in 704-703, he could have realized that his chances of success had seriously diminished, and he probably prepared to withstand an Assyrian attack. If Isa 30:6-7 was written in 704-702, it would mean that the Judean and Philistine allies paid a generous gift in order to obtain Egyptian support; however, Rabshakeh warned Hezekiah against such an alliance: "There you are relying on that broken reed, Egypt, which pricks and pierces the hand of the person who leans on it. That is what Pharaoh king of Egypt is like to all who rely on him" (Isa 36:6).[126] The chronology of the third campaign given in the Assyrian inscriptions is in conflict with that of the Bible, for example, concerning the dates of Ezekiah's and Sennacherib's reigns.[127] The most reliable chronology appears, in this case, to be the one given in the Assyrian inscriptions, in particular because of the yearly eponym lists and the dated campaigns in the annals.

The Assyrian inscriptions report Sennacherib's military attack against Judah as coming directly after the reestablishment of Padî on the throne of Ekron: "(As for) Hezekiah of the land of Judah, I surrounded (and)

---

124. See Gallagher, *Sennacherib's Campaign to Judah*, 270-74 (with bibliography).

125. See p. 53.

126. See Gallagher, *Sennacherib's Campaign to Judah*, 274; J. Blenkinsopp, "Hezekiah and the Babylonian Delegation: A Critical Reading of Isa. 39:1-8," in Amit, Ben Zvi, Finkelstein, and Lipschits, *Essays on Ancient Israel in Its Near Eastern Context*, 115-17.

127. See, for example, Nadav Na'aman, "Historical and Chronological Notes on the Kingdoms of Israel and Judah in the Eighth Century BC," *VT* 36 (1986): 73-74; Gershon Galil, *The Chronology of the Kings of Israel and Judah*, SHCANE 9 (Leiden: Brill, 1996), 100-101; Ernst Axel Knauf, "The 'Low Chronology' and How Not to Deal with It," *BN* 101 (2000): 59; Bob Becking, "Chronology: A Skeleton without Flesh? Sennacherib's Campaign as a Case-Study," in Grabbe, *"Like a Bird in a Cage,"* 46-72.

3. ACCESSION AND PRIORITY CAMPAIGNS (705–701)   73

conquered forty-six of his fortified walled cities and small(er) settlements in their environs, which were without number, by having ramps trodden down and battering rams brought up, the assault of foot soldiers, sapping, beaching, and siege engines."[128] The partly corresponding biblical passages are the following ones: "Sennacherib king of Assyria advanced and invaded Judah, and laid siege to the fortified cities, intending to demolish them"; "Sennacherib king of Assyria advanced on all the fortified cities of Judah and captured them" (2 Chr 32:1; Isa 36:1). The figure of forty-six given for the fortified cities of Judah conquered was probably exaggerated, because it is doubtful that they were so numerous. Exaggerating the number of conquered cities, prisoners of war, items of booty was part of the propaganda in the royal inscriptions. None of the cities conquered are named in the sources, as they were in the first campaign, possibly because Babylonian cities were better known and more important from Sennacherib's point of view than the Judean cities. However, the description of their capture is quite detailed. Only Lachish, Jerusalem, and Libnah (possibly Tel Burna, located northwest of Lachish) are mentioned by name in the sources relating to the Judean campaign (2 Kgs 19:8).[129] Turning to the archaeological evidence, the Shephelah of Judah and the northern Negev appear to have been the areas most assaulted during Sennacherib's campaign. However, there is a discussion over what archaeological data might be associated with this campaign, with one of the main problems being that there is no agreement on the terminology of the chronology. The attack and capture of Lachish seem to be confirmed by the remains; nothing similar exists for Jerusalem, but there is evidence regarding sites not far from Jerusalem, such as Ramat Raḥel.[130] A number of other sites in the region were destroyed at this time, and several of them have yielded jars with *lmlk* seal impressions. According to one of the theories proposed, their production and use were limited to a narrow time frame,

---

128. RINAP 3.1:65, 4.49–50.

129. David Ussishkin, *The Renewed Archaeological Excavations at Lachish (1973–1994)*, vol. 1 (Tel Aviv: Tel Aviv University Press, 2004), in particular 695–742; Ussishkin, "Sennacherib's Campaign to Judah: The Archaeological Perspective with an Emphasis on Lachish and Jerusalem," in Kalimi and Richardson, *Sennacherib at the Gates of Jerusalem*, 98–101.

130. Grabbe, "Introduction," 3–20 (with bibliography); David Ussishkin, "The Assyrian Attack on Lachish: The Archaeological Evidence from the Southwest Corner of the Site," *TA* 17 (1990): 53–86.

in the context of the rebellion of Hezekiah, who had stockpiled liquid foodstuffs in anticipation of the subsequent Assyrian attack.[131] Identifying the reliefs of Sennacherib's palace related to the Judean campaign is a difficult task: for example, the relief of Room I, slab 1, is not related to the third campaign, as has been proposed, but rather to the fifth campaign.[132]

The reliefs depicting the siege of Lachish, clearly identified by an epigraph, constitute the best testimony of Sennacherib's military action against Judah.[133] Many studies have been devoted to the Lachish reliefs, but I shall focus on the following issues: Why is Lachish, so well depicted in the reliefs, not mentioned in the Assyrian inscriptions? Why is Lachish's sacking and capture not represented in the reliefs? What was the meaning of these reliefs for Sennacherib? The representation of the conquest of Lachish on the reliefs, in a narrative progression on twelve slabs, was obviously important for Sennacherib, as it was probably used for the decoration of the throne room. If it was so important for him, why did he never mention the name of Lachish in the royal inscriptions? It figures in the Bible: "Then Hezekiah king of Judah sent this message to the king of Assyria at Lachish" (2 Kgs 18:14). First, Lachish was one of the unnamed forty-six fortified cities mentioned in the inscriptions; second, some other cities from these forty-six are possibly depicted in the reliefs but cannot be identified. Moreover, there are other conquered cities represented in the reliefs and absent in the inscriptions.[134] Lachish is not mentioned because it did not meet the criteria that the other cities mentioned possessed: it was not a royal city, it was not annexed by Assyria, people were not resettled

---

131. Jeffrey A. Blakely and James W. Hardin, "Southwestern Judah in the Late Eighth Century B.C.E.," *BASOR* 326 (2002): 52–53; Israel Eph'al, *The City Besieged: Siege and Its Manifestations in the Ancient Near East* (Leiden: Brill, 2009), 71.

132. Russell, *Sennacherib's Palace without Rival at Nineveh*, 160–64; Markus Wäfler, *Nicht-Assyrer neuassyrischer Darstellungen*, AOAT 26 (Neukirchen-Vluyn: Neukirchener Verlag, 1975), 112 n. 578; Frahm, *Einleitung in die Sanherib-Inschriften*, 124–25, T39; Gallagher, *Sennacherib's Campaign to Judah*, 13–14.

133. See, e.g., Ussishkin, *Conquest of Lachish by Sennacherib*; Barnett, Bleibtreu, and Turner, *Sculptures from the Southwest Palace of Sennacherib at Nineveh*, 47–144; Russell, *Sennacherib's Palace without Rival at Nineveh*, 252–53 and fig. 130; Christoph Uehlinger, "Clio in a World of Pictures: Another Look at the Lachish Reliefs from Sennacherib's Southwest Palace at Nineveh," in Grabbe, *"Like a Bird in a Cage,"* 221–305.

134. Russell, *Writing on the Wall*, 135, 140–43, 283–92; Matty, *Sennacherib's Campaign against Judah and Jerusalem in 701 B.C.*, 74–82.

3. ACCESSION AND PRIORITY CAMPAIGNS (705–701) 75

in it, and no battle took place there.[135] In fact, Lachish was not an exceptional city, and the victory against it was not considered by Sennacherib to be the high point of his western campaign. This city was chosen among several others to illustrate the efficiency of Assyrian tactics against a strong fortress and the victory as a great military achievement. This interpretation is confirmed by the representation of Sennacherib sitting on a magnificent throne, holding the bow and arrows of a conqueror, who oversaw the capture of Lachish, the seizing of the booty, and the procession of the deported inhabitants from a distant hill: "Sennacherib, king of the world, king of Assyria, sat upon a throne (while) the booty of Lachish passed in front of him."[136] It could also mean that Sennacherib had established his tactical operational center in Lachish, as shown by the Assyrian camp represented. Strangely enough, the sculptor did not depict the Assyrian soldiers entering the city and sacking it; the whole battle is shown outside the city, alongside the walls.[137] No doubt it was the choice of Sennacherib to depict the external battle, the military strategy, and the deportation of Judean families after the conquest of the city, but not its sack and destruction. As a matter of fact, destruction was not his objective, because he intended to leave loyal allies and vassals behind him, and not to create certain enemies. Lachish was treated just like the forty-six other Judean cities conquered: "I brought out of them 200,150 people, young (and) old, male and female, horses, mules, donkeys, camels, oxen, and sheep and goats, which were without number, and I counted (them) as booty."[138] Then, the Assyrian inscriptions focused directly on the attack against Hezekiah in

---

135. Matty, *Sennacherib's Campaign against Judah and Jerusalem in 701 B.C.*, 82, mentioning other unconvincing hypotheses.

136. Mayer, "Sennacherib's Campaign of 701 BCE," 197; Paul Collins, *Assyrian Palace Sculptures* (London: British Museum, 2008), 75–95; Guillaume Sence, *Les bas-reliefs des palais assyriens: Portraits de rois du 1er millénaire av. J.-C.* (Rennes: Presses Universitaires de Rennes, 2014), 144.

137. David Ussishkin, "Destruction of Judean Fortress Portrayed in Dramatic Eighth-Century B.C. Pictures," *BAR* 10 (1984): 48–73; Ussishkin, *The Renewed Archaeological Excavations at Lachish (1973–1994)* (Tel Aviv: Tel Aviv University Press, 2004), 2:695–767; Ussishkin, "Sennacherib's Campaign to Judah," 75–103.

138. RINAP 3.1:65, 4.51: Ziony Zevit, "Implicit Population Figures and Historical Sense: What Happened to 200,150 Judahites in 701 BCE?," in *Confronting the Past: Archaeological and Historical Essays on Ancient Israel in Honor of William G. Dever*, ed. Seymour Gitin, J. Edward Wright, and J. P. Dressel (Winona Lake, IN: Eisenbrauns, 2006), 357–66.

Jerusalem. It is uncertain whether the siege of Lachish was finished by then or continued during the episode against Jerusalem. Anyway, even if the siege ramps and siege machines took some time to be set up, it was a brief siege, as the entire third campaign only lasted less than a year.

The problem of the siege of Jerusalem, the capital city of Judah, has long been a *crux interpretum*, especially due to the contradictory Assyrian and biblical sources. Many authors now consider that no siege of Jerusalem ever took place in 701 BCE, but only a blockade, as is clearly specified in the Assyrian inscriptions: "As for him (Hezekiah), I confined him (*e-sir-šu*) inside the city of Jerusalem, his royal city, like a bird in a cage. I set up blockades (*ḫal-ṣu*.MEŠ) against him. Anyone going out of the city gate, I turned back to his misery."[139] The verb *esēru* means "to enclose, to confine," whereas the verb for besieging a city is *lamû*. Did the choice to set up a blockade instead of a siege mean that Sennacherib was unable to capture Jerusalem, because the siege techniques were not as advanced as is commonly believed or because they could be just as prejudicial for the assailants as for the besieged?[140] Was the city of Jerusalem so well fortified that the Assyrian king could not capture it?[141] It seems likely that Sennacherib could have done the same for Jerusalem as he did for Lachish, both cities being strong Judean fortified cities. In fact, the blockade technique was an Assyrian strategy already used, for example, by Tiglath-pileser III against King Rezin of Damascus.[142] A blockade would have entailed surrounding fortified structures over a larger area than for a siege, with the intention of cutting the city off from its sources

---

139. Luckenbill, *Annals of Sennacherib*, 33, col. iii, ll. 27–30; RINAP 3.1:165, 4.52. See Mayer, "Sennacherib's Campaign of 701 BCE," 179–81; Fales, "Road to Judah," 243–47.

140. As stated by some authors, for example Andreas Fuchs, "Über den Wert von Befestigungsanlagen," *ZA* 98 (2008): 45–98; Eph'al, *City Besieged*, 1–2.

141. Ann E. Killebrew and Andrew G. Vaughn, "Jerusalem in Bible and Archaeology: Dialogues and Discussions," in Vaughn and Killebrew, *Jerusalem in Bible and Archaeology*, 1–10; Nadav Na'aman, "When and How Did Jerusalem Become a Great City? The Rise of Jerusalem as Judah's Premier City in the Eighth-Seventh Centuries B.C.E.," *BASOR* 247 (2007): 21–56; Matty, *Sennacherib's Campaign against Judah and Jerusalem in 701 B.C.*, 109–14.

142. RINAP 1:59, 20.13'–14'; Davide Nadali, "Sieges and Similes of Sieges in the Royal Annals: The Conquest of Damascus by Tiglath-pileser III," *KASKAL* 6 (2009): 137–49; Fabrice Y. De Backer, *L'Art du siège néo-assyrien* (Leiden: Brill, 2013): see the critical review of Lionel Marti in *RA* 111 (2017): 188–89.

3. ACCESSION AND PRIORITY CAMPAIGNS (705–701)

of food, water, and other supplies, and from the support of its allies. A place called "Camp of the Assyrians" was still attested in Josephus's time.[143] In the meantime, the Assyrian army could quietly continue its rampage throughout the Judean countryside, attacking and capturing more cities. The blockade would have left the city gates free for parleys with the Assyrian officers such as the ones recorded in the Bible. The aim of the blockade was not to capture the city but to put pressure on Hezekiah in order to make him surrender. The Bible adds several accounts not recounted in the Assyrian inscriptions. Hezekiah expected to be submitted to a siege: "Hezekiah, realising that Sennacherib's advance was the preliminary to an attack on Jerusalem, consulted his officers and warriors" (2 Chr 32:2–3). Therefore, he was carefully preparing for it. Some of his preparations are alluded to after Hezekiah's submission in the Assyrian inscriptions: "He had the auxiliary forces (LÚ.úr-bi) (and) his elite troops whom he had brought inside to strengthen the city of Jerusalem, his royal city, and who had provided support."[144] According to the Bible, while Sennacherib was busy with the siege of Lachish or perhaps just after Lachish was captured, Hezekiah offered him unconditional surrender; this passage is in contradiction with his later refusal to surrender (2 Kgs 18:13–16; 2 Chr 32:1–8). Many authors have dealt with the contradictions between the different parts of the biblical account and with the intertextual relationships between the accounts in Kings, Isaiah, and Chronicles.[145] The Bible emphasizes the mission of Assyrian emissaries: Tartan, the commander-in-chief (turtānu), Rabsaris, probably the chief eunuch (rab ša-rēši), and Rabshakeh, the chief cupbearer (rab šāqê), who were dispatched to Jerusalem to demand Hezekiah to surrender (2 Kgs 18:17). The question of the historicity of this mission has been much debated. Are there parallels for this negotiation-based strategy in Assyrian inscriptions? There is no example in those of Sennacherib, but there

---

143. David Ussishkin, "The 'Camp of the Assyrians' in Jerusalem," *IEJ* 29 (1979): 137–42; Fales, "Road to Judah," 245–47.

144. RINAP 3.1:66, 4.55. The particular ethnosocial group of the LÚ.úr-bi was interpreted in different manners: Habiru-like bands, mercenaries, or Arabs, possibly auxiliary troops sent in the frame of a coalition: Fales, "Road to Judah," 241–43 (with bibliography).

145. For a summary of the different theories, see Gallagher, *Sennacherib's Campaign to Judah*, 8–9; Matty, *Sennacherib's Campaign against Judah and Jerusalem in 701 B.C.*, 3–9.

is in the Nimrud letters, where the Assyrians sent emissaries to Babylon in rebellion and possibly in a relief from the palace of Khorsabad representing the siege of Harhar.[146] However, Rabshakeh's speech comprised common biblical language rather than reflecting actual Assyrian speech and propaganda; hence it could have been free composition on the part of the biblical writer.[147] Therefore, this mission is plausible, but this does not prove its historicity. In its present form, the speech appears to be a piece of Judean propaganda, and it remains unproven that there was a historical kernel behind it, even though it is not excluded.

The consequences of Jerusalem's blockade are mentioned in the Assyrian inscriptions without actually having indicated the issue of the blockade itself: "I detached from his land (of Hezekiah) the cities of his that I had plundered and I gave (them) to Mitinti, the king of the city of Ashdod, and Padî, the king of the city of Ekron, (and) Silli-Bêl, the king of the land of Gaza, (and thereby) made his land smaller. To the former tribute, their annual giving, I added the payment (of) gifts (in recognition) of my overlordship and imposed (it) upon them."[148] This statement, which does not figure in the Bible, seems to be plausible because it was usual for the Assyrian kings to remove some parts of the territory from a rebellious vassal and to give them to a loyal vassal. For example, at the beginning of his third campaign, Sennacherib gave to Ittobaal, the new king of Sidon, the greatest part of the territory of Lulî, who had fled to Cyprus. The result of the blockade of Jerusalem is not mentioned explicitly in the Assyrian inscriptions, while the biblical accounts claim the success of Hezekiah against Sennacherib, with the help of Yahweh, for example through the prophecy of Isaiah: "He will not enter this city, will shoot no arrow at it, confront it with no shield, throw up no earthwork against it. By the road by which he

---

146. Saggs, "Nimrud Letters, 1952: Part II," 23–26; Evans, *Invasion of Sennacherib in the Book of Kings*, 179–81 (with bibliography); Dubóvský, *Hezekiah and the Assyrian Spies*, 10–31; Zevit, "Implicit Population Figures and Historical Sense," 361; Frederick Mario Fales, *Guerre et paix en Assyrie* (Paris: Cerf, 2010), 12–13, 185 fig. 42.

147. See for example Chaim Cohen, "Neo-Assyrian Elements in the First Speech of the Biblical Rab-šaqe," *IOS* 9 (1979): 36–37; Evans, *Invasion of Sennacherib in the Book of Kings*, 179–81; Peter Machinist, "The *Rab-Šāqēh* at the Wall of Jerusalem: Israelite Identity in the Face of the Assyrian 'Other,'" *HS* 41 (2000): 151–68; Gabriel A. Sivan, "The Siege of Jerusalem: Part II: The Enigmatic Rabshakeh," *JBQ* 43 (2015): 163–71; Gallagher, *Sennacherib's Campaign to Judah*, 261, proposes a reconstruction of the order of events, integrating the negotiations between Sennacherib and Hezekiah.

148. RINAP 3.1:65, 4.53–54.

3. ACCESSION AND PRIORITY CAMPAIGNS (705–701)

came, by that he will return; he will not enter this city, declares Yahweh. I shall protect this city and save it for my sake and my servant David's sake" (Isa 37:33–35; 2 Kgs 19:21b).[149]

Anyhow, according to the Assyrian inscriptions, Sennacherib fulfilled his aim against Hezekiah. Thus, the king of Judah was afraid: "Fear of my lordly brilliance overwhelmed him"; he paid tribute, he submitted: "I made Hezekiah ... bow down at my feet." His territory was ruined and considerably reduced: "I ruined the wide district of the land of Judah," and a large part of its population was deported.[150] His tribute is described in great detail:

> 30 talents of gold, 800 talents of silver, choice antimony, large blocks of *sandu*-stones, ivory beds, armchairs of ivory, elephant hide(s), elephant ivory, ebony, boxwood, garments with multicolored trim, linen garments, blue-purple wool, utensils of bronze, iron, copper, tin, (and) iron, chariots, shields, lances, armor, iron belt-daggers, bows and *uṣṣu*-arrows, equipment, (and) implements of war, (all of) which were without number, together with his daughter(s), his palace women, male singers, (and) female singers.[151]

Hezekiah's tribute is difficult to categorize among the different kinds of tribute known. It was one of the largest tributes received by Sennacherib in all his campaigns. It is amazing in the case of Judah, a country that comprised a tiny, landlocked area that lacked natural resources, had a subsistence agrarian economy, and did not benefit from a particularly strategic location to encourage trade to pass through the area. The difficulty for Hezekiah to pay such an amount is expressed in the Bible in this way: "Hezekiah gave him all the silver in the temple of Yahweh and in the palace

---

149. See, e.g., Ronald E. Clements, *Isaiah and the Deliverance of Jerusalem: A Study of the Interpretation of Prophecy in the Old Testament*, JSOTSup 13 (Sheffield: Sheffield Academic, 1980); Klaas A. D. Smelik, "Distortion of Old Testament Prophecy. The Purpose of Isaiah xxxvi and xxxvii," in *Crisis and Perspective: Studies in Ancient Near Eastern Polytheism, Biblical Theology, Palestinian Archaeology and Intertestamental Literature*, ed. A. S. van der Woude, Oud testamentische Studiën 24 (Leiden: Brill, 1985), 70–93; Alessandro Catastini, *Isaia ed Ezechia: Studio di Storia della Tradizione di II Re 18–20//Is. 36–39* (Rome: Università degli Studi di Roma "La Sapienza," 1989); Gallagher, *Sennacherib's Campaign to Judah*, 140–41, 238–39.

150. RINAP 3.1:65–66, 4.55–58; 3.1:210, 26.12′–13′; 3.1:222, 34.15; RINAP 3.2:69, 44.20b–22a.

151. RINAP 3.1:66, 4.56–58, and n. 58 (MUNUS.DUM-*šú*, "his daughter"); 2 Kgs 18:14 (three hundred talents of silver and thirty talents of gold).

treasury. At which time, Hezekiah stripped the facing from the leaves and jambs of the doors of the temple of Yahweh, which an earlier king of Judah had put on, and gave it to the king of Assyria" (2 Kgs 18:15–16). How did Hezekiah acquire such wealth to be able to meet Sennacherib's demands? Alternative sources of revenue did contribute substantially to the payment of his tribute, such as the income from tithes and taxes as a result of his religious reforms; a possible additional tax imposed on the "men of Judah"; an efficient, intense distribution system over large distances; and tolls and customs duties levied on international trade.[152] Why did Hezekiah pay such a tribute to Sennacherib? The conquest and destruction of Lachish, and of many other settlements in Judah, may have been a terrible military and moral blow inflicted on Hezekiah. His tribute was more than a surrender tribute with the purpose of showing his complete submission to Sennacherib. He also sent his daughter(s) to the Assyrian court. Other examples of sending members of the defeated king's family are reported in Assyrian inscriptions. This custom of having hostages at the Assyrian court guaranteed obedience of the defeated king and also ensured the fulfillment of the imposed obligations.[153]

One question is much debated: Why did Hezekiah send his tribute to Nineveh only after the departure of Sennacherib? The Assyrian inscriptions are not clear enough to know whether Hezekiah brought the tribute to Nineveh himself or whether he sent a messenger with it: "Hezekiah ... brought into Nineveh, my capital city, and he sent a mounted messenger of his to me to deliver (this) payment and to do obeisance."[154] According to some authors, Sennacherib returned to Nineveh because he accepted the large tribute that Hezekiah had offered. Other authors wonder why Hezekiah brought tribute if, after the departure of Sennacherib, the third campaign was finished. It is more likely that the king of Judah paid the tribute to appease Sennacherib so that he would not go back to Judah.[155]

---

152. Gail A. Röthlin and Magdel Leroux, "Hezekiah and the Assyrian Tribute," *VeEc* 34 (2013): 1–8.

153. Stefan Zawadski, "Hostages in Assyrian Royal Inscriptions," in *Immigration and Emigration within the Ancient Near East: Festschrift E. Lipiński*, OLA 65 (Leuven: Peeters, 1995), 449–58; Matty, *Sennacherib's Campaign against Judah and Jerusalem in 701 B.C.*, 58–64.

154. RINAP 3.1:66, 4.58. In 2 Kgs 18:13, Hezekiah brings the tribute to Sennacherib at Lachish.

155. Matty, *Sennacherib's Campaign against Judah and Jerusalem in 701 B.C.*, 141–48 (with bibliography).

However, the return of Sennacherib to Nineveh must be understood in the context of Assyrian military practices. The king did not move with all his army, comprising masses of slow-moving infantry; he was accompanied only by his mounted retinue and guards. Other units accompanied the booty garnered from campaigns, together with prisoners and deportees: it was a caravan of thousands of people traveling on foot or in carts drawn by oxen, which was extremely slow moving.[156] Another reason could have motivated Hezekiah to bring tribute to Nineveh: he may have been under constant threat from the Assyrian troops left in Judah to continue the blockade of Jerusalem. However, if this were the case, Hezekiah could not have gotten out of Jerusalem.

As a matter of fact, the main question, still debated, is: For what reason did Sennacherib leave Jerusalem without capturing it, returning to Nineveh instead? The account of Assyrian inscriptions ends abruptly with what Sennacherib did with the booty. According to the usual stereotyped formula, he distributed it in order to give the appearance of being a just and generous king: "From the booty of those lands that I had plundered, I conscripted 10,000 archers (and) 10,000 shield bearers and added (them) to my royal contingent. I divided up the rest of the substantial enemy booty like sheep and goats among my entire camp and my governors, (and) the people of my great cult centers."[157] Conversely, the Bible is quite wordy about Sennacherib's departure. The scholarly debate has focused on four points mentioned in the Bible.[158] The first point is Hezekiah's tribute payment to Sennacherib so that his forces might withdraw (2 Kgs 18:13–16): if he had paid tribute in Nineveh, it cannot have been the tribute that made Sennacherib return, as he was already in Nineveh at that time. The second point involves a rumor that was heard: Isaiah prophesized that Yahweh would put a spirit in Sennacherib to cause him to hear a rumor and return to Assyria, where he was killed (2 Kgs 19:7). Several authors have various opinions about what the rumor was, but the authenticity of the rumor is studied within the ambit of the authenticity of the oracle of salvation. As the rumor is mentioned in a theological context and as we are unaware of the complete set of events that took place in 701, there is no way of knowing whether it had a historical origin. The third point is

---

156. Mayer, "Sennacherib's Campaign of 701 BCE," 181.
157. RINAP 3.1:66, 4.59–60.
158. Matty, *Sennacherib's Campaign against Judah and Jerusalem in 701 B.C.*, 117–88 (with bibliography).

the Egyptian-Kushite aid: "The king had already left Lachish on hearing that Tirhakah king of Cush was on his way to attack him" (2 Kgs 19:8–9). Because of Sennacherib's devastating action in the southern Levant and in particular in Judah, even if the Egyptian-Kushite army came to confront him, it would not have prompted his departure to Nineveh. The fourth point concerns the intervention of the angel of Yahweh: "That same night the angel of Yahweh went out and struck down a hundred and eighty-five thousand men in the Assyrian camp. In the early morning when it was time to get up, there they lay, so many corpses. Sennacherib struck camp and left; he returned home and stayed in Nineveh" (2 Kgs 19:35–36). He was then killed by his sons. Some authors dismiss the whole account because of its theological framework. Others try to link it with a historical occurrence. Their main theory is that a plague was devastating the region on a large scale, disrupting the whole campaign and forcing Sennacherib to return to Assyria before entering Jerusalem. They relate the plague theory to the story of Herodotus, according to which the Egyptians confronted Sennacherib's army but were delivered because, during the night, mice gnawed away and rendered the weapons and armor of the Assyrian army useless: "One night a multitude of field mice swarmed over the Assyrian camp and devoured their quivers and their bows and the handles of their shields likewise, insomuch that they fled the next day unarmed and many fell."[159] Unfortunately, the story of Herodotus is used to help explain the biblical passage and vice versa: it is nothing more than circular reasoning. In fact, the mice in Herodotus's story suggest neither a plague nor any other kind of epidemic, the event does not concern Judah but Egypt, and the army of Sennacherib is presented as being composed of Arab troops.[160]

Now, what are the reasons for Sennacherib not seizing Jerusalem, for leaving Hezekiah on the throne and returning to Nineveh? Two ideologies are confronted here: in the Assyrian royal inscriptions, an Assyrian king, in this case Sennacherib, never suffered a military defeat; in the Bible, Hezekiah was a pious king whose actions resulted in the salvation

---

159. Herodotus, *Hist.* 2.141; my trans. of Philippe-Ernest Legrand, *Histoires: Livre 2, Euterpe* (Paris: Belles Lettres, 1936).

160. Cornelis Van Leeuwen, "Sanchérib devant Jérusalem," *OTS* 14 (1965): 264–65; Lester L. Grabbe, "On Mice and Dead Men: Herodotus 2.141 and Sennacherib's Campaign in 701 BCE," in Grabbe, *"Like a Bird in a Cage,"* 119–40.

of his capital city.¹⁶¹ Some authors consider that the defeat of Sennacherib helps explain why Jerusalem was not captured and Hezekiah was allowed to retain his throne, in spite of his prominent role in the rebellion.¹⁶² However, the campaign of Judah was not a defeat but a success for Sennacherib because he had achieved his aims. He intended to suppress Hezekiah's revolt and used the tactics of the blockade, which were suited to the situation, in order to force him to surrender: after having chastised him, Jerusalem returned to its vassal status intact. Lachish was besieged and captured for illustrating the might of the Assyrian army and the uselessness of resistance.¹⁶³ It was useless to besiege and capture Jerusalem, but it was sufficient to leave troops there to continue the blockade of the city until Hezekiah understood the lesson and surrendered. Some authors wonder why Judah was not turned into an Assyrian province or at least controlled by Assyrian administration.¹⁶⁴ This was not necessary because the status of a vassal state, severed of an important part of its territory and ruled by a king obliged to be loyal, was the best solution. There are several examples, in the Assyrian inscriptions, of rebellious vassals, submitted and then forgiven, who were allowed to keep their throne, such as Ullusunu, king of Mannea, maintained by Sargon on the throne after his submission: "Ullusunu, the Mannean, … seized my feet. I had mercy upon them. I forgave his transgression, on the royal throne [I placed him]."¹⁶⁵ Judah was henceforth harmless with its reduced territory; once the Shephelah was removed from Hezekiah's control, his economic base was destroyed. He no longer controlled the trade route to Egypt because the strategic part of his territory had been given to the Philistine cities of Ekron, Ashkelon, and Gaza, and Judah was not as economically significant to the Assyrian

---

161. Baruch A. Levine, "Assyrian Ideology and Israelite Monotheism," *Iraq* 67 (2005): 411–27.

162. Evans, *Invasion of Sennacherib in the Book of Kings*, 185. According to Stephanie Dalley, Sennacherib's tolerance toward Jerusalem is explained by the fact that Atalia, originating from Judah, was his mother, but this hypothesis is unlikely (see p. 13): "Yabâ, Atalyā and the Foreign Policy of Late Assyrian Kings," 97.

163. Mayer, "Sennacherib's Campaign of 701 BCE," 181; Fales, "Road to Judah," 248; Ussishkin, "Sennacherib's Campaign to Judah," 102–3.

164. Peter Zilberg, "The Assyrian Empire and Judah: Other Historical Documents," in *From Shaʿar Hagolan to Shaaraim: Essays in Honor of Yosef Garfinkel*, ed. S. Ganor, Igor Kreimerman, Katharina Streit, and Madeleine Mumcuoglu (Jerusalem: Israel Exploration Society, 2016), 396–97.

165. *ARAB* 2.10.

Empire as the Philistine cities were. However, it was useful for Sennacherib as a loyal vassal state because it belonged to the bloc of buffer states that, together with the Philistine states, were against Egypt.[166]

In reality, as Frederick Mario Fales stresses, "the campaigns preceding the expedition to the Levant seem to show ... a number of traits that may be compared with the campaign of 701 BCE. These common features suggest that the latter is somewhat less unique than previously perceived."[167] Sennacherib's policy continued that of his father, Sargon: it was directed at the suppression of uprisings in various sectors of the empire. As such, Hezekiah's rebellion had to be suppressed, all the more so if he was the leader of a western anti-Assyrian coalition, with Egyptian and Babylonian connections, which remained to be proved. Therefore, for Sennacherib, the attack against Hezekiah of Judah was a routine military operation, for which there was no different account in the Assyrian royal inscriptions; for example, it is put on the same level as the attack against Lulî of Tyre, which is even more developed.[168] However, for the Judeans, Sennacherib's attack was considered as a major event in the history of Judah, and this we know because of the abundant biblical accounts. One may well wonder whether Sennacherib's attack was not also considered by the Tyrians as a major event in the history of Tyre, and whether there were not also abundant accounts in the annals of Tyre, unfortunately lost. In short, Sennacherib was probably much more worried by the troubles in Babylonia than by the situation in Judah, which he had stabilized. One of the reasons for his sudden return to Nineveh could have been information received regarding unrest in Babylonia, which obliged him to undertake a second campaign in this region the following year, in 700.[169] One objection to put forward has been that the threat from Babylonia was not a major one, as the fourth campaign had proved, but Sennacherib did not know that before going to Babylonia.[170] Another objection has been that the phrase "Sennacherib went down to Akkad" in the Babylonian chronicles would indicate that

---

166. Ernst Axel Knauf, "701: Sennacherib at the Berezina," in Grabbe, *"Like a Bird in a Cage,"* 141–49. On the buffer states, see Benedikt Otzen, "Israel under the Assyrians," in *Power and Propaganda*, ed. Mogens Trolle Larsen, Mesopotamia 7 (Copenhagen: Akademisk, 1979), 251–61; Elayi, "Buffer States in the Neo-Assyrian Empire."

167. Fales, "Road to Judah," 235, 247–48.

168. RINAP 3.2:48, 42.7b–11a; 3.2:69, 44.17–22a.

169. See p. 90.

170. Laato, "Assyrian Propaganda and the Falsification of History," 215–16.

he came from Assyria and that he did not rush directly from Palestine: in reality, the usual itinerary of the Assyrian army did not cross the desert of Syria but went northward, then eastward to the heartland of Assyria.

The last question also much debated is: was there a second Assyrian campaign against Judah? For about a century and a half now, authors have failed to reach a consensus because of the contradictions between the biblical accounts themselves and with the Assyrian inscriptions. Some of them have suggested a way to resolve the contradictions by surmising that these reports relate to two separate campaigns: the first one in 701 BCE, in which Sennacherib was victorious and received a large tribute from Hezekiah, who, in return, was allowed to retain his throne; and the second campaign against Judah, in which Sennacherib suffered a setback around 688, in any case before 686, the date of Hezekiah's death.[171] The idea of two campaigns was already proposed by George Rawlinson in 1858 and is still accepted by Albert Kirk Grayson and Donald B. Redford, for example.[172] Among the contradictions of the biblical accounts are the following examples: Hezekiah made peace with Sennacherib and agreed to pay an enormous tribute, then the Assyrian king sent messengers to demand his capitulation; he resisted the Assyrian attack; he allied in 701 with King Taharqa, who became king of Kush only in 690; when Sennacherib returned to Nineveh, he was murdered by his sons, which occurred twenty years later, in 681. Therefore, William H. Shea proposed allocating the biblical accounts to the first campaign and siege of Jerusalem in 701 or to the second campaign of 688.[173] Even though

---

171. See, e.g., William F. Albright, *From the Stone Age to Christianity*, 2nd ed. (Garden City, NY: Doubleday, 1957), 314; John Bright, *A History of Israel*, 2nd ed. (Philadelphia: Westminster, 1972), 296–308; Siegfried H. Horn, "Did Sennacherib Campaign Once or Twice against Hezekiah?," *AUSS* 4 (1966): 1–28; William H. Shea, " Sennacherib's Second Palestinian Campaign," *JBL* 104 (1985): 401–18; Shea, "Jerusalem under Siege: Did Sennacherib Attack Twice?," *BAR* 25.6 (1999): 36–44, 64. According to Jeremy Goldberg, there were two campaigns, the second in 701 and the first in 712, when Sargon suppressed the revolt of Ashdod (in fact in 711), in which Judah was implicated: "Two Assyrian Campaigns against Hezekiah and Later Eighth Century Biblical Chronology," *Bib* 80 (1999): 360–90.

172. George Rawlinson, *The Five Great Monarchies of the Ancient Eastern World: The Second Monarchy; Assyria* (London: Murray, 1864), 2:430–46; Grayson, "Assyria," 111; Donald B. Redford, *Egypt, Canaan, and Israel in Ancient Times* (Princeton: Princeton University Press, 1992), 351–59.

173. Shea, "Jerusalem under Siege," 41: 2 Kgs 18:13–16 (first campaign); 2 Kgs 18:7, 19–21, 25; 19:1, 5–10, 15, 19–20, 32, 35–37 (second campaign).

only one campaign is mentioned in the Assyrian inscriptions, the hypothesis of a second campaign is not contradicted by the annals of Sennacherib's reign, which are missing for the last decade; hence we do not know what activities he engaged in during that period. The main arguments used by the supporters of the two-campaigns theory are the following: the mention of King Taharqa, king only in 690; a new text of Taharqa claiming a military victory against an unnamed adversary occurred before the great flood of the Nile in 685/684; the siege of Jerusalem is mentioned in the biblical account after the reference to Taharqa, therefore after 690; the great siege ramp used to conquer Lachish is absent on the reliefs and was found in the excavations of the city, so it is attributed to a later attack on Lachish; the new Jerusalem's fortifications and the Siloam tunnel, defensive preparations built by Hezekiah, were initiated after 701.[174]

These arguments were convincingly criticized by the supporters of the one-campaign theory.[175] The majority of authors have agreed that the biblical narrative is a composite literary creation, created by combining three different sources. The biblical account is by no means chronological; a critical evaluation shows that some elements are late and/or legendary, referring, for example, to the later Assyrian conquest of Egypt by Sennacherib's successors, and therefore cannot be accepted as evidence. Taharqa was old enough in 701 (twenty years old) to be able to lead the Kushite army as a commander.[176] The Azekah inscription cannot be used, as it is uncertain whether it was written during the reign of Sargon or that of Sennacherib.[177] The verse "I dried up with the sole of my foot all the rivers of Maṣor" (2 Kgs 19:24; Isa 37:25) cannot be used as an argument because *maṣor* is not connected with Egypt, nor the Adon papyrus, which should be better dated at the end of the seventh century BCE and would rather concern

---

174. See, for example, Shea, "Jerusalem under Siege," 38–44.

175. Mordechai Cogan, "Sennacherib's Siege of Jerusalem," *BAR* 27 (2001): 40–45, 69; Cogan, "Cross-Examining the Assyrian Witnesses to Sennacherib's Third Campaign," 51–74; Dan'el Kahn, "Tirhakah, King of Kush and Sennacherib," *JAEI* 6 (2014): 29–41; Frank J. Yurco, "The Shabaka-Shebitku Coregency and the Supposed Second Campaign of Sennacherib against Judah: A Critical Assessment," *JBL* 110 (1991): 35–45.

176. See p. 66.

177. See, e.g., Bob Becking, *The Fall of Samaria: An Historical and Archaeological Study* (Leiden: Brill, 1992), 52–54 and n. 30; Gershon Galil, "A New Look at the 'Azekah Inscription,'" *RB* 102 (1995): 327–28; Goldberg, "Two Assyrian Campaigns against Hezekiah and Later Eighth Century Biblical Chronology," 363.

a king of Byblos than a Judean king.[178] The Egyptian references used for the theory of the two campaigns are not relevant.[179] The fragment of stela recording Taharqa's victory was probably against some Libyan group.[180] It is inconceivable that, after the terrible ravage of Babylon by Sennacherib in 689, a western king had dared to revolt against Assyria. Moreover, when Esarhaddon acceded to the throne in 680, he himself would have campaigned against Judah if his father Sennacherib had suffered a failure: on the contrary, he inherited a subdued and quiescent empire.[181] Therefore, even if some questions still remain unanswered, it is unlikely that Sennacherib conducted a second campaign against Hezekiah of Judah.

During this first part of his reign (704–701), especially as regards international relations, the policy adopted by Sennacherib showed a basic continuity with that of Sargon or, at least, it did not deviate from the guidelines of territorial control and exploitation established by his father. Even if his plans for the future of the empire differed from those of Sargon when he was crown prince, his early campaigns were aimed at putting down the uprisings and at restoring Assyrian control, direct or indirect, in the whole empire.[182] At least from the time of Tiglath-pileser III, wars for consolidating and expanding the empire were institutionalized in the form of annual campaigns and became part of the traditional values of Assyrian society. Therefore, at the beginning of his reign, Sennacherib carried on the traditional military activity of his predecessors. He began with the priority campaigns, all of them defensive in character, intended to consolidate, not to expand the empire. The campaign against the Kulummeans in 704 was special: it is not mentioned in the Assyrian inscriptions, probably because it was not conducted by Sennacherib but by his magnates and because it was not a success. However, he had to undertake it in order to avenge his father, who had been killed in this area. The first campaign against Babylonia in 704–703 was

---

178. Bezalel Porten, "The Identity of King Adon," *BA* 44 (1981): 36–52; Elayi, *Histoire de la Phénicie*, 205–7.

179. Kahn, "Tirhakah, King of Kush and Sennacherib," 33–35.

180. Donald B. Redford, "Taharqa in Western Asia and Libya," *ErIsr* 24 (1993): 188*–91*; Cogan, "Sennacherib's Siege of Jerusalem," 40–43.

181. Cogan, "Cross-Examining the Assyrian Witnesses to Sennacherib's Third Campaign," 73–74.

182. Jana Pečírková, "Assyria under Sennacherib," *ArOr* 61 (1993): 2–3; Fales, "Road to Judah," 232–36.

a priority campaign because of the instability of its political situation, which was dangerous for the Assyrian Empire. Sennacherib did not solve the Babylonian problem by installing on the throne Bêl-ibni, a native of Babylon who had grown up at the Assyrian court, as he did not have much authority over the Babylonians and as Merodach-baladan was not yet captured. The second campaign against the Zagros region in 702 was directed against the Kassites and Yasubigallians, insubordinate mountain dwellers, and was also aimed at suppressing the revolt of Ellipi. In 701, Sennacherib undertook his third campaign to the west in order to submit rebellious western rulers of Phoenicia, Philistia, and Judah. His priority was to defeat Lulî, whose island of Tyre had been unsuccessfully blockaded by Sargon from 709 to 705. He conquered all the continental territories of Lulî, not the island, but nevertheless, he considered his Phoenician campaign as a success because all the Phoenician cities were again submitted. He also succeeded in pacifying the Philistine cities, maintaining the status quo of pro-Assyrian vassals, forming a bloc of buffer states against the increasing pressure of Egypt, which was behind most of the anti-Assyrian revolts. He was also successful against Hezekiah of Judah, even though he did not conquer Jerusalem: he did not need to conquer it. He restored the balance of power between the different buffer states of the region by giving parts of the Judean territory to loyal Philistine vassals. After having suppressed the secessionist tendencies of the Levantine kings, he forced them to renew their oaths of allegiance to Assyria, and he gained an immense amount of booty and tribute, particularly from Judah. His third campaign was a success because he had restored the political and economic order established by Sargon and his predecessors in the west of the empire, which provided an important part of its resources. Thus, Sennacherib restored the Pax Assyriaca there for a long time and made new campaigns in this region unnecessary during his reign.[183]

---

183. For different theories on the Assyrian policy in the west, see, e.g., Simo Parpola, "Assyria's Expansion in the Eighth and Seventh Centuries and Its Long-Term Repercussions in the West," in *Symbiosis, Symbolism, and the Power of the Past*, ed. William G. Dever and Seymour Gitin (Winona Lake, IN: Eisenbrauns, 2003), 99–111; Angelika Berlejung, "The Assyrians in the West: Assyrianization, Colonialism, Indifference, or Development Policy?," in *Congress Volume Helsinki 2010*, ed. M. Nissinen (Leiden: Brill, 2012), 21–59; Ariel M. Bagg, "Palestine under Assyrian Rule: A New Look at the Assyrian Imperial Policy in the West," *JAOS* 133 (2013): 119–43.

4
Consolidating the Empire (700–695)

After having put a great deal of effort into military campaigns during the first phase of his reign (705–701 BCE), Sennacherib continued to do what was necessary to consolidate the Assyrian Empire. During the second phase of his reign (700–695), the Assyrian campaigns were no longer priority campaigns, but they were shorter, not annual, and did not always require the presence of Sennacherib. However, there was no respite after his third campaign against the western rulers, as he immediately undertook his fourth campaign in 700 against Babylonia. This means that the Assyrian army had not been decimated by a plague or any other epidemic in Judah in 701, as some authors have proposed.[1] It also means that Sennacherib was not obsessed by Judah, as he had succeeded in pacifying all the western states until the end of his reign. Conversely, it is more and more apparent from his inscriptions that he had another obsession: Babylonia. After the fourth campaign in Babylonia in 700, the fifth campaign took place in 697 in the north of the empire, against Mount Nipur and Ukku. There is no information about what Sennacherib did during years 699 and 698, either in the royal inscriptions or in the eponym list.[2] New rebellions broke out in the northwest of the empire, in Que, Hilakku, and Tabal, which necessitated two campaigns in 696 and 695. Those two campaigns were not numbered as the other ones were and were conducted not by Sennacherib but by his magnates.

---

1. See p. 82.
2. SAAS 2:49, no. 61.

4.1. Second Babylonian Campaign

The fourth campaign of 700 is not recorded in the Rassam Cylinder, which is dated from the same year, at the beginning of the eponymy of Mitûnu, governor of Isâna; it may not have been completed when the Rassam Cylinder was inscribed. This campaign is mentioned in the eponym list in a lacunary passage.[3] It is recorded in Cylinder C, inscribed in 697; in the Octagonal Clay Prisms, dated from 697–691; in later inscriptions such as the bull inscriptions, dated from ca. 694/693; the Chicago Prism, inscribed in 691; and the Nebi Yunus inscription, probably dated from around 690–689.[4] In the nonroyal inscriptions, the campaign is recorded in some king lists and in the Babylonian Chronicles.[5] Sennacherib's so-called fourth campaign was in fact his second campaign against Babylonia, after a first one in 704–703. The motive of the campaign is not indicated, whereas for the other campaigns it is usually mentioned: "On my fourth campaign, the god Assur, my lord, encouraged me so that I mustered my numerous troops and ordered the march to the land of Bît-Yakin."[6] In 703, Sennacherib had installed Bêl-ibni on the throne of Babylon, a native from Babylon, who ruled for three years. However, his authority seems to have diminished, as is shown by the variations in territories entrusted to him.[7] He may have lost his authority over the region of Sumer around 701, because mentions of him in the texts dated from 702 and those dated from 700 and 699 have been modified. In the texts inscribed in 702, he is "appointed ... as king of the land of Sumer and Akkad," while in the texts inscribed in 700–699, he is only "entrusted ... with the people of Akkad."[8] This change clearly shows that Bêl-ibni was no longer able to rule over the land of Sumer, which means that this region had rebelled

---

3. SAAS 2:49, no. 61.

4. RINAP 3.1:97–98, 15.iv.15′–v.17; 3.1:116–17, 16.iv.38–69; 3.1:133–34, 17.iii.82–iv.17; 3.1:151–52, 18.iii.1′–30′; 3.1:177, 22.iii.50–74: 3.1:221, 34.6b–12a; RINAP 3.2:68, 44.7b–14; 3.2:81, 46.33–36.

5. Grayson, "Königslisten und Chroniken B. Akkadisch," 6:93, 101, 120, 122; Grayson, *Assyrian and Babylonian Chronicles*, 77, chr. 1, 26–31.

6. RINAP 3.1:133, 17.iii.82–84.

7. *PNA* 1.2:306.

8. RINAP 3.1:36, 1.54; 3.1:42, 2.13; 3.1:51, 3.13; RINAP 3.2:61, 4.11; 3.2:76, 8.11. See Brinkman, "Merodach-baladan II," 26 and n. 149; Brinkman, "Bēl-ibni's Letters in the Time of Sargon and Sennacherib," 175–76; Levine, "Sennacherib's Southern Front," 40–41; Manfred Dietrich, "Bēl-ibni, König von Babylon (702–700)," in *Dubsar anta-*

4. CONSOLIDATING THE EMPIRE (700–695)   91

against Assyria and not against Bêl-ibni, as has been suggested. It was a good reason for Sennacherib to intervene, which explains why the Assyrian army was heading toward the south of Babylonia. In the first part of his campaign, Sennacherib fought against the Chaldean Shûzubu: "In the course of my campaign, I defeated Shûzubu, a Chaldean who lives in the marshes, in the city of Bittûtu. As for him, terror of doing battle with me fell upon him and his heart pounded. He fled alone like a lynx and his (hiding) place could not be found."[9] He advanced through the marshes of Babylonia and tried to capture Shûzubu, but he failed in this. Shûzubu (Mushezib-Marduk) was a Chaldean leader of the Bît-Dakkûri tribe who at first seems to have been a loyal subordinate of the Assyrian governor of Lahiru.[10] Bît-Dakkûri was one of the three Chaldean territories, along with Bît-Amukâni and Bît-Yakin, which probably occupied the cultivated areas along the river from Borsippa (modern Birs Nimrud) to Marad (modern Diwaniyah).[11] When Shûzubu was defeated by the Assyrian king because of his rebellion, he probably sought refuge in Elam, and on his return he was made king of Babylon (692–689).[12]

In the second part of his campaign, Sennacherib led his army toward the land of Bît-Yakin, the tribe of Merodach-baladan, probably because he threatened to seize the throne of Babylon again, having already occupied it twice, in 721–710 and in 703.[13] He was probably a middle-aged man at that time, but he had not given up his anti-Assyrian fight. There are two different versions of this episode. The bull inscriptions seem to mix different episodes: "In a pitched battle, I repulsed Merodach-baladan, the king of Karduniash (Babylon), (and) took away his rulership. I killed with the sword all of the Chaldeans, together with the massed body of Elamite troops, his allies."[14] In fact, Ashur-nâdin-shumi, Sennacherib's son, replaced Bêl-ibni and not Merodach-baladan on the throne of Baby-

---

men: Studies zur Altorientalistik; Festschrift für W. H. P. Römer, ed. Manfred Dietrich and Oswald Loretz (Münster: Ugarit-Verlag, 1998), 81–108; *PNA* 1.2:305–6.

9. RINAP 3.1:133–34, 17.iii.85–91.

10. *PNA* 3.2:1297–98.

11. Frederick Mario Fales, "Moving around Babylon: On the Aramean and Chaldean Presence in Southern Mesopotamia," in *Babylon: Wissenskulturin Orient und Okzident*, ed. Eva Cancik-Kirschbaum, Margarete van Ess, and Joachim Marzahn (Berlin: de Gruyter, 2008), 96–97.

12. See p. 116.

13. *PNA* 2.2:705–11.

14. RINAP 3.2:48, 42.5; 3.2:68, 44.11; 3.2:81, 46.37.

lon, and the Elamites did not intervene in 700. All the other inscriptions gave a different version, which seems to be more reliable: Merodach-baladan preferred to flee instead of confronting Sennacherib's army: "He, whom I had defeated (and) whose forces I had scattered during my first campaign, became frightened by the clangor of my mighty weapons and my fierce battle array. He fled away like a bird to the city of Nagîte-raqqi, which is in the midst of the sea."[15] Nagîte-raqqi (Nagîtu) was a district of Elam, probably located at or near the point where the River Ulâya emptied into the Persian/Arabian Gulf.[16] In 700, Sennacherib did not try to pursue him across the sea, as he did later, when he launched an attack on the coast of Elam, in his campaign of 694. He contented himself with seizing prisoners and operating some deportations: "I brought his brothers, the seed of his father's house, whom he had abandoned at the shore of the sea, together with the rest of the people of his land, out of the land of Bît-Yakin, which is in the swamps (and) marshes, and I counted (them) as booty."[17] The configuration of this region has changed a great deal since antiquity, when the Persian/Arabian Gulf penetrated further into the mainland, probably up to the border of Bît-Yakin.[18] As a result, Bît-Yakin was not inland but on the seashore. That is why Sennacherib blamed Merodach-baladan for having abandoned his family on the coast instead of taking them on board the ship, which enabled him to flee to Elam. While he probably succeeded in seizing Merodach-baladan's family, it is dubious that he could catch the rest of the people of his land, scattered and hidden in the swamps and marshes. The results of the two parts of this campaign were quite meager, especially as he needed to collect at least some booty: "Once again (as in his first campaign), I destroyed (and) devastated his cities, (and) turned (them) into ruins."[19] Moreover,

---

15. RINAP 3.1:134, 17.iii.9–iv.1–5.

16. RINAP 3.1:83, 46.81b–90; 3.1:98, 15.v.5; 3.1:117, 16.iv.65; 3.1:134, 17.iv.13; 3.1:152, 18.iii.28'; 3.1:178, 22.iii.72; 3.1:195, 23.iii.63. See Levine, "Sennacherib's Southern Front," 40–41.

17. RINAP 3.1:134, 17.iv.5–9.

18. *ARAB* 2.43, 54; Paul Sanlaville, "Considérations sur l'évolution de la basse Mésopotamie au cours des derniers millénaires," *Paléorient* 15 (1989): 5–27; Paul Sanlaville and Rémi Dalongeville, "L'évolution des espaces littoraux du golfe Persique et du golfe d'Oman depuis la phase finale de la transgression post-glaciaire," *Paléorient* 31 (2005): 10–11 (map), 19; Joannès, *Dictionnaire de la civilisation mésopotamienne*, 793 (map).

19. RINAP 3.1:134, 17.iv.10.

4. CONSOLIDATING THE EMPIRE (700–695)

he was conscious that he had not confronted his Elamite enemy, probably not by cowardice but because he was not prepared for an expedition across the Persian/Arabian Gulf. Nevertheless, he boasted having frightened the king of Elam: "I poured out awe-inspiring brilliance upon his ally, the king of the land of Elam."[20] The Elamite kingdom was a powerful state, but the main threat came from Elam's connection with Babylonia, as Sargon had already experienced previously.

Coming back from Bît-Yakin to Babylon, Sennacherib was obliged to instigate another governmental procedure because his policy of partial appeasement by appointing a native Babylonian had failed. As a matter of fact, he had not dealt with the Chaldean component of the Babylonian problem. He decided to adopt a policy of more direct control by appointing his son Ashur-nâdin-shumi, who was also the crown prince: "On my return march, I placed Ashur-nâdin-shumi, my first-born son, offspring of my loins, on his lordly throne and entrusted him with the wide land of Sumer and Akkad."[21] He made no reference to the dethronement of Bêl-ibni, whose name disappeared from Sennacherib's inscriptions written after 700. The reason for this silence in the Assyrian sources was possibly an attempt to give the impression that the previous Assyrian decision to install Bêl-ibni on the throne of Babylon was not wrong.[22] Other sources gave information about what happened to Bêl-ibni after he had been dethroned by Sennacherib. According to the Babylonian Chronicles: "He led away to Assyria Bêl-ibni and his officers," and according to Berossus, a priest who lived in Babylon under Antiochus I, he took Belibos (Bêl-ibni) and his friends prisoner and deported them to Assyria.[23]

Even if Sennacherib's fourth campaign was not a great military success, his decision to place his son Ashur-nâdin-shumi on the throne of Babylon ensured Assyrian control over Babylonia for the next six years.[24]

---

20. RINAP 3.1:134, 17.iv.11–12.

21. RINAP 3.1:134, 17.iv.13–17.

22. Levine, "Sennacherib's Southern Front," 40–41; Laato, "Assyrian Propaganda and the Falsification of History," 204; Marc Van De Mieroop, "Revenge, Assyrian Style," *PaP* 179 (2003): 11–15; Ben Dewar, "Rebellion, Sargon II's 'Punishment' and the Death of Aššur-nādin-šumi in the Inscriptions of Sennacherib," *Journal of Ancient Near Eastern History* 3 (2016): 34–35.

23. Grayson, *Assyrian and Babylonian Chronicles*, chr. 1, ll. 28–29; Felix Jacoby, *Die Fragmente der griechischen Historiker* (Leiden: Brill, 1968), 386F 7c; *PNA* 1.2:306.

24. *PNA* 3.1:1119.

However, he knew, even at this early date in his reign, that Elam was part of the southern problem and that it had to be solved.

4.2. Fifth Campaign to the North

The fifth campaign took place in 697, after a void of two years (699 and 698). The silence of the sources concerning these two years leads us to suppose that there was no military campaign, either led by Sennacherib or by his magnates. In other words, the Pax Assyriaca lasted two years. The fifth campaign was conducted by Sennacherib toward the north of the empire, against some cities of Mount Nipur and against Ukku, certainly not in winter because the region, blocked in by the snow, was not accessible then. This campaign was first recorded in the same year on the spot, in what is referred to as Judi Dagh inscriptions. Sennacherib had them written on the face of Mount Judi Dagh in eastern Anatolia, near the Tigris. Eight sculpted panels were found: six near the village of Shakh, and two near the village of Hasanah. Two of them are unfinished; the remaining six panels, duplicated, have inscriptions and carved figures of the Assyrian king but were badly damaged.[25] They only record the fifth campaign, in a more detailed manner than in the later inscriptions. Sennacherib presents himself as the king who, thanks to his gods, made the insubmissive lands and disobedient people of the mountains bow down at his feet: "At that time, the cities of Tumurrum, Sharum, Halbuda, Kibshu, Ezâma, Qûa, (and) Qana, which were on the border of the land of Katmuhu, which were situated like the nests of eagle(s) on the peaks of Mount Nipur, (and) which since time immemorial were strong and proud, not knowing the fear of (Assyrian) rule during (the reigns of) the kings, my ancestors—during the reign of my lordship, their gods abandoned them and made them *vulnerable*."[26] The rebellious cities are not identified, but they were located on Mount Nipur, which has been identified with certainty with Cudi Dağlari in Turkey because of the so-called Judi Dagh inscriptions made by Sennacherib near the village of Shakh in the mountains around 14 kilometers northeast of Cizre.[27] The mention of Katmuhu is unclear: it cannot

---

25. Frahm, *Einleitung in die Sanherib-Inschriften*, 150–51; RINAP 3.2:307–10, 222.1–52 (with bibliography).

26. *ARAB* 2.295; RINAP 3.2:308–9, 222.12–24a.

27. Karen Radner, "Between a Rock and a Hard Place: Muşaşir, Kumme, Ukku and Šubria—The Buffer States between Assyria and Urartu," in *Biainili-Urartu*, ed.

be read Kutmuhu/Kummuhu (Commagene), as has been proposed,[28] because it is too far away to be bordering on Mount Nipur. It may designate Kumme, which was in the neighborhood, or another unknown place in this region. In some inscriptions, insistence is put on the city of Tumurrum: "[The Tumurr]ai dwelling in Nipur, [a rugged mountain, with] the sword I slew."[29] The rest of the account of the fifth campaign is very lacunary but can be restored from the other inscriptions.

Sennacherib pitched his camp at the foot of Mount Nipur, and then he climbed up the mountain, accompanied only by his select combat troops. The description of the climb is an admirable propaganda text to boast the courage, strength, and endurance of the king, who compares himself to a fierce wild bull in this steep, rugged mountain, very difficult to access: "I proceeded through the gorges of the streams, the outflows of the mountains, (and) rugged slopes in (my) chair. Where it was too difficult for (my) chair, I leapt forward on my (own) two feet like a mountain goat. I ascended the highest peaks against them. Where my knees became tired, I sat down upon the mountain rock and drank cold water from a water skin to (quench) my thirst."[30] The description is realistic, probably because this first inscription was made on the spot, by engravers who had accompanied him on the climb. Sennacherib was perfectly well acquainted with the problems of this area because he had been closely involved in the affairs of the north of the empire when he was crown prince;[31] however, he probably never went there before because he did not used to accompany his father on his military campaigns. The account of the campaign is quite short: "I pursued them on the peaks of the mountains and defeated them. I conquered, plundered, destroyed, devastated, (and) burnt with fire their cities."[32] It is probably true that he destroyed the rebellious cities but more doubtful that he could have reached and confronted their dwellers

---

Stephan Kroll, Claudia Gruber, Ursula Hellwag, Michael Roaf, and Paul E. Zimansky (Leuven: Peeters, 2012), 255 (with bibliography on the other wrong identifications).

28. *ARAB* 2.295; Luckenbill, *Annals of Sennacherib*, 64, v.15; RINAP 3.1:117, 16.iv.75, 78; 3.1:134, 17.iv.22, 24; 3.1:152, 18.iii.3", 5"; 3.1:178, 22.iii.78, 80; 3.1:195, 23.iii.69, 71; 3.1:210, 26.i.14'; 3.1:225, 34.73; RINAP 3.2:48, 42.11; 3.2:69, 44.22; 3.2:81, 46.38; 3.2:94, 49.7'; 3.2:97, 50.7'; 3.2:98, 51.6; 3.2:208, 152.o.11.

29. Reginald Campbell Thompson, "A Selection from the Cuneiform Historical Texts from Nineveh (1927–32)," *Iraq* 7 (1940): 95.

30. RINAP 3.1:117, 16.v.1–7.

31. See p. 36.

32. RINAP 3.1:117, 16.v.8–11a.

in such rugged mountains. However, after having destroyed the rebellious cities of Mount Nipur, he had a stela made: "Then, ... I had a stele made and had written (on it) the mighty victories of (the god) Assur, my lord. I er[ected (it) for] ever [after] on the peak of Mount Nipur."[33] It is difficult to know whether this stela corresponds with the panels of the Judi Dagh inscriptions or not. The malediction against whoever might alter it, which ends the inscription, suggests that it was the stela mentioned in it, but it is uncertain whether its location on the peak of Mount Nipur corresponds to the place where the Judi Dagh inscriptions were discovered.

The second part of Sennacherib's campaign was directed against Ukku, and the reason—to suppress a revolt—is given straightaway: "I turned around and took the road against Maniye, the king of the city of Ukku (and) an insubmissive mountain dweller."[34] His experiences with Ukku at the time when he was crown prince, as is shown in two letters,[35] had possibly also influenced his decision to lead a campaign against this state, which must be seen in the context of Assyria's relationship with Urartu. However, this aggression on the Urartian border does not seem to have resulted in any direct conflict between Urartu and Assyria, probably because of the weakening of Urartu after Sargon's campaign of 714 and of the ephemeral character of Sennacherib's invasion into Ukku; it was also a warning to Urartu not to interfere in Assyrian affairs. He asserted that he was the first Assyrian king to reach Ukku through the rugged mountains. Sargon had relations with Ukku, but he may not have gone there personally. Ukku was located north of the Judi Dagh, in the region where the Turkish provinces of Siirt and Hakkari intersect.[36] Ukku possibly corresponds to modern Hakkari, on the Greater Zab River, and was situated between Assyria and Urartu, opposite a Urartian province of unknown name, in one of the most rugged mountain areas of southeastern Turkey.[37] This geographic position gave Ukku its special political status. Permanent control was impossible because the high mountain passes leading to this territory were completely snowbound in winter.[38] Moreover, the transportation of chariots and other

---

33. RINAP 3.2:310, 222.48b–51a.
34. RINAP 3.1:117, 16.v.11b–15.
35. See pp. 36–37.
36. Parker, *Mechanics of Empire*, 94–97.
37. Radner, "Between a Rock and a Hard Place," 257–60.
38. The lacunary letter SAA 5:201, no. 285, is interpreted as referring to an overwhelming amount of snow by Giovanni Battista Lanfranchi and Simo Parpola.

4. CONSOLIDATING THE EMPIRE (700–695)

military equipment across these rugged mountains would have been too difficult and time consuming for the Assyrians. Those difficulties explain why Sargon had not annexed Ukku.[39] Another reason was no doubt the proximity of this state to Urartu: an Assyrian occupation of Ukku would have provoked a direct confrontation with Urartu, which would have been risky in this logistically difficult zone. Sargon considered it much more valuable to keep Ukku as a buffer state between Kumme, his loyal vassal, and the border of Urartu, and forced the king of Ukku to send spies to gather information. At the same time, he had obligations toward the Urartians, giving them information on the Assyrians. After Sargon's campaign of 714 and the weakening of Urartu, he tried to impose some vassal obligations on the Ukkeans, such as tribute and services; for example, one hundred Ukkean laborers were reported to be transporting logs for Assyrians.[40] Assyria's relations with Ukku illustrate a method of control other than vassalage or annexation: the manipulation of independent states as buffers between Assyria and its enemies. However, whatever the terms of the treaty concluded between Ukku and Assyria, they appear to have been unacceptable for the Ukkeans, who clearly chose to disregard them after Sargon's death.

Sennacherib's attack against Ukku is more succinctly reported than the previous one against Mount Nipur, possibly because it was repetitive: "I had my camp pitched at the foot of Mount Anara and Mount Uppa, mighty mountains, and I myself, in a (sedan) chair, with my seasoned warriors, entered their narrow passes with great difficulty and ascended with great difficulty the steep mountains peaks."[41] In the sources covering Sargon's reign, the king of Ukku is not known by name but only referred to as "the Ukkean"; his crown prince was named Bazia.[42] King Maniye, who revolted against Sennacherib, was possibly the same individual, already on the throne, at least at the end of Sargon's reign. He was afraid at the arrival of the Assyrian army: "He saw the dust cloud (stirred up) by the feet of my troops, then he abandoned the city of Ukku, his royal city, and fled afar. I surrounded, conquered, (and) plundered the city of Ukku. I brought out

---

39. Elayi, *Sargon II, King of Assyria*, 122–26.
40. SAA 5:87, no. 111.
41. RINAP 3.1:117–18, 16.v.16–22; 3.1:135, 17.iv.40, 53, 55; 3.1:152, 18.iv.6; 3.1:178, 22.iv.13, 24–25; 3.1:196, 23.iv.8, 19–20; 3.1:210, 26.i.16′; 3.1:222, 34.16; RINAP 3.2:48, 42.12; 3.2:69, 44.23; 3.2:82, 46.42, 45; 3.2:192, 143.o.i.3′.
42. SAA 5:136, no. 190; Parker, *Mechanics of Empire*, 95 and n. 237.

of it every kind of possession (and) property, the treasures of his palace, and I counted (it) as booty."[43] The destruction of Ukku is presented as particularly violent in the bull inscriptions: "I destroyed the city of Ukku, together with every one of its settlements, (so that they looked) like a ruin hill (created by) a hurricane."[44]

The campaign against Ukku is also documented in the reliefs of the Nineveh palace. Sennacherib had the city depicted on the western wall of the throne room of his palace, and it is identified by a lengthy epigraph: "Maniye, king of Ukku, feared the onslaught of my battle and deserted Ukku, his power base, and fled to distant parts. I pursued the people dwelling therein who had like birds flown to the summit of the inaccessible mountains and defeated them at the summit. I burned his royal city of Ukku."[45] The partly damaged relief shows the city in front of a massive mountain, unfortified, but the buildings are represented as tower-like structures having small windows. They were flanking an impressive building that was apparently the royal palace. It was built out of enormous stone blocks; it had several floors, three gateways on the first level, and several openings on the second level. This type of architecture was very different from the Assyrian mud-brick constructions and seems to be well suited for the harsh winters. The Assyrian army is depicted below the city on three levels, capturing horses and carrying off equipment and loot from the city. The seizure of the unfortified city of Ukku is represented differently from the siege of the fortified city of Lachish. The next relief slabs show Assyrian soldiers in a mountain landscape, rounding up fleeing Ukkeans, capturing or slaughtering them, then leading the captives down to an Assyrian fort.[46] According to Joshua Jeffers, Rooms XXXVIII and XLVIII also contained representations of Sennacherib's fifth campaign.[47] The different slabs, more or less preserved, also depict an unfortified city, fully ablaze, in the midst of high mountains, soldiers descending the mountain with booty, other soldiers capturing some inhabitants, killing others, and counting the decapitated heads of the enemy. This program's imagery would have

---

43. RINAP 3.1:118, 16.v.23–28.
44. RINAP 3.2:48, 42.11b–12a.
45. Frahm, *Einleitung in die Sanherib-Inschriften*, 124–25; Russell, *Writing on the Wall*, 283–84.
46. Radner, "Between a Rock and a Hard Place," 258–60 (with bibliography).
47. Joshua Jeffers, "Fifth-Campaign Reliefs in Sennacherib's 'Palace without Rival' at Nineveh," *Iraq* 73 (2011): 87–116.

been consistent with the devastation that Sennacherib wreaked during his fifth campaign to the north. The broad river represented would be the Greater Zab, along which the Assyrian king advanced into the territory of Ukku. Finally, dismantling the small state of Ukku as an indirect warning to Urartu would have been a more significant military operation than the defeat of a few small cities on Mount Nipur.[48]

After the destruction of Ukku, Sennacherib pursued the conquest of other cities of the area, probably without difficulty because they were not fortified: "Moreover I conquered thirty-three cities on the borders of his district and carried off from them people, donkeys, oxen, and sheep and goats. Then I destroyed (them), devastated (them), (and) burned (them) with fire."[49] At the end of the record of the fifth campaign, he made an evaluation of the results: he conscripted twenty thousand archers and fifteen thousand shield bearers. Then, to present an image of himself as a just and generous king, he mentions the distribution of the booty with the usual stereotyped sentence: "I divided up the rest of the substantial enemy booty like sheep and goats among my entire camp and my governors, (and) the people of my great cult centers."[50] The fifth campaign is said to have been initiated in the Assyrian tradition for territorial expansion, in a place where preceding kings had never gone. The inscriptions gave him the opportunity to praise his personal heroism. However, the isolated incursion into the mountains north of Assyria represented no more than token acknowledgment of the traditional duty of the king to expand the border. Sennacherib was not overtly an expansionist, and this attempt at territorial expansion in Mount Nipur and Ukku was limited and ephemeral. After the departure of his army, it is quite likely that the situation reverted to what it had previously been. Neither inscriptions nor reliefs reveal anything about the fate of Maniye, king of Ukku. If Sennacherib had captured or killed him, he would have boasted about this success. Maniye had probably managed to escape to Urartu and eventually returned later to Ukku.[51] The fifth campaign was obviously necessary to secure the northern border of the empire, but it was not a great and spectacular campaign with a substantial amount of booty, compared, for example, with Sargon's

---

48. Jeffers, "Fifth-Campaign Reliefs in Sennacherib's 'Palace without Rival' at Nineveh," 100–101.
49. RINAP 3.1:118, 16.v.29–32.
50. RINAP 3.1:118, 16.v.37–40.
51. *PNA* 2.2:677–78.

eighth campaign against Urartu, but Assyrian propaganda tried to demonstrate the contrary.

4.3. Campaign against Cilicia

Another Assyrian campaign was directed against Cilicia. This campaign took place "in the eponymy of Shulmu-Bêli, governor of the city of Talmusu," precisely dated in 696.[52] Instead of being dated in terms of Sennacherib's own campaigns (*gerru*), which were numbered, the Cilician campaign was dated in terms of eponyms, in an old-fashioned manner.[53] In the Nebi Yunus inscription, probably written around 690–689, Sennacherib boasts that he led the campaign himself: "I struck down with the sword the people of the land of Hilakku, who live in the mountains. I destroyed, devastated, (and) burned with fire their cities."[54] However, this inscription is a propaganda text obviously intended to summarize and celebrate the many accomplishments of the Assyrian king on the battlefield. The King/Heidel Prism contains a detailed account of the campaign written shortly after the event, in 694. It is clearly specified that Sennacherib made the decision for the campaign to be launched, but he did not participate in it: "I sent against them archers, shield and lance bearers, chariots, (and) horses of my royal contingent";[55] it is not indicated whether this contingent was coordinated by one of his magnates or by the Assyrian governor of Que. The campaign was conducted in Hilakku and Que. In Sennacherib's inscriptions, Que probably corresponded to the plain of Cilicia Pedias. It was bounded by the Mediterranean to the south, the Taurus mountains to the north, the Amanus range to the east and, to the west, the mountains of Cilicia Traccheia, which could correspond, at least partly, to Assyrian Hilakku.[56] The main passes by which entry could

---

52. RINAP 3.1:135, 17.iv.61–62; SAAS 2:50, 61.

53. Tadmor, "World Dominion," 61.

54. RINAP 3.1:222, 34.17b–18. See also Bull inscriptions: "The people of Hilakku, who dwell in the high mountains, I slaughtered like lambs" (*ARAB* 2.239).

55. RINAP 3.1:135, 17.iv.69–70.

56. Κιλικία: Olivier Casabonne, *La Cilicie à l'époque achéménide* (Paris: De Boccard, 2004), 21–49, 67; Afif Erzen, *Kilikien bis zum ender der Perserherrschaft* (Leipzig: Noske, 1940); John Daniel Bing, *A History of Cilicia during the Assyrian Period* (Ann Arbor, MI: University Microfilms, 1969); Paolo Desideri and Anna M. Jasink, *Cilicia: Dall' età di Kizziwatna alla conquista macedone* (Turin: Le lettere, 1990); Elizabeth French, "Cilicia," in *The Philistines and Other "Sea Peoples" in Text and Archaeology,*

be gained into Que were few, except for the southern coastline: the so-called Cilician Gates and Amanus Gates. The Que campaign, directed by Sargon in 715, had resulted in the cities that had been captured by Midas being reconquered, defeating the Ionians and turning Que into an Assyrian province; in 709, the Assyrian governor of Que had made three raids against Midas in a mountainous region, probably Hilakku: the Phrygian king was defeated and decided to submit, then behaving as a docile vassal.[57]

The motive of the campaign in 696 is clearly mentioned: "Kirûa, the city lord (*bēl āli*) of Illubru, a servant who belonged to me, whom his gods had abandoned, incited the population of Hilakku to rebel and prepare for battle. The people living in the cities of Ingirâ and Tarzu aligned themselves with him, then seized the road through the land of Que (and) blocked (its) passage."[58] Kirûa was formerly a loyal Assyrian vassal, but for an unknown reason, he revolted against Assyria and caused two Cilician cities to revolt. His city of Illubru could be identified with Byzantine Lampron, modern Çamlıyayla; Ingirâ may correspond to Anchialè, and Tarzu was probably Tarsus.[59] More than the revolt of some Cilician cities, the blockade of the Cilician Gates was intolerable for the Assyrians who followed this road when they were en route for Tabal. It was also the access route to the riches of Anatolia. As for the Amanus Gates, the Assyrians also needed to use them in order to exploit the wood of the Amanus for Sennacherib's building projects.

The campaign against Cilicia comprised three operations, presented in an order that is possibly chronological. First, "in rugged mountains, they (the Assyrians) defeated the population of Hilakku"; second, "they conquered and plundered the cities of Ingirâ (and) Tarzu."[60] The two Cilician cities were not fortified, otherwise it would be mentioned, and therefore they were easy to capture; the population of Hilakku was not sheltered inside fortifications but benefited from the ruggedness of the terrain where

---

ed. Ann E. Killebrew and Gunnar Lehmann, ABS 15 (Atlanta: Society of Biblical Literature, 2013), 479–83.

57. Elayi, *Sargon II, King of Assyria*, 87–90; *PNA* 2.2:755–56.

58. RINAP 3.1:135, 17.iv.63–68.

59. Avienus, *Descr.* 1040; Xenophon, *Anab.* 1.2.23; Plutarch, *Demetr.* 47; Cicero, *Fam.* 2.17.1, 12.13.4; Lucanus, *Pharsalia* 3.225; Stephanie Dalley, "Sennacherib and Tarsus," *AnSt* 49 (1999): 73–80; Casabonne, *La Cilicie à l'époque achéménide*, 67, 85, and n. 331.

60. RINAP 3.1:135, 17.iv.73–76.

they fought. Whatever the chronological order of these two operations, the siege of the fortified city of Illubru was the most difficult and probably followed on from the other action: "As for him (Kirûa), they besieged him in the city of Illubru, his fortified city, and cut off his escape route. They defeated him by means of bringing up battering rams, siege machines and (special) siege engines, (and) the assault of foot soldiers, and they took possession of the city."[61] If the Assyrians were able to carry these different kinds of siege machines, it means that the city of Illubru was not located on the summit of the rugged mountains of Hilakku but in a more accessible place. It is uncertain whether the siege of Illubru is represented in the reliefs of the palace of Nineveh—maybe not, as the siege was not conducted by Sennacherib himself. Anyhow, after the victorious campaign of Cilicia, all the booty and the rebellious vassal and people were brought to Sennacherib: "They brought Kirûa, the city ruler, together with booty from his cities and the inhabitants of Hilakku who had aligned themselves with him, as well as donkeys, oxen, and sheep and goats to Nineveh, before me. I flayed Kirûa."[62] The image of justice is always present: only the guilty people were punished, and the punishment of the leader of the revolt was the worst. The other prisoners were employed in building projects: "The people of the lands of Que and Hilakku, who had not submitted to my yoke, I deported, made them carry baskets (of earth) and they made bricks."[63] To replace the deported Illubru population, people from other conquered lands were settled in the city. The expression used, *ú-ter-ma*, "once again" is not quite clear: it could refer to a previous campaign undertaken by Sennacherib in this area, which is not mentioned in his inscriptions; to a campaign during the reign of Sargon (715 or 709), but this does not seem very likely; or it means that this kind of operation was usual when a city had been captured. After Sennacherib had reorganized the city of Illubru as was customary, he adds: "I installed the weapon of the god Assur, my lord, inside it. I had a stele of alabaster made and I erected (it) in front of it."[64] The GIŠ.TUKUL (*kakku*), the weapon of god Assur, was usually the bow and quiver with arrows; it was recognized as a symbol representing the god. The erection of a stela in front of it, which probably related Sennacherib's exploits, in particular the victorious campaign

---

61. RINAP 3.1:136, 17.iv.77–81.
62. RINAP 3.1:136, 17.iv.82–86.
63. *ARAB* 2.364, 383; RINAP 3.1:137, 17.v.53–55.
64. RINAP 3.1:136, 17.iv.89–91.

4. CONSOLIDATING THE EMPIRE (700–695)   103

of Cilicia, meant that all these achievements were made with the help of Assur. Even though it is written that the Assyrian king was present for the installation of the weapon and the stela inside the fortified city of Illubru, it was probably not true.

There exists another source relating the campaign of Cilicia of 696: the Greek historian Eusebius had transmitted two fragments of text attributed to the Babylonian priest Berossus. They were attributed to Polyhistor and Abydenus as intermediaries.[65] He reports that Sennacherib defeated Greeks/Ionians (*Graeci* in the Latin text, *Join* in the Armenian text), invaders of Cilicia, either on the land or in a sea battle. Then, according to the version of Polyhistor: "As a memorial of this victory he left a statue of himself on the battlefield and ordered that an account of his courage and heroic deed be inscribed in Chaldean script for future times. And Sennacherib built the city of Tarson after the model of Babylon, and he gave it the name of Tharsin."[66] According to the version of Abydenus, he built the temple of Sandes and erected bronze pillars. Is there any historical kernel in this source? Tarsus was not built by Sennacherib, possibly only rebuilt, because archaeological evidence has shown its existence as early as the Bronze Age.[67] Sennacherib's inscriptions mention, on one occasion, Ionian sailors whom he had captured and ordered to sail down the Tigris during the sixth campaign.[68] Therefore, even if it was not explicitly mentioned in the Assyrian inscriptions, it is possible that Sennacherib's battle against the Ionians in Cilicia really did take place.[69] The treatment of Tarsus by the Assyrian king presents some elements of similarity with the treatment of Illubru, for example, the inscribed memorial. The mention of bronze pillars is reminiscent of the pillars that Sennacherib was proud of having cast and placed in the arsenal (*ekal kutalli*) of Nineveh.[70] According to Stephanie Dalley, Berossus gave some accurate information, probably based on

---

65. Jacoby, *Die Fragmente der Griechischen Historiker*, 3Cl 268–70, F43–44; Robert Drews, "The Babylonian Chronicles and Berossus," *Iraq* 37 (1975): 39–55; Stanley Mayer Burstein, *Babyloniaca of Berossus*, 23–26; Gerald P. Verbruggte and John M. Wickerstam, *Berossos and Manetho: Introduced and Translated* (Ann Arbor: University of Michigan Press, 1996).

66. Burstein, *Babyloniaca of Berossus*, 24.2a

67. Dalley, "Sennacherib and Tarsus," 73–80 (with bibliography).

68. See p. 108; RINAP 3.1:165, 20.7–8; RINAP 3.2:82, 46.60–61.

69. Josette Elayi and Antoine Cavigneaux, "Sargon II et les Ioniens," *OrAnt* 18 (1979): 68–70.

70. See p. 180.

contemporary Mesopotamian sources in Akkadian or Aramaic: the cuneiform incantation tablets found at Tarsus may come from the house of the priest Nabû-dur-ilishu during Assyrian occupation, and the Tarsus god Sanda resembled great Assyrian gods.[71]

In short, the Cilician campaign was not a major campaign, but it was necessary and useful for pacifying this region on the northwestern border of the empire, for clearing the road passing through the Cilician Gates to Anatolia, and for bringing back booty and restoring the tribute of Que and Hilakku. Sennacherib also benefited from the captives as laborers in his building projects and as seafarers in his fluvial and maritime expeditions, such as the one against Elam in 694.[72] In sum, he benefited from all the advantages of this campaign without being involved.

4.4. Campaign against Tabal

Clearing the road that crossed the Cilician Gates led naturally to Tabal. It was probably not a mere coincidence if the following year's campaign took place in Tabal. It occurred "in the eponymy of Ashur-bêlu-usur, governor of the land of Katmuhi," that is, in 695,[73] with the same old-fashioned manner of dating as for the preceding campaign. Sennacherib boasts of having led the campaign himself: "Tîl-Garimmu, which is on the border of Tabalu, I captured and turned into ruins."[74] However, this text of propaganda is offset by the King/Heidel Prism, written in 694, just after the event, which gives a detailed account of the campaign. It is clearly stated that the Assyrian king did not participate in it: "I sent archers, shield and lance bearers, chariots, (and) horses of my royal contingent against it";[75] it is not indicated which official led the operation. The location of the campaign was Tabal, more particularly Til-Garimmu/e, a city on the border of Tabal, and Urdutu, the royal city of Gurdî. Til-Garimmu may be another spelling of Kulummu/Kulummayu in the Eponym Chronicle; it would

---

71. Albrecht Goetze, "Cuneiform Inscriptions from Tarsus," *JAOS* 59 (1939): 1–16; Hetty Goldman, "The Sandon Monument of Tarsus," *JAOS* 60 (1940): 544–57; Dalley, "Sennacherib and Tarsus," 74–78.

72. See p. 108.

73. RINAP 3.1:136, 17.v.1–2; SAAS 2:50, 61.

74. *ARAB* 2.329, 349. On Tabal, see Elayi, *Sargon II, King of Assyria*, 98–103 (with bibliography).

75. RINAP 3.1:136, 17.v.6–8.

4. CONSOLIDATING THE EMPIRE (700–695)

be written Tîl-karme in Tiglath-pileser III's inscriptions, possibly corresponding to Tekarama in Hittite and to the biblical Togarma.[76] It has been ingeniously suggested that a scribal wordplay was used in the King/Heidel Prism between the name of Til-Garimmu and the formula mentioning the destruction of the city: *ana tili ù kar-me (ú-ter-ru)*, "they turned (it) into a mound and ruins."[77] There are two interpretations of *alū urdūtu*: either it was the place name Urdutu, or it meant "a vassal city";[78] both interpretations seem plausible. In any event, the location of Til-Garimmu and, eventually, of Urdutu, is unknown.

The motive of the 695 campaign is indicated: "I ... against the city of Tîl-Garimmu, a city on the border of the land of Tabal where Gurdî, king of the city of Urdutu (or of the vassal city), had mobilized his weapons."[79] It is quite possible that the Gurdî in question is to be identified with Gurdî the Kulummean, who, in 705, defeated the Assyrian army and killed Sargon.[80] In this case, he was on the throne at the time of the first campaign led by Sennacherib's magnates in 704.[81] The fortified city of Til-Garimmu was seized after a siege: "They besieged that city and took possession of it by means of piling up earth, bringing up battering rams, (and) the assault of foot soldiers.... They destroyed (and) devastated that city."[82] It can be noticed that no siege machines were used, maybe because this city was located in a mountainous area, difficult to access. The booty collected in Til-Garimmu was, as usual, a vast number of prisoners: "From the booty of those lands that I had plundered, I conscripted 30,000 archers (and)

---

76. Frahm, *Einleitung in die Sanherib-Inschriften*, 76 and n. 12; Giovanni Battista Lanfranchi, "The Ideological and Political Impact of the Assyrian Imperial Expansion on the Greek World in the Eighth and Seventh Centuries BC," in *The Heirs of Assyria*, ed. Sanna Aro and Robert M. Whiting (Helsinki: Neo-Assyrian Text Corpus Project, 2000): 24 and n. 68 (with bibliography).

77. Rykle Borger, *Handbuch der Keilschriftliteratur* (Berlin: de Gruyter, 1967), 1:319.

78. RINAP 3.1:136, 17.v.4 and n. 72; Simo Parpola, *Neo-Assyrian Toponyms*, AOAT 6 (Neukirchen-Vluyn: Neukirchener Verlag, 1970), 373 (first interpretation); Alexandra Heidel, "The Octagonal Sennacherib Prism in the Iraq Museum," *Sumer* 9 (1953): 251; PNA 2.1:431 (second interpretation).

79. RINAP 3.1:136, 17.v.2–5.

80. Elayi, *Sargon II, King of Assyria*, 210–13 (with bibliography).

81. See p. 44.

82. RINAP 3.1:136, 17.v.9–13.

20,000 shield bearers and added (them) to my royal contingent."[83] Either these numbers are exaggerated or they represent the captives of both the 696 and 695 campaigns. What is original concerning the booty of Til-Garimmu is that he counted the gods of the city as well as its inhabitants as booty; it could be in retaliation against Gurdî to avenge his father's death. The description of this campaign ends with the usual distribution of booty by Sennacherib between Assyrian soldiers, provincial governors, and people of the large cities, the aim being to present an image of himself as a just and generous king.

The silence of the inscriptions on the fate of Gurdî, in contrast with the capture and killing of Kirûa, probably means that he had escaped. It represented a bitter failure for Sennacherib, not simply because Gurdî was a rebellious vassal but mainly because he was possibly the one responsible for Sargon's death. Therefore, the Tabalian campaign was only a partial success: Sennacherib had suppressed the rebellion of a Tabalian state, he had collected booty and captured many prisoners, including the gods of the city, but he could not capture Gurdî, a failure that he tried to dissimulate in his inscriptions. In 695, it can be said that the Assyrian Empire had been consolidated in the north and in the northwest. No other trouble had occurred in the western part of the empire, which was pacified. Sennacherib no longer had any problems with the powerful states of Urartu and Egypt. However, the situation in the east of the empire was alarming because of the threat always represented by Elam, with its possible connection with Babylonia against Assyria. For the time being, the situation in Babylonia seemed to be under control by Ashur-nâdin-shumi, Sennacherib's son, placed on the throne of Babylon since 700. However, Sennacherib was conscious that it was a precarious equilibrium, as is shown, for example, by the fact that he undertook his sixth campaign in 694 against Elamite cities where the people of Bît-Yakin had taken refuge.

---

83. RINAP 3.1:136, 17.v.15–19.

5
Focusing on Babylonia and Its Allies (694–689)

After having secured the western, northwestern, and northern parts of the Assyrian Empire, Sennacherib was then ready to focus on Babylonia and its allies, which represented his major problem and obsession. He had already undertaken two campaigns against Babylonia, in 704 and 700, without any substantial and definitive result. His strategy always consisted in defeating first Elam, the main ally of Babylonia: this was the aim of his sixth campaign, in 694. However, things did not turn to his advantage, the main shock for him being the capture and killing of his son Ashur-nâdin-shumi, whom he had named king of Babylon. This act ruined his plans and required retribution that would be costly and time-consuming. In 693, he undertook a second campaign against Elam, which he called his seventh campaign. The ever-growing tensions between Assyria and Babylonia pressed Sennacherib into undertaking a third campaign against Babylonia, which he called his eighth campaign, which escalated into the fierce battle of Halulê, which started in 691 and ended in 689. A short expedition in 690 against the Arabs was probably intended to prevent them from supporting the Babylonians. The final outcome of the crisis between Assyria and Babylonia took place in 689. After a long, unsuccessful siege of Babylon (more than fifteen months), Sennacherib decided to put an end to his protracted struggle against Babylonia at any cost: it was his fourth and final campaign against Babylonia, in 689, and the last campaign of his reign.

5.1. First Phase of the Campaign against Elam

The chronology of the years 694 and 693 is somewhat difficult to establish, due to the complexity of the events and to several contradictions in the documents, between the Assyrian royal inscriptions, the Babylonian

Chronicles, and private documents.[1] In 694, he undertook a mostly maritime expedition against Elam, which he numbered his sixth campaign. In fact, during his fourth campaign against Babylonia he did what he had not done in 700. Then he had devastated the rebels' territories of southern Mesopotamia and put to flight Merodach-baladan and Shûzubu, who took refuge in Elam by boat.[2] At that time, he was not ready for a maritime expedition in the Persian/Arabian Gulf, but in 694 he was. In the Chicago/Taylor Prism, he recalls this previous episode: "The rest of the people of the land of Bît-Yakin, who had groveled like onagers before my mighty weapons, dislodged the gods of the (full) extent of their land from their abodes, then crossed the Great Sea of the rising sun and set up their residences in the city of Nagîtu of the land of Elam."[3] He presents this little glorious episode in which he was not able to capture the enemies by turning it to his advantage, despising their cowardice. The motive given for justifying the sixth campaign is that, encouraged by his god, Assur, he wanted to capture the fugitive people of Bît-Yakin. Apparently, he delighted in this maritime expedition, because he describes its successive steps very lengthily, particularly in the inscription of one of the human-headed winged bull colossi, which were stationed in the main entrance of his throne room, composed in late 694 or early 693, that is, just after the event. He records in detail how he used prisoners from Tyre, Sidon, and Ionia (or Cyprus), who were experienced sailors, and ships of Hatti to sail down the Tigris and across the Bitter Sea, which was the Persian/Arabian Gulf: "They skillfully built (in Nineveh and Til Barsip) magnificent ships, a product characteristic of their land.... They (my troops) let (the sailors) sail down the Tigris with them downstream to the city of Opis. Then, from the city of Opis, they lifted them (the boats) up onto dry land and dragged th[em] on *rollers t*[*o Sippar* and] guided them into the Arahtu canal, (where) they let them sail downstream to the canal of Bît-Dakkûri, which is in Chaldea."[4] Then Sennacherib had the boats loaded with troops and provisions, grain, and straw. While the Assyrian warriors sailed down the Euphrates on the boats, he accompanied them on dry land, through the city of Bâb-salimenti, not yet identified. He relates a colorful adventure, which occurred in the marshes because of the rising sea tide, which

---

1. Levine, "Sennacherib's Southern Front," 41–48.
2. See p. 121.
3. RINAP 3.1:179, 22.iv.32–36; 3.1:109, 26.i.1'–5'; 221, 34.8–11.
4. RINAP 3.2:82–84, 46.56–64.

5. FOCUSING ON BABYLONIA AND ITS ALLIES (694–689) 109

surrounded his camp, even entering his tent: "For five days and nights, on account of the strong [wate]r, all of my soldiers had to sit curled up as though they were in cages."[5] Finally, the boats and the soldiers reached the Bitter Sea: "The boats of my warriors reached the marshy area at the mouth of the river, where the Euphrates debouches its water in[to] the roiling [s]ea."[6] Sennacherib chose the moment they reached the seashore to perform sacrifices, as was the custom in Assyrian tradition. He cast into the sea a gold boat, a gold fish, and a gold crab, for Ea, associated with purification rituals.

Then he immediately had his boats cross over the sea to the city of Nagîtu on the Elamite coast. They landed on an unsuitable shore, very difficult for ships to dock, for horses to climb, and for soldiers to have a stable footing on. The inhabitants of Chaldea living in the cities of Nagîtu and Nagîtu-dibina and the Elamites of the lands of Hilmu, Pillatu, and Hupapanu saw the arrival of the Assyrian army and prepared for battle. They gathered a countless force and drew up in battle line at the mouth of the Ulâya, a river with secure shores. The battle is described as easy for the Assyrians in spite of the vast number of enemy troops: "My warriors reached the quay of the harbor (and) like locusts swarmed out of the boats onto the shore against them and defeated them."[7] They conquered, devastated, and burned all the cities mentioned above, belonging to the king of Elam. Then, "they carried off their garrisons, the population of Chaldea, the gods of all the land of Bît-Yakin, [together with] their property, and the people of (the) Elamite (king), wagons, [horses], mules, (and) donkeys."[8] They loaded all the booty onto the boats and brought it to the city of Bâb-salimenti, on the other side of the Persian/Arabian Gulf, to hand over to Sennacherib, who had gone back across the sea before the end of the expedition, possibly in order to let his warriors loot the conquered cities as much as they wished. From the booty obtained, he conscripted 30,500 archers and 20,200 shield bearers, whom he added to his royal contingent. Then comes the usual stereotyped sentence: "I divided up the rest of the substantial enemy booty like sheep and go[ats] among my ent[ire] camp

---

5. RINAP 3.2:83, 46.74–75.
6. RINAP 3.2:83, 46.76–78.
7. RINAP 3.2:83–84, 46.91–93; Grayson, *Assyrian and Babylonian Chronicles*, 78, chr. 1, ii.36–38.
8. RINAP 3.2:84, 46.94–98.

and my governors, (and) the people of my cult centers."⁹ Even if the objective of his expedition was limited, Sennacherib was very proud to have won this battle, which he had in mind since his campaign of 700, and, in a poetic manner, he boasts that his warriors had "poured out deathly silence over the wide land of Elam."

In fact, the Assyrian attack on Elam, which was the first phase of the sixth campaign, is presented in the bull inscription as a positive action because it was written at that time and the scribe did not yet know what was going to happen subsequently. Other inscriptions, such as the Nebi Yunus inscription, treat the campaigns of 694 and 693 differently, as they were normally divided into the sixth and the seventh campaigns.¹⁰ The account of the sixth through the eighth campaign is twice presented with the adverb *arka*, "afterwards," which served as a formal device to delimit sections of the narrative, sometimes combining the section that followed with the preceding one. Thus, the first half of the sixth campaign was separated from the second half, which was itself combined with the seventh campaign. The fact that the Assyrians themselves could combine or separate events, using different principles at different times, means that the attempts at periodization depended on the purpose of each inscription. A reconstruction of the events of years 694 and 693 was proposed by John A. Brinkman, Albert Kirk Grayson, and Louis D. Levine.¹¹

After the beginning of the first phase, which was victorious, Sennacherib's good fortune changed. Hallushu, the king of Elam, did not accept his defeat and decided to counterattack northern Babylonia. There is a debate among historians concerning this king: either "Hallushu" was an abbreviated rendering in Akkadian of the Elamite name Hallutash-Inshushinak, or there were two different kings, one of them being abbreviated as Hallushu.¹² According to the Babylonian Chronicles, Hallushu

---

9. RINAP 3.2:84, 46.104–6.

10. RINAP 3.2:222–23, 34.19–43.

11. John A. Brinkman, "Ur: 721–605 B.C.," *Or* 34 (1965): 243–46; Grayson, *Assyrian and Babylonian Chronicles*, 78–79; Levine, "Sennacherib's Southern Front," 41–48.

12. Friedrich Wilhelm König, *Die elamischen Königsinschriften*, AfOB 16 (Graz: Weidner, 1965), no. 77; Florence Malbran-Labat, *Les inscriptions royales de Suse: Briques de l'époque paléo-élamite à l'empire néo-élamite* (Paris: Éditions de la Réunion des musées nationaux, 1995), no. 58 (first hypothesis); François Vallat, "Šutruk-Nahunte, Šutur-Nahunte et l'imbroglio néo-élamite," *NABU* (1995): 44; Vallat, "Nouvelle analyse des inscriptions néo-élamites," in *Collectanea Orientalia Histoire, Arts de l'espace et industrie de la terre: Études offertes en hommage à Agnès Spycket*, ed.

5. FOCUSING ON BABYLONIA AND ITS ALLIES (694–689)

(Hallutash-Inshushinak I), the brother of Ishtarhundu (Shutruk-Nahhunte II), usurped the throne of Elam by force in 698 and ruled until 693.[13] The Assyrian army, which was still in the depths of southern Babylonia, found itself trapped by an Elamite counterattack across its rear. Hallushu used both Elamite and Chaldean troops, "marched to Akkad and entered Sippar at the end of the month Tashrîtu (October). He slaughtered (its) inhabitants. Shamash did not leave Ebabbarra."[14] The capture of Ashur-nâdin-shumi is reported laconically in the Babylonian Chronicles: "Ashur-nâdin-shumi was taken prisoner and transported to Elam" (ᵐAššur-na-din-šumi ṣabit-ma ana KUR.elámti a-bi-ik). Although there are few documents relating to the reign of Ashur-nâdin-shumi, his years of reign over Babylon seem to have been quiet ones.[15] Sennacherib's inscriptions mention Ashur-nâdin-shumi several times, but only in relation with his installation on the throne of Babylon.[16] However, there is not a word about his capture, maybe because his father was too much afflicted with his loss, and he considered it as divine punishment, a reminder of the sin of Sargon.[17] From a later letter of Shamash-shumu-ukîn to his father, Esarhaddon, we learn that Ashur-nâdin-shumi was not captured by the Elamites, as was supposed from the Babylonian Chronicles, but by the Babylonians, who handed him to the Elamites.[18] As he is no longer mentioned, he was probably killed in Elam, but we do not know exactly when he died; Sennacherib made an inquiry through extispicies about his fate.[19]

Hermann Gasche and Barthel Hrouda (Neuchâtel: Recherches et publications, 1996), 385–95; SAAS 12:24–30.

13. Grayson, *Assyrian and Babylonian Chronicles*, 77–79, chr. 1, ii.32–iii.8.

14. Grayson, *Assyrian and Babylonian Chronicles*, 78, chr. 1, ii.39–41.

15. Geoffrey Neate, "A Fragment from Kish with the Name of Aššur-nādin-šumi," *Iraq* 33 (1971): 54–56; John A. Brinkman, "Documents Relating to the Reign of Assurnadin-šumi," *Or* 41 (1972): 245–48.

16. RINAP 3.1:98, 15.v.5; 3.1:117, 16.iv.65; 3.1:134, 17.iv.13; 3.1:152, 18.iii.28′; 3.1:178, 22.iii.72; 3.1:178, 23.iii.63; RINAP 3.2:48, 42.5; 3.2:68, 44.11; 3.2:81, 46.37.

17. Van De Mieroop, "Revenge, Assyrian Style," 3–23; Dewar, "Rebellion, Sargon II's 'Punishment' and the Death of Aššur-nādin-šumi," 34–35.

18. Simo Parpola, "A Letter from Šamaš-šumu-ukin to Esarhaddon," *Iraq* 34 (1972): 22, 32–33 (from the context of the letter, *nišē*, "people," designed Babylonians); John A. Brinkman, "Sennacherib's Babylonian Problem: An Interpretation," *JCS* 25 (1973): 92 n. 18.

19. Israel L. Finkel, "A Report on Extispicies Performed for Sennacherib on Account of His Son Aššur-nadin-šumi," *SAAB* 1 (1987): 53; SAAS 9:17 and n. 29.

It is difficult to know how the different forces in presence were positioned in the vicinity of Sippar and Babylon during the last months of 694, and which area each of them controlled exactly: the first phase of the campaign ended without a clear decision for either side.

5.2. Second Phase of the Campaign against Elam

Shûzubu (Nergal-ushezib), son of Gahal, ascended the throne of Babylon, thus marking the beginning of the second phase of Sennacherib's campaign. According to the Babylonian Chronicles, he was put on the throne by the king of Elam.[20] The Nebi Yunus inscription and stone tablets confirm that the king of Elam placed him on the throne of Babylon. However, other Assyrian inscriptions see it as the result of a popular uprising: he was "a citizen of Babylon who had taken the lordship of the land of Sumer and Akkad for himself during the confusion in the land."[21] It is difficult to know exactly what happened, but this period was undoubtedly confused, facilitating usurpation, although an intervention by the king of Elam is also possible. The date of this usurpation is not known precisely: at the end of 694 or at the beginning of 693. It seems more plausible to interpret the length of his reign given in the Babylonian Chronicles (MU I VI) as six months rather than as a year and a half.[22] He captured Nippur, plundered it, and sacked it on the sixteenth day of the month of Tammuz (July). His purpose was probably to consolidate his rule by taking central and southern Babylonia, and to destroy the Assyrian army entrapped in the far south.[23] The following two military operations, a battle against the Elamites and a battle against Shûzubu, are presented in a different order according to the sources. Either the battle against the Elamites (and Babylonians?) occurred first: "I ordered archers, chariots, (and) horses of my royal contingent to confront the king of the land of Elam. They killed

---

20. Grayson, *Assyrian and Babylonian Chronicles*, 78, chr. 1, ii.44–45; *PNA* 3.2:1297.

21. RINAP 3.1:179, 22.iv.47–48; 3.1:197, 23.iv.40; 3.1:222, 34.28–29; 3.1:230, 35.o.7′–8′; RINAP 3.2:204, 149.14–16.

22. Grayson, *Assyrian and Babylonian Chronicles*, 79, chr. 1, iii.5–6; Brinkman, *Political History of Post-Kassite Babylonia 1158–722 B.C.*, 64–68; Brinkman, "Ur: 721–605 B.C.," 245 and n. 1; Levine, "Sennacherib's Southern Front," 43.

23. Grayson, *Assyrian and Babylonian Chronicles*, 78, chr. 1, ii.46–47; Levine, "Sennacherib's Southern Front," 43–44.

many troops, including his son, and he retreated. They marched to Uruk (and) carried off ... the gods who live in Uruk, together with their property (and) possessions, which are without number."[24] If the kingship in Elam had not yet changed between the reigns of Hallushu and Kudur-nahhunte, the killing of the Elamite king's son was, for Sennacherib, probably revenge for the killing of his own son by the Elamites. The battle against Shûzubu is reported afterwards: "On their return march, in a pitched battle, they captured Shûzubu, the king of Babylon, alive. They threw him unto a neck-stock (and) fetters and brought him before me. At the Citadel Gate of Nineveh, I bound him with a bear."[25] This account switches from first-person singular to third-person plural as if Sennacherib had ordered the expedition but did not lead it. The Babylonian Chronicles seem to follow the same order of events.[26] According to an epigraph on a palace relief, Shûzubu fell off his horse in fear of Sennacherib's approach.[27] In other Assyrian inscriptions, the capture of Shûzubu preceded the battle against the king of Elam: "I captured him (Shûzubu) alive, bound him with tethering ropes and iron fetters, and brought him to Assyria. I defeated the king of the land of Elam, who had aligned himself with him and come to his aid. I dispersed his forces and scattered his assembled host."[28] Whatever the order of events, the battle between the Assyrian and Babylonian armies in the district of Nippur was to be the decisive and final battle of the second phase of the campaign: the Babylonian army was defeated, Shûzubu was captured, there was no longer a king in Babylon, and the Assyrians were finally liberated from their trapped position in the south. Sennacherib seems then to have taken the upper hand, having brought together the forces of the two parts of his army.

5.3. Third Phase of the Campaign against Elam

Then came the third part of the campaign, labeled in some inscriptions as the seventh campaign. Whether or not Sennacherib intended to attack Elam, an incident occurred on the twenty-sixth day of Tashrîtu (October), less than three weeks after his victory against the Babylonian army, that

---

24. RINAP 3.1:223, 34.29b–33a.
25. RINAP 3.1:223, 34.33b–36a.
26. Grayson, *Assyrian and Babylonian Chronicles*, 79, chr. 1, iii.2–5.
27. Luckenbill, *Annals of Sennacherib*, 156, col. xxiv, ll. 14–17.
28. RINAP 3.1:179–80, 22.iv.46b–53.

made him decide to launch an attack against Elam. The subjects of Hallushu, king of Elam, rebelled against him: "They shut the door in his face (*bāba ina pāni-šú ip-ḫu-ú*) (and) killed him."[29] This expression is possibly an Elamite idiom meaning "they threw him in prison." He was replaced on the throne by Kud/tur-nahhunte, his brother.[30] Sennacherib took advantage of the unsettled situation in Elam to attack its northwest flank; the starting date of this attack is not recorded, but it was in winter, possibly in Arahsammu (November). At the beginning of his expedition he regained the territory on the border of Assyria, conquered by the Elamites during the reign of Sargon; he brought it back within Assyria under the authority of the garrison commander of Dêr.[31] According to Levine, Sennacherib's original objective was a limited one, but the success of his initial attack was sufficient to enable him to broaden his objective and to continue to advance into northern Elam. Without forgetting his revenge for the capture of his son Ashur-nâdin-shumi, he was always conscious of the fact that, if he wanted to reconquer Babylon, he had to defeat Elam. That is why he mentions in detail, with obvious satisfaction, the thirty-four fortified cities, together with their small settlements, that he conquered in the western part of Elam: "I surrounded, conquered, plundered, destroyed, devastated, (and) burned with fire.... I made the smoke from their conflagration cover the wide heavens like a heavy cloud."[32] The Babylonian Chronicles also mention that he ravaged and plundered Elam from Rashi to Bit-Burnaki, this last city also appearing in the Assyrian list of conquered cities. The Heyderabad relief was found in 2009 near the source of the Sarabe Mishkhas river; its inscription, if any, has been obliterated. However, it is similar to the Shikaft-i Gulgul relief, carved around 11 kilometers away and possibly related with one of Sennacherib's campaigns.[33]

The Elamite king Kudur-nahhunte was unable to organize an effective resistance to the Assyrian attack because he "heard about the conquest

---

29. Grayson, *Assyrian and Babylonian Chronicles*, 79, chr. 1, iii.6–8, and 77, ii.33.
30. *PNA* 2.1:645.
31. RINAP 3.1:180, 22.iv.54–61a; Levine, "Sennacherib's Southern Front," 45.
32. RINAP 3.1:180, 22.iv.61b–81. In fact, he listed thirty-six cities but wrote thirty-four. See also Parpola, "Letter to Sennacherib Referring to the Conquest of Bit-Ha'iri and Other Events of the Year 693," 559–77; SAA 17:xx and 105–6, no. 120.
33. Alibaigi, Shanbehzadeh, and Hossain Alibaigi, "Discovery of a Neo-Assyrian Rock-Relief at Mishkhas, Ilam Province (Iran)," 29–40; Albert Kirk Grayson and Louis D. Levine, "The Assyrian Relief from Shikaft-i Gulgul," *IrAnt* 11 (1975): 29–38; Julian E. Reade, "Shikaft-i Gulgul: Its Date and Symbolism," *IrAnt* 12 (1977): 33–48.

5. FOCUSING ON BABYLONIA AND ITS ALLIES (694–689) 115

of his cities and fear fell upon him. He brought (the people of) the rest of his cities into fortresses. He abandoned the city of Madaktu, his royal city, and took the road to the city of Haydala (Hidalu), which is in the distant mountains."[34] There are numerous questions regarding the location of these two cities, the political relationship between them, and whether they were centers of independent kingdoms or regional power bases in a united kingdom.[35] The way to Madaktu was free, and Sennacherib wanted to take advantage of this opportunity, so he ordered his army to march into the heart of Elam. Suddenly, however, he changed his mind because he came up against a serious problem: "In the month Tamhîru/Kislimu (December), bitter cold set in and a severe rainstorm sent down its rain. I was afraid of the rain and snow in the gorges, the outflows of the mountains, (so) I turned around and took the road to Nineveh."[36] The Zagros Mountains were in fact difficult to access in winter; moreover, the Assyrians were not accustomed to low temperatures, storms, and snow, and they were probably not well equipped with warm clothes and winter shoes. This brought the campaigns of 694–693 to a conclusion, with the Assyrian army returning to Nineveh.

In 692, Sennacherib did not undertake any military campaign, as far as we know from the Assyrian inscriptions, which do not mention any event. However, the Babylonian Chronicles report that Mushezib-Marduk ascended the throne of Babylon and that significant changes took place in Elam: "On the seventeenth day of the month of Ab (August), Kudur-(nahhunte), king of Elam, was taken prisoner in a rebellion and killed. For ten months Kudur-(nahhunte) ruled Elam. Humban-nimena (Humban-menânu) ascended the throne in Elam."[37] The Assyrian inscriptions give Sennacherib's version of the Elam events, explaining them by a divine intervention, not by a rebellion of Elamite people: "At that time, by the command of the god Assur, my lord, Kudur-nahhunte, the king of the land of Elam, did not last three months and suddenly died a premature

---

34. RINAP 3.1:180–81, 22.iv.81b–v.5; 3.1:198, 23.iv.72–76. See SAAS 12:31–33.

35. Pierre de Miroschedji, "La localisation de Madaktu et l'organisation politique de l'Elam à l'époque néo-élamite," in *Fragmenta Historiae Elamicae: Mélanges offerts à M.-J. Steve*, ed. Leon de Meyer, Hermann Gasche, and François Vallat. (Paris: Editions Recherche sur les civilisations, 1986), 209–22; François Vallat, *Les noms géographiques des sources suso-élamites*, RGTC 11 (Wiesbaden: Reichert, 1993), 96, 162; SAAS 12:33.

36. RINAP 3.1:181, 22.v.6–11a.

37. Grayson, *Assyrian and Babylonian Chronicles*, 80, chr. 1, iii.13–15.

death. After him, Humban-menânu, who does not have sense or insight, his younger brother, sat on his throne."[38] The discrepancy in the length of Kudur-nahhunte's reign—ten months in the Babylonian Chronicles and three months in the Assyrian inscriptions—is not easy to explain. At the beginning of the account of his eighth campaign in 691, Sennacherib paints a rapid portrait of the new Babylonian and Elamite kings. Shûzubu (Mushezib-Marduk) should not be confused with Shûzubu (Nergal-Ushezib), the previous king of Babylon. He was "a Chaldean, a person of lowly status, a coward (literally 'who has no knees'), (and) a servant who belonged to the governor of the city of Lahîru," whom he had defeated during his fourth campaign against Babylonia in 700.[39] His portrait is as pejorative as that of Humban-menânu, who "does not have sense or insight," taking decisions "without thinking."[40] He was the brother of Kudur-nahhunte and the son of Hallushu. In 692, after the defeat of Shûzubu (Nergal-Ushezib) and the disarray in Elam because of its internal problems of royal succession, one might have assumed that Babylonia would have then come firmly under Sennacherib's control. The scarce sources that we have do not seem to support this assumption. Shûzubu (Mushezib-Marduk) ascended the throne in Nisan (April), only a few months after the departure of the Assyrian army, on his own initiative and not installed by Sennacherib. Nor was his accession opposed by the Assyrian king. However, as the Assyrian inscriptions refer to him as having revolted in 691, it would imply that he had been loyal to Assyria before.[41]

5.4. First Two Phases of the Eighth Campaign

The reasons given in the sources as explanation for the eighth campaign of 691 are confused. According to the Babylonian Chronicles, "in an unknown year (šatti la idi), Humban-menânu mustered the troops of Elam (and) Akkad and did battle against Assyria in Halulê."[42] It reflects a gap in its sources, but from Assyrian sources, we know that it occurred in 691.[43] The Assyrian inscriptions report at great length that the reason

---

38. RINAP 3.1:181, 22.v.11b–16; *PNA* 2.2:748.
39. See p. 90. RINAP 3.1:181, 22.v.20–22; *PNA* 3.2:1297–98.
40. RINAP 3.1:181–82, 22.v.33–34, 40–41 (repeated twice in the account).
41. Levine, "Sennacherib's Southern Front," 47–48.
42. Grayson, *Assyrian and Babylonian Chronicles*, 80, chr. 1, iii.16–17.
43. SAAS 12:33–34.

5. FOCUSING ON BABYLONIA AND ITS ALLIES (694–689) 117

for the eighth campaign was the revolt of Shûzubu (Mushezib-Marduk). Before beginning the account of the eighth campaign, the scribe introduces an account of the previous history of Shûzubu: "He had rebelled and the citizens of Babylon, evil *gallû*-demons, had locked the city gates, they plotted to wage war. Arameans, fugitives, runaways, murderers, (and) robbers rallied around Shûzubu … and they went down into the marshes and incited rebellion."[44] After that Sennacherib had besieged him in 700, he was obliged to flee to Elam. The following passage is ambiguous and has been translated in various ways: "When there were conspiracy and treachery (*ri-kil-ti ù gíl-la-ti*) against him, he hurried out of the land of Elam and entered Shuanna (Babylon). The Babylonians inappropriately placed him on the throne (and) entrusted him with the lordship of the land of Sumer and Akkad."[45] The translation of *rikiltu* as "treaty," presumably between Assyria and Elam, is unlikely. Yet the translation by "conspiracy" is not clear either: if Shûzubu were driven out of Elam by conspiracy, it would have been difficult for him to be able to acquire significant Elamite support for a battle against Assyria,[46] unless his new status of king of Babylon, and in addition the gold and silver of the Babylonian gods, had changed the Elamite view of him.

According to the Assyrian inscriptions, Shûzubu initiated the revolt against Assyria by looking for an alliance with Elam. He sent huge treasures from the Esagil of Babylon as a bribe (*ṭa'tu*)[47] to Humban-menânu, with the following message: "Gather your army, muster your forces, hurry to Babylon, and align yourself with us! Let us put our trust in you."[48] According to M. W. Waters, the large scale of the battle and its direction by the king of Elam suggest strategic objectives,[49] in contrast to what Sennacherib said, that the king of Elam acted without thinking. He assembled an impressive army composed of Elamites, Iranians, Chaldeans, and Arameans to join the Babylonians, even people from Ellipi, which was traditionally pro-Assyrian: "a large host formed a confederation (*kitru*)

---

44. RINAP 3.1:181, 22.v.17–24a.
45. RINAP 3.1:181, 22.v.24b–30; SAA 17:150–51, no. 170.
46. SAAS 12:34.
47. *AHw*, 1382; Klaas R. Veenhof, *Aspects of Old Assyrian Trade and Its Terminology*, Studia et Documenta ad Iura Orientis Antiqui Pertinentia 40 (Leiden: Brill, 1972), 223; Frame, *Babylonia 689–627 B.C.*, 182.
48. RINAP 3.1:181, 22.v.35.
49. SAAS 12:34–35.

with him."⁵⁰ Humban-undasha (Huban-untash?) was the "commander" of his army (LÚ.*tur-ta-nu-šú*). Information about the Elamite king's political relationship with all these peoples and groups is lacking, but the Assyrian account would imply that Humban-menânu had significant influence, if not political authority, over these regions. It would be more likely that the Chaldean and Aramean tribes, such as Bît-Adini, Bît-Amukâni, Bît-Shilâni, Puqudu, and Gambulu, for example, were assembled by the Chaldean Shûzubu. Anyway, together, they all joined forces against Sennacherib, who described their arrival like an epic fresco: "Like a spring invasion of a swarm of locusts, they were advancing towards me as a group to do battle. The dust of their feet covered the wide heavens like a heavy cloud in the deep of winter."⁵¹

The account of the fierce battle of Halulê was written within months of the event and was incorporated into the prism edition, although the eighth campaign as a whole was not yet completed. The Chicago/Taylor Prism is dated from the twentieth day of Addaru (March) 691, giving a *terminus ante quem* for the battle. Sennacherib clearly viewed this battle as a major achievement of his reign, explaining why the account of it formed the centerpiece of the later editions of his annals. The battle is described in more detail than any other Assyrian battle, written in elevated poetic language, and constitutes one of finest pieces of Assyrian royal literature. Moreover, the creative royal scribe seems to make literary allusions to Enūma Eliš, the Babylonian Epic of Creation, as a means of transfiguring the battle's reality into mythic spheres, by suggesting a demonic portrait of the Babylonians, in order to enhance the anti-Babylonian propaganda.⁵² After having reported how the enemy army was recruited and composed, the place of the battle is specified: "While drawing up in battle line before me at the city of Halulê, which is on the bank of the Tigris, they blocked my passage and sharpened their weapons."⁵³ Halulê has not been identified, but we know that it was located in the plain, on the left side of the Tigris, probably somewhere near Samarra,

---

50. See p. 51.

51. RINAP 3.1:182, 22.v.56–59.

52. Elnathan Weissert, "Creating a Political Climate: Literary Allusions to Enūma Eliš in Sennacherib's Account of the Battle of Halule," in *Assyrien im Wandel der Zeiten*, ed. Hartmut Waetzoldt and Harold Hauptman, RAI 39 (Heidelberg: Heidelberger Orientverlag, 1997), 191–202.

53. RINAP 3.1:182, 22.v.60–61.

which is 130 kilometers north of Baghdad and may correspond to the city of Sûr-marrati.⁵⁴

As usual before a battle, Sennacherib prayed to Assur and all the other gods who supported him, for victory over his strong enemy. Then he prepared himself for battle, first psychologically, by raging up like a lion, then he put on his armor and placed his helmet on his head. He rode in his battle chariot, with his weapons: "I took in my hand the mighty bow that the god Assur had granted to me (and) I grasped in my hand an arrow that cuts off life."⁵⁵ He started his attack on his chariot with his fierce battle array, simultaneously targeting the flanks and front lines of the enemy troops. He forced them to turn back in retreat. He shot at them using two kinds of arrows: *uṣṣu* and *mulmullu*, possibly indicating two categories of wood from which they were made. The result of this violent attack was rapid: he slaughtered and defeated Humban-undasha, the commander of the Elamite troops, together with his magnates. Their clothing is described in a colorful and caricatured manner: they "wear gold (decorated) belt-daggers and have reddish gold sling straps fastened to their forearms, like fattened bulls restrained with fetters."⁵⁶ Then follows the description of one of the worst slaughters of the Assyrian inscriptions, with poetic comparisons. He slit the throats of his enemies and produced a flow of blood over the earth. He wanted to represent a nightmarish vision of his chariot crossing this flow of blood: "The swift thoroughbreds harnessed to my chariot plunged into floods of their blood (just) like the river ordeal. The wheels of my war chariot, which lays criminals and villains low, were bathed in blood and gore."⁵⁷ The large plain of Halulê was filled with the enemies' corpses. This slaughter was not sufficient for Sennacherib; he wanted, in addition, to mutilate them, cutting their lips and hands in order to destroy their pride. Then the Assyrian warriors spoiled the corpses, taking away all the precious ornaments and weapons from them. This barbaric description was intended for the palace circle of Nineveh to celebrate his glorious feats as a warlord and, through other channels, such as great sanctuaries for the common people, to dissuade anyone from attacking him.⁵⁸ Even if it is partly accurate because it was

---

54. *PNA* 3.1:1120; RINAP 3.2:328.
55. RINAP 3.1:183, 22.v.71–73.
56. RINAP 3.1:183, 22.v.84–88.
57. RINAP 3.1:183, 22.vi.5–9.
58. Liverani, "Critique of Variants and the Titulary of Sennacherib," 251; Fales,

customary in warfare, it is not certain that he accomplished all the horrible deeds related in the account.

Then he described the rendition of the rest of the magnates, including Nabû-shuma-ishkun, a son of Merodach-baladan, whom he failed to capture in his fourth campaign, of 700. Capturing his son was maybe a kind of revenge for Sennacherib for the capture of his own son. As these magnates had raised their arms because they were terrified of doing battle with him, he captured them alive and probably later took them back to Assyria. The last action carried out before terminating the battle was to reassemble all the chariots with their horses, whose drivers had been killed and which galloped back and forth. The description does not mention when the battle started and how long it lasted but at what time it stopped: "after the second double hour" (*a-di 2 bîri*) of the night. The night was divided into three "parts" (*maṣṣartu*) and six "double hours" (*bêru*): the first one, which contained two double hours, corresponded to twilight.[59] Therefore, after the second double hour meant just after twilight, at the very beginning of the night. The last part of the description of the battle is devoted to the fate of the leaders of the enemy troops: Humban-menânu, the king of Elam, Shûzubu (Mushezib-Marduk), the king of Babylon, and all the sheikhs of Chaldea who had joined them. Their attitude is described in a very contemptuous manner, and with some contradictions between the different inscriptions, which means that he may not have captured them. Overwhelmed by the terror of waging battle with Sennacherib, they abandoned their tents and, to be able to run away more quickly, they trampled the corpses of their troops, passed their urine hotly, and released their excrement inside their chariots, which are clinical symptoms of extreme fear. According to the Chicago/Taylor and the Jerusalem prisms, written in 691, Sennacherib ordered his chariots and horses to pursue and kill them with the sword wherever they caught them.[60] However, the two kings were not killed in 691, as they were still alive in 689. The Bavian

---

Guerre et paix en Assyrie, 63–65; Van De Mieroop, "Metaphors of Massacre in Assyrian Royal Inscriptions," 299–309.

59. RINAP 3.1:184, 22.vi.22–23; Jean-Robert Kupper, "Les différents moments de la journée, d'après les textes de Mari," in *Tablettes et images aux pays de Sumer et d'Akkad: Mélanges offerts à Monsieur H. Limet*, ed. Ö. Tunca and D. Deheselle (Liège: Université de Liège, 1996), 79–85; Joannès, *Dictionnaire de la civilisation mésopotamienne*, 528–29.

60. RINAP 3.1:184, 22.vi.29b–35; 3.1:201, 23.vi.25–30.

inscriptions, probably written ca. 688, give a different version: the king of Elam and the king of Babylon "fled to their (own) land(s) and did not return ever again."[61]

On the battlefield, Sennacherib collected the skulls of the enemies and piled them up like pyramids so that no one would ever forget; next to them, he had a stela erected: "I had a stele made, had all the victorious conquests that I achieved over my enemies with the support of the great gods, my lords, written on it, and I erected (it) on the plain of the city of Halulê."[62] The stela itself has not been found, but the text engraved on it is known through two limestone tablets, possibly originating from Samarra, written in 690 and commemorating the city wall of Sûr-marrati.

The main problem concerning the battle of Halulê is knowing who was victorious. On the one hand, Sennacherib lengthily claims his victory. On the other hand, the Babylonians claim victory in a laconic manner: "He (Humban-menânu) effected an Assyrian retreat."[63] Who was lying? There is a great debate on the subject, a frequent conclusion being that the Babylonian Chronicles are an objective document and that the Assyrian claim to victory is a prodigious falsehood.[64] What is the historical value of the Babylonian Chronicles? Whatever its record in terms of accuracy, it can also be biased because it was seen through Babylonian eyes. However, in this case, its testimony is probably exact. It must be stressed that it mentions a retreat, not a defeat, which is something quite different. From the viewpoint of the Babylonians, before the battle, the Assyrian troops were marching toward Babylon; after the battle, they were no longer marching to Babylon, hence this possibly being seen as a retreat. If they had been

---

61. RINAP 3.2:316, 223.38b–40.
62. RINAP 3.2:335, 230.112–14, and 327–29 (with bibliography).
63. Grayson, *Assyrian and Babylonian Chronicles*, 80, chr. 1, iii.18.
64. See, e.g., Albert Kirk Grayson, "Problematic Battles in Mesopotamian History," in *Studies in Honor of Benno Landsberger on His Seventy-Fifth Birthday April 21, 1965*, ed. Hans G. Güterbock and Thorkild Jacobsen, AS 16 (Chicago: University of Chicago Press, 1965), 342; Walter Mayer, "Sanherib und Babylonien: Der Staatsmann und Feldherr im Spiegel seiner Babylonienpolitik," in *Vom Alten Orient Zum Alten Testament: Festschrift für Wolfram Freiherrn von Soden zum 85. Geburtstag am 19. Juni 1993*, ed. Manfred Dietrich and Oswald Loretz (Neukirchen-Vluyn: Neukirchener Verlag, 1995), 305–32; JoAnn Scurlock, "Neo-Assyrian Battle Tactics," in *Crossing Boundaries and Linking Horizons: Studies in Honor of Michael C. Astour on His Eightieth Birthday*, ed. Young and Mark W. Chavalas (Bethesda, MD: CDL, 1997), 514; SAAS 12:36–37; Fales, *Guerre et paix en Assyrie*, 199–203.

defeated, the Babylonian Chronicles would undoubtedly have mentioned it.[65] Now, concerning the Assyrian viewpoint, the Assyrian kings used to keep silent on their defeats, or to present them as victories, but briefly. It would not have been understandable that Sennacherib had described in his royal inscriptions in such detail and in such length a battle that he had lost, much more lengthily than other battles that he had won. If we review the events that followed the battle, even if the sources are scarce, it must be noticed that Sennacherib does not appear as somebody who had been defeated, first of all because he stayed on the spot to erect a stela. Before analyzing the following events of 690 and 689, let us try to evaluate the true result of the battle of Halulê. It was a victory, but a mitigated victory for Sennacherib, having both positive and negative consequences. As he was not personally a great warlord, he was very proud to have succeeded in defeating such a great coalition of peoples, mainly Babylonians and Elamites, his two worst enemies. He could also boast of taking back to Nineveh several spoils seized on the battlefield: precious weapons and ornaments, chariots, and horses. His army had, however, endured some losses, but not that many, because he was ready to continue his campaign soon afterwards. The main drawback was that the kings of Elam and Babylon remained on their thrones, and that the Babylonian problem had not been resolved.

Did Sennacherib, or his magnates, attack the border areas of Elam after the battle of Halulê? This attack is possibly recorded by the Bavian inscriptions, written in 689 or 688, in the following passage: "Fear (and) terror fell upon all the Elamites and they abandoned their land, and (then), in order to save their lives, they betook themselves to a rugged mountain like eagle(s) and their hearts throbbed like (those of) pursued birds. Until they died, they did not make their way (back) and they no longer made war."[66] This passage follows the flight of the king of Elam after the battle of Halulê. The next sentence is ambiguous and is translated differently by Daniel David Luckenbill: "Thereupon Sennacherib became violently angry and he ordered (his army) to turn toward Elam," and by Albert Kirk Grayson: "Perhaps Sennacherib, king of Assyria, is so angry that he will return to the land of Elam," a translation which seems more likely.[67] In any

---

65. Levine, "Sennacherib's Southern Front," 49–51.

66. RINAP 3.2:316, 223.41–43a.

67. Luckenbill, *Annals of Sennacherib*, 82, l. 40; RINAP 3.2:316, 223.39–40. See Levine, "Sennacherib's Southern Front," 50 and n. 66.

case, if there was a further attack against Elam in 690, it was limited and not worthy of being recorded precisely after the dazzling narrative of the battle of Halulê. For the year 689 (the fourth year of Mushezib-Marduk), the Babylonian Chronicles mention: "On the fifteenth day of the month Nisan (April), Humban-menânu, king of Elam, was stricken by paralysis and his mouth was so affected that he could not speak," then, on the seventh day of the month Addaru (March), he died and was replaced by Humban-haltash I, who reigned from 689 to 681.[68]

5.5. Expedition against the Arabs

In two fragmentary stone tablets, probably inscribed around 690–689, a summary of Sennacherib's accomplishments on the battlefield is recorded: after the battle of Halulê, directly and without mentioning any attack on the Elamite border, an expedition against the Arabs is reported.[69] It has been argued that the Assyrian expedition against the Arabs occurred in about 688, after the destruction of Babylon, in order to vanquish the Babylonian allies, which would have been impossible before Babylon collapsed.[70] However, after such a drastic conclusion as the destruction of Babylon, an expedition against the Arabs would have been unnecessary, whereas before attacking Babylon this expedition would probably have been intended to prevent them from supporting the Babylonians. The first Arab leader attacked by the Assyrians was Te'elhunu, queen of the Arabs; she is called Apkallatu in the inscriptions of Esarhaddon, apparently a title that was misunderstood to be her name.[71] The second Arab leader, allied with her, was Hazail, whose title is not preserved in Sennacherib's inscriptions but who was known later as king of the Arabs in the inscriptions of Esarhaddon and Ashurbanipal, and as king of the Qedarites in other Ashurbanipal inscriptions.[72] The account is lacunary but understandable: "Teelhu]nu, queen of the Arabs, in the middle of the desert [...] I took away [...] thousand camels from her. She [...] with Hazail. [Terror of doing battle wi]th me overwhelmed them. They aban-

---

68. Grayson, *Assyrian and Babylonian Chronicles*, 80–81, chr. 1, iii.19–21, 25–27; SAAS 12:36–37.
69. RINAP 3.1:232, 35.r.53′–59′, 1″–9″.
70. Alois Musil, *Arabia Deserta: A Topographical Itinerary* (New York, 1927), 480–81; Fales, "Moving around Babylon," 91–111.
71. PNA 3.2:1322; Israel Eph'al, *The Ancient Arabs* (Leiden: Brill, 1982), 118–25.
72. PNA 2.1:468; Eph'al, *Ancient Arabs*, 118–19.

doned their tents and fled for (their) lives [to *the city* ...] *and* the city of Adummatu."[73] The city of Adummatu/Dumetu/Adumu is described as a fortified city in the midst of the desert and which the Assyrians captured by treading down ramps. It is usually identified with Dûmat al-Jandal (possibly biblical Dumah), the main oasis in the Jauf depression in Wadi Sirhân, mentioned by classical and Arab authors from the first century BCE onwards as an important oasis.[74] It was the most important oasis in the whole of North Arabia, located halfway between Syria and Babylonia, a main stopping point on the roads to Damascus, Medina, and Hîra (near Kûfa), on the western border of Babylonia.[75] This expedition far into the desert was probably not led by Sennacherib but by his magnates, even though the first person is used in the account. The Assyrians took the stronghold of Adummatu; they captured Te'elhunu and carried her off to Assyria, together with her gods, precious stones, wood, and all types of aromatics, Arab trading products.[76] Esarhaddon later returned her gods to the Arabs because such desert cities could not be kept under control by the Assyrians.[77] Sennacherib's inscriptions do not specify that Hazail was also captured by the Assyrian army because, as we learn from Esarhaddon's inscriptions, he surrendered and sent him tribute. One of the Nineveh gates, which usually bore the names of gods, was called "The Desert Gate Through Which the Presents of the People of Têma and Sumuel Enter."[78] Several onyx and agate stones found at Nineveh testify to these presents as they were inscribed: "palace of Sennacherib ... Booty of the city of Dumetu."[79] The city of Kapânu mentioned in the lacunary inscription of the expedition against the Arabs has been identified with modern Kaf.[80] Herodotus's mention that Sennacherib was "king of the Arabs and Assyrians" is possibly related to this expedition.[81]

---

73. RINAP 3.1:232, 35.o.53′–56′. On a tribute of camels, see SAA 17:7, 4.3.
74. Musil, *Arabia Deserta*, 532–53; Eph'al, *Ancient Arabs*, 120–121 and map 241 (with bibliography); RINAP 3.2:152, no. 111.
75. Eph'al, *Ancient Arabs*, 121–22.
76. RINAP 3.1:232, no. 35.r.5″–9″; Eph'al, *Ancient Arabs*, 123–24.
77. RINAP 4:30, 2.ii.46–62.
78. RINAP 3.1:143, 17.vii.95–viii.1; 3.1:159, 18.vii.37–38.
79. RINAP 3.2:152, 111.5; 3.2:153, 112.7 and 113.2; 3.2:154, 114.3; 3.2:155, 115.2; Eckart Frahm, "Perlen von den Rändern der Welt," in *Languages and Cultures in Contact: At the Crossroads of Civilizations in the Syro-Mesopotamian Realm*, ed. Karel Van Lerberghe and Gabriela Voet, RAI 42 (Leuven: Peeters, 1999), 79–99.
80. Eph'al, *Ancient Arabs*, 42–43; *PNA* 3.1:1120.
81. Herodotus, *Hist.* 2.141; Eph'al, *Ancient Arabs*, 137–42.

5.6. Siege and Destruction of Babylon

In fact, the eighth campaign was long and presumably arduous, lasting at least two years, from 691 to 689. It comprised three phases: the battle of Halulê, which occurred before the twentieth day of Addaru (March) 691; the attack, by Assyrian forces, possibly of the Elam border to the east of Babylonia, and of the Arabs to the west of Babylonia; and the protracted siege, fall, and destruction of Babylon. Sennacherib's ultimate aim was to attack Babylon, which eventually fell on the first day of Kislimu (December) 689; however, the siege had already started in 690.[82] It can be noticed that his first, second, fourth, six, seventh, and eighth campaigns were directed toward the south of Assyria, four of which targeted Babylonia: the first, in 704–702, consisted of an initial attack against the Babylonians. The second campaign, in 700, represented a limited action to suppress a revolt of the Chaldean tribes. The third campaign, stretching out over the years 694–693, was a complex action against the Elamite-Babylonian coalition for final control of southern Babylonia. The fourth campaign against Babylonia (691–689) was the final struggle.

Why did Sennacherib want to put an end to the Babylonian problem? As a related question, why did such a coalition of Babylonians and allies gather against Assyria? The bulk of the sources being Assyrian, it is through Assyrian eyes that we can answer these questions. Concerning Sennacherib's motives, they can be postulated quite easily. Several motives have been listed, all of which are true: his unsuccessful attempts at governing Babylonia; recurring revolts; the loss of his eldest son; three protracted unsuccessful offensives and a series of related shorter campaigns, which were costly and time consuming, represented frustrations and taxed the patience of the Assyrian king.[83] Was there also an economic motive? Military campaigns were necessary to maintain the empire and the economic base that it encompassed. Tribute, booty, and the prospect of new markets and trading opportunities were also needed for his ambitious building projects. However, these campaigns were very expensive and took the king and his magnates away from the administrative center for protracted

---

82. Levine, "Sennacherib's Southern Front," 50–51.
83. Brinkman, "Sennacherib's Babylonian Problem," 94; Levine, "Sennacherib's Southern Front," 53–55; Frederick Mario Fales, "Arameans and Chaldeans: Environment and Society," in *The Babylonian World*, ed. Gwendolyn Leick (New York: Routledge, 2007), 288–98.

periods of time, implying that they must have had detrimental effects on the functioning of the imperial bureaucracy. Moreover, little mention is made of booty in the southern campaigns until the final one. The continued flow of revenue from Babylonia, which stopped paying tribute after 694, must have been a motive. The Assyrian Empire was very prosperous under Sennacherib, and the only limitation to its prosperity was the Babylonian problem. Chauvinism on Assyria's part was not excluded: Babylon was a prestigious capital that overshadowed Nineveh, even at the time when it was included in the Assyrian Empire. In reality, Sennacherib was never fascinated by Babylon, as is shown by the fact that he never wanted to be crowned as the city's king, and he consequently had no scruples about destroying it.[84] Another motive could have been his fear of a rival state in the south that might one day challenge Assyrian supremacy. Total devastation of Babylon would stop further trouble in the south, remove the symbol of Babylonian aspirations, and suppress any fear of a resurgent challenge from the south.

The siege, fall, and destruction of Babylon are, unexpectedly, not described in detail in Sennacherib's inscriptions, as was the battle of Halulê, even though it was a major historical event for Assyria. It is only reported in three texts: the Bavian inscriptions, written just after the event, in around 688, after the description of the battle of Halulê; the fragment of Prism K 1634, an edition of 688 or later; and it is briefly mentioned in a stone tablet from Assur describing the construction of the *akītu* house, written after 689.[85] There are brief mentions in the Babylonian Chronicles and in some king lists.[86]

According to the Babylonian Chronicles, "On the first day of the month Kislev/Kislimu (December) the city was captured. Mushezib-Marduk was taken prisoner and transported to Assyria. For four years Mushezib-Marduk ruled over Babylon."[87] The Chronicles are laconic, as usual, but they are valuable because they give the date of the capture of Babylon.

---

84. Marc Van De Mieroop, "A Tale of Two Cities: Nineveh and Babylon," *Iraq* 66 (2004): 1–5; Marti, "Sennachérib, la rage du prince," 57–59.

85. RINAP 3.2:316, 223.43b–54a; 3.2:248, 168.36b–42; Luckenbill, *Annals of Sennacherib*, 83–84; see Julian E. Reade, "Sources for Sennacherib: The Prisms," *JCS* 27 (1975): 194.

86. Grayson, *Assyrian and Babylonian Chronicles*, 80–81, chr. 1, iii.22–24; Grayson, "Königslisten und Chroniken B. Akkadisch," 6:93, 101, 122.

87. Grayson, *Assyrian and Babylonian Chronicles*, 80–81, chr. 1, iii.22–24.

A legal document in the Yale collection depicts the conditions of life in Babylon during the siege: "In the time of Mushezib-Marduk, king of Babylonia, the land was gripped by siege, famine, hunger, want, and hard times. Everything was changed and reduced to nothing. Two *qa* of barley (sold for) one shekel of silver. The city gates were barred, and a person could not go out in any of the four directions. The corpses of men, with no one to bury them, filled the squares of Babylon."[88] This text is dated to 690, fifteen months before the fall of Babylon, on the first day of Kislimu (December) 689, at the end of summer 690, when the siege was already well advanced. The description in the Bavian inscriptions began with a small, poetic introduction: "On my second expedition, I marched quickly to Babylon, which I planned to conquer, and (then) I blew like [the onset] of a storm and enveloped it like a (dense) fog."[89] *I-na* 2-i KASKAL-*ia* does not mean "my second campaign," as translated by Grayson, because this action still took place in the eighth campaign. Sennacherib probably meant that his expedition to Halulê was the first and that the other expedition was the second, both in the scope of his eighth campaign. He did not take into account the possible expedition to the Elam border and the expedition against the Arabs, because they were led not by him but by his magnates. The account of the long siege, of the fall of the city, and of the subsequent slaughter of its inhabitants is reported in only two sentences: "I besieged the city; then, by means of sapping and ladders, I [captured (it)] (and) plundered [*the city*]. Its people, young and old, I did not spare, and I filled the city squares with their corpses."[90] Then he briefly mentions the fate of the Babylonian king: "I carried off alive to my land Shûzubu (Mushezib-Marduk), the king of Babylon, together with his family (and) his […]." A longer description is devoted to the plundering of Babylon. First, he handed to his soldiers the riches of the city: silver, gold, and choice stones. Then he targeted the Babylonian gods, who were also inhabitants of the city. His soldiers seized and smashed the gods, and took the riches of their temples. Sennacherib does not want to describe himself as an impious king. He boasts of having accomplished a just and pious action related to the Assyrian gods: "The god Adad (and) the goddess Shala, gods of the city of Ekallâtum whom Marduk-nâdin-ahhê, king of Akkad, had taken and brought to Babylon during the reign of Tiglath-pileser (I), king of Assyria—I had

---

88. YBC 11377. See Brinkman, "Sennacherib's Babylonian Problem," 93–94.
89. RINAP 3.2:316, 223.43b–44.
90. RINAP 3.2:316, 223.45.

(them) brought out of Babylon after 418 years and I returned them to the city of E[kallâtum], their (proper) place."[91] The chronology is problematic because 689 plus 418 makes 1107, but Marduk-nâdin-ahhê, Babylonian king of the Second Dynasty of Isin, reigned later, from 1099 to 1082. The two statues were probably dilapidated during their sojourn in Babylonia and needed to be repaired, as shown from a letter of Marduk-shakin-shuni to King Esarhaddon, which represents another chronological problem, as they were no longer in Babylonia.[92]

The destruction of Babylon is described in a few lines. Following the usual phraseology, Sennacherib destroyed, devastated, and burned the city, which was moreover pulled down, from its foundation to its crenellations and from the inner wall to the outer wall, including the temples and the ziggurat. He threw the ruins into the Arahtu River. The most barbarous part of his action is described methodically, as with the cold rage of revenge against the Babylonians: "I dug canals into the center of that city and (thus) leveled their site with water. I destroyed the outline of its foundations and (thereby) made its destruction surpass that of the Deluge. So that in the future, the site of that city and (its) temples will be unrecognizable, I dissolved it in water and annihilated (it), (making it) like a meadow."[93] In the stone tablet of Assur, he describes a consequence of the destruction of Babylon: the earth of the destroyed city was carried to the sea by the Euphrates. This dirt reached Dilmun and frightened its inhabitants, prompting them to send audience gifts to Sennacherib. Moreover, "they sent people mustered from their land, corvée workers, (with) bronze spades (and) bronze plowshares, tools manufactured in their land, in order to demolish Babylon."[94] In order to pacify the god Assur and to serve as a reminder of the power of Assyria, Sennacherib removed some of the dirt from Babylon and piled it up in heaps and mounds in the *akītu* house. Even though he claims to have completely suppressed Babylon, first himself, then with the help of people from Dilmun, it was such a large city, which was thereafter rebuilt by Esarhaddon, that its total

---

91. RINAP 3.2:316, 223.48–49. However, in the stone tablet of Assur (3.2:248, 168.36b), he also states that he smashed the gods.

92. Waterman, *Royal Correspondence of the Assyrian Empire*, 662; Brinkman, *Political History of the Post-Kassite Babylonia 1158–722 BC*, 83–85, 124–26; Frame, *Babylonia 689–627 B.C.*, 53; PNA 2.2:719.

93. RINAP 3.2:316–17, 223.50b–54a.

94. RINAP 3.2:248, 168.36b–44a.

destruction is inconceivable. As usual, it is a literary topos in Sennacherib's inscriptions.

Esarhaddon's inscriptions testify to the destruction and depopulation of Babylon, justifying his rebuilding and resettlement of the city. They report that the Arahtu River overflowed its banks, swept its waters destructively across the city and its dwellings, and turned them into ruins: "The gods dwelling in it flew up to the heavens like birds; the people living in it were hidden in another place and took refuge in an [unknown] land."[95] Esarhaddon does not mention the name of Sennacherib in this account because he did not wish to criticize his father's actions. A letter from Ubaru, governor of Babylon, to Esarhaddon refers to the fact that he had returned prisoners and booty taken from Babylon, and repopulated the city.[96] Other later texts testify to the destruction and depopulation of Babylon, such as a Babylonian inscription dating from the reign of Nabopolassar, or another one from the time of Nabonidus, which states that Sennacherib was punished for his actions by being killed by his son.[97] Did archaeological excavations find any traces of the destruction of Babylon? According to Oskar Reuther, the Merkes residential quarter of Babylon may support the hypothesis that the city was devastated, partly burned, and probably abandoned for a time.[98] However, he did not find any evidence that this area was destroyed by flooding. Thus, there is no proof of a systematic destruction of the entire city. Possibly Sennacherib focused his attention on the religious and administrative quarters and on the fortifications. Anyway, the results of excavations are difficult to interpret because of the rebuilding of the city.[99]

One question has been shelved: Why was there such a difference in the Assyrian inscriptions between the account of the battle of Halulê and that of the destruction of Babylon? It is not enough to say that they were not written by the same scribe. In fact, the standard accounts make no mention of the actions following the battle. Maybe Sennacherib saw his victory over the great southern coalition, the largest assembled during his reign, as the crowning triumph of his military exploits. This was the glorious

---

95. RINAP 4:196, 104.i.34–ii.9a.
96. Waterman, *Royal Correspondence of the Assyrian Empire*, 418.
97. Frame, *Babylonia 689–627 B.C.*, 54–55 (with bibliography).
98. Oskar Reuther, *Die Innenstadt von Babylon (Merkes)*, WVDOG 47 (Leipzig: Hinrichs, 1926), 21–25, 60–64.
99. Frame, *Babylonia 689–627 B.C.*, 55–56.

end he wanted to be written as a conclusion to his annals.[100] The rhetoric used for describing the battle of Halulê became superfluous once Babylon had been sacked, and it was unnecessary to mention the frustration and hatred felt toward the Babylonians after the final victory.[101] Another explanation could be that he was always mindful of the divine punishment of his father, and he was afraid that, if he boasted about it, his action against the gods of Babylon could be a "sin" and he would be punished.[102]

Finally, the period 694–689 was entirely intended by Sennacherib to be devoted to crushing the allies of Babylon, Elam and secondarily the Arabs, and finally to capturing and destroying Babylon. All his actions during this period reveal plenty of clear thinking and calculation; they progressed in line with his planning, albeit with some delays and disturbances. The sixth and seventh campaigns were devoted to fighting against Elam. After a short break in 692, the fight against Elam started again, ending in 691 in the battle of Halulê with a defeat of the anti-Assyrian coalition. Possibly an additional limited expedition in 690 to the border of Elam was necessary to neutralize the Elamite ally definitively. A short expedition, also in 690, against the Arabs, prevented them from giving their support to the Babylonians. Sennacherib could implement the final phase of his plan: the conquest of Babylon, initiating its siege in spring or summer 690. The annihilation of Babylon, the most prestigious religious and significant political center of Mesopotamia, was a drastic action that had considerable consequences for the future relationship between Babylonia and Assyria, and for the evolution of the Assyrian Empire.[103] More personally, he had lost a son and incurred the hatred of the Babylonians. He dreaded receiving divine punishment for having destroyed the Babylonian gods. However, the destruction of Babylon also had positive consequences for him: he was no longer frustrated because he had realized all his military objectives, he was recognized as a glorious warlord by the Assyrians, and he had established a Pax Assyriaca in the Assyrian Empire, with Babylonia and Elam posing no further threat to Assyria during the remaining eight years

---

100. Levine, "Sennacherib's Southern Front," 51.

101. Weissert, "Creating a Political Climate," 202.

102. Victoire Moinard, *Les mauvais traitements envers les dieux en Mésopotamie au premier millénaire av. J.-C.* (Saarbrücken: Éditions universitaires européennes, 2006), 65–75.

103. Frame, *Babylonia 689–627 B.C.*, 52–53; Eckart Frahm, "Assyria's Downfall," in Frahm, *Companion to Assyria*, 191–93.

of his reign.[104] Finally, he had substantially increased the prosperity of the empire, which allowed him to carry out his prestigious building projects and innovating activities.

---

104. Frederick Mario Fales, "On *Pax Assyriaca* in the Eighth–Seventh Centuries BCE and Its Implications," in Cohen and Westbrook, *Swords into Plowshares*, 17–35; Fales, *Guerre et paix en Assyrie*, 219–28.

6
END OF REIGN (688–681)

The period from the destruction of Babylon in 689 until the death of Sennacherib in 681 is poorly known. There are very few texts and in particular no information in the royal inscriptions about Assyrian foreign politics. It was probably a period of relative peace, Pax Assyriaca, even though some problems may have occurred. The main question is what became of Babylon after its destruction. Even if Sennacherib was not involved in military campaigns, it is interesting to know how his relations with his previous enemies, Elamites, Babylonians, and Chaldeans, had evolved. In fact, the main difficulties that the king of Assyria encountered were not outside Assyria but at his own court: his domestic situation became more and more unstable during these last eight years. There was an increasingly severe struggle between his sons for the succession. Sennacherib mismanaged this difficult situation, leading to the consequence that he was killed by one of his sons.

6.1. Babylon after Its Destruction

In 688, Sennacherib was not far short of sixty years old[1] and was probably tired after fifteen years of military campaigns with few breaks. As all his objectives had been attained, no doubt he wanted to rest and devote himself entirely to the activities that interested him most, such as building and innovating, as is shown in his inscriptions. What was the situation of Babylonia at that time? The relative lack of documentation covering this period may be an accident of archaeological discoveries, but it may also

---

1. Parpola, *Letters from Assyrian Scholars to the Kings Esarhaddon and Assurbanipal*, 239 and n. 390; *PNA* 3.1:1116; Elayi, *Sargon II, King of Assyria*, 28–29.

correspond to a period of uncertainty and weakness in this region.² Moreover, it was the will of Sennacherib neither to mention Babylon anymore in his inscriptions nor to depict it in the reliefs of his palace. A fragmentary hexagonal prism from Nineveh probably represents the last edition of his annals, dated from 687 or later.³ A clay tablet recording the text that was to be inscribed on a lapis lazuli seal gives an idea of the difficulty in interpreting certain documents.⁴ The first owner was the Kassite king Shagarakti-Shuriash, who reigned over Babylon. The second owner, Tukultî-Ninurta I, king of Assyria from 1243 to 1208, brought it from Babylon. Afterward, the seal returned to Babylon, and then Sennacherib took it from the booty collected in 689: "This seal found some hidden way from Assyria to hostile Akkad. I, Sennacherib, king of Assyria, after 600 years, took Babylon, and from the wealth of Babylon, I selected it."⁵

Unexpectedly, the Babylonian Chronicles are not primarily concerned with the destruction of Babylon or its later rebuilding by Esarhaddon but with the presence or absence of the great god Marduk: "For eight years (during the reign of) Sennacherib, for twelve years (during the reign of) Esarhaddon—twenty years (altogether—Bêl (Marduk) stayed [in B]altil (Assur) and the *akītu* festival did not take place."⁶ Whether the statue of Marduk was destroyed or not in 689 remains uncertain. Sennacherib's inscriptions state that the gods of Babylon were destroyed along with the city, without any specific mention of Marduk: "My people seized and smashed the gods living inside it (Babylon)."⁷ However, the presence of Marduk in Assyria is attested in Esarhaddon's inscriptions, for example, in clay tablets, copied from the base of the statue of Marduk: "Written on the pedestal of (the statue of) the god Bêl (Marduk)."⁸ It is clearly mentioned in Ashurbanipal's inscriptions that Marduk took up residence in Assyria under the reign of an unnamed previous Assyrian king: "The great lord Marduk, who in the reign of a former king, took up his abode in

---

2. Frame, *Babylonia 689–627 B.C.*, 61–63.

3. Julian E. Reade, "Sources for Sennacherib," 194–95; Frahm, *Einleitung in die Sanherib-Inschriften*, 107–8, T19; RINAP 3.1:209–10, no. 26.

4. Frahm, *Einleitung in die Sanherib-Inschriften*, 217–19, T180; *PNA* 3.2:1181.

5. *ARAB* 2.359–61. The date "six hundred years" is very approximate.

6. Grayson, *Assyrian and Babylonian Chronicles*, 127, chr. 14, ll. 31–32; 131, chr. 16, ll. 1–4.

7. RINAP 3.2:316, 223.48–49.

8. RINAP 3.2:100, 44.r.18'; 3.2:101, 45.iv.13'–14'.

the presence of the father, his begetter (Assur), in Assyria."[9] However, it is uncertain whether the original statue of Marduk was brought to Assyria at the time of Sennacherib's capture of Babylon, or whether copies of the statue were made by the Assyrian kings. According to different Esarhaddon inscriptions, either a statue of Marduk (copy or original?) was sent to Babylon or Marduk was said to have been born in Assyria. A statue of Marduk (copy or original?) was also sent to Babylon in 668.[10] In fact, Sennacherib and his successors made use of Marduk for political-ideological reasons.[11]

How was Babylonia governed after 689? Sennacherib never took the title of "king of Babylon," unlike his predecessors, or "viceroy of Babylon" or "king of Sumer and Akkad." Only one of Sennacherib's royal inscriptions can be considered as Babylonian: it was found on paving stones from Babylon, and it merely mentions "Sennacherib, king of Assyria."[12] This inscription possibly came from his first reign over Babylonia (704–703). Three Babylonian economic texts are dated by Sennacherib's regnal years, that is to say, 686, 685, and 681, and also refer to him as "king of Assyria."[13] Sennacherib officially left Babylonia rulerless. Part of northern Babylonia was possibly reduced to the status of an Assyrian province, as could be inferred from two tablets found at Dur-Kurigalzu and dated by reference to the official eponym for 682.[14] During the entire period 689–681 or part of it, Nabû-zêr-kitti-lîshir had been appointed by Sennacherib as governor of the Sealand (area of Bît-Yakin). He was the son of Merodach-baladan; it is known that he was installed by Sennacherib, maybe shortly after 689, from an inscription said to come from Nineveh (Kuyunjik) on an onyx cylinder-shaped bead: "[Palace of] Sennacherib, king of [Assyria: (This is) the aud]ience gift that (Nabû)-zêr-kitti-[lîshir, son of] Marduk-apla-iddina (II) (Merodach-baladan) presented to me."[15] He occupied the same

---

9. *ARAB* 2.962.

10. Frame, *Babylonia 689–627 B.C.*, 56–57 (with bibliography).

11. See p. 169.

12. Grant Frame, *Rulers of Babylonia from the Second Dynasty of Isin to the End of the Assyrian Domination (1157–612 BC)* (Toronto: University of Toronto Press, 1995), 153–54.

13. Brinkman and Kennedy, "Documentary Evidence for the Economic Base of Early Neo-Babylonian Society," 14, C.

14. Brinkman, "Sennacherib's Babylonian Problem," 95 and n. 33.

15. Frame, *Babylonia 689–627 B.C.*, 60 and n. 41; Frahm, *Einleitung in die Sanherib-Inschriften*, 146, T96; RINAP 3.2:150, 109.1–7.

position at the beginning of Esarhaddon's reign, as is apparent in Esarhaddon's inscriptions and letters.[16] Then he rebelled against Esarhaddon, because he wanted to build up his position in the south: "At that time, Nabû-zêr-kitti-lîshir, son of Merodach-baladan, governor of the Sealand, who did not keep his treaty (*adê*) nor remember the agreement of Assyria, forgot the good relations of my father."[17] Taking advantage of the disturbances in Assyria, he mustered his troops and besieged Nikkal-iddin, the "governor of the land" (*šakin māti*) of Ur and a loyal servant of the Assyrian king. When hearing of the approach of the Assyrian army, he fled to Elam but was killed because he had transgressed against the gods. Nikkal-iddin had probably been appointed governor of Ur by Sennacherib, before or after the period 694–689, and he is mentioned in several documents: royal inscriptions, letters, and legal and administrative texts dated from Esarhaddon's reign.[18]

No letter can be securely dated from the period 688–681, but later letters may refer to events that occurred at that time. For example, in a letter to Esarhaddon, the governor of Nippur complains that the governor of Babylon denied Nippur access to the Banîtu canal although Sennacherib had granted the city this access.[19] This authorization was possibly granted during the period 688–681, after the destruction of Babylon, which no longer needed this waterway. A Babylonian astronomical text possibly refers to a revolt in 686, but it is too fragmentary to permit an interpretation.[20] Only a few economic documents can be ascribed to this period, but none refer to Sennacherib as king of Babylonia.[21] Two texts from Nippur and one from Hursagkalama refer to Sennacherib as king of Assyria. Two texts from Borsippa are dated respectively from the twelfth and thirteenth year after the deceased Ashur-nâdin-shumi, that is, 688 and 687.[22] This dating means that Ashur-nâdin-shumi was the last ruler of Babylon who was considered legitimate in both Assyrian and Babylonian eyes. Two texts

---

16. *PNA* 2.2:906 (with bibliography).

17. RINAP 4:15, 1.ii.40–45.

18. Frame, *Babylonia 689–627 B.C.*, 60–61; *PNA* 2.2:961 (with bibliography).

19. Waterman, *Royal Correspondence of the Assyrian Empire*, no. 327; SAA 18:53–55, no. 70.

20. *LBAT* 1417.i′.1; Frame, *Babylonia 689–627 B.C.*, 60 and n. 40.

21. Frame, *Babylonia 689–627 B.C.*, 61 (with bibliography).

22. Francis Joannès, *Archives de Borsippa: La famille Ea-ilûta-bâni* (Geneva: Droz, 1989), 255–56, L 1672; John A. Brinkman, "A Legal Text from Borsippa Dated Posthumously under Aššur-nādin-shumi," *NABU* (1992): 68–69, no. 88.

6. END OF REIGN (688–681)

from Ur are dated from the eighth and twelfth year of Nikkal-iddin, governor of Ur, which can tentatively be dated from 681 and 677 respectively if he was appointed governor in 689. Esarhaddon had to deal with some unrest in Bît-Dakkûri at the very beginning of his reign because its king, Shamash-ibni, had gained power by encroaching on fields of the citizens of Babylon and Borsippa.[23] Assyrian control under Sennacherib had possibly been somewhat lax, encouraging Bît-Dakkûri to appropriate fields now lying vacant around Babylon.

Other events occurred during the period 688–681, reported in the Babylonian Chronicles: the death of the Elamite king Humban-menânu on the seventh day of Addaru (March) 689, and the accession of Humban-haltash I; the death of Humban-haltash I on the twenty-third day of Tashrîtu (October) 681, and the accession of Humban-haltash II.[24] According to the Babylonian Chronicles: "On the third day of the month Tammuzu (July 681), the gods of Uruk went from [Ela]m into Uruk."[25] As there is no record of a new campaign against Elam in 681, peaceful relations seem to have been established between Assyria and Elam during this period. In fact, the affair of the gods of Uruk is not quite clear. An entry in the Babylonian Chronicles for the year 693 states that the gods of Uruk were removed from the city. There is a contradiction between the fact that "the army of Assyria entered Uruk (and) plundered the gods and inhabitants of Uruk" and that "the Elamites had come and carried off the gods and inhabitants of Uruk."[26] Albert Kirk Grayson considers that it was the Elamites who carried off the gods of Uruk in 693 and that Humban-haltash I allowed them to return from Elam to Babylonia in 681 in order to establish or confirm peaceful relations with Sennacherib.[27] However, it seems more plausible that the Assyrians, who had plundered Uruk, also removed its gods to Assyria, and that, in 681, they returned them from Assyria, not from Elam.[28] It is possible that Sennacherib returned the statues of the gods to the city in order to alleviate some of the anti-Assyrian

---

23. RINAP 4:18, 1.iii.62–70.
24. Grayson, *Assyrian and Babylonian Chronicles*, 81, chr. 1, iii.30–33; SAAS 12:33–40.
25. Grayson, *Assyrian and Babylonian Chronicles*, 81, chr. 1, iii.28–29.
26. Grayson, *Assyrian and Babylonian Chronicles*, 78–79, chr. 1, ii.48–iii.1–2.
27. Grayson, *Assyrian and Babylonian Chronicles*, 16 and 79, chr. 1, iii.1–2.
28. The name of the country is badly damaged. See Levine, "Sennacherib's Southern Front," 44–45 and n. 52; Frame, *Babylonia 689–627 B.C.*, 59–60 and n. 37.

feeling there. A later document from the time of Ashurbanipal stated that he gave some Puqudians to the deities Ishtar and Nanaya of Uruk, which means that he may have had some respect for Uruk and its deities.[29] Delegates from faraway countries came to visit Sennacherib, for example, a Sabean embassy, which brought spices and precious stones to Assyria, and six beads as audience gifts from Karib-il, king of Saba.[30] Other audience gifts were found in Nineveh, for example, those of Abibaal, king of Samsimuruna, and Nabû-zêr-kitti-lîshir, governor of the Sealand.[31]

6.2. Problem of Succession

In this period of relative peacefulness, Sennacherib had a major concern: the problem of his succession arrangement. His father, Sargon, had correctly settled this problem by designating Sennacherib as crown prince at the very beginning of his reign.[32] Sennacherib seems to have designated several of his sons as crown prince. Who the first one was is not quite clear. Logically, his eldest son, Ashur-nâdin-shumi, who had received a house in Assur from his father,[33] should have been designated as crown prince. However, in 700, Sennacherib installed him as king of Babylon, and his rule lasted for six years, until his capture and deportation to Elam in 694. Therefore, he could probably not be king of Babylon and crown prince of Assyria at the same time. The status of "heir apparent" without being formally inducted into the succession house, proposed by Sarah C. Melville, is not documented.[34] The need to settle the succession issue must have become pressing for Sennacherib, who probably made a permanent arrangement after 700. The title *mār šarri* literally meant "king's

---

29. BIN 2:132, nos. 1–4; Frame, *Babylonia 689–627 B.C.*, 60 and n. 38.

30. Frahm, "Perlen von den Rändern der Welt," 79–99; RINAP 3.2:146–50, nos. 103–8.

31. See p. 136; Frahm, *Einleitung in die Sanherib-Inschriften*, 16–18, 146, T 96; Frahm, "Perlen von den Rändern der Welt," 83, 89–90; RINAP 3.2:145, 102.1–5; 3.2:150, 109.1–7; *PNA* 3.1:1121.

32. See p. 30.

33. RINAP 3.2:285, 205.1–7. Andrew Knapp questions it in *Royal Apologetic in the Ancient Near East* (WAWSup 4 [Atlanta: SBL Press, 2015]), 302–4), giving two arguments. First, he would have been too old to succeed Sennacherib one day, but his age is unknown. Second, Sennacherib would have not elevated him over Babylonia; however, this decision was made years later, as an emergency solution.

34. SAAS 9:19–20.

son" or "prince" in general and also "crown prince." This second meaning was always that of contemporary letters, reports, and administrative texts, while the other sons of the king were regularly referred to by their names only. Theodore Kwasman and Simo Parpola examined how far this usage also applied to legal texts.[35] After having shown that it applied to texts dated from Esarhaddon's and Ashurbanipal's reigns, they examined six texts dating from 683–681. Text 103 belonged to the archive of Aplaya. He was "third man" (that is, shield bearer on a chariot) of "Urdu-Mullissu the crown prince."[36] Urdu-Mullissu was Sennacherib's "second son" (*māru tardennu*). He had been given a house by his father, which has been discovered in the excavations. It was situated at the eastern wall of Assur and was under construction around 700. Several religious objects were found inside, together with some inscriptions, indicating that the prince had some priestly function in the Assur temple.[37] An inscribed stone vessel, given to him by Sennacherib, seems to indicate that he lived in Assur but also spent some time at the royal court of Nineveh.[38] Text 103 is dated from the eponymy of Ilu-isse'a, that is, 694, on the twelfth day of Tashrîtu (October). The earliest document of the Aplaya archive, text 100, concerning a major real-estate purchase, is dated from the tenth day of Simânu (June) of the eponymy of Shulmu-sharri, that is, 698.[39] If the name of Urdu-Mullissu can be restored in a lacuna, it would mean that he was already crown prince at that time, which would have been a logical decision on the part of Sennacherib after the installation of Ashur-nâdin-shumi as king of Babylon. Two other texts, number 130, dated from 696, and number 85, dated from the ninth day of Tebêtu (January) 692, mentioning the title *mār šarri*, could also refer to Urdu-Mullissu.[40] The fact that Urdu-Mullissu swore an oath of fealty to Esarhaddon, the new crown prince, does not mean that he was not the previous crown prince but that he had no other choice but to swear oath.[41] Moreover, it is quite unlikely that Sennacherib did not designate a crown prince before 683, after twenty-one years of reign.

---

35. SAA 6:xxvii–xxxiv.
36. SAA 6:93, 103.4–5; Simo Parpola, "The Murderer of Sennacherib," in *Death in Mesopotamia*, ed. Bendt Alster, RAI 26 (Copenhagen: Akademisk, 1980), 174–75.
37. RINAP 3.2:260–67, nos. 179–85; *PNA* 1.1:189 (with bibliography).
38. Walker, "Some Mesopotamian Inscribed Vessels," 84–86 (BM 93088).
39. SAA 6:90–91, no. 100.
40. SAA 6:73–74, 85.r.7; 117–18, 130.r.11.
41. SAAS 9:22–23.

However, four other texts concerning royal charioteers, dated from 694 to 693, raise a difficulty. Three of them (nos. 37, 39, and 40) mention "Sama', horse raiser of the *mār šarri*" as witness of the transaction, while text 41 mentions "Sama', horse raiser of Nergal-shumu-[…]."[42] It is important to note that text 37 (694-VII-1) was practically contemporary with text 103 (694-VII-12), referring to Urdu-Mullissu, the crown prince. As Sama' was mentioned alternatively as "horse raiser of the crown prince" and "of Nergal-shumu-[ibni]" in 694 and 693, it could mean that Nergal-shumu-ibni was then crown prince of Babylonia (?), in parallel with Urdu-Mullissu, crown prince of Assyria, in view of the later parallel of Ashurbanipal and Shamash-shumu-ukîn.[43]

Thus, Urdu-Mullissu was probably appointed crown prince of Assyria at least from 698. It has to be confirmed whether Nergal-shumu-ibni was appointed as crown prince of Babylonia in 693. Even if we have no information on the crown prince(s) during the following years, it leads one to suppose that there was no change. Therefore, when did Esarhaddon in turn become crown prince? Two later texts concern Se'madi, village manager of the crown prince: text 109, dated from 683, and text 110, dated from the sixteenth of Addaru (March) 681, just twelve (or two) days before Esarhaddon's accession.[44] The following text of Se'madi, number 111, dated from Tashrîtu (October) 680, no longer mentions his title of village manager of the crown prince.[45] These texts have been interpreted as follows: the crown prince referred to in the two texts dated from 683 and 681 was Esarhaddon, and his title has disappeared from the third text because he had then become king of Assyria. It has been suggested that the nomination of Esarhaddon took place either in Nisannu (April) 683 or in 682.[46] According to the preceding legal texts, it is possible to propose 683 as the most likely time for the appointment of Esarhaddon as crown prince of Assyria, possibly in the month of Nisannu (April), during the New Year Festival at the Akîtu temple of Assur. In the twenty-second year of Sen-

---

42. SAA 6:40, 37.r.7; 41–42, 39.16; 42–43, 40.r.4; 43–44, 41.r.5.

43. *PNA* 2.2:956; SAA 6:xxxii–xxxiv and n. 59. Nergal-shumu-ibni was restored on the basis of SAA 6:150, 186.7', dated from 683.

44. SAA 6:xxxiii–xxxiv, 100, 109.6; 100–101, 110.7; Grayson, *Assyrian and Babylonian Chronicles*, 82, chr. 1, iii.38 (eighteen or twenty-eight).

45. SAA 6:101–2, 111.9.

46. Simo Parpola, "Neo-Assyrian Treaties from the Royal Archives of Nineveh," *JCS* 39 (1987): 164–70; SAA 9:lxxii.

nacherib (683), he dedicated personnel to the newly built Akîtu temple, possibly in relation with Esarhaddon's appointment.[47] This appointment could also be related with a gift made by Sennacherib to his son, golden bracelets, a golden crown and necklace, and rings for the upper arm: "I gave to Esarhaddon, my son, who henceforth shall be called Ashur-etellu-ilâni-mukîn-apli, as a token of love. (From) the booty of Bît-Amukâni."[48] The inscription is undated, but it is stated that his name shall be changed to Ashur-etellu-ilâni-mukîn-apli, "Assur, prince of the gods, is establishing an heir," which means that the gift was made at the time of his promotion to crown prince. The booty from Bît-Amukâni refers to one of Sennacherib's Babylonian campaigns, the last one being in 689. However, it gives no indication of the date of the gift. A small stone lion head from Sippar or Nineveh, given by Sennacherib to Esarhaddon, is also undated: in a damaged passage, he is called DUMU-šú GAL?, translated as "his senior-ranking son," which would mean that the gift was offered after his official nomination as heir designate.[49]

How can the nomination of Esarhaddon as crown prince be explained? This choice was not obvious, first because he was Sennacherib's youngest son, and second because he had a chronically debilitating illness that ultimately killed him and that was already visible when he was crown prince.[50] Esarhaddon himself gives an explanation of his father's choice: "I am my older brothers' youngest brother (and) by the command of the gods Assur, Sîn, Shamash, Bêl, and Nabû, Ishtar of Nineveh, and Ishtar of Arbela, (my) father, who engendered me, elevated me firmly in the assembly of my brothers, saying: 'This is the son who will succeed me.' He questioned the gods Shamash and Adad by divination, and they answered him with a firm 'yes,' saying: 'He is your replacement.'"[51] Beyond this divine explanation, what was the true reason for Sennacherib's choice? Most authors considered that Naqi'a/Zakûtu, one of his wives, had such influence over him that she convinced him to do this unprecedented deed.[52] However, while

---

47. SAA 12:104–8, no. 86.
48. SAA 12:xv and n. 10, and 109, no. 88. The copyist has omitted *ilāni*.
49. RINAP 3.2:339–40, no. 233 and fig. 30.
50. SAA 10:266–67, 328.15–18; Grayson, *Assyrian and Babylonian Chronicles*, 86, chr. 1, iv.30–31.
51. RINAP 4:11–12, 1.i.8–14.
52. See p. 16; also, e.g., Hildegard Lewy, "Nitokris-Naqi'a," *JNES* 11 (1952): 271–72; Reade, "Was Sennacherib a Feminist?," 142; Albert Kirk Grayson, "Assyrian Civi-

her important role is documented during the reigns of her son Esarhaddon and grandson Ashurbanipal, evidence is lacking for the reign of Sennacherib; hence Melville does not consider that Naqi'a was entirely responsible for Sennacherib's choice.[53] She probably supported his son's advancement, but she was not representing a minor because, in 683, Esarhaddon was about thirty years old. Therefore, Naqi'a probably had played a role in Sennacherib's decision, but Esarhaddon most likely did too, meaning that it was a combination of factors that explained the king's decision. According to Parpola, Esarhaddon was possibly the only son born after the usurped accession of Sargon, while his elder brothers were born before, but it was not a usurpation.[54] Esarhaddon seems to have had a "messianic" dimension: he was regarded as the legitimate heir by the prophets; he had been raised by his divine mother, the goddess Mullissu.[55] In addition, he had a human mother, whose name Naqi'a ("pure," "innocent") reminds one of the holy goddess herself: in the eyes of the prophets, he was the god-chosen Assyrian king to defeat the forces of evil, to restore order, and to save the country.

Sennacherib's decision caused a great deal of internal strife. The most strongly shocked was probably Urdu-Mullissu, the next-oldest son, especially if he had been crown prince for some fifteen years. Sennacherib must have been aware of the trouble his decision provoked, and he decided to contain it by imposing an oath of loyalty. This succession treaty was found in the excavations of Assur, but its state is fragmentary, and it is impossible to say how much is missing. The name of Sennacherib is preserved, but the name of Esarhaddon is missing: "You shall protect [*Esarhaddon*, the crown prince designated, and] the other princes [whom Sennacherib, king of Assyria, had presen]ted to you."[56] This treaty is mentioned in the inscriptions of Esarhaddon: "Before the gods Assur, Sîn, Shamash, Nabû, (and) Marduk, the gods of Assyria, the gods who live in heaven and netherworld, he (Sennacherib) made them swear their solemn oath(s)

---

lization," in *The Assyrian and Babylonian Empires and Other States of the Near East, from the Eighth to the Sixth Centuries B.C.*, ed. John Boardman et al., 2nd ed., CAH 3.2 (Cambridge: Cambridge University Press 1991), 121.

53. SAAS 9:22–29.
54. SAA 9:xliii and n. 206; Elayi, *Sargon II, King of Assyria*, 25–32.
55. SAA 9:xlii–xliv (with bibliography).
56. SAA 2:18, no. 3.

concerning the safe-guarding of my succession."⁵⁷ No doubt everybody, including Urdu-Mullissu and his brothers, was obliged to take the oath. This succession treaty was followed by Esarhaddon's admission into the house of succession: "In a favorable month, on a propitious day, in accordance with their sublime command, I joyfully entered the House of succession, an awe-inspiring place within which the appointment to kingship (takes place)."⁵⁸ Apparently, Sennacherib felt that he could control the situation, because he did not estrange his other sons from Nineveh. They remained at the court of Nineveh in close contact with Esarhaddon, and they caused him trouble by plotting behind his back, as he reports in his inscriptions: "Evil rumors, calumnies they started against me, (and) slander about me against the will of the gods, and they were constantly telling insincere lies, hostile things behind my back. They alienated the well-meaning heart of my father from me against the will of the gods, (but) deep down he was compassionate and his eyes were permanently fixed on my exercising kingship."⁵⁹ According to Parpola, the rumors spread by Esarhaddon's brothers concerned his illness.⁶⁰ The king's illness could not be kept secret because it was visible and was known at the court of Nineveh. Moreover, it is possible that, during this period, Esarhaddon suffered a bout of illness that would have handicapped him for reigning.⁶¹ Anyway, when the aim is to bring discredit on somebody, it is always easy to spread all kinds of calumnies and false rumors. His brothers tried to discredit him in particular before Sennacherib in order to make the king change his mind. This period lasted from the appointment of Esarhaddon as crown prince and the loyalty oath in 683 to his departure in Nisannu (April) 681. Esarhaddon held out against the calumnies of his brothers, probably with the help of his mother, Naqi'a. After an ideal period where the future was assured for her and her son, opposition to the nomination of Esarhaddon started to gain momentum. No doubt she was striving to counteract the negative reports about Esarhaddon that were reaching Sennacherib. In particular, she resorted to extispicy, astrology, and oracles to obtain favorable signs. Several oracles were consulted by her

---

57. RINAP 4:12, 1.17–19.
58. RINAP 4:12, 1.20–22; SAA 9:lxxii.
59. RINAP 4:12, 1.25–31; SAA 9:lxxii.
60. Parpola, *Letters from Assyrian Scholars to the Kings Esarhaddon and Assurbanipal*, 235.
61. SAA 10:266, 328.o.15–18.

and Esarhaddon because of the severity of the situation and the necessity to get a prognostication concerning the future of the kingship.[62] Bêl-ushezib, a well-known Babylonian astrologer, sent a letter to Esarhaddon, two months after his accession, in which he reminded him what he had done to support him earlier: "I told the omen of the kingship of my lord Esarhaddon the crown prince, to the exorcist Dadâ, and to the mother of the king."[63]

At the beginning of 681, around Nisannu (April), the conspiracy against Esarhaddon for succession was more severe, and the situation became very dangerous for the crown prince. He was obliged to run away from Nineveh. The explanation that he reported in his inscriptions was based on a divine intervention. After having thought it over, he became sure that his brothers could not do anything against the will of the gods. Therefore, he prayed to the god Assur, king of the gods, and Marduk, the Babylonian god taken from Babylon, who hated treacherous talk. They answered his prayers and saved his life for his future kingship: "By the command of the great gods, my lords, they settled me in a secret place (*ašar niṣirti*) away from the evil deeds, stretched out their pleasant protection over me, and kept me safe for (exercising) kingship."[64] In what conditions did Esarhaddon leave Nineveh? Was it an exile? Was it a protective measure taken by Sennacherib in favor of the crown prince for safety's sake? Authors do not agree on this point: Esarhaddon would have been exiled either because he was temporally in disfavor or was himself complotting against his father (and finally killing him).[65] This theory is unlikely because Sennacherib did not change the crown prince, who remained Esarhaddon, as he claimed in his inscriptions. His decision to protect the crown prince by sending him away seems to be more logical due to the fact that he had not chosen another heir.[66] Esarhaddon's removal from the court of Nineveh lasted approximately nine months. Where he stayed during this long period is

---

62. SAAS 7:14–34.

63. SAA 10:109; René Labat, "Asarhaddon et la ville de Zaqqap," *RA* 53 (1959): 113–18; Parpola, "Murderer of Sennacherib," 179 n. 41; SAAS 7:89–95.

64. RINAP 4:12, 1.i.32–42.

65. Frame, *Babylonia 689–627 B.C.*, 63–64; Benno Landsberger and T. Bauer, "Zu neuveröffentlichen Geschichtsquellen der Zeit von Asarhaddon bis Nabonid," *ZA* 37 (1927): 69; Wolfram Von Soden, *Herrscher im alten Orient*, Verständliche Wissenschaft 25 (Berlin: Springer, 1954), 118.

66. SAAS 9:24–25; Labat, "Asarhaddon et la ville de Zaqqap," 113–18.

not revealed in Esarhaddon's inscriptions. The location of this place has been much debated: for example, it has been suggested that the crown prince found a safe haven with family in Harrân.⁶⁷ In the meantime, in Nineveh, the situation was so disrupted that the traditional institution of eponymate was perturbed. An Assyrian document is dated on the fifth of Ayyaru (May) of the "eponymy after Nabû-sharru-usur," that is, in 681: this situation of unrest may have prevented the appointment of the new eponym at the right time.⁶⁸ What happened to Naqi'a during this period? Based on the assumption that she had immense influence over Sennacherib, some authors suggested that she wielded a new power, for example, as governor of Babylonia.⁶⁹ However, this theory is not documented.⁷⁰ It has also been suggested that Sennacherib gave her a new status, involving her at his side in religious ceremonies, in the context of his religious reform.⁷¹

6.3. Sennacherib's Murder

Esarhaddon's absence created a stalemate for his brothers. He had been removed, but the succession remained unchanged as Sennacherib persisted in his decision: Esarhaddon was still the crown prince, and he had supporters in Nineveh, in particular among the prophets and soothsayers who delivered several oracles in his favor.⁷² These supports probably prompted his brothers to act. As a matter of fact, they could not achieve anything by waiting; consequently they opted for action. This moment is described

---

67. Erle Leichty, "Esarhaddon's Exile: Some Speculative History," in *Studies Presented to Robert D. Biggs*, ed. Martha T. Roth, Walter Farber, and Matthew W. Stolper, AS 27 (Chicago: Oriental Institute of the University of Chicago, 2007), 189–91; Mordechai Cogan, "Sennacherib and the Angry Gods of Babylon and Israel," *IEJ* 59 (2009): 164.

68. Mogens Trolle Larsen, "Unusual Eponymy-Datings from Mari and Assyria," *RA* 68 (1974): 22; C. H. W. Johns, *Assyrian Deeds and Documents Recording the Transfer of Property, Including the So-Called Private Contracts, Legal Decisions and Proclamations Preserved in the Kouyunjik Collections of the British Museum Chiefly of the 7th Century B.C.* (Cambridge: Deighton Bell, 1898–1923), no. 213; Frame, *Babylonia 689–627 B.C.*, 63.

69. Lewy, "Nitokris-Naqi'a," 272–77.

70. Rykle Borger, review of Benno Landsberger, *Brief des Bischofs von Esagila an König Asarhaddon*, in *BiOr* 29 (1972): 34–35.

71. See p. 165; Reade, "Was Sennacherib a Feminist?," 142–45; SAAS 9:25–28.

72. SAAS 9:28–29 (with bibliography).

in Esarhaddon's inscriptions: "Afterwards, my brothers went out of their minds and did everything that is displeasing to the gods and mankind, and they plotted evil, girt (their) weapons, and in Nineveh, without the gods, they butted each other like kids for (the right to) exercise kingship."[73] Sennacherib was killed on the twentieth of Tebêtu (January) 681. The date is provided by the Babylonian Chronicles: "On the twentieth day of the month Tebêtu, Sennacherib, king of Assyria, was killed in a rebellion. For [*twenty-four*] years Sennacherib ruled Assyria."[74] Sennacherib's murder is only alluded to in veiled terms in Esarhaddon's inscriptions: "The gods ... saw the deeds of the usurpers which had done wrongly against the will of the gods and they did not support them."[75] However, this event, which had a deep and lasting impact on the people of the ancient Near East, is recorded in numerous sources, all of them later, except for a letter dated from 680, possibly to Esarhaddon, and for the contemporaneous Babylonian Chronicles.[76] It can be understood that the Babylonians were not worried that Sennacherib was dead after his destruction of Babylon.

Where was he killed and how? According to the inscriptions of Ashurbanipal, he was killed in his palace of Nineveh, next to the colossi: "The rest of the people, alive, by the colossi, between which they had cut down Sennacherib, the father of the father who begot me,—at that time, I cut down those people there, as an offering to his shade. Their dismembered bodies I fed to the dogs, swine, wolves, and eagles, to the birds of heaven and the fish of the deep."[77] This action of revenge occurred during his sixth campaign, against the rebels of Babylonia, some thirty years after the murder of Sennacherib. It is not specified who these people responsible for the murder of the king of Assyria were: Esarhaddon's brothers, or other persons involved in the plot? According to the Bible also, the murder took place in Nineveh: "He returned home and stayed in Nineveh. One day when he was worshiping in the temple of his god Nisroch, his sons Adrammelech and Sharezer struck him down with the sword and escaped into the territory of Ararat. His son Esarhaddon succeeded him" (2 Kgs 19:36-37; Isa 37:38); "When he went into the temple of his god, some of his own

---

73. RINAP 4:12, 1.i.42–44.

74. Grayson, *Assyrian and Babylonian Chronicles*, 81, chr. 1, iii.34–36.

75. RINAP 4:13, 1.i.45–48.

76. SAA 16:xix, 88–89, 95.3; Ivantchik, *Les Cimmériens au Proche-Orient*, 53–57, 1.10; *PNA* 3.1:1121 (with bibliography).

77. *ARAB* 2.795.

sons there struck him down with the sword" (2 Chr 32:21). Instead of an unknown Assyrian god, Nisroch (Nusku or Ninurta?), Edward Lipiński proposed to read *byt srk(n)*, Bet-Sarruk(in), Sargon's new capital (Dûr-Sharrukîn/Khorsabad), and to correct *mištaḥaweh*, "worshiping," into *mišteh*, "banquet."[78] This interpretation seems to be unlikely because it is based on two corrections of the text. The biblical statement according to which Sennacherib was killed with a sword (*b-ḥrb*) might be a pun on the king's name.[79] It has also been suggested that he was possibly crushed alive under a winged bull-colossus guarding the temple where he was praying at the time of the murder.[80]

The question as to who was (were) the murderer(s) of Sennacherib has been much debated.[81] A first consideration of good sense is that a plot against a king by the king's son does not usually involve more than one prince because, if the plot succeeds, the new king would be tempted to kill his brother(s), accomplice(s), and potential rivals. Esarhaddon himself was suspected because of the silence of his inscriptions with regard to the circumstances that led to the murder of his father, because he was the one who benefited most from the crime, because his banishment for safety is a unique phenomenon, because Esarhaddon's succession lasted only six weeks, and because he completely reversed his father's policy.[82]

---

78. Edward Lipiński, "Bet-Sarruk(in)," in *Dictionnaire Encyclopédique de la Bible* (Paris: Brépols, 1987), 208–9; followed by Stefan Zawadski, "Oriental and Greek Tradition about the Death of Sennacherib," *SAAB* 4 (1990): 69.

79. Garsiel, *Biblical Names*, 47.

80. Maximilian Streck, *Assurbanipal und die letzten assyrischen Könige bis zum Untergange Niniveh's*, VAB 7.1–3 (Leipzig: Hinrichs, 1916), 38, iv, ll. 70–71; Parpola, "Murderer of Sennacherib," 175 and n. 44.

81. Friedrich Schmidtke, *Asarhaddons Statthalterschaft in Babylonien und seine Thronbesteigung in Assyrien 681 v. Chr.*, AOTU 1.2 (Leiden: Brill, 1916), 105, with earlier literature; Landsberger and Bauer, "Zu neuveröffentlichen Geschichtsquellen der Zeit von Asarhaddon bis Nabonid," 65–69; Hans Hirschberg, *Studien zur Geschichte Esarhaddons König von Assyrien* (Ohlau in Schlesien: Eschenhagen, 1932); Von Soden, *Herrscher im alten Orient*, 118–26; Parpola, "Murderer of Sennacherib," 171–82; Oded Tammuz, "Punishing a Dead Villain: The Biblical Accounts of the Murder of Sennacherib," *BN* 157 (2013): 101–5 (with bibliography).

82. Landsberger and Bauer, "Zu neuveröffentlichen Geschichtsquellen der Zeit von Asarhaddon bis Nabonid," 69; Von Soden, *Herrscher im alten Orient*, 118–26; Knut L. Tallqvist, "Arad-Bēlit," in *Assyrian Personal Names*, Acta Societatis Scientiarum Fennicae 43.1 (Helsinki: Societas Orientalis Fennica, 1918), 25b; Tammuz, "Punishing a Dead Villain," 103; M. J. De Jong, " 'Fear Not, O King!' The Assyrian

However, all these arguments are not decisive, and this hypothesis is groundless if we accept that Esarhaddon was the crown prince: he had no interest to kill his father, and moreover he was far from Nineveh at the time of his murder. The name of the murderer is not known from any cuneiform text, and the names mentioned by the Bible and Berossus were obviously textually corrupted. Following an ancient theory, these names would have been corruptions of Ardi/Arad-Ninlil, a son of Sennacherib, known from a contemporary legal document.[83] Parpola was the first author to identify Sennacherib's murderer in a letter dealing with a conspiracy against the king, which was misunderstood by Leroy Waterman, its editor.[84] A group of Babylonian inhabitants heard about the conspiracy, and one of them tried to inform Sennacherib about it. This informer conformed to an Assyrian law allowing subjects to appeal to the king as the supreme judge. Therefore he requested an audience with the king and was received by two officials, Nabû-shuma-ishkun and Sillâ. He was led before the supposed king, who, as usual, had his face covered, and he said: "Urdu-Mullissu, your son, is going to kill you!" Unfortunately, the two officials were members of the conspiracy, and the informer was taken not to Sennacherib but to Urdu-Mullissu himself. He was killed, and the attempt to inform the king about the conspiracy against him was thwarted. Parpola reconsidered the two names mentioned in the Bible: the name Adrammelek (*'drmlk*) differs from the Assyrian name only in two respects: the metathesis of *r* and *d*, and the replacement of *š* by *k* at the end of the name. The second biblical name, Sharezer (*śr'ṣr*), is not a name but ironically meant "God save the king" (*šarru-uṣur*); an alternative speculative hypothesis is that the biblical name could be identified with Nabû-sharru-usur, governor of Marash/Marqasi, eponym of the year 682 and possibly another of Sennacherib's sons.[85] Ardumuzan, mentioned by

---

Prophecies as a Case for a Comparative Approach," *JEOL* 38 (2003–2004): 113–15; Stephanie Dalley, *Esther's Revenge at Susa: From Sennacherib to Ahasuerus* (Oxford: Oxford University Press, 2007), 37–41; Knapp, *Royal Apologetic in the Ancient Near East*, 320–24.

83. Johns, *Assyrian Deeds and Documents*, no. 201:5; Schmidtke, *Asarhaddons Statthalterschaft in Babylonien und seine hronbesteigung in Assyrien 681 v. Chr.*, 105 (with bibliography).

84. Waterman, *Royal Correspondence of the Assyrian Empire*, no. 1091; Parpola, "Murderer of Sennacherib," 172–75; SAA 18:82, no. 100.

85. *PNA* 3.1:1115; SAA 6:xli and n. 59; Tammuz, "Punishing a Dead Villain," 101–5.

Berossus, and Adremelos, mentioned by Abydenus, are both referring to Urdu-Mullissu.[86] The names Andromachos and Seleukaros, given by Josephus, are distorted.[87] The account of the assassination of Semiramis, as presented by Nicolaus of Damascus, provides proof in agreement with real facts concerning the circumstances of the death of Sennacherib.[88] Even if "it cannot be definitively proven," as stated by Grayson,[89] Parpola's theory regarding Esarhaddon's noninvolvement in the death of his father is the most likely in the present state of documentation.

What were the reasons for Sennacherib's murder? Several reasons are provided by the different sources. When news of the murder reached Babylonia and Judah, it was probably perceived as divine punishment imposed by the gods for his misdeeds. According to an inscription of the Babylonian king Nabonidus: "He (Sennacherib) planned evil; he thought out crimes [agai]nst the country; he had no mercy for the people [of Babylon]. With evil intentions he advanced on Babylon, he turned his sanctuaries to waste; he made the ground plan unrecognizable; he desecrated the cultic rites. He led the lord Marduk away and brought him to the city of Assur."[90] For the Babylonians, Sennacherib was the savage king who had destroyed Babylon and spread havoc throughout the land eight years earlier. The murder of Sennacherib was received by the Judeans in the same way as by the Babylonians, because they too had suffered greatly at the hands of the Assyrian conqueror, even though twenty years had elapsed between the end of the Assyrian military campaign against Judah and the murder of 681. The two events are juxtaposed in the Bible in order to create the impression of immediacy and to persuade readers that Yahweh always punishes evil deeds (2 Kgs 19:36–37). Isaiah answers to Hezekiah's ministers: "Yahweh says this: 'Do not be afraid of the words which you have heard or the blasphemies which the king of Assyria's minions have uttered against me. Look, I am going to put a spirit

---

86. Burstein, *Babyloniaca of Berossus*, 24–25; Tammuz, "Punishing a Dead Villain," 101–5 (with bibliography).

87. Josephus, *A.J.* 10.23.

88. Friedrich Wilhelm König, *Die Persika des Ktesias von Knidos*, AfOB 18 (Graz: Im Selbstverlage des Heraugebers, 1972), 40; Zawadski, "Oriental and Greek Tradition about the Death of Sennacherib," 71–72.

89. Grayson, "Assyrian Civilization," 121.

90. Hanspeter Schaudig, *Die Inschriften Nabonids von Babylon und Kyros' des Grossen*, AOAT 256 (Münster: Ugarit-Verlag, 2001), 516–22; Cogan, "Sennacherib and the Angry Gods of Babylon and Israel," 165–68.

in him and, on the strength of a rumour, he will go back to his own country, and in that country I shall make him fall by the sword'" (2 Kgs 19:6–7).

In fact, Sennacherib is depicted as playing a contradictory role, both in the Bible and in the Babylonian inscriptions. According to Isaiah, Yahweh used Sennacherib to punish his people: "Woe to Assyria, rod of my anger, the club in their hands is my fury! I was sending him against a godless nation, commissioning him against the people who enraged me, to pillage and plunder at will and trample on them like the mud in the streets" (Isa 10:5–6). Marduk also wanted to punish Babylon through the agency of Sennacherib, as is stated in Nabonidus's inscriptions: "The king of Subartu (Sennacherib), who in accord with Marduk's anger, had laid waste to the country, his very own son struck him down."[91] How could he be at one and the same time the executor of divine punishment of angry gods and the object of divine judgment?[92] In the text mentioning the "sin" of Sargon, he is accused of having been punished because he had built a statue of Assur, but not a statue of Marduk, as he had promised; moreover, he did so on the advice of the scribes.[93] Esarhaddon tries very skillfully to mask the major fault of the sacrilege of Sennacherib under a minor fault he was not even responsible for, as he had been misled by the scribes.

When Esarhaddon came to the throne of Assyria in 680, he needed to provide an explanation for his reversal of his father's policy toward Babylon. He rewrote the account of the destruction of Babylon, where he masked the fault of Sennacherib in accusing the Babylonians of being responsible for this destruction. They rebelled against Assyria and committed a sacrilege by taking out the treasure of the Esagil in order to pay for Elamite support: "They opened the treasure of Esagil and s[ent] my gift(s)—the silver, gold, (and) precio[us stones that] I had given as presents [to the god Bêl (Marduk) and the goddess Zarpanîtu] the property (and) possession(s) of the temple of the[ir] gods—[as a bribe (ṭa-a'-tú)] to Humban-menânu, the king of the land of Elam."[94] Moreover, the Baby-

---

91. Schaudig, *Die Inschriften Nabonidus von Babylon und Kyros' des Grossen*, 516–22.

92. Cogan, "Sennacherib and the Angry Gods of Babylon and Israel," 170–72.

93. Van De Mieroop, "Revenge, Assyrian Style," 15–17; Tadmor, Landsberger, and Parpola, "Sin of Sargon and Sennacherib's Last Will," 3–51; Elayi, *Sargon II, King of Assyria*, 213–17.

94. RINAP 3.2:198, 146.10–13; 3.2:200, 147.10–13; 3.2:330, 230.13b–14a; Moinard, *Les mauvais traitements envers les dieux*, 72–74.

lonians performed evil deeds: they "split into factions, plotting rebellion, [forsaking their gods], abandoning [the worship] of the goddess of their cult, and going away to other (lands)"; Marduk, their protective god, was very angry at them: "For the overthrow of the land and the destruction of its people he devised evil plans."[95] It was not Sennacherib but Marduk who planned to destroy Babylon, not by weapons but by using natural elements such as the Arahtu canal. The gods were not crushed by Sennacherib, as he said in his inscriptions; they decided to leave: "The gods (and) goddesses, who dwelt therein, went up to heaven."[96] The aim of Esarhaddon was to exonerate his father from any aspect of impiety, by imposing a religious and nonhistorical perspective on the destruction of Babylon: it was the fault of the Babylonians and the decision of Marduk. The only thing that Sennacherib did was to obey Marduk's orders. Esarhaddon intended to rewrite history in order to reconcile Assyria and Babylonia, following a pro-Babylonian trend. He was also distressed by his father's crimes, and hence he was anxious to dissociate himself from them, and he tried to minimize and repair them throughout the whole of his reign.

Now, what were the true reasons for Sennacherib's murder? Above all, it has to be put in the larger context of ancient Near Eastern dynasties, for example, in Mesopotamia, Egypt, and Persia. Such murders, regicide and parricide, were favored by the ambiguity of the succession rules, the multiplication of possible legitimate heirs, the rivalry between the different wives and family branches, and by harem intrigues.[97] Urdu-Mullissu, the legitimate heir, did not accept the prospect of being supplanted by Esarhaddon, his father's youngest son. Whatever the other possible reasons for Sennacherib's choice, the influence of Naqi'a probably played a role, and Esarhaddon was possibly, or pretended to be, of the same political opinions as his father.[98] Anyhow, he was clever enough to obtain the support of the religious circles at the court of Nineveh. Yet there was a general agreement against him: the opposition was led by Sennacherib's other sons, starting with Urdu-Mullissu, the second-oldest son after Shamash-shumu-ukîn, his deceased brother. The murder of Sennacherib occurred

---

95. *ARAB* 2.649.
96. *ARAB* 2.642.
97. Sharif Bujanda Viloria, "Regicidio e intrigas de harén: Las muertes de Ramsés III y de Senaquerib, fuentes antiguas, perspectivas modernas," *Fuentes Humanísticas* 29.51 (2015): 109–21.
98. Pečirková, "Assyria under Sennacherib," 10.

on the twentieth of Tebêtu (January) 681, and Esarhaddon ascended the throne on the twenty-eighth/eighteenth of Addaru (March). There was a time lapse of more than six weeks. Esarhaddon was undoubtedly in close contact with Naqi'a and his supporters and was immediately apprised of what had occurred in Nineveh. First, he had to return from the place where he had been living for the last nine months, and he had to assemble his army and supporters. Most of the time was probably devoted to crushing the rebellion. It is clearly mentioned in the Babylonian Chronicles: "The rebellion continued in Assyria from the twentieth day of the month Tebêtu until the second day of the month Addaru."[99] From the second day of Addaru, when the rebellion was crushed, to the twenty-eighth/eighteenth day, when he acceded to the throne, there must have been a fair amount of "cleaning up" to do in Nineveh.[100] Judging from the scope of the rebellion, the rebels must have had the support of a large part of Assyrian society. They were probably joined not only by the military party of the court and by cities profiting from imperial wars but also by all the people to whom Assyrian tradition, in particular for royal succession, was sacred.[101] Why did Urdu-Mullissu not take advantage of his murder to seize power, as he had planned to do at the outset? Probably because he had to fight against his brothers, who were also ambitious, and he was unable to assert his influence over them. Esarhaddon defeated the rebels and won this war of succession.[102] He stressed the loyalty treaty established by his father in 683, guaranteed by the gods: "The people of Assyria, who had sworn by the treaty, an oath bound by the great gods, concerning me, came before me and kissed my feet."[103] However, the opposition was so strong that he was obliged to abandon the political aims of his father. This could have been another reason for the murder of Sennacherib: the majority of society regarded his efforts to adapt tradition to the new historical reality of the Assyrian Empire as an offense to the gods, a danger to the existing order.[104]

---

99. Grayson, *Assyrian and Babylonian Chronicles*, 81, chr. 1, iii.36–37.
100. SAAS 9:28–29.
101. Pečirková, "Assyria under Sennacherib," 10.
102. On the place where the rebels took refuge, see Nadav Na'aman, "Sennacherib's Sons' Flight to Urartu," *NABU* (2006): 4–5; Cogan, "Sennacherib and the Angry Gods of Babylon and Israel," 164.
103. RINAP 4:14, 1.i.80–81.
104. See p. 171.

7
Traditions and Reforms

Albert T. Olmstead passed a severe judgment on Sennacherib that persists even now as a stereotyped image: "Sennacherib has been given the fame, in all probability never to be lost, of a savage warrior and nothing more."[1] In the most recent research, this Assyrian king who had the bad idea of destroying Babylon and attacking Judah has been rehabilitated to some extent by several authors, such as Jana Pečirková: "It is a pity that Sennacherib's interesting personality has been overshadowed by his destruction of the sacred city of Babylon."[2] He did have an interesting personality, rather exceptional among Assyrian rulers, particularly because, instead of systematically following tradition without thinking, he tried to adapt it to the new historical reality of the Assyrian Empire. He was a farsighted and open-minded king who attempted to create a stable imperial structure immune from traditional recurrent problems. Even though, for more than fifteen years, he was a loyal and obedient crown prince, it is clear that, after Sargon's death, he did not adhere to all the political views of his father. Sennacherib's reign marked a major break with the past, in particular because he rejected Sargon's pro-Babylonian policy and adopted a vigorous Assyrocentric policy.[3] When he came to the throne, even though suddenly and unexpectedly, he was a man of great administrative and political experience. He seems to have already decided on the strategy of his reign, and maybe had still earlier, when he was crown prince. When he became king, he understood that it was impossible to reform the Assyrian Empire

---

1. Albert T. Olmstead, *History of Assyria* (Chicago: University of Chicago Press, 1923), 334.

2. Pečirková, "Assyria under Sennacherib," 7. See also Julian E. Reade, "Studies in Assyrian Geography. Part I: Sennacherib and the Waters of Nineveh," *RA* 72 (1978): 47; Reade, "Was Sennacherib a Feminist?," 139–45; *PNA* 3.1:1123–24.

3. Tadmor, "Sennacherib, King of Justice," 388–89.

immediately and on a large scale. Therefore, the beginning of his reign was not marked by any radical changes in imperial politics but by some discreet and progressive changes.

7.1. Main Reforms

First, he omits mention of his royal parentage in his inscriptions. Genealogy is missing only in cases of usurpation, and he was not a usurper. The tradition was respected, as he was the oldest son of Sargon and his legitimate successor. The omission of his genealogy is possibly a means of showing right away his antagonism to the political-religious orientation of his father. Moreover, he was not strictly observing the traditional right of succession to the throne: for example, Bêl-ibni, the puppet king whom he installed on the throne of Babylon, was "the son of a builder." Finally, he chose as crown prince Esarhaddon, his youngest son, whose health was bad, whereas tradition required that serving the gods for example necessitated being perfect in body.[4] In the text related to the "sin" of Sargon, the fact that he attempted to find out the reason for his death through extispicy was maybe a means to distance himself from his father's policy, which had provoked his death.[5]

As war and expansion were institutionalized in the form of annual campaigns, Sennacherib did not make any radical change in this matter, creating opportunities to enrich Assyrian society through booty and trading possibilities. However, his campaigns did not occur systematically each year, and he changed their dating system, not yearly, as in Sargon's inscriptions, but by numbering them. Moreover, almost all the campaigns that he undertook were defensive, intended to consolidate the empire, and not offensive, for its expansion, as his predecessors did. Sennacherib did not add any new province to the Assyrian Empire.[6] In fact, the Assyrian

---

4. Hayim Tadmor, "Autobiographical Apology in the Royal Assyrian Litterature," in *History, Historiography and Interpretation*, ed. Hayim Tadmor and Moshe Weinfeld (Jerusalem: Magnes, 1983), 36–57; Oded, *War, Peace and Empire*, 74; Pečirková, "Assyria under Sennacherib," 10.

5. SAA 3:76, no. 33.

6. Karen Radner, "The Assur-Nineveh-Arbela Triangle, Central Assyria in the Neo-Assyrian Period," in *Between the Cultures: The Central Tigris Region from the Third to the First Millennium*, ed. Peter A. Miglus and Simone Mühl (Heidelberg: Heidelberger Orientverlag, 2011), 327.

Empire bequeathed by Sargon was more stable and stronger, but not easy to control, because of the minor upheavals in the recently annexed areas and of the major problem of Babylon. On the basis of the approximate figures given in the inscriptions, he deported and resettled more people than his predecessors, close to half a million, with almost half of them coming from Babylonia and most of the deportees being destined for Nineveh.[7] Instead of creating new Assyrian provinces, he preferred to keep some states, after having suppressed their revolts, as buffer states, for example, in the southwest of the Assyrian Empire against the increasing pressure of Egypt. Either he maintained the king who had revolted on the throne, such as Hezekiah on the throne of Judah, or he replaced him by a pro-Assyrian king, such as Sharru-lû-dâri, who took the place of Sidqâ on the throne of Ashkelon.[8] To ensure that the system functioned well, Sennacherib paid attention that the buffer states had roughly the same power, by distributing equal territories among them.

Concerning the Babylonian problem, Sennacherib began to deal with it in the traditional Assyrian way.[9] He kept Babylonia as a vassal state that he ruled personally, but as king of Assyria and not as king of Babylonia, as his predecessors.[10] Yet his reign, once established, did not prove effective. After two successive revolts and a campaign where he regained most of Babylonia, he abandoned his policy and tried a new strategy. He installed on the throne a puppet king, Bêl-ibni, a native Babylonian, supposedly loyal to Assyria. After the failure of Bêl-ibni's three-year reign, Sennacherib attempted a third method of governing Babylonia: he installed on the throne his eldest son, Ashur-nâdin-shumi. This solution lasted without apparent disturbance for six years. Then the loss of his son, the recurring revolts, and his unsuccessful attempts at governing Babylon prompted him to apply the final solution: the destruction of the city.

We lack documents regarding the development of the army under Sennacherib's reign. However, military reforms are referred to in two administrative texts, which involve dividing the royal units between leading members of the royal family.[11] They are also reflected in some terms

---

7. Bustenay Oded, *Mass Deportations and Deportees in the Neo-Assyrian Empire* (Wiesbaden: Reichert, 1979), 20–21, 116–35; SAAS 3.
8. See p. 63.
9. Brinkman, "Sennacherib's Babylonian Problem," 89–95.
10. See p. 135.
11. Stephanie Dalley and John Nicholas Postgate, "New Light on the Composi-

for professions among the witnesses to contracts. For example, the royal units were assigned to the crown prince and to the "household of the Lady of [the House]," that is to say, the queen.[12] In a text dated to the ninth of Simânu (June) of the eponymy of Bêl-êmurrani, that is, 686, two of the witnesses are Mannu-kî-assâr-lê'i and Banûnu, "cohort commanders of the queen"; Nabû-sharru-usur is the "third man of the queen."[13] During Sennacherib's reign, the occurrence of the queen's military units became more frequent.[14] The "royal cohort" (*kiṣir šarrūti*) represented the royal core of the Assyrian army. However, the *kiṣir šarri*, attested as the profession of four witnesses to a slave sale dating to 682, possibly refers here to a much smaller body of troops closely attached to the king.[15] The "royal cohort" was a variety of fighting men, sent on several occasions by Sennacherib to assist governors with local campaigns in Cilicia, Til-garimmu, and Elam.[16] He also created the so-called new cohort of Sennacherib, which appears in the title of Nabû-sharru-usur, governor of Marash/Marqasi.[17] According to John Nicholas Postgate, Sennacherib added troops to the royal cohort, with a governor and a separate "review palace" (*ekal māšarti*). It was a body of troops not commanded via the provincial governors but under the separate command of the king. During the reign of Sennacherib, it was probably based at the seat of the government in Nineveh, a few hundred meters from the principal royal palace.[18]

During his sixth campaign, against Elam in 694, Sennacherib elaborated a new military strategy: a large-scale amphibious assault, having ships made and transported to the mouth of the Euphrates, whence they embarked for the Elamite coast.[19] He enjoyed this campaign, which was a kind of aquatic adventure. He was also a warlord eager to take a city without bloodshed if possible, and to bring it into the Assyrian orbit

---

tion of Sargon's Army," in *The Tablets from Fort Shalmaneser* (Oxford: British School of Archaeology in Iraq, 1984), 28; Fales, *Guerre et paix en Assyrie*, 140–45.

12. SAA 7:6, no. 3; 7, 4.ii.r.7, 12.

13. SAA 6:138, 164.r.3; 138–39, 165.r.6 (date not preserved).

14. Svärd, "Changes in Neo-Assyrian Queenship," 163.

15. SAA 6:153, 192.5–8; 194–95, 246.r.1–2; Postgate, "Invisible Hierarchy," 347; SAAS 11:154.

16. Luckenbill, *Annals of Sennacherib*, 61, ll. 69–71; 62, ll. 6–8; 87, ll. 29–30.

17. SAA 7:6, 3.5–6; 7, 4.7–8.

18. Walther Manitius, "Das stehende Heer der Assyrerkönige und seine Organisation," ZA 24 (1910): 114–17; Postgate, "Invisible Hierarchy," 348–49, 353.

19. See p. 108.

by peaceful means, such as parleys with Judah.[20] In the representations of military events in his palace of Nineveh, there are some of the most remarkable images of camps, quite different from those of Shalmaneser III, for example.[21] The spatial shape of Sennacherib's camps was an elliptical defensive perimeter with walls and towers, enclosing a space containing various items: for example, a representation of the king sitting on a throne, two priests celebrating a ritual, tents, accommodation for the soldiers and the people following the army on campaign. The space was divided into two or three sections. The shape had changed from quadrangular to elliptic between Shalmaneser III and Sennacherib. The elliptic or circular perimeter presented the advantage of not creating dangerous corners, thus preventing the possibility of danger during an assault of the camp: the corner was the most exposed and weakest place, as it broke the defense line of the besieged.[22] The towers were no longer outside the perimeter walls but integrated inside the walls, which gave a smooth outer line of defense for the camp, hence providing better protection. In addition, Sennacherib's camps are represented in a mountainous environment, for assuring a constant and accessible water supply.[23] The function of the two types of representations was different: the role of Salmaneser III's camp seems to be connected with the exaction and collection of tribute and booty by the king; Sennacherib's camp does not seem to be linked to military activities but represents the final conclusion of the narrative of the reliefs.[24]

Scholars have long claimed that Sennacherib reformed the economy of the Assyrian Empire by minting half-shekels, the first coins in antiquity, of which no example has been discovered.[25] This generally accepted

---

20. See p. 77.

21. Maria Gabriella Micale and Davide Nadali, "The Shape of Sennacherib's Camps: Strategic Functions and Ideological Space," *Iraq* 66 (2004): 163–75.

22. Israel Ephaʿal, "The Assyrian Siege Ramp at Lachish: Military and Lexical Aspects," *TA* 11 (1984): 60–61.

23. Micale and Nadali, "Shape of Sennacherib's Camps," 164–65.

24. Micale and Nadali, "Shape of Sennacherib's Camps," 173.

25. Leonard William King, *Cuneiform Texts from Babylonian Tablets in the British Museum* (London: Trustees of the British Museum, 1909), 26:26 and plate 28, l. 18; Sidney Smith, "A Pre-Greek Coinage in the Near East?," *NumC* 5/2 (1922): 177–78; Smith, *Early History of Assyria* (London: Chatto & Windus, 1928), 395; R. Campbell Thompson, *On the Chemistry of the Ancient Assyrians* (London: Luzac, 1925), 62; A. Leo Oppenheim, *Ancient Mesopotamia* (Chicago: University of Chicago Press, 1964),

interpretation among Assyriologists was followed by most numismatists.[26] The basis of the interpretation was a much-quoted passage of the bull inscriptions in which the Assyrian king explains how he created molds for casting copper works, for example, twelve raging lions and twelve magnificent bull colossi. Daniel David Luckenbill translates the key passage as follows: "I built a form of clay and poured bronze into it as in making half-shekel pieces and finished their construction."[27] The ambiguous passage *ki-i pi-ti-iq* 1/2 GÍN.TA.ÀM had been interpreted as evidence for the existence of coinage minted under Sennacherib's reign. The weight of half a shekel was around four grams, which represented a small reference in the comparison used by Sennacherib. The first interpretation of the passage was then "like the casting of half-shekels," related to coins.[28] The second interpretation was that this passage constituted a mere hyperbole, Sennacherib's aim being to exaggerate his competence in bronze casting and to illustrate his simple and effective new method.[29] The third interpretation proposed a translation with a correction to the

---

87; Oppenheim, "Trade in the Ancient Near East," in *Fifth International Congress of Economic History* (Moscow: Academy of Sciences, 1970), 32–34 and n. 55; E. Weidner, "Geld," *RlA* 3:198b; Daniel C. Snell, "Methods of Exchange and Coinage in Ancient Western Asia," in *Civilizations of the Ancient Near East* (New York: Scribner, 1995), 3:1491; Karen Radner, "Money in the Neo-Assyrian Empire," in *Trade and Finance in Ancient Mesopotamia*, ed. Jan Gerrit Dercksen (Leiden: Netherlands Institute for the Near East, 1999), 127 n. 2. On the economy of the Assyrian Empire, see John Nicholas Postgate, "The Economic Structure of the Assyrian Empire," in *Power and Propaganda: A Symposium on Ancient Empires*, ed. Mogens Trolle Larsen, Mesopotamia 7 (Copenhagen: Akademisk, 1979), 193–221.

26. Miriam S. Balmuth, "Remarks on the Appearance of the Earliest Coins," in *Studies Presented to G. M. A. Hanfmann*, ed. David G. Mitten et al. (Cambridge: Harvard University Press, 1971), 3; Andreas Furtwängler, "Neue Beobachtungen zur frühesten Münzprägung," *Schweizerische Numismatische Rundschau* 65 (1986): 157; Christopher Howgego, *Ancient History from Coins* (London: Routledge, 1995), 13. See, however, the reservation of Georges Le Rider, *La naissance de la monnaie: Pratiques monétaires de l'Orient ancien* (Paris: Presses Universitaires de France, 2001), 22.

27. Luckenbill, *Annals of Sennacherib*, 109, l. 18; 123, l. 29.

28. Henry William Frederick Saggs, *The Might That Was Assyria* (London: Sidgwick & Jackson, 1984), 171.

29. Edward Lipiński, "Les temples néo-assyriens et les origines du monnayage," in *State and Temple Economy in the Ancient Near East*, OLA 5–6 (Leuven: Departement Orientalistiek, 1979), 565 and n. 2; Marvin A. Powell, "Money in Mesopotamia," *JESHO* 39 (1996): 231.

text: "as in pouring into one-shekel pieces," insisting on the simplicity of the operation, just as easy for making huge colossi as small figurines.[30] The fourth interpretation was related to objects: "Just like the cast work (of an object weighing only) a half-shekel."[31] The first interpretation is not likely, even if the idea is not impossible, as the minting of coins did take place in Lydia in the seventh century and Carchemish could have played a hub role between the two areas.[32] However, it is inconceivable that the metal of the first coins was copper or bronze and not a precious metal (silver or electrum), as in other mints, and that the coins were cast, not struck, as usual at this time. Moreover, the system of payment used in the Near East before the invention of coinage was weighed silver, as is shown in the nonmonetary hoards discovered in the Levant, Mesopotamia, Iran, and Egypt, which give an idea of the different shapes of weighed metal: bar-shaped ingots, sometimes stamped, intact or cut into various fragments when needed; rings; jewels; plates, both intact or fragmented; and various fragments melted or hacked.[33] Payments in weighed silver were so common in the region that they were still in use even after the diffusion of Greek and Persian coinages, for example in Babylonia, where it was the only currency until the Seleucid period.[34] The second

---

30. Peter Vargyas, "Sennacherib Alleged Half-Shekel Coins," *JNES* 61 (2002): 111–15.

31. Stephanie Dalley, "Neo-Assyrian Textual Evidence for Bronzeworking Centres," in *Bronzeworking Centres of Western Asia c. 1000–539 B.C.*, ed. John Curtis (London: Kegan Paul, 1988), 104; Stephanie Dalley and John Peter Oleson, "Sennacherib, Archimedes and the Water Screw: The Context of Invention in the Ancient World," *Technology and Culture* 44 (2003): 7; RINAP 3.2:51, 42.29'–31'; 3.2:62, 43.82–83; 3.2:72, 44.59–60.

32. Lipiński, "Les temples néo-assyriens et les origines du monnayage," 558 (with bibliography).

33. Lipiński, "Les temples néo-assyriens et les origines du monnayage," 575–78; Peter Calmeyer and Paul Naster, "Münzen," *RlA* 8:404–6; Josette Elayi and Alain G. Elayi, *The Coinage of the Phoenician City of Tyre in the Persian Period* (Leuven: Peeters, 2009), 325–28 (with bibliography).

34. Francis Joannès, "Métaux précieux et moyens de paiement en Babylonie achéménide et hellénistique," *Transeu* 8 (1994): 137–44; Peter Vargyas, "Silver and Money in Achaemenid and Hellenistic Babylonia," in *Assyriologia et Semitica: Festschrift für J. Oelsner*, AOAT 252 (Neukirchen-Vluyn: Neukirchener Verlag, 2000), 513–21; Salvatore Gaspa, "Silver Circulation in the Development of the Private Economy in the Assyrian Empire (Ninth–Seventh Centuries BCE): Considerations on Private Investments, Prices and Prosperity Levels of the Imperial *Elite*," in *Dynamics of Production in*

interpretation is theoretically possible, but no precise translation is provided for the ambiguous passage. The third interpretation would be acceptable for the meaning, but it is based on inaccurate corrections of the text.[35] The fourth interpretation seems to be the most likely, even though all the problems of reading are not solved. The sense of the passage is clear: Sennacherib boasted of having made huge metallic colossi by using clay molds, as easily as others used the same technique for small metallic objects. These objects are said to weigh one-half of a shekel. If he chose to refer to the half-shekel, and not to the shekel, it was not as a unit of weight but as a very small weight, even less than the shekel. Weights of half-shekel, not even as frequent as weights of one shekel, existed,[36] and people knew how light they were. The small metallic objects evoked by Sennacherib could be figurines of animals or animal-shaped weights, which would have been in the same field of comparison as the huge statues. Therefore, there is nothing in the passage of the bull inscriptions that would imply minting coins, and it is generally acknowledged today that the alleged half-shekel coins by Sennacherib never existed.[37]

After moving his capital to Nineveh, he relocated the administrative centers from Nimrud and Khorsabad there. He had implemented some administrative reforms. He had first intended to limit the influence of court officials. This was already a problem for Sargon, who had simply tried to maintain equilibrium of power between them, whose influence neutralized one another and stabilized the empire. Sennacherib decided to give up the eponymate (*limmu*) altogether, because holding the eponymate gave the official more prestige and considerably strengthened his position. Power concentrated in the hands of his closest magnates represented a strong threat for the king, all the more so since, apart from holding court offices, they also controlled their own provinces. The traditional order in the list of eponyms, after the king, was: the "commander-in-chief" (*turtānu*), "palace

---

the Ancient Near East 1300–500 BC, ed. Juan Carlos Moreno García (Oxford: Oxbow, 2016), 125–66.

35. Eckart Frahm, "Wer den Halbschekel nicht ehrt," *NABU* (2005): 50, no. 45.

36. Wilfred G. Lambert, "Another Babylonian Weight," *NABU* (2002): 57, no. 57 (4.0177 grams).

37. Gaspa, "Silver Circulation in the Development of the Private Economy," 127–28. The "Ishtar heads," supposed coins minted by Neo-Assyrian temples, also did not exist: Albert T. Olmstead, "Materials for an Economic History of the Ancient Near East," *Journal of Economic and Business History* 2 (1930): 226, 231; Lipiński, "Les temples néo-assyriens et les origines du monnayage," 566, 569–75.

herald" (*nāgir ekalli*), "chief cupbearer" (*rab šāqê*), "treasurer" (*mašennu*), "governor of the land" (*šakin māti*), "chief eunuch" (*rab ša rēši*), then provincial governors. This order had already been modified by Sargon, who retained only, after the king, the treasurer and the governor of the land, yet under the restrictive name "governor of the Inner city (Assur)" (*šakin Libbi-āli*).[38] Instead of being the first in the list, Sennacherib decided to become eponym seventeen years later, in 687. His decision should probably be linked with a completely changed political situation. By taking up the office of eponym and resigning the composition of new annals, he probably wanted to demonstrate that, after a period of wars, a period of peace had commenced.[39] Assyrian order was introduced into the whole of Babylonia, and military actions on a large scale were no longer necessary. After taking up the office of eponym in 687, Sennacherib did not restore the previous order of succession. The only exception was, in 686, Bêl-êmuranni, "commander of the right" (*turtān imitti*). It is noticeable that, from 692 to 681, the office was taken up exclusively by governors of provinces from the west and northwest: Arpad, Carchemish, Samaria, Hatarikka, Simirra, Que, Kullania, Supite, Marash, and Samal. It is not impossible that there were no more governors of Assyria proper because they had already been in the list and that some of them ruled over noneponymate provinces. However, the most likely explanation is that the order of the list was Sennacherib's deliberate choice. On the one hand, maybe he wished to demonstrate that these provinces were no less important for him than those of Assyria proper. On the other hand, his choice was probably motivated by the strong tension existing between him and the influential people from heartland Assyria. The background to this tension could have been the opposition to his hostile politics toward Babylonia and finally the question of his succession.

Sennacherib's mistrust toward the court officials is also expressed through the disappearance of traditional large-scale processions of officials

---

38. SAAS 2:61; Simonetta Ponchia, "Administrators and Administrated in Neo-Assyrian Times," in *Organization, Representation, and Symbols of Power in the Ancient Near East*, ed. Gernot Wilhelm, RAI 54 (Winona Lake, IN: Eisenbrauns, 2012), 213–24; Heather D. Baker, *Neo-Assyrian Specialists, Crafts, Offices, and Other Professional Designations*, PNA 4.1 (Helsinki: Neo-Assyrian Text Corpus Project, 2017), professions index; Elayi, *Sargon II, King of Assyria*, 42–43.

39. Stefan Zawadski, "The Question of the King's Eponymate in the Later Half of the Eighth Century and the Seventh Century BC," in *Assyria 1995*, ed. Simo Parpola and Robert M. Whiting (Helsinki: Neo-Assyrian Text Corpus Project, 1997), 387–88.

from the reliefs of his palace.[40] It is also significant that he reduced the place of the eunuchs in the reliefs, in contrast to Sargon, who had promoted them as high officials, in particular as military commanders, their physical inability to father children increasing their loyalty to the king.[41] In Sennacherib's reliefs, the eunuchs, recognizable because they were conventionally beardless, are depicted in menial roles, such as carrying equipment.[42] However, in 702, he sent the "chief eunuch" (*rab ša rēši*) to Kish, against Merodach-baladan, as the governors were unable to handle the assault.[43] In 701, he sent him with the "chef cupbearer" (*rab šāqê*), and the "commander-in-chief" (*turtānu*) to Hezekiah of Judah for parleys.[44] The office of "second vizier" (*sukallu šaniu*) was possibly created by him, as it is first attested in around 684 and became eponym in 676.[45] Two damaged administrative texts mentioning Sennacherib[46] comprised a list of high officials: Ashur-gimilli-tirri, treasurer; Aplay]a, palace herald; Shamash-sharru-usur, chief eunuch; Man-ki-Harran, majordomo; and also a chief of the *equipment*, a chief of the replacements, a chief confectioner, and a chief of the accounts, "in all, 49 higher-ranking magnates of the crown prince."[47] Who was this crown prince? Not Sennacherib, as its mention is separated from his name. It could be Urdu-Mullissu or Esarhaddon. Governors, who had a lesser hierarchic position than that of the high officials, are also listed in these two texts: governors of Nineveh, Arbela, (U)pumu, Kulimmeri, Rasappa, Barhalza, T[ushhan], and [Hindana]. The high officials supported Sennacherib in governing Assyria. They were given the royal seal as a manifestation of authority and a sign of trust: every document bearing the impression of the royal seal had the same value as a direct command from the king. An unusual small text from the British Museum, probably a draft, concerns the making of Sennacherib's royal seal.[48] In spite of the protection of high

---

40. Ursula Magen, *Assyrische Königsdarstellungen-Aspekte der Herrschaft: Eine Typologie* (Mainz am Rhein: von Zabern, 1986), 40.
41. Elayi, *Sargon II, King of Assyria*, 35, 248.
42. Julian E. Reade, "Ideology and Propaganda in Assyrian Art," in *Power and Propaganda*, 339 and fig. 18 (BM 93019).
43. SAAS 11:74.
44. SAAS 11:59, 125, 155, 163.
45. SAAS 11:165; *PNA* 1.2:263.
46. See p. 155.
47. SAA 7:xvii–xviii, 6, no. 3; 7:7, no. 4.
48. Albert Kirk Grayson and J. Ruby, "Instructions for Inscribing Sennacherib's Seal," *Iraq* 59 (1997): 89–91; Karen Radner, "The Delegation of Power: Neo-Assyrian

officials and of his personal protection guard (*maṣṣartu*), his murder by his son proved that the king needed more protection. Therefore, Esarhaddon, his successor, created two new offices, "gate keeper" and "lock master," to control access into the Assyrian palace.⁴⁹

Sennacherib was also protected by a team of exorcists (*āšipu*) residing in Nineveh who played a substantial role in the problem of the succession. Six of them were Balassû, Aplaya, Adad-shumu-usur, Bêl-ushêzib, and two others whose names are lost.⁵⁰ Most of them were permanently in office until the reign of Esarhaddon. Bêl-ushêzib was also a scholar, judging from his letters, mainly expert in astronomy and astrology.⁵¹ Sargon had contributed to the rise of court scholars, an initiative that was continued by Sennacherib and reached its apogee during Esarhaddon's and Ashurbanipal's reigns. Nabû-zuqup-kênu was a famous scribe active from 716 to 683, under Sargon's and Sennacherib's reigns. He used his vast erudition to help strengthen and centralize the power of the Assyrian king. He belonged to a highly placed scribal family who had possibly worked in Nimrud before moving to Nineveh; his sons, such as Nabû-zêru-lêshir, were also scribes of Sennacherib.⁵² Just like his father and his successors, Sennacherib developed the libraries. However, literary texts were different from archive texts, as they were carefully copied, sometimes in several duplicates and kept for ages, but the borderline between the two was fluid, for example, for prophecies. The fact that the Assyrian king undertook some renovation work in the Nabû temple in Nimrud was evidence of his interest for this god, who was the divine scribe of destinies.⁵³ A library

---

Bureau Seals," in *L'archive des fortifications de Persépolis: État des questions et perspectives de recherches*, ed. Pierre Briant, Wouter F. M. Henkelman, and Matthew W. Stolper, Persika 12 (Paris: De Boccard, 2008), 481–515.

49. Karen Radner, "Gatekeepers and Lock Masters: The Control of Access in Assyrian Palaces," in *Your Praise Is Sweet: A Memorial Volume for Jeremy Black from Students, Colleagues and Friends*, ed. Heather D. Baker, Eleanor Robson, and Gábor Zolyomi (London: British School of Archaeology in Iraq, 2010), 269–80; Lionel Marti, "Rois visibles, rois inaccessibles, le changement dans l'idéologie royale assyrienne," *DoArch* 348 (2011): 60–61; Pierre Villard, "Quelques aspects du renseignement militaire dans l'Empire néo-assyrien," *HIMA* 3 (2016): 95.

50. Cynthia Jean, "Le petit monde des exorcistes de Ninive," *Iraq* 66 (2004): 77–81; *PNA* 1.1:38, 116; 1.2:257, 338.

51. *PNA* 1.2:338 (with bibliography).

52. *PNA* 2.2:911–13.

53. *PNA* 3.1:1123; Charpin, *La vie méconnue des temples mésopotamiens*, 122 and fig. 4–4.

(*gerginakku*) was discovered next to the Nabû temple.⁵⁴ As Sennacherib lived for most of the time in Nineveh, first as crown prince, then as king, the city, which was first an administrative center, then the royal capital of the empire, must have concentrated a large quantity of documents, repatriated from other capitals. They are now in the Kuyunjik collection.⁵⁵ Archival texts of all types were found mixed with library texts. It has to be known that much, if not most, of the contents of these archives is now lost because material other than clay was used, all of it perishable: wax-covered writing boards, papyrus, and leather. The Southwest Palace of Sennacherib contained a royal library (which seems to have been somewhat smaller in size that the one of Ashurbanipal), including a large collection of nine hundred archival texts from the reigns of Sennacherib, Esarhaddon, and Ashurbanipal. Out of 120 legal texts, twenty-five are dated to Sennacherib's reign. Another collection of six hundred tablets comes from the Southwest Palace, with an almost total absence of tablets attributed to his reign (only two legal texts).⁵⁶ Two of Sennacherib's letters as crown prince were discovered in the north palace, which was used as the house of succession.⁵⁷ If the stocking of texts in the royal archives was largely conditioned by the presence of the king, where are Sennacherib's correspondence and administrative files? It is always possible to imagine that they could still be found in some unexcavated part of the southwest and north palaces, where he had successively lived. Simo Parpola first suggested that Sennacherib's archives were purposely destroyed in antiquity; in this case, it implies that the royal archives were stored chronologically; otherwise it would have been impossible for destroyers to select them.⁵⁸

---

54. Black, "Libraries of Kalhu," 262; Antoine Jacquet, "Assarhaddon et Assurbanipal, la collecte des savoirs," *DoArch* 348 (2011): 62–67.

55. Parpola, "Royal Archives of Nineveh," 223–36 (with bibliography).

56. Parpola, "Royal Archives of Nineveh," 230–32 (two isolated tablets also date from the reign of Sennacherib); Laura Battini, "La localisation du palais sud-ouest de Ninive," *RA* 90 (1996): 33–40 (the tablets probably fell from an upper floor during the collapse of the palace).

57. Waterman, *Royal Correspondence of the Assyrian Empire*, nos. 197, 198+; SAA 1:31–32, 31.29.

58. Simo Parpola, "Assyrian Royal Inscriptions and Neo-Assyrian Letters," in *Assyrian Royal Inscriptions: New Horizons in Literary, Ideological, and Historical Analysis*, ed. Frederick Mario Fales, OAC 17 (Rome: Istituto per l'Oriente, 1981), 120.

However, he has recently changed his opinion because many letters may remain unidentified in the archives.[59]

The social action of Sennacherib also has to be underlined. In contrast with the preceding kings, throughout his entire reign he adopted a series of titles extolling his role as a king of justice: "guardian of the truth who loves justice, renders assistance, goes to the aid of the weak, (and) strives after good deeds."[60] This new title was possibly polemical, directed against Sargon: he was trying to say that, in contrast to his father, he dispensed justice to all his subjects without exception and not just to the privileged elite of the Babylonian temple cities.[61] Far from being a feminist, however, Sennacherib did in some way modify the position of royal women. He wrote a paean of praise for Tashmêtu-sharrat, his favorite wife. Instead of being inscribed in the women's quarters, it was unexpectedly incorporated in an official inscription.[62] A bronze relief, now in the Louvre museum, represents the king, probably in a religious ceremony, followed by a woman identified by an epigraph as Naqi'a, another of his wives. This relief has been ascribed to Sennacherib, but this attribution is questioned.[63] However, a similar composition appears on two seal impressions, found in his Southwest Palace in Nineveh: the Assyrian king is in worship before a goddess, probably Mullissu, and behind him the queen is represented with her mural crown.[64] Julian E. Reade considers that Naqi'a was fully integrated into the religious rite and suggests that this new status was a reflection of Sennacherib's religious reform concerning the female companion (Mullissu) attributed for the first time to the god Assur.[65] Sarah C. Melville has objected to this theory that the attribution of the bronze relief is uncertain, that the role of queens in religious ceremonies is unknown, and that

---

59. Parpola, "Letter to Sennacherib Referring to the Conquest of Bit-Ha'iri," 559–77; see also SAA 17:xix–xx.
60. RINAP 3.1:172, 22.i.4–7.
61. Tadmor, "Sennacherib, King of Justice," 385–90.
62. Reade, "Was Sennacherib a Feminist?," 141.
63. Jutta Börker-Klähn, *Altvorderasiatische Bildstelen und vergleichbare Felsreliefs*, BaF 4 (Mainz: von Zabern, 1982), 214, no. 220–21; Reade, "Was Sennacherib a Feminist?," 143. On the questioning of the identification, see André Parrot and Jean Nougayrol, "Asarhaddon et Naqi'a sur un bronze du Louvre (AO 20, 185)," *Syria* 33 (1956): 151–60; SAAS 9:25.
64. Reade, "Was Sennacherib a Feminist?," 144–45 and figs. 5–6 (the seal of fig. 7 is different, with two women worshiping the goddess).
65. Reade, "Was Sennacherib a Feminist?," 142–43 and fig. 3.

it is impossible to determine whether the new position of the queen was a by-product of the religious reform or vice versa.[66] As Sennacherib tried to break free from tradition in several fields, it seems likely that he acknowledged to some extent that the queen sustained him in his public role and became more independent, with her own military unit.[67]

7.2. Religious Reform

Sennacherib's major reform was, by far, his religious reform. If he had succeeded in solving the Babylonian problem without destroying Babylon, his religious reform would certainly have been different. But Babylon was destroyed and its gods crushed. The god Marduk was at the heart of the reform. Marduk (Bêl) was the son of Ea and Damkina, exalted to the kingship of gods as slayer of the forces of chaos (Tiâmat) and establisher of cosmic order. He was the father of Nabû. His main temple was the Esagil of Babylon. His cultic statue was taken away several times: by the Hittites in 1595 after the capture of Babylon by Murshili I, by Tukultî-Ninurta I (1243–1208), by the Elamite king Kutur-nahhunte in 1157, and finally by Sennacherib in 689; in each case, the statue was brought back to Babylon some time later.[68] What happened to the statue of Marduk in 689 and afterwards is not quite clear in the texts. According to Sennacherib's inscriptions, all the statues of gods were crushed by the Assyrian warriors when Babylon was seized; there is no particular mention of Marduk, which could mean that his statue was destroyed just like the other ones or that Sennacherib wanted to minimize his impious action toward this god. The first clear mention that Marduk resided in Assyria during his absence from Babylon is found in the inscriptions of Ashurbanipal, who brought his statue back to Babylon in 668.[69] However, it was possibly not the original statue, which could have been destroyed in 689. In order

---

66. SAAS 9:25.

67. See p. 156.

68. Walter Sommerfeld, *Die Stellung Marduks in der babylonischen Religion* (Neukirchen-Vluyn: Neukirchener Verlag, 1982); Joannès, *Dictionnaire de la civilisation mésopotamienne*, 493–96; Simo Parpola, "Monotheism in Ancient Assyria," in *One God or Many? Concepts of Divinity in the Ancient World*, ed. Barbara Nevling Porter (Chebeague Island, ME: Casco Bay Assyriological Institute, 2000), 177; Jennifer Finn, *Much Ado about Marduk* (Leiden: Brill, 2017), 97–104.

69. *ARAB* 2.988.

to show his concern for Babylonia, Esarhaddon might have restored the original statue or created a new statue for the god Marduk.[70] Whether this statue was destroyed or not in 689, Sennacherib used its destruction or its presence in captivity in Assyria to promote the god Assur and to realize his religious reform. In any event, the statue of Marduk was no longer in Babylon, as is mentioned in the Babylonian chronicles: "For eight years (during the reign of) Sennacherib, for twelve years (during the reign of) Esarhaddon—twenty years (altogether)—Bêl stayed [in B]altil (Assur) and the *akītu* festival did not take place."[71]

In his endeavor to reformulate older rituals and imbue them with new meaning, Sennacherib reintroduced into Assur the *akītu* festival, whose earliest evidence dates from the reign of Shamshi-Adad I (1807–1776).[72] As it was celebrated in Babylon, the *akītu* festival served to commemorate the victory of the god Marduk over the forces of chaos, which resulted in the creation of the cosmos and in his position as chief god of the Babylonian pantheon. Sennacherib's scholars elaborated a theological discourse centered on Assur, the chief god of the Assyrian pantheon. Assur replaced Marduk as the chief protagonist in the ritual of the *akītu*, accompanied by the king in his cosmic role as defender of the civilized world, annually consolidating the existing social and civic order.[73] Sennacherib first asked his scholars to rewrite the Epic of the Creation (Enūma Eliš) so that Assur, instead of Marduk, figured as the supreme god. He continued by writing Assur's name with the logogram AN.ŠÁR, which was the name of one of the gods preceding Marduk in Enūma Eliš.[74] Then he had to adapt mythical, theological concepts to the existing ground plan of the Assur temple. The temple had to be transformed to integrate the socle of destinies in the celebration of the *akītu* festival.[75] Then he built the *akītu* temple outside

---

70. Frame, *Babylonia 689–627 B.C.*, 56–59 (with bibliography).
71. Grayson, *Assyrian and Babylonian Chronicles*, 127, chr. 14, ll. 31–32.
72. ARMT 1:50.
73. SAA 20:lvi–lxiv.
74. George, "Sennacherib and the Tablet of Destinies," 133–46; Piotr Michalowski, "Presence at the Creation," in *Lingering over Words: Studies in Ancient Near Eastern Literature in Honor of William L. Moran*, ed. Tzvi Abusch, John Huehnergard, and Piotr Steinkeller (Atlanta: Scholars Press, 1990), 392; Wilfred G. Lambert, "The God Aššur," *Iraq* 45 (1983): 86; Lambert, "The Assyrian Recension of Enuma Eliš," in *Assyrian im Wandel der Zeiten*, ed. Hartmut Waetzoldt and Harold Hauptmann, HSAO 6 (Heidelberg: Heidelberger Orientverlag, 1997), 77–79.
75. RINAP 3.2:243, 166.8–12.

Assur in order to enact the procession according to the Babylonian model in Assyria, as it was symbolically associated with the steppe, the realm of chaos. Finally, on its gate, he represented Assur/Anshar, accompanied by the other gods and marching against Tiâmat. Marduk's ceremonial bed had been removed from Babylon in 689, set up in the temple of Assur, and rededicated to this god.[76]

The composition of the Marduk Ordeal, which appears to be connected with the captivity of Marduk in Assyria, places Assur/Anshar as being prior to the creation of heaven and earth, while Marduk only emerged after the building of Babylon, in order to establish Ashur's transcendent character, apparent also in his new epithet, "the one who creates himself" (*bānû ramānīšu*).[77] Several new cultic texts dealt with the *akītu* festival, with a precise description of the rituals to be performed during the festival.[78] These texts also fixed the hierarchy of the gods, who marched in procession alongside Assur, ten before Assur, eight inside, fifteen on the left and on the right.[79] "The gods whose places Sennacherib, king of Assyria, put in the mouths of the people through extispicy and their cups of veneration: Assur ... Marduk":[80] twenty-four gods separate Assur from Marduk in this hierarchic list (no. 52). This text is a highly significant document for reconstructing the cultic calendar of the Neo-Assyrian Empire, since it provided the precise dates on which specific cultic acts had to be performed, extending over eleven days, like the Babylonian festival. The group of texts called "Marduk Ordeal" describes the defeat and humiliation of the supreme Babylonian god Marduk, and they were probably not accepted by the Babylonians. In connection with his reform, Sennacherib adopted some Babylonian traditions, Babylonian features appeared on the

---

76. Frame, *Babylonia 689–627 B.C.*, 58 and n. 29.

77. Tikva Frymer-Kensky, "The Tribulations of Marduk: The So-Called 'Marduk Ordeal Text,'" *JAOS* 103 (1983): 131–41; Alasdair Livingstone, *Mystical and Mythological Explanatory Works of Assyrian and Babylonian Scholars* (Oxford: Clarendon, 1986), 205–53; Beate Pongratz-Leisten, *Ina šulmi īrub: Die Kulttopographische und ideologische Programmatik der akītu-Prozession in Babylonien und Assyrien im I. Jahrtausend V. Chr.*, BaF 16 (Mainz: von Zabern, 1994), 115–32; SAA 3:82–86, 34.54–55; Frahm, *Einleitung in die Sanherib-Inschriften*, 221–22, T 183:1.

78. SAA 20:103–10, no. 38.

79. SAA 20:148, 52.v.1–16. See also the relief of Maltai in Fales, *Guerre et paix en Assyrie*, 91, fig. 15.

80. SAA 20:155, 52.iv.24–26.

royal stelae, and new symbols, attributes, and forms can also be observed in the reliefs of his palace.[81]

Had Sennacherib really aimed at the Assyrianization of the Mesopotamian religious tradition? The fact that he omitted from his titles the most significant of all Assyrian titles, "priest of Assur" (*šangû Aššur*), intended to prove that he made an effort to amalgamate Babylonian and Assyrian cults.[82] According to Peter Machinist,[83] Sennacherib's reform of the Assur cult did not simply consist in interchanging the gods Marduk and Assur but in proving the superiority of Assur and a more ancient origin. It was a deliberate step to diminish the religious role of Babylon and to transfer it to Assur, the oldest capital and religious center of Assyria. However, Sennacherib's religious reform had a wider objective.[84] The fact that he stopped expanding the Assyrian Empire means that he was probably aware of its unstable conditions due to the growing economic burden of endless wars. By amalgamating Assyrian and Babylonian cults under the supremacy of the god Assur, he thought he could elaborate a cult capable of uniting all the local traditions in creating a common ideological framework. His emphasis on the Assur cult was not the expression of aggressive Assyrian nationalism, as has been stated,[85] but the ideological and religious expression of a very real political problem.

Must such a concentration on Assur, a single omnipotent god dominating the Assyrian state religion, be regarded as essentially monotheistic? In fact, the Assyrian concept of god implied a distinction between a transcendent universal god, the supreme god of the empire, and his powers and attributes, hypostatized as different gods; in other words, the god

---

81. Julian E. Reade, "Neo-Assyrian Monuments in Their Historical Context," in Fales, *Assyrian Royal Inscriptions*, 163–67; Magen, *Assyrische Königsdarstellungen-Aspekte der Herrschaft*, 64, 89–94.

82. Reade, "Ideology and Propaganda in Assyrian Art," 341; Jean Bottéro, *La plus vieille religion* (Paris: Gallimard, 1997), 122; Peter Machinist, "Kingship and Divinity in Imperial Assyria," in *Assur: Gott, Stadt und Land*, ed. Johannes Renger, CDOG 5 (Berlin: Harrassowitz, 2011), 406–9.

83. Peter Machinist, "The Assyrians and Their Babylonian Problem: Some Reflections," *WBJb* (1984–1985): 353–64.

84. Pečirková, "Assyria under Sennacherib," 7–8.

85. René Labat, "Das Assyrische Reich unter den Sargoniden," in *Fischer Weltgeschichte*, vol. 4, ed. Elena Cassin, Jean Bottéro, and Jean Vercoutter (Frankfurt am Main: Fischer Bücherei, 1967), 69.

Assur = "(all) the gods."[86] In reality, Sennacherib did not limit his religious reform to Assur but also integrated in it the other gods. For example, he gave a female companion to the god Assur: the goddess Mullissu, both being depicted roughly with the same presentation in the rock sculpture at Bavian, standing on the back of animals and on a much higher level than the Assyrian king who is worshiping them.[87] Sennacherib's *tākultu* text offers detailed ritual prescriptions to provide for the gods of the Emashmash, Ishtar's temple in Nineveh.[88] Ishtar of Nineveh played a central role in empowering the king in his office and in mediating between him and the god Assur through prophecy, enabling them to contribute jointly to the cosmic order. The *tākultu* ritual aimed at binding all the gods of the Assyrian Empire into a relationship of mutual obligation between the god Assur, the king, and each of the gods. The aim was to create a relational space in which all the cities with their gods would be tied to the imperial center, envisioning a large-scale, unified territory under divine guidance. The *tākultu* ritual mapped imperial territory with the same strategy as the royal inscriptions: to draw attention to the Assyrian heartland and its relation to the rest of the empire.[89] Sennacherib's religious reform was also expressed through the restoration and building works of the temples of Sin, Ningal, Shamash, and Haja in Nineveh; of Nergal in Tarbisu; and of Nabû in Nimrud.[90]

Finally, it is paradoxical that Sennacherib, who was considered by the Babylonians as an impious king for having destroyed all the Babylonian temples and the statues of the gods, had carried out such an important religious reform. However, his aim was not necessarily religious, as seen above, and maybe the religious reform appears to be the most important because it is the best documented. But one thing is clear: Sennacherib did not completely reject traditions, while at the same time, he was decidedly a reformer. One of his main original features was that he "restructured the center—and not the periphery, as had traditionally been the mode in the

---

86. Oded, *War, Peace, and Empire*, 187; Parpola, "Monotheism in Ancient Assyria," 165–66.

87. Reade, "Was Sennacherib a Feminist?," 142–43 and fig. 3.

88. SAA 20:xxxviii and 103–10, no. 38; Wilfred G. Lambert, "Ištar of Nineveh," *Iraq* 66 (2004): 35–39.

89. SAA 20:xliv and 103–10, no. 38.

90. See p. 189.

Assyrian Empire."[91] In fact, tradition was also a source of legitimacy of royal power, as a source of limitation. Assyrian history has demonstrated that the kings who had tried to change the tradition to some extent, such as Tukultî-Ninurta I, Shalmaneser III, and Sennacherib, finally failed and lost their lives.

---

91. Tadmor, "World Dominion," 61–62.

8
BUILDING AND INNOVATION

Compared to the other Assyrian kings, Sennacherib is the only one to have left such a vast quantity of inscriptions describing his building activities. No other royal Assyrian inscriptions give all the technical details so meticulously. He was a passionate builder and also an innovator who boasted of introducing a number of innovations in several fields. Most of his inscriptions where he relates his military campaigns are devoted, in one-third or half of them, to his building and innovating activities.[1] His great interest for these activities, which he probably considered among the most important undertakings of his reign, also appears through their representations on the reliefs of his palace in Nineveh.[2]

8.1. Building Activities

8.1.1. In Nineveh

His most ambitious building project was his palace, the so-called Southwest Palace in Nineveh. He had acquired a solid experience, when he was crown prince, in the building of the new capital of Khorsabad by his father, already interested in the techniques of mining, smelting and alloying. His name is mentioned in some building progress reports from the Nineveh archives, and Irene J. Winter is even persuaded that he was largely responsible for the building of Khorsabad while his father was often away on campaign.[3] In fact, his earliest building accounts are partly modeled on

---

1. RINAP 3.1:41–47, no. 2 (33 and 38 lines, respectively); 3.1:128–46, no. 17 (394 and 294 lines, respectively).
2. See pp. 192–93.
3. SAA 1:38–41, no. 39; SAA 11:18, no. 17; Elayi, *Sargon II, King of Assyria*, 201–10; Irene J. Winter, "Sennacherib's Expert Knowledge: Skill and Mastery as Com-

the palace building accounts of Sargon, as regards the length, wording, and some phrases of the building episodes.[4] Even the famous name of the Southwest Palace is taken from Sargon's inscriptions: "A palace of ivory, maple, boxwood, mulberry, cedar, cypress, juniper, pine and pistachio, the Palace Without Rival, for my royal abode I built therein."[5] It is almost the same formulation in Sennacherib's inscriptions: "I had a palace of elephant ivory, ebony, boxwood, mulberry, cedar, cypress, juniper, and terebinth, (a palace I named) *Egalzagdunutukua* ('Palace Without Rival'), constructed thereon as my royal residence."[6] It has been suggested that the famous scribe Nabû-zuqup-kênu was the author of some of Sargon's inscriptions and of some of Sennacherib's inscriptions.[7] Anyway, such a similar sentence would not have been written without Sennacherib's approval. Even if he did not agree with the political ideology of his father, he appears to have been influenced by him, at least in the building projects.

The first step for building his palace was the choice of the site. It was customary that each Assyrian king chose a new capital. In contrast with Sargon, who chose to build Khorsabad, an entirely new place,[8] Sennacherib chose Nineveh, the most famous Assyrian capital, located on the left bank of the Tigris, opposite modern Mosul. This city was a cult center, in particular of Ishtar: "a sophisticated place (and) site of secret lore in which every kind of skilled craftsmanship, all the rituals, (and) the secret(s) of the *lalgar* (cosmic subterranean water) are apprehended."[9] Sennacherib revealed his own identity, different from that of his father. He established

---

ponents of Royal Display," in *Proceedings of the Fifty-First Rencontre Assyriologique Internationale, Held at the Oriental Institute of the University of Chicago, July 18–22, 2005: Studies in Ancient Oriental Civilization 62*, ed. Robert D. Biggs, Jennie Myers, and Martha T. Roth, RAI 51 (Chicago: Oriental Institute of the University of Chicago, 2008), 335.

4. Russell, *Sennacherib's Palace without Rival at Nineveh*, 88–89; Barnett, Bleibtreu, and Turner, *Sculptures from the Southwest Palace of Sennacherib at Nineveh*.

5. Arthur Gotfred Lie, *The Inscriptions of Sargon II, King of Assyria*, part 1, *The Annals* (Paris: Geuthner, 1929), 76–77, v, ll. 13–14; *ARAB* 2.73.

6. RINAP 3.1:38, 1.79.

7. Eckart Frahm, "New Sources for Sennacherib's First Campaign," in *Assur und sein Umland: Im Andenken an die ersten Ausgräber von Assur*, ed. Peter A. Miglus and Joaquín Maria Córdoba, ISIMU 6 (Madrid: Universidad Autónoma de Madrid, 2003), 157–60; *PNA* 2.2:912–14.

8. Elayi, *Sargon II, King of Assyria*, 201–10.

9. RINAP 3.1:37, 1.65.

8. BUILDING AND INNOVATION

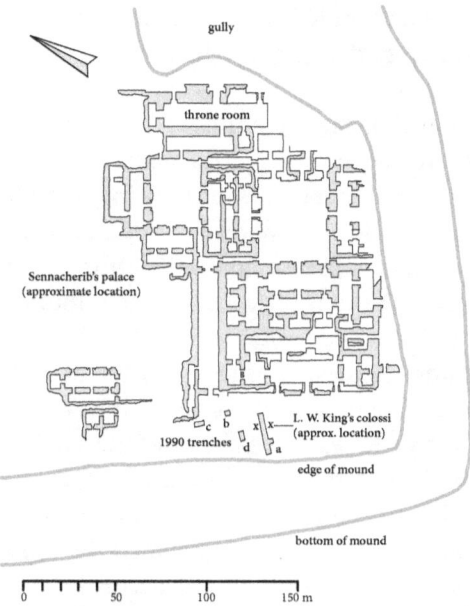

Fig. 8. Sennacherib's Southwest Palace, Nineveh. After John Malcolm Russell, "Some Painted Bricks from Nineveh, A Preliminary Report," *IrAnt* 34 (1999): 88 fig. 2.

continuity with the ancient traditions and associated his reign with those traditions: in Nineveh "since time immemorial earlier kings, my ancestors, before me exercised dominion over Assyria and ruled the subjects of the god Enlil."[10] He needed an immense labor force to accomplish his building projects. It was thanks to his military achievements that he obtained this labor force. His inscriptions provide a brief list of the different peoples conquered and incorporated into this force, which constitutes a direct link with the accounts of military campaigns in the preceding passages.[11]

Sennacherib first had to prepare the site as a necessary step for building his palace. The previous palace was badly kept and too small to be integrated into the project, and the fault lay with the preceding kings who dwelled in it: "Not one among them had paid heed to (or) shown interest in the palace inside it, the seat of lordly dwelling whose site had become too small."[12] Moreover, the Tebiltu River, "a tempestuous flood of water"

---

10. RINAP 3.1:37, 1.66.
11. RINAP 3.1:37, 1.71–72; Clifford Mark McCormick, *Palace and Temple: A Study of Architectural and Verbal Icons* (Berlin: de Gruyter, 2002), 55.
12. RINAP 3.1:37, 1.68.

(*a-gu-ú šit-mu-ru*),[13] had undermined the foundation platform of the old palace by erosion because the king who had carried out its construction did it inexpertly. The only solution was the complete destruction of the former palace and the removal of the threat posed by the river: "I tore down that small palace in its entirety. I diverted the course of the Tebiltu river from the center of the city and directed its outflow into the meadow behind the city."[14] It was confined with low water channels and was prevented from flowing against the walls of the foundation platform. In order to make the site even more secure, Sennacherib built a new foundation platform by raising its height and reinforcing its sides with slabs of limestone to guard against future erosion. He describes this new terrace, giving a lot of technical details and its dimensions, not easy to interpret: "I surrounded its damp course with large limestone slabs (and thereby) reinforced its base. Upon them, I filled in a terrace to a height of 160 courses of bricks, then added (it) to the dimensions of the former palace and (thus) enlarged its *structure*."[15] He underlines that he manipulated the topography of the site in order to accommodate his royal palace: according to a traditional idea, the Assyrian king could shape the world to fit his will.

The chronology of the building of the Southwest Palace is not easy to ascertain with any precision. Its construction started very early in Sennacherib's reign, as the earliest inscription mentioning it is dated to early in 702.[16] It had once been assumed that all the relief programs in the Southwest Palace depicted events solely from his first three military campaigns, that is, until 701.[17] However, representations of later campaigns might be expected to be included in the palace decoration. The representation of the fifth campaign (697) has now been identified.[18] Other sources mention the palace construction, for example the Bellino Cylinder, dated to 702; the Rassam Cylinder, dated to 700; the King Prism, dated to 694; and the

---

13. RINAP 3.1:54, 4.46.

14. RINAP 3.1:38, 1.75; 3.1:45, 2.44–48; 3.1:138, 17.iv.84–87; 3.2:70, 44.36–37; 3.2:85, 46.116–18.

15. RINAP 3.1:38, 1.77–78; Sylvie Lackenbacher, *Le palais sans rival, le récit de construction en Assyrie* (Paris: La Découverte, 1990); Russell, *Sennacherib's Palace without Rival at Nineveh*, 89–91; McCormick, *Palace and Temple*, 57; SAAS 3:58–62, 70.

16. Frahm, *Einleitung in die Sanherib-Inschriften*, 43, T1; RINAP 3.1:29, no. 1.

17. Russell, *Sennacherib's Palace without Rival at Nineveh*, 164–66.

18. Jeffers, "Fifth-Campaign Reliefs in Sennacherib's 'Palace without Rival' at Nineveh," 87–116.

8. BUILDING AND INNOVATION

Taylor Prism, dated to 691.[19] It is interesting to compare the description written in 702 with that written in 694 in order to understand the evolution of the construction.[20] There are no real differences between these two texts in the first steps of the building: choice of the site, description of the labor force, reference to the previous palace and preceding kings, preparation of the site, construction materials, and creation of the park. Then, for describing the decoration of the palace, such as the painting of the roofing timbers and the adornment of walls, the text written in 694 is more specific and far more extensive. Such differences can normally be attributed to the later document's inclusion of information on progress made in the intervening years.[21] By giving a lot of details about the subsequent decoration of the palace, Sennacherib grasped the opportunity to distinguish himself from his predecessors and to show that his palace was built from all the materials of his empire, thanks to his military conquests. The palace was the product of his creativity and was evidence of his might and radiance in the world. However, the comparison between the end of the two texts is surprising. The text of 702 ends in this way: "After I had finished the work on my lordly palace, broadened the squares, (and) brought light into the alleys (and) streets, making (them) as bright as day, I invited inside it (the palace) the god Assur, the great lord, (and) the gods and goddesses living in Assyria, then I made splendid offerings and presented my gift(s)."[22] The end of the text of 694 is similar, but it adds the inauguration of the palace and the invitation of his subjects to a great banquet. In fact, the invitation of the gods was already dissociated from the inauguration banquet, in Khorsabad, for example.[23] Even though the two texts are well dated, the first interpretation would be to consider that the end was added by a scribe as an update in a later compilation, as the so-called First Campaign Cylinder was copied several times.[24] An alternative interpretation is that a first stage of the palace was finished in 702, when Sennacherib took up residence, after inviting the gods. On the one hand, at the beginning of his reign, he could no longer dwell in the succession house (north palace), as

---

19. Julian E. Reade, "Foundations Records from the South-West Palace, Nineveh," *ARRIM* 4 (1986): 33–34; McCormick, *Palace and Temple*, 49–52 (with bibliography).
20. RINAP 3.1:37–40, no. 1; 3.1:137–46, no. 17.
21. McCormick, *Palace and Temple*, 58–59.
22. RINAP 3.1:39–40, 1.91–92.
23. Elayi, *Sargon II, King of Assyria*, 207–9.
24. A dozen exemplars are known: RINAP 3.1:29–30.

he did when he was crown prince. On the other hand, he could not dwell in the former royal Southwest Palace because he had destroyed it as the first step of his building project. During the first three years of his reign, there was enough time to build a first stage of his palace. Thus, one seal dated around 700 was part of a foundation deposit buried in this palace.²⁵ An eponym list gives the following entry for the year 700: "[The walls (?)] of the palace in the city [of Nineveh ...],"²⁶ pointing to the same date for the first building phase of the palace. It was urgent for Sennacherib to have a suitable place to dwell, probably not in Khorsabad, haunted by the ghost of his father. Provisionally, it could have been Assur, Nimrud, or Tarbisu where he undertook one of his earliest building projects. No doubt he prompted the building of his palace in Nineveh, his favorite city. After his installation in the new Southwest Palace, he had enough time to have the decoration completed and its final form established. The total length of time required for finishing the construction of the palace, until 691, when it was said to be officially completed, was twelve or thirteen years, as the precise date for the start of the project is unknown.

The Southwest Palace, located in the artificial tell of Kuyunjik, was sporadically excavated from 1847 to 1990. It was first excavated by English expeditions: in the period between 1845 and 1851 by Austen Henry Layard, who concentrated on Kuyunjik.²⁷ Some sporadic excavations were conducted from 1852 to 1932 by English expeditions.²⁸ T. Madhloon, from the Iraqi Department of Antiquities, resumed the excavations from 1965 to 1968. In the years 1980–1990, an American expedition continued the excavations, in particular with John Malcolm Russell, who excavated the *bīt-nakapti*, a structure that was a late addition around 693 to the Southwest Palace.²⁹

---

25. Dominique Collon, *First Impressions: Cylinder Seals in the Ancient Near East* (London: British Museum, 1987), 175, no. 812.

26. A. Ungnad, "Eponymen," *RlA* 2:435 (Eponym Canon C^{b}7); Russell, *Sennacherib's Palace without Rival at Nineveh*, 93: "The walls of the nucleus of the palace were built around 700 B.C."

27. Russell, *Sennacherib's Palace without Rival at Nineveh*, 34–44 (with bibliography); Russell, "Layard's Descriptions of Rooms in the Southwest Palace at Nineveh," 71–85; Geoffrey Turner, "Sennacherib's Palace at Nineveh: The Primary Sources for Layard's Second Campaign," *Iraq* 65 (2003): 175–220.

28. See p. 5.

29. Russell, *Sennacherib's Palace without Rival at Nineveh*, 85–93; Joannès, *Dic-*

8. BUILDING AND INNOVATION 179

One of the main difficulties in the building of this palace was quarrying and transport. The only Neo-Assyrian quarry known today is a limestone quarry near Bavian, Khinis, and the Gomel River. Sennacherib gives detailed information on his quarries: Tastiate, near Nineveh, "across the Tigris," which supplied white limestone for colossi; they could be transported to Nineveh by rafts on the Tigris, once a year, in spring. He discovered a new quarry near Nineveh, in the district of Balatai, generally identified with modern Eski Mosul (medieval Balad), on the right bank of the Tigris, some 35 kilometers northwest of Mosul.[30] The quarrying and transport of bull colossi in alabaster from Balatai is illustrated on reliefs from Courtyard VI.[31] Unusual stones were brought from farther-away places: Mount Nipur (Judi Dagh) to the north, near Cizre, which he discovered during his campaign of 697; Kapridargilâ, on the border of Til Barsip; and Mount Ammanâna, probably the Anti-Lebanon range.[32] Quarrying technique is illustrated in reliefs of Courtyard VI, with quarrymen crouching and kneeling around a block to be extracted.[33] Transportation of huge stones, such as the colossi, is illustrated several times in the reliefs of Courtyard VI. The colossus to be transported was put on a sledge moved by wooden rollers placed under the front of it, by a long, stout lever behind, and on each side by ropes pulled by teams of men. The king is represented high above the labor force but directly overseeing its progress.[34]

Sennacherib's inscriptions do not give a clear image of the palace itself but several times present the opportunity to distinguish the king from his predecessors in this building project: "Since times immemorial, the kings, my ancestors, created copper statues, replicas of their (own) forms, to be erected in temples, and through their manufacture they had exhausted

---

tionnaire de la civilisation mésopotamienne, 574–75; Diana Pickworth, "Excavations at Nineveh: The Halzi Gate," *Iraq* 67 (2005): 295–316.

30. Russell, *Sennacherib's Palace without Rival at Nineveh*, 94–116; Pier Luigi Bianchetti, "Sennacherib's Quarries and the Stones of the Southwest Palace Decoration," in *Nineveh the Great City: Symbol of Beauty and Power*, ed. Lucas P. Petit and Daniele Morandi Bonacossi, PALMA 13 (Leiden: Sidestone, 2017), 158–59.

31. Julian E. Reade, "Studies in Assyrian Geography. Part I: Sennacherib and the Waters of Nineveh," *RA* 72 (1978): 55–60.

32. Mordechai Cogan, "… From the Peak of Amanah," *IEJ* 34 (1984): 255–59; Josette Elayi, "L'exploitation des cèdres du Mont Liban par les rois assyriens et néo-babyloniens," *JESHO* 31 (1988): 14–41.

33. Russell, *Sennacherib's Palace without Rival at Nineveh*, 100–105 and fig. 50.

34. Russell, *Sennacherib's Palace without Rival at Nineveh*, 105–14 and figs. 54–61.

all of the craftsmen. Through ignorance (and) failure to give thought on the matter, they depleted the oil, wax, (and) wool in their lands for the work they desired."[35] The description of the palace follows a pattern influenced by a walk through the structure. The tour begins at the portals and doorways, with a long description of the fantastic creatures stationed at the doorposts, as protective guardians: bull colossi,[36] sphinxes of white limestone, bronze lions. After the entryways comes the description of the palace interior: the halls, doorways, ceilings, pillars, columns, and walls, all of them shining, as they were decorated with silver, copper, and glazed bricks.[37] Wood also played an important role in the construction of the palace: "beams of cedar (and) cypress, whose scent is sweet, products of Mount Amanus and Mount Sirâra, the holy mountains ... juniper and Indian wood."[38] Mount Sirâra is regarded as the southern part of the Anti-Lebanon range.[39] In contrast with other preceding Assyrian kings, only rarely did Sennacherib present himself as cutting down large trees, and sometimes they were cut down by the kings of Amurru; he is presented in the Bible as cutting down cedars (2 Kgs 19:23–24; Isa 37:25), but it could be only a stereotyped sentence.[40] Despite the archaeological publications of the different excavations, the plan of the Southwest Palace remains incompletely known, altered by the first excavations, tunneling through it in order to discover reliefs and tablets. The total length of the new palace was approximately 385 meters and 503 meters in its final form.[41] Like other Neo-Assyrian palaces, it was divided into suites of rooms that surrounded a central courtyard area, possibly open to the sky. According to

---

35. RINAP 3.1:140, 17.vi.80–88.

36. Hannes D. Galter, Louis D. Levine, and Julian E. Reade, "The Colossi of Sennacherib's Palace and Their Inscriptions," *ARRIM* 4 (1986): 27–34; Virginie Danrey, "Winged Human-Headed Bulls of Nineveh: Genesis of an Iconographic Motif," *Iraq* 66 (2004): 133–39.

37. John Malcolm Russell, "Some Painted Bricks from Nineveh: A Preliminary Report," *IrAnt* 34 (1999): 85–109.

38. RINAP 3.1:139, 17.vi.23–29.

39. John Pairman Brown, *The Lebanon and Phoenicia*, vol. 1 (Beirut: American University of Beirut, 1969).

40. RINAP 3.1:225, 34.70; William S. Morrow, "Water Control and Royal Propaganda: Sennacherib's Boast in 2 Kgs 19:24 (=Isa 37:25)," in *Thinking of Water in the Early Second Temple Period*, ed. Ehud Ben Zvi and Christoph Levin (Berlin: de Gruyter, 2014), 317–37.

41. Russell, *Sennacherib's Palace without Rival at Nineveh*, 80–86.

the restoration plan proposed by Russell, Courtyard VI was surrounded by suites on all sides, with the throne room (I) in a suite to the northwest of the courtyard.[42] Sennacherib's spatial arrangement and relief program were different from those of his predecessors and successors. He chose Courtyard VI for presenting his vast construction project, near his throne room, depicting himself as the direct overseer of the activity. By installing protective guardians, traditionally buried in the floor but here visible to palace visitors, he repeatedly reminded observers that his kingship was under the watchful protection of the gods. The colorful reliefs (blue, red, yellow) were not merely decorative, but they presented him as being creatively gifted by the gods and totally protected. They expressed the power of a king who controlled vast territories and could muster the labor force needed to create the colossi. The military conquests depicted on the reliefs clued up on the acquisition of foreign captive labor. The military representations connected with the construction representations in the same courtyard link the two inseparably. One may wonder why Lachish, a relatively minor city in the west, was chosen as representing the successful siege of a city (Room XXXVI), and not the prestigious city of Babylon. Military matters related to Babylon were treated extensively in the annals of Sennacherib, and not so for Lachish. The main reason was probably the chronology: Babylon's defeat was achieved long after the palace was completed. There was, in Sennacherib's palace, a palatial hall built for his royal wife Tashmêtu-sharrat.[43] To whom were addressed the messages included in the Southwest Palace? Theoretically, several groups of visitors could be concerned: after the king himself, the crown prince and royal family, courtiers, servants, foreign employees, foreign prisoners, Assyrians, provincials, and subject and independent foreigners, without omitting the gods who were invited inside the palace.[44]

Sennacherib, after completing his Southwest Palace, filled it with luxury, then proceeded to build a palace combined with an arsenal, situated on the nearby artificial tell of Nebi Yunus: "The Rear Palace (*ekal kutalli*)

---

42. Russell, *Sennacherib's Palace without Rival at Nineveh*, 78–88 and figs. 43–45; Russell, "Sennacherib's Palace without Rival Revisited: Excavations at Nineveh and in the British Museum Archives," in Parpola and Whiting, *Assyria 1995*, 295–306; Davide Nadali, "An Urban Perspective of Nineveh," *Mes* 50 (2015): 157–76 and fig. 3.

43. Frahm, *Einleitung in die Sanherib-Inschriften*, 121, T35; *PNA* 3.1:1122 (with bibliography).

44. Russell, *Sennacherib's Palace without Rival at Nineveh*, 223–40.

that earlier kings, my ancestors, had had built for the proper running of the military camp, the care of horses, (and) the overseeing of everything—its terrace did not exist, its site had become too small, and its construction was inexpert. With the passage of time, its base had fallen into disrepair, then its foundations had become loose (and) its superstructure had collapsed."[45] The two inscriptions mentioning this building date from 690–689. The name of Nebi Yunus was given to the tell where the prophet Jonah is said to have been buried; according to the Bible, Jonah had been ordered by Yahweh to vilify Nineveh and its inhabitants for their iniquity (Gen 10:11; Nah 1:9–11, 14; 2:4; 3:19).[46] First, Sennacherib tore down the old palace. Then he made a high terrace, filled in with fallow land from a meadow. On this terrace he laid the foundations of his new palatial hall of limestone and cedar, "replica of a palace of the land of Hatti."[47] On a relief depicting Nineveh, above three rings of fortifications, the *hilāni* façade of the palace can be seen and was visible from outside the city.[48] Sennacherib then enlarged the outer courtyard, used for breaking in his thoroughbred horses and reviewing the booty. He made this palace magnificent and extremely large and filled it with the tribute of all the lands and the booty, such as "the wagons, chariots, *vehicles of* the king of the Elamites, the king of Babylon and Chaldea."[49]

---

45. RINAP 3.1:184, 22.vi.39–44; 3.1:224, 34.55–59; John MacGinnis, "Some Inscribed Horse Troughs of Sennacherib," *Iraq* 51 (1991): 187–92; *PNA* 3.1, 1122; Julian E. Reade, "Assyrian Palace at Nebi Yunes, Nineveh," in *At the Dawn of History: Ancient Near Eastern Studies in Honour of J. N. Postgate*, ed. Yagmur Heffron, Adam Stone, and Martin Worthington (Winona Lake, IN: Eisenbrauns, 2017), 431–58.

46. Russell, *Sennacherib's Palace without Rival at Nineveh*, 59; Joannès, *Dictionnaire de la civilisation mésopotamienne*, 574–77. Deep inside looters' tunnels dug beneath the tomb of Jonah were discovered several royal inscriptions, some of them dated to Sennacherib's reign: https://tinyurl.com/SBL1730a.

47. RINAP 3.1:225, 34.64. On the possible incorporation of the *bīt hilāni* into Assyrian palaces, see, e.g., Russell, *Sennacherib's Palace without Rival at Nineveh*, 182–83; Karen Polinger Foster, "The Hanging Gardens of Nineveh," *Iraq* 66 (2004): 214. It was possibly connected with the *aptu* in the Ashur temple: David Kertai, "Embellishing the Interior Spaces of Assyria's Royal Palaces: The *Bēt Ḫilani* Reconsidered," *Iraq* 79 (2017): 85–104.

48. Mirko Novák, "From Ashur to Nineveh: The Assyrian Town-Planning Programme," *Iraq* 66 (2004): 184 and fig. 9.

49. RINAP 3.1:226, 34.85–90; Julian E. Reade, "The Assyrians as Collectors: From Accumulation to Synthesis," in *From the Upper Sea to the Lower Sea: Studies on the*

8. BUILDING AND INNOVATION

In Kuyunjik, Sennacherib also restored the temple of Sin, Ningal, Shamash, and Aja (four gods in one building) and the temple of Ishtar, as recorded on a damaged stone tablet dated to around 702 from the slope below the temple. Fragments of Sennacherib foundation cylinders found on the temple site are dated to 702 and 700. Inscriptions on two bricks and a stone slab fragment complete the modest documentation on the restoration of these two temples.[50] The restoration or construction of other temples in Nineveh is more uncertain, as the information is based on fragmentary inscriptions: the temple of Haja, god of the scribes, possibly related to the Nabû temple in Nineveh or situated in Assur, and the temple for the warlike Sebetti gods in Nineveh.[51]

Sennacherib completely transformed his capital of Nineveh: "I enlarged the site of Nineveh, my capital city."[52] He doubled the circumference of the city and built a huge wall 12 kilometers long around the city, which comprised, in its final stage, eighteen monumental gates: "I had an inner (and) outer wall built and I raised (them) as high mountains."[53] The great wall, 45 meters thick and about 20 meters high, was called "Wall Whose Brilliance Overwhelms Enemies" (*Bàd-ní-gal-bi-lú-kúr-ra-šú-šú*).[54] He opened up a foundation pit for the outer wall, which he called "Terrorizer of the Enemies" (*Bàd-níg-érim-ḫu-luḫ-ḫa*). Twelve of the fourteen gates of the city wall mentioned in a text dated to 697, and eighteen in a text dated to 691 were identified by the excavators; each had a name carefully recorded by Sennacherib, in relation with gods, demons, agricultural products, roads, cisterns, tributes, or armory.[55] One was Sennacherib's gate and was called "The One Who Flattens All Enemies."[56] He also built the citadel wall of Kuyunjik and a bridge: "I had a bridge constructed opposite

---

History of Assyria and Babylonia in Honour of A. K. Grayson, ed. Grant Frame (Leiden: Nederlands Instituut voor het Nabije Oosten, 2004), 255–68.

50. Julian E. Reade, "The Ishtar Temple at Nineveh," *Iraq* 67 (2005): 380–81.

51. Luckenbill, *Annals of Sennacherib*, 147; Frahm, *Einleitung in die Sanherib-Inschriften*, 110, T21; 106–7, T18.

52. RINAP 3.1:77, 8.14; 3.1:103, 15.vii.21–24; *PNA* 3.1:1122.

53. RINAP 3.1:103, 15.vii.14–20; RINAP 3.2:139, 94.1–3.

54. RINAP 3.1:77, 8.11′–12′; Frahm, *Einleitung in die Sanherib-Inschriften*, 62–64, 76–78, 82, 92–94, 141–42, T75–T80a.

55. RINAP 3.1:103–4, 15.vii.25–29; 3.1:158–59, 18.vii.10–40. On the functions of the gates, see, e.g., Laura Battini, "Les portes urbaines mésopotamiennes," *HIMA* 3 (2016): 223–47.

56. RINAP 3.1:122, 16.vii.43.

the Citadel Gate with paving limestone for my lordly chariot."[57] A brick found in Assur but supposed to have been brought from Nineveh mentions the building of a house for one of his sons: "Sennacherib, king of Assyria, built a house *at the same time as* the laying of the foundation(s) of Nineveh and gave (it) to Ashur-shumu-ushabshi, his son."[58] In Nineveh, he built the so-called royal road (*girru šarri*), up to the Park Gate, and he put stelae facing each other on each side of the road so that it could not be narrowed.[59] He also widened the squares of Nineveh and made the avenues and streets bright.[60] According to a fragmentary inscription found in Nineveh and dated to 690, Sennacherib built an *akītu* house, probably for Assur and Ishtar, maybe located in a park outside the city wall.[61] Finally, he embellished Nineveh with parks and gardens: "Beside the city, a botanical garden (one) *pānu* (in size and) a garden (one) *pānu* (in size) for a game preserve, I gathered every type of aromatic tree of the land of Hatti, fruit trees of [all lands], (and) trees that are the mainstay of the mountains and Chaldea. Upstream of the city, on newly tilled so[il], I planted vines, every type of fruit tree, and olive tre[es]."[62] Thanks to irrigation,[63] he also enlarged the yearly harvest by having grain and cereals grown in the fields around the city. He subdivided the meadowland upstream of the city into plots of two *pānu* each and gave them to the citizens of Nineveh.[64] He also created a kind of zoological garden: "I created [a m]arsh to moderate the flow of water for (these) gardens and had a canebrake planted (in it). I let loose in it herons, wild boars, (and) water buffalos (or roe deers).... Birds of the heavens, heron(s) whose [home(s)] are far away, [made] nest(s)."[65] The embellishment of his capital was a veritable imitation of Chaldea; Sennacherib brought Babylonian geography northwards, a highly symbolic

---

57. RINAP 3.1:68, 4.90; 3.1:77, 8.16'; 3.1:104, 15.viii.1'; *PNA* 3.1:1122.

58. RINAP 3.2:143, 99.1–3. For duplicates, see Frahm, *Einleitung in die Sanherib-Inschriften*, 142–43, T81–83; 180–81, T156.

59. Luckenbill, *Annals of Sennacherib*, 153, xvii, ll. 15–23; RINAP 3.1:159, 18.vii.49'–52'.

60. Luckenbill, *Annals of Sennacherib*, 101, ii, l. 61.

61. Ahmad and Grayson, "Sennacherib in the Akitu House," 187–89; Eckart Frahm, "Die Akītu-Häuser von Ninive," *NABU* (2000): no. 66; *PNA* 3.1:1122.

62. RINAP 3.1:68, 4.85–86; 3.1:123, 16.viii.3b–11.

63. See p. 194.

64. RINAP 3.1:68, 4.86.

65. RINAP 3.1:76, 8.5'–6'; 3.1:123–24, 16.viii.29–44.

action of his interest for this area.⁶⁶ It has been suggested that hanging gardens of the deeply sunken bed type first appeared in Nineveh.⁶⁷ Hanging gardens expressed the royal ideology through a complex mix of horticultural and technological achievement with spatial and conceptual manipulation. They may well have existed both in Nineveh and Babylon, as there was a classical confusion between the two cities, maybe initiated by Sennacherib himself.⁶⁸

8.1.2. In Assur

The second Assyrian city where Sennacherib developed his building projects was Assur, located in the south of the Assur-Nineveh-Arbela triangle.⁶⁹ At that time, the urban Assyrian landscape was characterized by a bipolar structure: Assur and Nineveh.⁷⁰ Ashur became an important trading center at the beginning of the second millennium, because of its situation on one of the major routes connecting Babylonia with the north, whereas for a long time Nineveh was not a major Assyrian city. However, in the seventh century, Nineveh became the capital of Assyria and the major city of the whole Near East, transformed by the most ambitious town-building program ever realized in Assyria. Assur was then a relatively small town, very different from the spacious metropolis of Nineveh, with its vast dwelling areas and huge palaces on top of high

---

66. John A. Brinkman, "Reflections on the Geography of Babylonia (1000–600 B.C.)," in *Neo-Assyrian Geography*, ed. Mario Liverani (Rome: Università di Roma "La Sapienza," 1995), 28–29.

67. Stephanie Dalley, "Ancient Mesopotamian Gardens and the Identification of the Hanging Gardens of Babylon Resolved," *Garden History* 21 (1993): 8–10; Dalley, "Nineveh, Babylon and the Hanging Gardens: Cuneiform and Classical Sources Reconciled," *Iraq* 56 (1994): 51–54; Dalley, "More about the Hanging Gardens," in *Of Pots and Plans: Papers on the Archaeology and History of Mesopotamia and Syria Presented to David Oates in Honour of His Seventy-Fifth Birthday*, ed. Lamia Al-Gailani Werr, John Curtis, Harriet Martin, Augusta McMahon, Joan Oates, and J. E. Reade (London: Nabu, 2002), 67–73; Dalley, "Sennacherib's Palace Garden at Nineveh, a World Wonder," in Bonacossi, *Nineveh the Great City*, 188–91; Polinger Foster, "Hanging Gardens of Nineveh," 217.

68. Marc Van De Miroop, "A Tale of Two Cities: Nineveh and Babylon," in Liverani, *Neo-Assyrian Geography*, 1–5.

69. Radner, "Assur-Nineveh-Arbela Triangle, Central Assyria in the Neo-Assyrian Period," 321–23.

70. Novák, "From Ashur to Nineveh," 177–85.

citadels. Assur remained the religious and ceremonial center of Assyria, whereas Nineveh was the king's seat of power. Assur was seen as the "vertical axis" of the world, connecting heaven, earth, and underworld, while the residential city of Nineveh was the "horizontal axis," the center of all the power in the world.[71]

Numerous texts of Sennacherib were found in Assur: clay prisms, horizontal stone prisms, a stela, a stone tablet, numerous stone blocks, stone door sockets, a sculpted water basin, bronze plating (possibly a dais for Assur), numerous bricks, and a clay tablet.[72] After the destruction of Babylon in 689, the Assyrian king rebuilt the Esharra, temple of the god Assur, which was the central temple of the Assyrian Empire. He imitated the Esagil complex in Babylon. He changed the orientation of the *cella* of the Assur temple, with its gate opening to the east instead of to the south.[73] He laid the foundation of the courtyard of the Esharra temple with white limestone.[74] The numerous works he accomplished in the Esharra are detailed in a foundation inscription on eight-sided horizontal stone prisms: in particular, he rebuilt the *šuḫūru* house with four bull-shaped bronze figures on the roof, two bronze daises, a bronze fish man, a bronze carp man, and a gate surrounded with a lion-man and scorpion-man figures.[75] He renovated several entrance gates to "The Courtyard of the Row of Pedestal for the Igīgū Gods," the gates of the *cella* and of the *šuḫūru* house, installing the gate doors in their sockets.[76] Several inscribed bricks record the embellishment of the frieze of the parapets of the Esharra.[77] Numerous bricks were baked in a ritually pure kiln for the *tikātu* house of the Assur temple: "I had the *tikātu* house of

---

71. Stefan Mario Maul, "Die altorientalische Hauptstadt: Nabel und Abbild der Welt," in *Die Orientalische Stadt: Kontinuität, Wandel, Bruch (Colloquien der Deutschen Orient-Gesellschaft 1)*, ed. Gernot Wilhelm (Saarbrücken: Saarbrücker Druckerei und Verlag, 1997), 109–24.

72. RINAP 3.2:233–88.

73. RINAP 3.2:243, 166.8b–13a; 3.2:274, 194.4′–6′.

74. RINAP 3.2:250, 169.1–5; 3.2:277–79, 198.1–6.

75. RINAP 3.2:243, 166.17b–22a; Otto Schroeder, "Ein Bericht über die Erneuerung des Ašur-Tempels unter Sanherib," *OLZ* 11–12 (1920): 244–46; Margaret Huxley, "The Gates and Guardians in Sennacherib's Addition to the Temple of Assur," *Iraq* 62 (2000): 109–37; SAA 10:73–74, no. 96.

76. RINAP 3.2:243–44, 166.22–29; 3.2:270, 190.6–11; 3.2:271, 191.3–16; 3.2:275, 195.1–5.

77. RINAP 3.2:275, 195.1–5.

the courtyard (where) the pedestals of the Igīgū gods (stand) in rows made anew and I raised (it) as high as a mountain."[78] Several inscriptions mention that he fashioned statues of the god Assur and of the other great gods.[79]

He built a new procession road linking the Assur temple to the *akītu* house outside the city. The *akītu* house was the second important temple built after the destruction of Babylon in 689, possibly in 683, as an imitation of its cultic topography.[80] A large inscribed stone tablet describes in detail the construction of this temple, which is said to have been forgotten for a very long time and to have fallen into disrepair. Sennacherib was commanded by the gods Shamash and Adad to rebuild it, and he chose a propitious day in a favorable month: "I laid its foundation with limestone, stone from the mountains, and I raised its superstructure.... I had two canals dug around each of its sides, and (then) I had it surrounded with a lush garden, an orchard with fruit, and place a splendid plantation around it."[81] He removed dirt from Babylon and piled it up in heaps in the *akītu* house.

Sennacherib also built the temple of Zababa, probably situated in the vicinity of the Assur temple.[82] He dedicated personnel to this new temple and also to the newly built *akītu* temple.[83] An octagonal clay prism, possibly dated to around 691–689, records the restoration of the old royal palace of Assur. Sennacherib criticizes his predecessors Tiglath-pileser I and Ashurnasirpal II, who did "inexpert" work, thereby obliging him to tear down the dilapidated sections.[84] He had a large private room constructed anew to be his lordly seat, through the craft of well-trained master builders, roofing it with beams of cedar from Mount Amanus and fastening metal bands on the cedar doors. He rebuilt with baked bricks the step

---

78. RINAP 3.2:276, 196.1–3.
79. RINAP 3.2:252, 170.1–3; 3.2:268, 186.1–5.
80. RINAP 3.2:244; *PNA* 3.1:1122; Pongratz-Leisten, *Ina šulmi īrub*, 60–64.
81. RINAP 3.2:248, 168.30b–36a; 3.2:252–59, nos. 171–76. There is an uncertain mention of a "temple of the god *Dagān*" in a damaged inscription: RINAP 3.2:274, 193.12.
82. RINAP 3.2:260, 177.1–3; *PNA* 3.1:1122; Hannes D. Galter, "Der Tempel des Gottes Zababa in Assur," *ARRIM* 2 (1984): 1–2.
83. SAA 12:104–9, nos. 86–87. See also 49–50, no. 48.
84. RINAP 3.2:234–35, 164.1–12.

gate of the old palace.[85] His rebuilding of the northern rooms (the throne room?) remains speculative.[86]

He had a house constructed for his eldest son, Ashur-nâdin-shumi, probably before he became king of Babylon in 700, in an unknown location in Assur. He also had a house constructed for his son Urdu-Mullissu, who was in the service of the god Assur, in the southeastern part of Assur, near to the city wall.[87] Several inscribed bricks mention that Sennacherib had built his own tomb during his lifetime and that he probably commemorated its construction. This "palace of rest" or "of sleep" (*ekal tapšuḫti* or *ṣalāli*) was presented alternatively as the mausoleum of the royal family and as Sennacherib's mausoleum.[88] Like the other royal tombs in Assur, this mausoleum was apparently situated under the renovated palace, together with other tombs of Assyrian kings; it was intentionally destroyed at a later date.[89] However, Ashurbanipal, his grandson, offered slaughtered Babylonians as a *kispu* sacrifice, not in the mausoleum but in the place where his grandfather was murdered. A late literary text, perhaps from Ashurbanipal's time, probably alludes to Sennacherib's ghost sojourning in the netherworld.[90]

8.1.3. In Other Places

Sennacherib carried out restoration and building works in other places, not only Nineveh and Assur, but they are less well documented. In Tarbisu, to which a road led from Nineveh through the Nergal gate, he entirely rebuilt the temple of the god Nergal (*é-gal-lam-mes*). This reconstruction occurred

---

85. RINAP 3.2:260, 178.1–5; 3.2:279, 199.1–3; 3.2:280–82, nos. 200-202; David Kertai, "The Multiplicity of Royal Palaces: How Many Palaces Did an Assyrian King Need?," in *New Research on Late Assyrian Palaces*, ed. David Kertai and Peter A. Miglus (Heidelberg: Heidelberger Orientverlag, 2013), 11–29.

86. Friedhelm Pedde, "Der Alte Palast in Assur: Ausgrabungen und Neubearbeitung," in *Assur: Gott, Stadt und Land*, ed. Johannes Renger, CDOG 5 (Berlin: Harrassowitz, 2011), 33–61; Peter A. Miglus, "Considerations on the East Palace at Ashur," in Kertai and Miglus, *New Research on Late Assyrian Palaces*, 50–51.

87. RINAP 3.2:285, 205.1–7; 3.2:260–67, nos. 179–85.

88. RINAP 3.2:283, 203.1–5; 3.2:285, 204.1–4; PNA 3.1:1123.

89. Frahm, *Einleitung in die Sanherib-Inschriften*, 181–82, T157–58; Steven Lundström, *Die Königsgrüfte im Alten Palast von Assur*, WVDOG 123 (Berlin: Harrassowitz, 2009), 181–83, 215–18; Miglus, "Considerations on the East Palace at Ashur," 50.

90. PNA 3.1:1123 (with bibliography); SAA 3:74, 32.r.22–25.

at the very beginning of his reign, as it is mentioned on two clay cylinders found in Tarbisu, probably written early in 702. He was very proud of his work: "For the god Nergal, who (lives) in the city of Tarbisu, my lord, I indeed did a splendid job, which surpassed previous (work) and was worthy of (high) praise."[91] He then settled Nergal in his new dwelling and held festivities inside that temple. He developed the cultivation of grain and sesame in the fields between Tarbisu and Assur.[92] The reconstruction of the Nergal temple may be linked to the violent death of his father, Sargon, and also to the fact that he possibly dwelled in this city, a short distance north of Nineveh, at the beginning of his reign.[93] Sennacherib also rebuilt the outer city wall of Kalzu/Kilîzu, modern Qasr Shemâmok, 28 kilometers west of Erbil, as is mentioned on numerous bricks and on a threshold slab found on this site; another short inscription mentions the "palace of Sennacherib."[94] He performed some renovation work on the Nabû temple in Nimrud (Kalhu), as can be deduced from an inscription of Ashurbanipal commemorating the building of the Nabû temple and mentioning that he found Sennacherib's inscriptions on the site.[95] During his campaign against Babylonia in 690, Sennacherib sojourned one night in Sûr-marrati (modern Samarra).[96] According to him, the city had been abandoned and had gone to ruin. Therefore, he decided to repopulate it, and he rebuilt the city wall: "Beside the wall, I dug a moat around its (entire) circumference. I planted palm grove(s and) grape vine(s) in the meadow."[97] According to several inscribed paving stones from Babylon, he had restored its processional road.[98] As Sennacherib's seals were found in the cities of Shibaniba, Tell Yarah, Beisan (Beth-Shean), and Tulul al-Lak, it has been suggested that the king may have conducted building operations in these cities.[99] Shibaniba is also mentioned in the Bavian inscriptions, written several times on a cliff

---

91. RINAP 3.2:299, 214.64–65; 3.2:300, 214.1; 3.2:302, 215.4; 3.2:303, 216.4; *PNA* 3.1:1123.
92. RINAP 3.2:314, 223.22.
93. See p. 18.
94. RINAP 3.2:304, 218.4; 3.2:306, 219.2; C. B. F. Walker, *Cuneiform Brick Inscriptions* (London: British Museum, 1981), nos. 174, 184; Frahm, *Einleitung in die Sanherib-Inschriften*, 190–91, T165, T166, T66; *PNA* 3.1:1123 (with bibliography).
95. *PNA* 3.1:1123 (with bibliography).
96. See p. 121.
97. RINAP 3.2:335, 230.118–20a.
98. *PNA* 3.1:1123 (with bibliography).
99. Frahm, *Einleitung in die Sanherib-Inschriften*, 191 D–G.

in stela-like panels as the point of departure of one of the eighteen canals that he had dug.[100] It is uncertain whether he undertook building work in a temple of the city of Shabbu, so far unidentified.[101]

8.2. Innovations

Sennacherib defined himself as a great builder and, at the same time, as an innovator, his interest in aspects of technology being remarkable: "the builder of Assyria, the one who brings its cult centers to completion…, the one who makes brickwork structures secure, from buildings for the living to tombs befitting the dead (made) from limestone, stone from the mountains, with which none of the kings of the past (who came) before me in Assyria had used."[102] However, he also employed skilled craftsmen, whose role he recognizes, in addition to his own role, in the realization of his works: "with my innate expertise (*nik-lat lib-bi-ia*), I had … a magnificent palace wing … built through the craft of well-trained master builders (^{m}*dim-gal-le-e en-qu-ti*), for my lordly residence."[103] Or he claims to have carried out the entire work himself, for example, the *akītu* temple in Assur: "of my [own initiat]ive I ski[llfu]lly built it from the foundation to the parapet."[104] In many respects, in his building works he proved to be the most innovative builder among the neo-Assyrian kings, in his creative ability and his innovative approach to old problems. Thus, for creating massive sculptures, he selected stones that had previously been used only for inlay and jewelry, such as alabaster for making bull colossi and sphinxes: "In the uplands of Mount Ammanâna, they (Assur and Ishtar) disclosed to me the location of alabaster, which in the time of [the king]s, my ancestors, was too expensive (even) for the pommel of a sword."[105] For making slabs and bowls, he used a new stone, brescia, which was discovered in Kapridargilâ, near Til Barsip.[106] Limestone was discovered in

---

100. See p. 196; RINAP 3.2:313, 223.9.

101. Frahm, *Einleitung in die Sanherib-Inschriften*, 241–42, ZT4, ZT5; SAA 12:23, no. 21; *PNA* 3.1:1123.

102. RINAP 3.2:247, 168.9–10, 17–20.

103. RINAP 3.1:185, 22.vi.51b–58a; for the meaning of the vocabulary, see Winter, "Sennacherib's Expert Knowledge," 333–38.

104. SAA 12:105, 86.17.

105. RINAP 3.2:37, 39.41b–43a; 3.2:41, 40.10″–12″; 3.2:61, 43.43–46a; McCormick, *Palace and Temple*, 58.

106. See p. 33.

abundance in Balatai, and he used it for making bull colossi and sphinxes. He described the basalt seats for palace door posts: "I brought back (with me) precious basalt (*kašurû*-stone), whose mountain is far away, and I installed (it) underneath the pivots of the door leaves of the gates of my palace."[107] Even though Sennacherib selected palace building stones for their novelty, he was also interested in their beauty and in their apotropaic qualities. For example, the "[*pendû*-stone—whose appearance is as finely granulated] as cucumber seeds, considered valuable [eno]ugh to be an amulet, [a stone for speaking (and) be]ing accepted, as well as [making] storms [pass by], (and) preventing [illn]ess from approaching a man—made [itse]lf known to me [at the foot of Mount Nipur]."[108] Finally, he added to his palace an element of foreign architecture: a house with double doors that was a replica of a Hittite palace.[109]

The figures that flanked the doorways of Sennacherib's palace were so exceptional that he invented a literary innovation for designating them. The sign KAL had two readings: ALAD2 (*šēdu*) and LAMA2 (*lamassu*); he combined them to produce a new Akkadian word: *aladlammû*.[110] He created a combination of different stones and metals: thus, he made bull colossi with metal features, for example by overlaying them with silver; he fastened bands of copper, or he added gold and silver inlays to wooden columns.[111] Copper statues had existed "since time immemorial," but they were apparently made by the lost-wax technique, which Sennacherib criticized.[112] He boasted of inventing a new technique for casting metal. Inspired by Ninshiku, the god of magic and wisdom, but with his own ideas and knowledge, he created clay molds of the large objects he wanted to obtain and he poured copper into them: "I created a cast work of copper and expertly carried out its artful execution."[113] In fact, he stated that he had adapted a technique previously used for small objects such as figurines.[114] By using this casting technique, he obtained tree trunks and date

---

107. RINAP 3.2:129, 86.1–6; McCormick, *Palace and Temple*, 59.
108. RINAP 3.2:94, 49.2′–7′; Russell, "Sennacherib's Palace without Rival Revisited," 300–301.
109. See p. 182; RINAP 3.2:85, 46.125a.
110. McCormick, *Palace and Temple*, 30; Huxley, "Gates and Guardians in Sennacherib's Addition to the Temple of Assur," 109–37.
111. RINAP 3.2:87, 46.148b–50a.
112. RINAP 3.2:86, 46.139b–41a.
113. RINAP 3.2:87, 46.143a.
114. See p. 158.

palms, twelve lions "open at the knees," twelve bull colossi, and twenty-two sphinxes. He knew how to make alloys, for example, "four bronze columns that were alloyed with one-sixth tin."[115] He was always seeking perfection: through its skilled craftsmanship and embellishment, a work had to be "perfect" (*šuklulu*). He appears to have enjoyed his metal-casting invention, which contributed to making his palace beautiful in order "to be an object of wonder for all of the people."[116] However, at that time, bronze working was mainly founded on royal patronage, and iron working was developing for common usage, as iron could not be used as easily as bronze and decayed more readily.[117]

Sennacherib gave his palace, built to live in and to carry out imperial business, particular characteristics that corresponded to his taste, such as the height of the ceilings and the dimensions of colossi, the redundancy of images and forms, and the color of the decorative programs.[118] He suppressed the fifth leg of the animal colossi, which made them more naturalistic. The innovations introduced in the reliefs were concerned with subject matters and composition. In addition to the traditional apotropaic figures, Sennacherib added new ones, such as the man with six large curls at the back of his head and a kilt, the man with a horned crown and a long tress, the lion-headed or eagle-footed men; in contrast, the "sacred tree" was completely absent. The narrative subjects of the reliefs also changed. Some subjects were omitted: processions of tribute bearers, royal banqueting, and hunting scenes, developed by his predecessors.[119] There was a

---

115. RINAP 3.1:226, 35.83–84.
116. RINAP 3.2:87, 46.152b.
117. J. E. Curtis, T. S. Wheeler, James D. Muhly, and R. Maddin, "Neo-Assyrian Ironworking Technology," *Proceedings of the American Philosophical Society* 123 (1979): 369–90; Theodore A. Wertime and James D. Muhly, *The Coming of the Age of Iron* (New Haven: Yale University Press, 1980); Peter Roger Stuart Moorey, *Ancient Mesopotamian Materials and Industries: The Archaeological Evidence* (Oxford: Clarendon, 1994), 290.
118. McCormick, *Palace and Temple*, 42–86.
119. Russell, *Sennacherib's Palace without Rival at Nineveh*, 179–89; McCormick, *Palace and Temple*, 78–86; Russell, "Sennacherib's Palace without Rival Revisited," 187–90; Nicolas Gillmann, *Les représentations architecturales dans l'iconographie néo-assyrienne* (Leiden: Brill, 2016), 82–84. Julian E. Reade, "Assyrian Architectural Decoration: Techniques and Subject-Matter," *BaghM* 10 (1979): 14–49, suggests that some traditional subjects were dropped because they offered little potential for narration: this is not true for hunting scenes.

game preserve in Nineveh, but whether Sennacherib was a great hunter or not, he did not consider hunting important for his royal image, hence hunting is almost completely absent from his reliefs and his inscriptions. The subject he emphasized most was the transport of building materials for the construction of his palace. He was the only Assyrian king who made his construction activity a central element in his royal image, just as his building texts were longer that those of any of his predecessors. He was involved in various aspects of the building process, which means that he seems to have viewed royal construction as a more significant component of his imperial policy than his predecessors did. He carried out several other changes: among which are that the flanking orthostats of his throne room were carved with a royal campaign instead of a procession; the division of the narrative reliefs into two registers was abandoned, as was the central band of text; the inscriptions on the thresholds were replaced by floral patterns. In brief, the Southwest Palace represented a complex fusion of tradition and innovation: the most spectacular example is his throne room, virtually identical to that of his father, following the same plan, but quite different in its content.

Sennacherib was also an innovator as far as town planning is concerned: the urban fabric of Nineveh.[120] It is clear that he worked by himself with the help of his architects.[121] Like all the preceding Assyrian residential cities, Nineveh had a more or less rectangular outline, dominated by a citadel, where the royal palaces and the main temples were situated. The public buildings on top of the citadel, partly visible from outside, were separated from the dwelling quarters of the common people. The king, as the main representative of the god Assur, lived above the city, close to the houses of the gods.[122] What changed in the conception of this capital city with Sennacherib? The first innovation was the creation of space. Streets directed traffic to the citadel through major gates, through an urban landscape full of variations. The inclusion of the high eastern terrace within

---

120. Stephen Lumsden, "On Sennacherib's Nineveh," in *Proceedings of the First International Congress on the Archaeology of the Ancient Near East*, ed. Paolo Matthiae, Lorenzo Nigro, Luca Peyronel, and Frances Pinnock (Rome: La Sapienza, 2000), 815–34; Lumsden, "The Production of Space at Nineveh," *Iraq* 66 (2004): 187–97; Novák, "From Ashur to Nineveh," 177–85; Marta Rivaroli, "Nineveh: From Ideology to Topography," *Iraq* 66 (2004): 199–205.

121. RINAP 3.1:185, 22.vi.51b–58a.

122. Novák, "From Ashur to Nineveh," 184.

the walled city, a feature unknown in Nimrud and Khorsabad, provided an unprecedented viewpoint, different from the high view from the citadel or temple platform.[123] Sennacherib intentionally created a new perception of the city seen from the viewpoint of the panorama, easier to understand. This new perception corresponded to the panoramic view introduced in the reliefs: there was a connection between this imperial reorientation and the change of viewpoint in the reliefs.[124]

The founding or refounding of an Assyrian city was the expression of the state's renewal and of the reconstitution of the cosmic order. Nineveh was presented as the new center of the world, replacing Babylon, as Assur replaced Marduk. Sennacherib had undertaken the refoundation of Nineveh, justified by the god's decision. The first step intended to reestablish order, with reference to a mythical foundation:[125] to totally demolish the previous small palace and to canalize the potentially destructive Tebiltu River. Then he could move on to the next phase: to build his incomparable palace, to create a park associated with the palace, conceived to look like the forest of Mount Amanus. Then he enlarged the city, straightened the roads, dug out canals, and planted an orchard. Sennacherib had doubled the urban area by including within the walls part of the outside territory, having built a double city wall.[126] Perhaps his new urban space can be seen as part of a larger project, including both the Assyrian tradition of territorial expansion and the restructuring of Nineveh, the center of the empire.[127]

Another of Sennacherib's important innovations was his various waterworks. One of the main problems in a huge city such as Nineveh was the shortage of water, and he was conscious of the importance of his water projects: he claimed to be "the one who has canals dug, the one who opens streams, the one who makes watercourses gush, the one who establishes abundance and plenty in the wide plains of Assyria, the one who provides

---

123. Lumsden, "Production of Space at Nineveh," 190–92.

124. Lumsden, "Production of Space at Nineveh," 195–96. His interpretation is based on Henri Lefebvre's theory (*The Production of Space* [Oxford: Blackwell, 1991], 33–46). According to Sennacherib's inscriptions found recently inside looters' tunnels dug beneath the tomb of Jonah, this king "had the inner wall and outer wall of Nineveh built anew and raised as high as mountains": https://tinyurl.com/SBL1730a.

125. Rivaroli, "Nineveh: From Ideology to Topography," 200–202 (with bibliography).

126. See p. 183.

127. Russell, "Sennacherib's Palace without Rival Revisited," 250–51; Tadmor, "World Dominion," 61–62; Lumsden, "Production of Space at Nineveh," 196.

irrigation water in the meadows of Assyria—which from the days of yore no one in Assyria had seen or known canals and artificial irrigation and which none in bygone times had used."[128] His motivations are interpreted in different ways: as luxuries with regard for any requirement of the economy, for his personal legitimization, as a demonstration of technical expertise, or in emulation with the Babylonian irrigation system.[129] Maybe all of these interpretations are correct to some degree. First, he knew how to exploit ground water by digging a deep pit: "I dug down forty-five *nindanu* and made (it) reach the water table. I bound together strong mountain stone in the water below and above I expertly carried out its construction with large limestone (blocks) up to its copings."[130] He constructed four main canal systems at different stages of his reign: the Kisiru canal in 702, the Musri system in 694, the northern system around 690, and the Khinis canal around 690–688.[131] In fact, the soils of the plain to the north and east of Mosul had a high agricultural potential. Through his ingenious system, Sennacherib attempted to redirect springs, rivers, and wadis onto those soils in order to convert the hydrology of the area into a form that would be more amenable to human control, by reducing the risks of insufficient rainfall.[132] People who had no knowledge of artificial irrigation would no longer have to permanently focus their eyes on the sky in the hope of rain and showers.[133] The Kisiru canal is mentioned in several inscriptions, first in clay cylinders dated to early in 702: "I cut with iron picks a canal straight through mountain and *valley*, from the border of the city of Kisiru to the plain of Nineveh. I caused an inexhaustible supply of water to flow

---

128. RINAP 3.2:247, 168.11–16.

129. Reade, "Studies in Assyrian Geography. Part I: Sennacherib and the Waters of Nineveh," 174; Julian E. Reade, "Some Assyrian Representations of Nineveh," *IrAnt* 33 (1998): 81–94; Brinkman, "Reflections on the Geography of Babylonia (1000–600 B.C.)," 29; Ariel M. Bagg, *Assyrische Wasserbauten* (Mainz am Rhein: von Zabern, 2000), 223–24; Stephanie Dalley, "Water Management in Assyria from the Ninth to the Seventh Centuries B.C.," *Aram* 13–14 (2001–2002): 443–60; Tony J. Wilkinson, *Archaeological Landscapes of the Near East* (Tucson: University of Arizona Press, 2003), 130; Lumsden, "On Sennacherib's Nineveh," 815–34.

130. RINAP 3.1:144, 17.viii.8–12.

131. Jason Ur, "Sennacherib's Northern Assyrian Canals: New Insights from Satellite Imagery and Aerial Photography," *Iraq* 67 (2005): 317–45 and table 1.

132. P. Buringh, *Soils and Soil Conditions in Iraq* (Baghdad: Ministry of Agriculture, 1960), 218; Ur, "Sennacherib's Northern Assyrian Canals," 319–20.

133. RINAP 3.2:313, 223.6–7.

there for a distance of one and a half leagues from the Husur river (and) made (it) gush through feeder canals into these gardens."[134] The original departure point of this canal was Al-Shallalat, and it stretched for 13.4 kilometers; it could have irrigated a maximum area of 11.8 square kilometers.[135] The Mount Musri canals are only known from the inscriptions. He claimed to have mounted an expedition to search for water at the foot of Mount Musri (modern Jebel Bashiqa).[136] He enlarged the openings of several springs near the cities of Dûr-Ishtar, Shibaniba (possibly modern Tell Billa), and Sulu. Then he cut through rugged mountains with picks and directed the outflow into the plain of Nineveh, adding it to the waters of the Husur River. As a result, "in summer, I enabled all of the orchards to be irrigated. In winter, I annually had water provided to 1,000 seeded fields in the plains upstream and downstream of the city."[137]

The northern system and the Khinis canal were true engineering accomplishments on an even larger scale than the first two. The so-called northern system has been hypothesized as being part of a single system; all the canals were probably among the eighteen canals listed in the Bavian inscriptions, which summarize the four stages of Sennacherib's hydrological works.[138] The total length of the canals of the northern system is estimated at 46.4 kilometers, including those of Maltai, Faida, Bandwai, Tel Uskof, and Tarbisu, south of Jebel al-Qosh. The canals of Maltai, Faida, and Bandwai were associated with carved reliefs of Sennacherib.[139] A Tigris canal to Tarbisu was not mentioned in Sennacherib's inscriptions, but it is probably to be integrated in the northern system. The waters of these canals were partly added to the Khosr River.[140] The Khinis system

---

134. RINAP 3.1:39, 1.89–90; RINAP 3.2:63, 43.94–96; Frahm, *Einleitung in die Sanherib-Inschriften*, 60; Lionel Marti, "Les monuments funéraires—Birûtu," in *Florilegium marianum VIII: Le culte des pierres et les monuments commémoratifs en Syrie amorrite*, ed. Jean-Marie Durand (Paris: SEPOA, 2005), 196–97.

135. Ur, "Sennacherib's Northern Assyrian Canals," 321–23 and figs. 3–4.

136. RINAP 3.1:144, 17.viii.31–35; Ur, "Sennacherib's Northern Assyrian Canals," 323–25.

137. RINAP 3.1:145, 17.viii.43–45.

138. RINAP 3.2:313–15, 223.8–33; Reade, "Studies in Assyrian Geography," 157–68.

139. Rainer Michael Boehmer, "Die neuassyrischen Felsreliefs von Maltai (Nordirak)," *JdI* 90 (1975): plates 25–95; Boehmer, "Bemerkungen bzw. Ergänzungen zu Ğerwan, Khinis and Faidhi," *BaghM* 28 (1997): 245–49; Reade, "Studies in Assyrian Geography," 160–65 and figs. 10b, 11a, 11b, 12a, 13a, and 13b.

140. Ur, "Sennacherib's Northern Assyrian Canals," 325–35.

preserves two important building inscriptions *in situ*. First, the Bavian inscriptions, carved on a cliff near the village of Khinis, give a detailed description of the excavations and inauguration of the Khinis canal and an overview of the three other canal systems. Sennacherib is said to have dug eighteen canals, giving them the names of the nearby cities. He boasts of digging the Kisiru canal with only seventy men within a year and six months; in case someone does not believe him, he swears by the god Assur that he is telling the truth. The canals he had dug enabled planting around Nineveh gardens, vines, fruit trees, trees from all over the world, spices, olive trees, grain, and sesame. He describes in detail the inauguration of the Khinis canal, in the presence of an exorcist and a singer. He prayed and made offerings to "the god Ea, the lord of undergrounds waters, cisterns…, (and to) the god Enbilulu, the inspector of canals, (and) to the god En'e'imdu, the lord of [dike(s) and canal(s)]."[141] After the opening of the gate of the watercourse, he inspected the canal himself in order to make sure that its construction had been accomplished correctly. Then he offered abundant sacrifices and rewarded the workers: "I clothed those men who dug out this canal with linen garments (and) garments with multi-colored trim, (and) I placed gold rings (and) gold pectorals on them."[142] A number of inscriptions on stone blocks were discovered at Jerwan, in the Dohuk region of Iraqi Kurdistan. These blocks originally formed part of an aqueduct constructed by Sennacherib to convey water to Nineveh. This monument is preserved on a length of 280 meters and on a width of 22 meters, with a maximum height of 9 meters.[143] The inscriptions are divided into four types. Inscriptions of Type A are very short: "Palace of Sennacherib, king of the world, king of Assyria."[144] Among the hypotheses, these blocks were brought from the palace of Nineveh, or Sennacherib had a summer residence next to Jerwan. Inscriptions of Types B and C celebrate the building and the hydraulic function of the aqueduct: "For a long distance, adding to it the water of the two Hazur

---

141. RINAP 3.2:315, 223.27–29.

142. RINAP 3.2:315, 223.32–33.

143. Thorkild Jacobsen and Seton Lloyd, *Sennacherib's Aqueduct at Jerwan* (Chicago: University of Chicago Press, 1935); Frederick Mario Fales and Roswitha Del Fabbro, "Back to Sennacherib's Aqueduct at Jerwan: A Reassessment of the Textual Evidence," *Iraq* 76 (2014): 65–72 and figs. 1–6.

144. RINAP 3.2:317–19, nos. 224–25; Fales and Del Fabbro, "Back to Sennacherib's Aqueduct at Jerwan," 72–73.

rivers…, I had a canal dug to the meadows of Nineveh. Over deep-cut wadis, I had an aqueduct (*titurru*) of white stone blocks made, (and) those waters I caused to pass over it."[145] The inscriptions of Type D are scattered on 202 stone blocks found in Jerwan in secondary usage and not well preserved. They comprise at least seventy-eight lines and record some of Sennacherib's military campaigns.[146] There was also a badly preserved relief on the rock depicting a cultic scene with him but subsequently erased for the carving of a rider of Hellenistic or Parthian date.[147]

Other canals were dug in Assyria, not all of them destined for Nineveh, but it is difficult to say which ones were dug by Sennacherib. For example, several stone blocks formed the entrance to a tunnel that was part of an aqueduct built to divert water from the Bastura River (a tributary of the Upper Zab) to Arbela. The inscription records: "The three watercourses which (flow) from Mount Hâni, a mountain above the city of Arbela, I dug out the springs which are on the right and left banks of those watercourses and (thus) added (the springs' water) to them. I dug a (subterranean watercourse and directed (all of) their course(s) inside the city of Arbela."[148] This underground tunnel to bring high-quality water for the inhabitants was built like a *qanat*, an underground aqueduct with shafts to the surface at intervals.[149] The construction of an artificial marsh to accommodate surges in the water flow was also an excellent solution that

---

145. RINAP 3.2:319, 226.1–9; Fales and Del Fabbro, "Back to Sennacherib's Aqueduct at Jerwan," 74–77 and n. 44 for the discussion on *titurru*.

146. RINAP 3.2:323–26, no. 228, fragments A to K; Fales and Del Fabbro, "Back to Sennacherib's Aqueduct at Jerwan," 81–96.

147. Julian E. Reade and Julie Renee Anderson, "Gunduk, Khanes, Gaugamela, Gali Zardak: Notes on Navkur and Nearby Rock-Cut Sculptures in Kurdistan," ZA 103 (2013): 96–117.

148. RINAP 3.2:327, 229.1–8; Fuad Safar and Faraj Basmachi, "Sennacherib's Project for Supplying Erbil with Water," *Sumer* 2 (1946): 50–52; *Sumer* 3 (1947): 23–25; Reade, "Studies in Assyrian Geography," 170–73.

149. Dalley, "Water Management in Assyria from the Ninth to Seventh Centuries B.C.," 443–60. See Pierre Briant, ed., *Irrigation et drainage dans l'Antiquité: Qanats et canalisations souterraines en Iran, en Égypte et en Grèce* (Paris: Thotm Éditions, 2001); Peter Magee, "The Chronology and Environmental Background of Iron Age Settlement in Southeastern Iran and the Question of the Origin of the Qanat Irrigation System," *IrAnt* 40 (2005): 217–31.

has recently been reinvented: this kind of marsh absorbs and delays flow, filters the water, and attracts wildlife.[150]

Was Sennacherib the inventor of the so-called Archimedes water screw? It consists of a cylinder containing several continuous helical walls that, when the entire cylinder is rotated on its longitudinal axis, scoop up water at the open lower end and dump it out through the upper end.[151] The invention of the water screw is attributed to Archimedes in several classical sources because he wrote a mathematical treatise on spirals, for which the main possible application at his time was the water screw: "the inhabitants (of the Nile Delta) irrigate the whole region by means of a certain device that Archimedes the Syracusan invented, called the screw (κοχλίας) on account of its design."[152] The passage concerning Sennacherib's invention is included in the inscriptions on bull colossi, dated between late 694 and early 693, where he describes at great length his achievements in Nineveh: a palace, a palace garden, and various measures for water control. Stephanie Dalley proposes the following translation: "In order to draw water up all day long I had ropes, bronze wires and bronze chains made, and instead of shadufs (*makâte*) I set up the great cylinders (*gišmaḫḫu*) and *alamittu* palms over cisterns."[153] Then Sennacherib boasts of raising the height of the surroundings (or the superstructures) of the palace to be a wonder for all peoples. He gave it the name "Palace without Rival." Then he describes the park that he laid out next to the palace, imitating the Amanus Mountains, with all kinds of aromatic plants and fruit trees. The vocabulary conveys the difficulty of finding appropriate technical terms in the languages of preindustrial cultures. For example, *gišmaḫḫu*, which means literally "great tree trunk,"

---

150. RINAP 3.1:123–24, 16.viii.29–44; Stephanie Dalley and John Peter Oleson, "Sennacherib, Archimedes, and the Water Screw: The Context of Invention in the Ancient World," *Technology and Culture* 44 (2003): 6.

151. John Peter Oleson, *Greek and Roman Mechanical Water-Lifting Devices: The History of Technology* (Toronto: University of Toronto Press, 1984), 291–94; Oleson, "Water-Lifting," in *Handbook of Ancient Water Technology*, ed. Orjan Wikander (Leiden: Brill, 2000), 242–47.

152. Diodorus Siculus, *Bib. hist.* 1.34.2. See Wilbur R. Knorr, "Archimedes and the Spirals: The Heuristic Background," *History of Mathematics* 5 (1978): 43–75. For an analysis of the classical sources, see Dalley and Oleson, "Sennacherib, Archimedes, and the Water Screw," 17–24.

153. RINAP 3.1:142, 17.vii.45–49; RINAP 3.2:87, 46.151b–53b; Dalley and Oleson, "Sennacherib, Archimedes, and the Water Screw," 7.

is also the word used for a cylinder in mathematical-problem texts. The term *alamittu*, identified as *Chamaerops humilis* in the *Chicago Assyrian Dictionary*, would be used metaphorically to indicate the spiraling helix of such a water screw. The spiral form was familiar to Mesopotamian engineers since the Middle Bronze Age and was used, for example, in mud-brick columns constructed of trapezoidal bricks laid in a decorative pattern, some of them still visible in Sennacherib's day.[154] Therefore, the passage would mean that a helical form was hidden inside a cylinder, used to raise water. Hollow bronze cylinders from Susa, dated to the twelfth century, could indicate the technological heritage that Sennacherib could draw on in casting his cylindrical water-lifting devices,[155] but without using the lost-wax technique. The casting of a helix inside a cylinder was not easy, but the diameter was probably larger than the cylinders of Susa, and Sennacherib had at his disposal the metallurgical skills needed to produce large bronze water screws.

There was an attempt to reconstruct Assyrian casting procedures in a simple open-air furnace by casting a small-scale water screw, using 60 kilograms of bronze.[156] There did not appear to be any technical obstacles to the casting of a large water screw other than the difficulties inherent in any large casting project, such as the weight. Of course, the Roman wooden water screws were much lighter.[157] Therefore, it seems likely that Sennacherib invented the water screw based, like most inventors, on a long accumulation of human experience. His invention was possibly illustrated in the Nineveh garden relief of Ashurbanipal, but the panel is badly damaged and is only 35 percent complete.[158] The absence of representations of water screws before the time of Archimedes could mean that this device fell out of use and was reinvented almost five hundred years later, by Archimedes. At the request of the Ptolemies, he allegedly solved irrigation problems in the Nile Delta using the water screw. In fact, there were

---

154. Dalley and Oleson, "Sennacherib, Archimedes, and the Water Screw," 8 (with bibliography).

155. Prudence Harper, Joan Aruz, and Françoise Talon, *The Royal City of Susa* (New York: Metropolitan Museum of Art, 1992), 132–35: the one on display in the Louvre is 4.36 meters long and 0.18 meters thick.

156. Dalley and Oleson, "Sennacherib, Archimedes, and the Water Screw", 10–11: the attempt was made by A. Lacey.

157. Dalley and Oleson, "Sennacherib, Archimedes, and the Water Screw," 8.

158. Dalley and Oleson, "Sennacherib, Archimedes, and the Water Screw," 13–14 and fig. 3.

similar conditions in seventh-century Nineveh and third-century Alexandria, depending on exogenous river systems to supply water for irrigating their rich, alluvial soils, and on technologies and regulations that facilitated irrigation agriculture.

Another of Sennacherib's water-related innovations was an automatic sluice at the departure of the Khinis canal, mentioned in the Bavian inscriptions: "This (sluice) gate of the watercourse opened by itself [without (the help)] of spade or shovel and let an abundance of water flow through. Its (sluice) gate was not ope[ned] through the work of human hands."[159] It shows that he had mastered, with the help of his experts, the principles of hydraulic engineering.

Another of his innovations seems to have been the introduction of the cotton culture, as related in the detailed description of Nineveh's new plantations: "They picked cotton (and) wove (it) into clothing."[160] *Iṣ-ṣu na-áš ši-pa-a-ti* meant literally "trees bearing wool." There is no Akkadian or Sumerian word to designate cotton (genus *Gossypium*; family *Malvaceae*), as the plant was introduced late in Mesopotamia, apparently by Sennacherib. Its origin is not indicated in his inscriptions: possibly the Indus Valley, where cotton was cultivated from the third millennium at least; seeds were even found in Baluchistan in a context dated to the fifth millennium.[161] In the fifth century, Herodotus vaunted the qualities of Indian cotton, which he also compared to wool.[162]

Concerning warfare, it does not seem that Sennacherib introduced substantial innovations, as it was not his major center of interest. The accurate representation of the siege material in the reliefs at Lachish does not show any new machines.[163] There was no catapult, even though some authors had attributed its invention to Ashurnasirpal II, based on the drawing of a relief, lost today, and on the unidentified siege-engine

---

159. RINAP 3.2:315, 223.30–31; Ariel M. Bagg, "Assyrian Technology," in Frahm, *Companion to Assyria*, 514–17.

160. RINAP 3.1:142, 17.vii.57; 3.1:145, 17.viii.64.

161. Joannès, *Dictionnaire de la civilisation mésopotamienne*, 207; C. Wayne Smith and J. Tom Cothren, *Cotton: Origin, History, Technology, and Production* (New York: Wiley, 1999); Christophe Moulherat, Margareta Tengberg, Jérôme-F. Haquet, and Benoît Mille, "First Evidence of Cotton at Neolithic Mehrgarh, Pakistan: Analysis of Mineralized Fibres from a Copper Bead," *Journal of Archaeological Science* 29 (2002): 1393–1401.

162. Herodotus, *Hist.* 3.106.

163. See p. 74.

kabānātu, literally "great wall flies."[164] It was probably a misinterpretation.[165] However, the shape of shields was changed, and the length of the tip of the battering ram was increased.[166] There was a novelty in the representation of groups of warriors in the reliefs of Sennacherib's palace: these tactical units were made up of different military specialists, whereas previously each tactical unit was composed of warriors having one specialty, for example bowmen.[167] It is difficult to know whether it was a simple novelty in the representation of the reliefs or an innovation of the Assyrian king in warfare tactics.

In short, Sennacherib was a great builder who participated personally in the planning and realization of large building projects, not only in Nineveh but throughout the Assyrian Empire. These building realizations gave him the opportunity to express another important aspect of his personality: he was clearly a highly innovative ruler who was fond of experiments. He was conscious and very proud both of his building activities and of his innovations in various fields. He could be compared to his father Sargon for the building activities, but he was unique among the Assyrian kings as an innovator.

---

164. T. Madhloom, "Assyrian Siege-Engines," *Sumer* 21 (1965): 11; Madhloom, *The Chronology of Neo-Assyrian Art* (London: Athlone, 1970), 35 and plate X, 2; Chaim Herzog and Mordechai Gichon, *Battles of the Bible* (London: Greenhills Books, 2002), 247–53; Luckenbill, *Annals of Sennacherib*, 62, iv, l. 79; RINAP 3.1:136, 17.iv.79.

165. Fabrice Y. De Backer, "Note sur les 'catapultes' néo-assyriennes," *Acta Orientalia Belgica* 21 (2008): 197–208.

166. H. W. F. Saggs, "Assyrian Warfare in the Sargonic Period," *Iraq* 25 (1963): 145–54; Erkki Salonen, *Die Waffen der alten Mesopotamier* (Helsinki: Societas Orientalis Fennica, 1965), 198 (similar to the Roman *scutum*); Fales, *Guerre et paix en Assyrie*, 187–88.

167. Fabrice Y. De Backer, "Les archers de siège néo-assyriens," in *Organization, Representation, and Symbols of Power in the Ancient Near East*, ed. Gernot Wilhelm, RAI 54 (Winona Lake, IN: Eisenbrauns, 2012): 429–48 and figs. 12–14.

9

CONCLUSION:
ASSESSMENT OF SENNACHERIB'S REIGN

Who exactly was Sennacherib? He was different from the negative image conveyed to us through the centuries because he attacked Judah and destroyed Babylon. He was also different from the propaganda image that he wanted to promote through his royal inscriptions and his palace reliefs: an image of intelligence, ability, justice, piety, benevolence, and energy. In fact, these two converse images are not completely false, as they contain some elements of his personality. He was certainly intelligent, skillful, with an ability of adaptation and a capacity to concede failures; he was an educated and experienced man, and an aesthete; he was passionate in his undertakings, affectionate, and thoughtful in some circumstances. He was a realist. His sense of justice consisted in rewarding his loyal subjects and punishing his enemies. His sense of piety was contradictory, as, on the one hand, he impiously destroyed the statues of gods and temples of Babylon while, on the other hand, he used to consult the gods before acting and prayed to them. One major deficiency was his irascible, vindictive, and impatient character. When he was dominated by his feelings, he was pushed to take irrational decisions. He was excessively proud, stubborn, and somewhat influenceable. He was able to commit atrocities, not by sadism but following the line of traditional Assyrian warfare.

The question of Sennacherib's relationship with his father is complex. All the letters he wrote to him as crown prince during more than fifteen years give the impression that he was both respectful and friendly. He never discussed the royal orders but scrupulously obeyed Sargon, consulting him as often as possible. He learned a lot from his father about governing the empire, as he replaced him during his frequent absences, and he participated in the building of Khorsabad.[1] However, in spite of the apparent good relationship between father and son, some elements indicate certain difficulties. Sennacherib was possibly frustrated, as he was never associated with his father's campaigns or entrusted with military operations. Even though he was not very interested in warfare, he could have been sensitive to the glory attached to war feats. However, he was not ambitious enough to conduct a coup in order to seize power illegitimately. He wanted to keep his distance from Sargon, as most of the time he did not reside in the same place as him: when he was crown prince, while Sargon resided in Nimrud, he chose to reside mainly in Nineveh, on the pretext that the house of succession was there, but he probably followed his father to Khorsabad from 706 to 705. After his father's death, he did not want to reside in Khorsabad. He never mentions Sargon in his genealogy, as his successors did, and never celebrated his memory. He had to preserve appearances and to maintain his rank, but he possibly felt overshadowed by his father because both had strong, different personalities, and he was relieved, after this long period living in the shadow of Sargon, to be allowed to exist by himself and to express his differences. Even though Sargon had undertaken several reforms, he was essentially a conservative. Conversely, Sennacherib was basically a reformer, but he knew that he was obliged to also be conservative in certain circumstances. How did he react to his father's violent and inauspicious death on the battlefield? The fact that his body was not retrieved and could not be buried according to tradition shocked Sennacherib, who had to ponder what sin(s) his father had committed to deserve such an infamous death. He probably tried to avenge his murder, first in 704 by sending his magnates against the Kulummeans, responsible for Sargon's death. This campaign does not seem to have been successful, as it is not mentioned in the royal inscriptions, and another campaign was conducted against the Kulummeans in 695.

Did Sennacherib have a clear plan or program at the beginning of his reign, or did he respond to various challenges in different areas, as and when they arose? Even though his plans for the future of the empire differed from those of Sargon, his policy showed a basic continuity with that of his father or, at least, did not deviate from the guidelines of territorial control and exploitation established by him. His first campaigns

---

1. Elayi, *Sargon II, King of Assyria*, 201–10.

9. CONCLUSION: ASSESSMENT OF SENNACHERIB'S REIGN

were aimed at putting down the uprisings and at restoring Assyrian control, direct or indirect, throughout the entire empire. Even though he was not primarily a warlord, he carried on the traditional military activity of his predecessors, institutionalized in the form of annual campaigns. He began with the priority campaigns, all of them being defensive in character, intended to preserve, not to expand, the empire. After the campaign against the Kulummeans, which was special, his first campaign in 704–703 was directed against Babylonia: the instability of its political situation was dangerous for the Assyrian Empire. As a first solution to solve the Babylonian problem, he installed Bêl-ibni, a native pro-Assyrian of Babylon, on the throne. His second campaign in 702 was directed against insubordinate mountain dwellers of the Zagros and the rebellious Ashpa-bara, king of Ellipi, installed on the throne by Sargon. In 701, Sennacherib undertook his third campaign, to the west, in order to submit rebellious rulers of Phoenicia, Philistia, and Judah. Even though he did not conquer the island of Tyre, he succeeded in subjugating all the Phoenician and Philistine cities. He was also successful against Hezekiah of Judah, even though he did not conquer Jerusalem. He restabilized the balance of power between the different buffer states of the region, separating Assyria and Egypt. He had restored the political and economic order established by Sargon and his predecessors over the west of the empire, which provided an important part of its resources.

After devoting significant effort to military campaigns during the first period of his reign (705–701), Sennacherib modified his strategy during the second period (700–695). There were no more priority campaigns, but it was still necessary to consolidate the empire. Therefore, he adapted his military action to the evolution of the situation: the campaigns were shorter, no longer annual, and they did not always require his presence. However, Babylonia appeared to be more and more threatening for Assyria. He undertook his fourth campaign in 700 against Babylon and Bît-Yakin, still failing to capture his great enemy, Merodach-baladan. As his policy of appointing a native Babylonian had failed, he was obliged to find another procedure of government by appointing his eldest son, Ashur-nâdin-shumi, to the throne of Babylon. Then he undertook his fifth campaign, in 697 against the insubmissive people of Mount Nipur and against Maniye, the rebellious king of Ukku. He sent his magnates to repress the revolts of Que and Hilakku in 696, and against Tabal in 695, but Gurdî, the Tabalian ruler, was able to escape. The Assyrian Empire was henceforth pacified in the west, the northeast, and the north. However, the situation in the east was alarming because of the threat always represented by Elam, with its possible connection with Babylonia against Assyria. Sennacherib was conscious that the situation in Babylonia, under the control of his son Ashur-nâdin-shumi, was a precarious equilibrium, and it became an obsession for him to find out how to resolve the Babylonian problem definitively.

He elaborated a new strategy, which consisted in first defeating Elam in order to deprive Babylonia of its main ally. This was the aim of his sixth campaign, against Elam in 694. However, things did not turn out to his advantage, the main shock for him being the capture of his son Ashur-nâdin-shumi by the Babylonians, who delivered him to the Elamites. In spite of the loss of his son, Sennacherib did not change his strategy: he continued to campaign against Elam from 694 to 691 (and possibly 690), with short breaks, until he neutralized the Elamite ally of Babylon definitively. A short expedition, in 690, against the Arabs, prevented them from supporting the Babylonians. Sennacherib could then implement the final phase of his plan: the conquest of Babylon, starting its siege in spring or summer 690 and destroying the city in 689.

Even though he had incurred the hatred of the Babylonians and dreaded receiving a divine punishment for destroying the Babylonian gods, the destruction of Babylon also resulted in positive consequences for him: he was no longer frustrated because he had realized all his military goals, he was recognized as a glorious warlord by the Assyrians, and he had established a Pax Assyriaca in the entire Assyrian Empire for the remaining eight years of his reign. He had substantially increased the prosperity of the empire, which allowed him to carry out his building and innovating activities. However, the main difficulties he encountered then were no longer outside Assyria but at his court, as his domestic situation became more and more unstable. There was an increasingly severe struggle between his sons for his succession. He had mismanaged this difficult situation by designating Esarhaddon, his youngest son, as the crown prince, possibly under the influence of his wife Naqi'a.

Let us now compare the extension of the empire that Sennacherib inherited in 705 and that of the empire that he left to his son and successor Esarhaddon in 681.[2] It was almost the same, except for the annexation

---

2. Giovanni Battista Lanfranchi, "Consensus to Empire: Some Aspects of Sargon's II Foreign Policy," in *Assyrien im Wandel der Zeiten*, ed. Hartmut Waetzoldt and Harold Hauptmann, RAI 39 (Heidelberg: Heidelberger Orientverlag, 1997), 87.

of a few cities in the Zagros, which he placed under the authority of the governor of Arrapha. He also annexed the Ellipean district of Bît-Barrû, with Elenzah as capital city, which he renamed Kâr-sin-ahê-eriba, "Sennacherib-burg," entrusting it to the governor of the Assyrian province of Harhar. He boasted about this expansionist action: "And I added this area to the territory of Assyria."[3] His attempt at territorial expansion in Mount Nipur and Ukku was limited and ephemeral. He did not expand the Assyrian Empire as it was institutionalized as part of the traditional values of Assyrian society. However, he succeeded in consolidating the empire and establishing a Pax Assyriaca. It was an achievement for the king, who was not primarily a warlord. Yet he preferred to work more for the embellishment of the empire than for its expansion. In fact, he was curious about everything and happy with life. He was an aesthete, an expert and even a scholar, and a reformer.

Instead of systematically following tradition without thinking, he tried to adapt it to the new historical reality of the Assyrian Empire. With farsighted and open-minded views, he attempted to create a stable imperial structure immune from traditional recurrent problems. However, he understood that it was not possible to reform the Assyrian Empire immediately and on a large scale. Therefore, he operated progressive changes, not really noticeable at the beginning of his reign. The military campaigns were no longer dated yearly but by the number. Instead of creating new Assyrian provinces, he preferred to keep some states as buffer states. He divided the royal cohorts among leading members of the royal family, including the queen. He elaborated a new military strategy: a large-scale amphibious assault. He modified the shape of military camps from quadrangular to elliptic. He had tried to limit the influence of court officials by giving up the eponymate for them to the benefit of the governors of western and northwestern provinces. He suppressed the processions of officials on the reliefs and reduced the place of the eunuchs. Far from being a feminist, Sennacherib modified the position of royal women in Assyrian society. His major reform was by far his religious reform. By amalgamating the Assyrian and Babylonian cults under the supremacy of the god Assur, superior to Marduk, he thought he could elaborate a cult capable of uniting all the local traditions and creating a common ideological framework. His emphasis on the Assur cult was the ideological and

---

3. RINAP 3.2:79, 46.15.

religious expression of a very real political problem. He considered that tradition was both a source of legitimacy of royal power and a source of limitation; therefore, he did not completely reject it but wanted to impose his reforms.

Sennacherib was a passionate builder and an innovator who boasted of introducing a number of innovations in several fields. His most ambitious building project was his southwest palace in Nineveh, which he called "Palace without Rival."[4] He boasted of being different from his predecessors, who were ignorant and failed in their building activities.[5] In the relief program of his palace, besides his military conquests, a large place was reserved for the representation of the construction, with the king as the direct overseer of the activity. He completely transformed his capital Nineveh by enlarging and embellishing it. He also developed his building projects in Assur, the religious and ceremonial center of Assyria, and in several other places of the empire.

His interest in aspects of technology was remarkable. He used his "innate expertise ... and the craft of well-trained master builders."[6] For creating massive sculptures, he selected stones that had previously been used only for inlay and jewelry. The figures that flanked the doorways of his palace were so exceptional that he invented a new term for designating them: *aladlammû*.[7] Sennacherib boasted of inventing a new technique for casting metal. In fact, he had adapted a technique previously used for small objects such as figurines for making big objects such as bull colossi. He also knew how to make alloys. He was an innovator as far as town planning is concerned. In Nineveh, he created a new perception of the city seen from the point of view of the panorama, and this new panoramic view was introduced in the reliefs. Other important innovations of Sennacherib were related to water, one of the main problems of Nineveh and more generally Assyria. He knew how to use the water table. He invented an automatic opening of a sluice at the departure of a canal. He constructed four main canal systems at different stages of his reign: the Kisiru canal, the Mount Musri canal, the northern system, and the Khinis canal, eighteen canals in all, according to his inscriptions. He built the Jerwan aqueduct,

---

4. RINAP 3.1:38, 1.79.

5. RINAP 3.1:140, 17.vi.80–88.

6. RINAP 3.1:185, 22.vi.51b–58a; Winter, "Sennacherib's Expert Knowledge," 333–38.

7. McCormick, *Palace and Temple*, 30.

9. CONCLUSION: ASSESSMENT OF SENNACHERIB'S REIGN

an impressive monument in Iraqi Kurdistan, to convey water to Nineveh. Sennacherib was probably the inventor of the so-called Archimedes water screw, a metallic cylinder containing a spiraling helix for dumping out water. It was used for irrigating the hanging gardens of Nineveh, which predated the famous hanging gardens of Babylon. Finally, he seems to have introduced the cotton culture into Assyria: "trees bearing wool."[8]

When assessing Sennacherib's reign, his main failure was certainly the destruction of Babylon, but maybe he had no other solution for neutralizing the city. It was heavy with consequences, even if Esarhaddon did his best to rectify his father's action by reconstructing Babylon and conducting a pro-Babylonian policy. It was undoubtedly one of the reasons for the collapse of the Assyrian Empire, because the Babylonians could not forget this destruction, and they wanted to take revenge on the Assyrians.[9] Among Sennacherib's successes are ranked his building and innovating activities and his reforms. He could be compared with his father, Sargon, for the building activities, but he was unique among the Assyrian kings as an innovator. His major action as a reformer was probably one reason for his murder because the majority of society regarded his efforts to adapt tradition to the new historical reality of the Assyrian Empire as an offense to the gods and a danger for the existing order. Indeed, the hostility of societies to reform themselves is a phenomenon that has traveled down through the ages.

---

8. RINAP 3.1:142, 17.vii.57; 3.1:145, 17.viii.64.

9. For the other reasons, see, e.g., Paul Garelli and André Lemaire, *Les empires mésopotamiens, Israël*, Nouvelle Clio (Paris: Presses universitaires de France, 1997), 125; David Stronach, "Notes on the Fall of Nineveh," in Parpola and Whitting, *Assyria 1995*, 307–24; Francis Joannès, "La stratégie des rois néo-babyloniens contre l'Assyrie, de 616 à 606 av. J.-C.," in *Les armées du Proche-Orient ancien (IIIe-Ier millénaires av. J.-C.)*, BAR International Series 1855 (Oxford: Hedges, 2008), 207–18.

Selected Bibliography

General Works

Dietrich, Manfred. *The Neo-Babylonian Correspondence of Sargon and Sennacherib*. SAA 17. Helsinki: Helsinki University Press, 2003.
Frahm, Eckart. *Einleitung in die Sanherib-Inschriften*. AfOB 26. Vienna: Institut für Orientalistik, 1997.
Grayson, Albert Kirk, and Jamie Novotny. *The Royal Inscriptions of Sennacherib, King of Assyria (704–681 BC)*. 2 vols. RINAP 3.1–2. Winona Lake, IN: Eisenbrauns, 2012–2014.
Luckenbill, Daniel David. *The Annals of Sennacherib*. OIP 2. Chicago: University of Chicago Press, 1924.
Russell, John Malcolm. *Sennacherib's Palace without Rival at Nineveh*. Chicago: University of Chicago Press, 1991.

Chapter 1

Barnett, Richard D., Erika Bleibtreu, and Geoffrey Turner. *Sculptures from the Southwest Palace of Sennacherib at Nineveh I–II*. London: British Museum, 1998.
Borger, Rykle. "König Sanheribs Eheglück." *ARRIM* 6 (1998): 5–11.
Dalley, Stephanie. "The Identity of the Princesses in Tomb II and a New Analysis of Events in 701 BC." Pages 171–75 in *New Light on Nimrud: Proceedings of the Nimrud Conference Eleventh–Thirteenth March 2002*. Edited by John Curtis, Henrietta McCall, Dominique Collon, and Lamia al-Gailani Werr. London: British Institute for the Study of Iraq, 2008.
Frahm, Eckart. "Family Matters: Psychohistorical Reflections on Sennacherib and His Times." Pages 179–81 in *Sennacherib at the Gates of Jerusalem: Story, History and Historiography*. Edited by Isaac Kalimi and Seth Richardson. Leiden: Brill, 2014.

Kertai, David. "The Queens of the Neo-Assyrian Empire." *AoF* 40 (2013): 108–24.
Laato, Antii. "Assyrian Propaganda and the Falsification of History in the Royal Inscriptions of Sennacherib." *VT* 45 (1995): 198–226.
Liverani, Mario. "Critique of Variants and the Titulary of Sennacherib." Pages 225–57 in *Assyrian Royal Inscriptions: New Horizons in Literary, Ideological, and Historical Analysis*. Edited by Frederick Mario Fales. OAC 17. Rome: Istituto per l'Oriente, 1981.
Marti, Lionel. "Sennacherib, la rage du prince." *DoArch* 348 (2011): 54–59.
Melville, Sarah C. "Neo-Assyrian Royal Women and Male Identity: Status as a Social Tool." *JAOS* 124 (2004): 37–57.
Ornan, Tallay. "The Godlike Semblance of a King: The Case of Sennacherib's Rock Reliefs." Pages 161–78 in *Ancient Near Eastern Art in Context: Studies in Honor of Irene J. Winter by Her Students*. Edited by Jack Cheng and Marian H. Feldman. Leiden: Brill, 2007.
Russell, John Malcolm. *Sennacherib's Palace without Rival at Nineveh*. Chicago: University of Chicago Press, 1991.
Tadmor, Hayim. "Sennacherib, King of Justice." Pages 385–90 in *The Moshe Weinfeld Jubilee Volume*. Edited by Chaim Cohen, Avi Hurvitz, and Shalom M. Paul. Winona Lake, IN: Eisenbrauns, 2004.

Chapter 2

Ahmad, Ali Yaseen, and Albert Kirk Grayson. "Sennacherib in the Akitu House." *Iraq* 61 (1999): 187–89.
Çifçi, Ali. *The Socio-economic Organization of the Urartian Kingdom*. Leiden: Brill, 2017.
Dubóvský, Peter. *Hezekiah and the Assyrian Spies: Reconstruction of the Neo-Assyrian Intelligence Services and Its Significance for 2 Kings 18–19*. Rome: Pontifical Biblical Institute, 2006.
Elayi, Josette. *Sargon II, King of Assyria*. ABS 22. Atlanta: SBL Press, 2017.
Hunger, Hermann. *Babylonische und Assyrische Kolophone*. AOAT 2. Neukirchen-Vluyn: Neukirchener Verlag, 1968.
Ivantchik, Askold I. *Les Cimmériens au Proche-Orient*. OBO 127. Göttingen: Vandenhoeck & Ruprecht, 1993.
Parker, Bradley. J. *The Mechanics of Empire: The Northern Frontier of Assyria as a Base of Imperial Dynamics*. Helsinki: Neo-Assyrian Text Corpus Project, 2001.

Parpola, Simo. "The Royal Archives of Nineveh." Pages 223–36 in *Cuneiform Archives and Libraries*. Edited by Klaas R. Veenhof. Leiden: Nederlands Historisch-Archaeologisch Instituut te Istanbul, 1986.
Tadmor, Hayim, Benno Landsberger, and Simo Parpola. "The Sin of Sargon and Sennacherib's Last Will." *SAAB* 3 (1989): 3–51.

Chapter 3

Bagg, Ariel M. "Palestine under Assyrian Rule: A New Look at the Assyrian Imperial Policy in the West." *JAOS* 133 (2013): 119–43.
Blenkinsopp, Joseph. "Hezekiah and the Babylonian Delegation: A Critical Reading of Isa. 39:1–8." Pages 115–17 in *Essays on Ancient Israel in Its Near Eastern Context: A Tribute to Nadav Na'aman*. Edited by Yairah Amit, Ehud Ben Zvi, Israel Finkelstein, and Oded Lipschits. Winona Lake, IN: Eisenbrauns, 2006.
Elayi, Josette. "Les relations entre les cités phéniciennes et l'Empire assyrien sous le règne de Sennachérib." *Sem* 35 (1985): 19–26.
Evans, Paul S. *The Invasion of Sennacherib in the Book of Kings: A Source-Critical and Rhetorical Study of 2 Kings 18–19*. Leiden: Brill, 2009.
Fales, Frederick Mario. "The Road to Judah: 701 B.C.E. in the Context of Sennacherib's Political-Military Strategy." Pages 223–48 in *Sennacherib at the Gates of Jerusalem: Story, History and Historiography*. Edited by Isaac Kalimi and Seth Richardson. Leiden: Brill, 2014.
Frahm, Eckart. *Einleitung in die Sanherib-Inschriften*. AfOB 26. Vienna: Institut fur Orientalistik, 1997.
Gallagher, William R. *Sennacherib's Campaign to Judah: New Studies*. SHCANE 18. Leiden: Brill, 1999.
Grabbe, Lester L., ed. *"Like a Bird in a Cage": The Invasion of Sennacherib in 701 BCE*. JSOTSup 363. Sheffield: Sheffield Academic, 2003.
Kahn, Dan'el. "Tirhaka, King of Kush and Sennacherib." *JAEI* 6 (2014): 29–41.
Kalimi, Isaac, and Seth Richardson, eds. *Sennacherib at the Gates of Jerusalem: Story, History and Historiography*. Leiden: Brill, 2014.
Lanfranchi, Giovanni Battista. "The Assyrian Expansion in the Zagros and the Local Ruling Elites." Pages 79–118 in *Continuity of Empire: Assyria, Media, Persia*. Edited by Giovanni B. Lanfranchi, Michael Roaf, and Robert Rollinger. Padova: Sargon, 2003.
Levine, Louis D. "Sennacherib's Southern Front: 704–689 B.C." *JCS* 34 (1982): 28–58.

Matty, Nazek Khalid. *Sennacherib's Campaign against Judah and Jerusalem in 701 B.C.: A Historical Reconstruction*. BZAW 487. Berlin: de Gruyter, 2016.

Nadali, Davide. "Sennacherib's Siege, Assault, and Conquest of Alammu." *SAAB* 14 (2002–2005): 113–32.

Prinsloo, Gert T. M. "Sennacherib, Lachish and Jerusalem: Honour and Shame." *OTE* 13 (2000): 348–63.

Radner, Karen. "After Eltekeh: Royal Hostages from Egypt at the Assyrian Court." Pages 473–79 in *Stories of Long Ago: Festschrift für Michael D. Roaf*. Edited by Heather D. Baker, Kai Kaniuth, and Adelheid Otto. AOAT 397. Münster: Ugarit-Verlag, 2012.

Sivan, Gabriel A. "The Siege of Jerusalem: Part II: The Enigmatic Rabshakeh." *JBQ* 43 (2015): 163–71.

Tadmor, Hayim. "History and Ideology in the Assyrian Royal Inscriptions." Pages 25–46 in *"With My Many Chariots I Have Gone Up the Heights of Mountains": Historical and Literary Studies on Ancient Mesopotamia and Israel*. Edited by Mordechai Cogan. Jerusalem: Israel Exploration Society, 2011.

Ussishkin, David. "Sennacherib's Campaign to Philistia and Judah: Ekron, Lachish, and Jerusalem." Pages 339–57 in *Essays on Ancient Israel in Its Near Eastern Context: A Tribute to Nadav Na'aman*. Edited by Yairah Amit, Ehud Ben Zvi, Israel Finkelstein, and Oded Lipschits. Winona Lake, IN: Eisenbrauns, 2006.

Van Der Brugge, Caroline. "Of Production, Trade, Profit and Destruction: An Economic Interpretation of Sennacherib's Third Campaign." *JESHO* 60 (2017): 292–335.

Younger, K. Lawson. "Assyrian Involvement in Southern Levant at the End of the Eighth Century B.C.E." Pages 235–63 in *Jerusalem in Bible and Archaeology: The First Temple Period*. Edited by Andrew G. Vaughn and Ann E. Killebrew. Atlanta: Society of Biblical Literature, 2003.

Zilberg, Peter. "The Assyrian Empire and Judah: Other Historical Documents." Pages 383–406 in *From Sha'ar Hagolan to Shaaraim: Essays in Honor of Yosef Garfinkel*. Edited by S. Ganor, Igor Kreimerman, Katharina Streit, and Madeleine Mumcuoglu. Jerusalem: Israel Exploration Society, 2016.

Chapter 4

Dalley, Stephanie. "Sennacherib and Tarsus." *AnSt* 49 (1999): 73–80.

Dewar, Ben. "Rebellion, Sargon II's 'Punishment' and the Death of Aššur-nādin-šumi in the Inscriptions of Sennacherib." *Journal of Ancient Near Eastern History* 3 (2016): 25–38.
Dietrich, Manfred. "Bēl-ibni, König von Babylon (702–700)." Pages 81–108 in *Dubsar anta-men: Studies zur Altorientalistik; Festschrift für W. H. P. Römer*. Edited by Manfred Dietrich and Oswald Loretz. Münster: Ugarit-Verlag, 1998.
Fales, Frederick Mario. "Moving around Babylon: On the Aramean and Chaldean Presence in Southern Mesopotamia." Pages 91–111 in *Babylon: Wissenskulturin Orient und Okzident*. Edited by Eva Cancik-Kirschbaum, Margarete van Ess, and Joachim Marzahn. Berlin: de Gruyter, 2008.
Jeffers, Joshua. "Fifth-Campaign Reliefs in Sennacherib's 'Palace without Rival' at Nineveh." *Iraq* 73 (2011): 87–116.
Lanfranchi, Giovanni Battista. "The Ideological and Political Impact of the Assyrian Imperial Expansion on the Greek World in the 8th and 7th Centuries BC." Pages 7–34 in *The Heirs of Assyria*. Edited by Sanna Aro and Robert M. Whiting. Helsinki: Neo-Assyrian Text Corpus Project, 2000.
Parker, Bradley J. *The Mechanics of Empire: The Northern Frontier of Assyria as a Case Study of Imperial Dynamics*. Helsinki: Neo-Assyrian Text Corpus Project, 2001.
Radner, Karen. "Between a Rock and a Hard Place: Muṣaṣir, Kumme, Ukku and Šubria—The Buffer States between Assyria and Urartu." Pages 243–64 in *Biainili-Urartu*. Edited by Stephan Kroll, Claudia Gruber, Ursula Hellwag, Michael Roaf, and Paul E. Zimansky. Leuven: Peeters, 2012.

Chapter 5

Alibaigi, Sajjad, Abdol-Malek Shanbehzadeh, and Hossain Alibaigi. "The Discovery of a Neo-Assyrian Rock-Relief at Mishkhas, Ilam Province (Iran)." *IrAnt* 47 (2012): 29–40.
Brinkman, John A. "Sennacherib's Babylonian Problem: An Interpretation." *JCS* 25 (1973): 89–95.
Fales, Frederick Mario. "On *Pax Assyriaca* in the Eighth-Seventh Centuries BCE and Its Implications." Pages 17–35 in *Swords into Plowshares: Isaiah's Vision of Peace in Biblical and Modern International Relations*.

Edited by Raymond Cohen and Raymond Westbrook. Basingstoke, UK: Macmillan, 2008.

Finkel, Israel L. "A Report on Extispicies Performed for Sennacherib on Account of His Son Aššur-nadin-šumi." *SAAB* 1 (1987): 53.

Frame, Grant. *Babylonia 689–627 B.C.: A Political History.* Leiden: Nederlands Instituut voor het Nabije Oosten, 1992.

Grayson, Albert Kirk. *Assyrian and Babylonian Chronicles.* TCS 5. Winona Lake, IN: Eisenbrauns, 2000.

Parpola, Simo. "A Letter to Sennacherib Referring to the Conquest of Bit-Ha'iri and Other Events of the Year 693." Pages 559–77 in *Ex Mesopotamia et Syria Lux: Festschrift für Manfred Dietrich.* Edited by Oswald Loretz, Kai A. Metzler, and Hanspeter Schaudig. Münster: Ugarit-Verlag, 2002.

Radner, Karen. "An Assyrian View on the Medes." Pages 38–58 in *Continuity of Empires: Assyria, Media, Persia.* Edited by Giovanni B. Lanfranchi, Michael Roaf, and Robert Rollinger. Padova: Sargon, 2003.

Van De Mieroop, Marc. "Metaphors of Massacre in Assyrian Royal Inscriptions." *KASKAL* 12 (2015): 291–317.

Weissert, Elnathan. "Creating a Political Climate: Literary Allusions to Enūma Eliš in Sennacherib's Account of the Battle of Halule." Pages 191–202 in *Assyrien im Wandel der Zeiten.* Edited by Hartmut Waetzoldt and Harold Hauptman. RAI 39. Heidelberg: Heidelberger Orientverlag, 1997.

Chapter 6

Cogan, Mordechai. "Sennacherib and the Angry Gods of Babylon and Israel." *IEJ* 59 (2009): 164–82.

Frahm, Eckart. "Perlen von den Rändern der Welt." Pages 79–99 in *Languages and Cultures in Contact: At the Crossroads of Civilizations in the Syro-Mesopotamian Realm.* Edited by Karel Van Lerberghe and Gabriela Voet. RAI 42. Leuven: Peeters, 1999.

Frame, Grant. *Rulers of Babylonia from the Second Dynasty of Isin to the End of the Assyrian Domination (1157–612 BC).* Toronto: University of Toronto Press, 1995.

Leichty, Erle. "Esarhaddon's Exile: Some Speculative History." Pages 189–91 in *Studies Presented to Robert Biggs.* Edited by Martha T. Roth, Walter Farber, and Matthew W. Stolper. AS 27. Chicago: Oriental Institute of the University of Chicago, 2007.

Parpola, Simo. "The Murderer of Sennacherib." Pages 171–82 in *Death in Mesopotamia*. Edited by Bendt Alster. RAI 26. Copenhagen: Akademisk, 1980.
Reade, J. E. "Was Sennacherib a Feminist?" Pages 139–45 in *La femme dans le Proche-Orient antique*. Edited by Jean-Marie Durand. RAI 33. Paris: ERC, 1986.
Tammuz, Oded. "Punishing a Dead Villain: The Biblical Accounts of the Murder of Sennacherib." *BN* 157 (2013): 101–5.
Zawadski, Stefan. "Oriental and Greek Tradition about the Death of Sennacherib." *SAAB* 4 (1990): 69–72.

Chapter 7

Battini, Laura. "La localisation du palais sud-ouest de Ninive." *RA* 90 (1996): 33–40.
Epha'al, Israel. "The Assyrian Siege Ramp at Lachish: Military and Lexical Aspects." *TA* 11 (1984): 60–70.
George, A. R. "Sennacherib and the Tablet of Destinies." *Iraq* 48 (1986): 133–46.
Grayson, Albert Kirk, and J. Ruby. "Instructions for Inscribing Sennacherib's Seal." *Iraq* 59 (1997): 89–91.
Machinist, Peter. "Kingship and Divinity in Imperial Assyria." Pages 405–30 in *Assur: Gott, Stadt und Land*. Edited by Johannes Renger. CDOGS 5. Berlin: Harrassowitz, 2011.
Micale, Maria Gabriella, and Davide Nadali. "The Shape of Sennacherib's Camps: Strategic Functions and Ideological Space." *Iraq* 66 (2004): 163–75.
Moreno García, Juan Carlos, ed. *Dynamics of Production in the Ancient Near East, 1300–500 BC*. Oxford: Oxbow, 2016.
Pečirková, Jana. "Assyria under Sennacherib." *ArOr* 61 (1993): 1–10.
Ponchia, Simonetta. "Administrators and Administrated in Neo-Assyrian Times." Pages 213–24 in *Organization, Representation, and Symbols of Power in the Ancient Near East*. Edited by Gernot Wilhelm. RAI 54. Winona Lake, IN: Eisenbrauns, 2012.
Postgate, John Nicholas. "The Invisible Hierarchy: Assyrian Military and Civilian Administration in the 8th and 7th Centuries BC." Pages 331–62 in *The Land of Assur and the Yoke of Assur: Studies on Assyria; 1971–2005*. Oxford: Oxbow, 2007.

Radner, Karen. "The Assur-Nineveh-Arbela Triangle, Central Assyria in the Neo-Assyrian Period." Pages 321–29 in *Between the Cultures: The Central Tigris Region from the Third to the First Millennium*. Edited by Peter A. Miglus and Simone Mühl. Heidelberg: Heidelberger Orientverlag, 2011.

Svärd, Saana. "Changes in Neo-Assyrian Queenship." *SAAB* 21 (2015): 162–69.

Vargyas, Peter. "Sennacherib Alleged Half-Shekel Coins." *JNES* 61 (2002): 111–15.

Villard, Pierre. "Quelques aspects du renseignement militaire dans l'Empire néo-assyrien." *HIMA* 3 (2016): 87–97.

Chapter 8

Barnett, Richard D., Erika Bleibtreu, and Geoffrey. *Sculptures from the Southwest Palace of Sennacherib at Nineveh*. London: British Museum, 1998.

Dalley, Stephanie. "More about the Hanging Gardens." Pages 67–73 in *Of Pots and Plans: Papers on the Archaeology and History of Mesopotamia and Syria Presented to David Oates in Honour of His Seventy-Fifth Birthday*. Edited by Lamia Al-Gailani Werr, John Curtis, Harriet Martin, Augusta McMahon, Joan Oates, and J. E. Reade. London: Nabu, 2002.

Dalley, Stephanie, and John Peter Oleson. "Sennacherib, Archimedes and the Water Screw: The Context of Invention in the Ancient World." *Technology and Culture* 44 (2003): 1–26.

Fales, Frederick Mario, and Roswitha Del Fabbro. "Back to Sennacherib's Aqueduct at Jerwan: A Reassessment of the Textual Evidence." *Iraq* 76 (2014): 65–98.

Lumsden, Stephen. "On Sennacherib's Nineveh." Pages 815–34 in *Proceedings of the First International Congress on the Archaeology of the Ancient Near East*. Edited by Paolo Matthiae, Lorenzo Nigro, Luca Peyronel, and Frances Pinnock. Rome: La Sapienza, 2000.

McCormick, Clifford Mark. *Palace and Temple: A Study of Architectural and Verbal Icons*. Berlin: de Gruyter, 2002.

Morrow, William. "Water Control and Royal Propaganda: Sennacherib's Boast in 2 Kgs 19:24 (= Isa 37:25)." Pages 317–37 in *Thinking of Water in the Early Second Temple Period*. Edited by Ehud Ben Zvi and Christoph Levin. Berlin: de Gruyter, 2014.

Nadali, Davide. "An Urban Perspective of Nineveh." *Mes* 50 (2015): 157–76.

Novák, Mirko. "From Ashur to Nineveh: The Assyrian Town-Planning Programme." *Iraq* 66 (2004): 177–85.

Polinger Foster, Karen. "The Hanging Gardens of Nineveh." *Iraq* 66 (2004): 207–20.

Reade, Julian E. "Assyrian Palace at Nebi Yunes, Nineveh." Pages 431–58 in *At the Dawn of History: Ancient Near Eastern Studies in Honour of J. N. Postgate*. Edited by Yagmur Heffron, Adam Stone, and Martin Worthington. Winona Lake, IN: Eisenbrauns, 2017.

———. "Studies in Assyrian Geography. Part I: Sennacherib and the Waters of Nineveh." *RA* 72 (1978): 47–72, 157–75.

Rivaroli, Marta. "Nineveh: From Ideology to Topography." *Iraq* 66 (2004): 199–205.

Russell, John Malcolm. *Sennacherib's Palace without Rival at Nineveh*. Chicago: University of Chicago Press, 1991.

Ur, Jason. "Sennacherib's Northern Assyrian Canals: New Insights from Satellite imagery and Aerial Photography." *Iraq* 67 (2005): 317–45.

Winter, Irene J. "Sennacherib's Expert Knowledge: Skill and Mastery as Components of Royal Display." Pages 333–38 in *Proceedings of the Fifty-First Rencontre Assyriologique Internationale, Held at the Oriental Institute of the University of Chicago, July 18–22, 2005: Studies in Ancient Oriental Civilization 62*. Edited by Robert D. Biggs, Jennie Myers, and Martha T. Roth. RAI 51. Chicago: Oriental Institute of the University of Chicago, 2008.

Index of Ancient Sources

Hebrew Bible/Old Testament

1 Kings
16:31	55

2 Kings
16:7	14
18:7–8	61
18–19	7 n. 25, 31 n. 10, 212–13
18:13–37	5 n. 14
19:1	85 n. 173
19:21b	79
19:24	86, 180 n. 40, 218
20:12–19	72

2 Chronicles
18–19	7 n. 25, 31 n. 10, 212–13
32:1–23	5 n. 14
32:31	72

Isaiah
10:5–6	150
29:5–9	5 n. 14
30:27–33	5 n. 14
31:5–8	5 n. 14
32:2–3	77
36–37	69
36:1	73
36:6	42
36:13–22	5 n. 14
37:1–38	5 n. 14
39:1–8	72 n. 126, 213

Micah
1:8–16	5 n. 14

Deuterocanonical Works

Tobit
1:18–22	5 n. 14

1 Maccabees
7:41–42	5 n. 14

2 Maccabees
8:19	5 n. 14
15:22–24	5 n. 14

Sirach
48:18–22	5 n. 14

Ancient Jewish Writers

Josephus, *Antiquitates Judaicae*
9.283–285	53 n. 50, 55 n. 58
10.1–23	5 n. 14, 69 n. 113, 149 n. 87

Greco-Roman Literature

Berossus, *Babyloniaca* 4, 15 n. 24, 47 n. 18, 93, 103 nn. 65–66, 148–49, 149 n. 86

Diodorus Siculus, *Bibliotheca historica*
1.34.2	199 n. 152

Herodotus, *Histories*
2.41	69 n. 113
2.141	4 n. 14, 82 nn. 159–60, 124 n. 81
3.106	201 n. 162

Index of Modern Authors

Adali, Selim   12
Ahmad, Ali Yaseen   x, 30 n. 5, 212
Albright, William F.   85 n. 171
Alibaigi, Hossain   50 n. 33, 114 n. 33, 215
Alibaigi, Sajjad   50 n. 33, 215
Al-Rawi, Farouk N. H.   13 n. 13
Anderson, Julie Renee   198 n. 147
Andrae, Walter   13 n. 14
Archer, Robin   22 n. 68
Aruz, Joan   200 n. 155
Bagg, Ariel M.   22 n. 67, 88 n. 183, 195 n. 129, 201 n. 159, 213
Baker, Heather D.   67 n. 107, 161 n. 38, 163 n. 49, 214
Balmuth, Miriam S.   158 n. 26
Bányai, Michael   66 n. 101
Barnett, Richard D.   7 n. 26, 11 n. 1, 12 n. 6, 74 n. 133, 174 n. 4, 211, 218
Basmachi, Faraj   198 n. 148
Battini, Laura   164 n. 56, 183 n. 55, 217
Bauer, T.   144 n. 65, 147 nn. 81–82
Becking, Bob   62 n. 127, 86 n. 177
Berlejung, Angelika   88 n. 183
Bianchetti, Pier Luigi   179 n. 30
Bikai, Patricia   59 nn. 77–78
Bing, John Daniel   100 n. 56
Black, Jeremy   24 n. 78, 163 n. 49
Blakely, Jeffrey A.   74 n. 131
Bleibtreu, Erika   7 n. 26, 11 n. 1, 12 n. 6, 74 n. 133, 174 n. 4, 211, 218
Blenkinsopp, Joseph   72 n. 126, 213
Boehmer, Rainer   196 n. 139
Borger, Rykle   16 n. 33, 17 nn. 39 and 44, 57 n. 69, 105 n. 77, 145 n. 70, 211
Börker-Klähn, Jutta   165 n. 63
Bostock, David   70 n. 115
Botta, Paul-Émile   5 n. 16, 6 n. 20, 319
Bottéro, Jean   169 nn. 82 and 85
Breasted, J. H.   69 n. 113
Briant, Pierre   163 n. 48, 198 n. 149
Bright, John   85 n. 171
Brinkman, John A. 45 nn. 10 and 13, 46 n. 16, 48 n. 23, 90 n. 8, 110 n. 11, 111 nn. 15 and 18, 112 n. 22, 125 n. 83, 127 n. 88, 128 n. 92, 135 nn. 13–14, 136 n. 22, 155 n. 9, 185 n. 66, 195 n. 129, 215
Brown, John Pairman   180 n. 39
Budge, E. A. Wallis   6 n. 18
Bujanda Viloria, Sharif   151 n. 97
Buringh, P.   195 n. 132
Burstein, Stanley Meyer   15 n. 24, 47 n. 18, 103 nn. 65–66, 149 n. 86
Byron, Lord   1 n. 1
Campbell Thompson, Reginald   6 n. 18, 95 n. 29, 157 n. 25
Casabonne, Olivier   100 n. 56, 101 n. 59
Catastini, Alessandro   79 n. 149
Cavigneaux, Antoine   103 n. 69
Charpin, Dominique   24 n. 78, 163 n. 53
Childs, Brevard S.   70 n. 118
Çifçi, Ali   37 n. 44, 212
Clements, Ronald E.   79 n. 149
Cogan, Mordechai   2 n. 3, 61 n. 85, 64 n. 92, 65 nn. 96–97, 68 n. 110, 70 n. 114, 86 n. 175, 87 nn. 180–81, 145 n. 67, 149 n. 90, 150 n. 92, 152 n. 102, 179 n. 32, 214, 216
Cohen, Chaim   21 n. 63, 22 n. 67, 78 n. 147, 131 n. 104, 212, 216

INDEX OF MODERN AUTHORS

Collins, Paul 75 n. 136
Collon, Dominique 13 n. 13, 24 n. 78, 178 n. 25, 211
Cothren, J. Tom 201 n. 161
Curtis, John E. 13 n. 13, 24 n. 78, 159 n. 31, 185 n. 67, 192 n. 117, 211, 218
Dalley, Stephanie 13 n. 13, 14 nn. 18–19, 61 n. 82, 66 n. 103, 83 n. 162, 101 n. 59, 103 n. 67, 104 n. 71, 148 n. 82, 155 n. 11, 159 n. 31, 185 n. 67, 195 n. 129, 198 n. 149, 199 nn. 150 and 152–53, 200 nn. 154 and 156–58, 211, 214, 218
Dalongeville, Rémi 92 n. 18
Danrey, Virginie 180 n. 36
De Backer, Fabrice Y. 76 n. 142, 202 nn. 165 and 167
Del Fabbro, Roswitha 7 n. 27, 197 nn. 143–44, 198 nn. 145–46, 218
De Miroschedji, Pierre 115 n. 35
De Odorico, Marco xii
Desideri, Paolo 100 n. 56
Dewar, Ben 93 n. 22, 111 n. 17, 215
Dietrich, Manfred 4 n. 11, 90 n. 8, 121 n. 64, 211, 215–16
Dothan, Trude 64 n. 96, 65 n. 97
Drews, Robert 103 n. 65
Dubóvský, Peter 31 n. 10, 78 n. 146, 212
Eide, Tormod 69 n. 113
Elayi, Alain G. 159 n. 33
Elayi, Josette 2 n. 4, 8 nn. 29 and 31, 9 n. 32, 15 n. 27, 18 n. 48, 20 n. 57, 30 n. 4, 32 nn. 11, 13 and 15, 33 n. 22, 34 nn. 24 and 26, 35 n. 31, 36 n. 34, 37 nn. 42–43, 39 n. 58, 43 nn. 2–3, 47 nn. 18 and 22, 49 n. 26, 50 n. 32, 51 n. 39, 52 n. 45, 53 n. 48, 55 nn. 52–53 and 55, 56 nn. 62 and 64, 58 nn. 72 and 74, 60 n. 80, 61 n. 83, 63 n. 86, 66 n. 101, 71 n. 120, 84 n. 166, 87 n. 178, 97 n. 39, 101 n. 57, 103 n. 69, 104 n. 74, 105 n. 80, 133 n. 1, 142 n. 54, 150 n. 93, 159 n. 33, 161 n. 38, 165 n. 41, 173 n. 3, 174 n. 8, 177 n. 23, 179 n. 32, 204 n. 1, 212–13

Eph'al, Israel 2 n. 3, 74 n. 131, 76 n. 140, 123 nn. 71–72, 124 nn. 74–76 and 80–81, 157 n. 22, 217
Erzen, Afif 100 n. 56
Evans, Paul S. 7 n. 25, 78 nn. 146–47, 83 n. 162, 213
Fales, Frederick Mario 3 n. 8, 4 n. 14, 7 n. 27, 16 n. 32, 21 n. 62, 27 n. 91, 43 n. 3, 44 nn. 6–7, 53 n. 47, 70 n. 114, 76 n. 139, 77 nn. 143–44, 78 n. 146, 86 n. 163, 84 n. 167, 87 n. 182, 91 n. 11, 119 n. 58, 121 n. 64, 123 n. 70, 125 n. 83, 131 n. 104, 156 n. 11, 164 n. 58, 168 n. 79, 169 n. 81, 197 nn. 143–44, 198 nn. 145–46, 202 n. 166, 212–13, 215, 218
Farber, Walter 33 n. 17, 145 n. 67, 216
Finkel, Israel L. 44 n. 6, 111 n. 19, 216
Finn, Jennifer 166 n. 68
Flandin, Eugène 31 n. 9
Fleming, Wallace Bruce 53 n. 48
Frahm, Eckart 1 n. 1, 2 n. 5, 4 nn. 10–14, 6 nn. 21–22, 7 nn. 24 and 28, 8 n. 30, 13 n. 15, 14 n. 16, 15 n. 29, 16 nn. 32 and 36, 17 n. 39, 30 nn. 6–7, 44 nn. 5–6, 57 n. 67, 74 n. 132, 94 n. 25, 98 n. 45, 105 n. 76, 124 n. 79, 130 n. 103, 134 nn. 3–4, 135 n. 15, 138 nn. 30–31, 160 n. 35, 168 n. 77, 174 n. 7, 176 n. 16, 171 n. 43, 183 nn. 51 and 54, 184 nn. 58 and 61, 188 n. 89, 189 nn. 94 and 99, 190 n. 101, 196 n. 134, 201 n. 159, 211, 213, 216
Frame, Grant 45 nn. 9 and 12, 117 n. 47, 128 n. 92, 129 nn. 97 and 99, 130 n. 103, 134 n. 2, 135 nn. 10, 12 and 15, 136 nn. 18 and 20–21, 137 n. 28, 138 n. 29, 144 n. 65, 145 n. 68, 167 n. 70, 168 n. 76, 183 n. 49, 216
French, Eva 100 n. 56
Frymer-Kensky, Tikva 168 n. 77
Fuchs, Alexander 76 n. 140
Furtwängler, Andreas 158 n. 26
Gadd, Cyril John 6 n. 18
Galil, Gershon 72 n. 127, 86 n. 177

Gallagher, William R.   7 n. 25, 56 n. 63, 57 nn. 66–69, 61 n. 81, 63 nn. 86 and 89–90, 64 nn. 93–94, 65 nn. 96 and 98, 66 n. 102, 67 n. 105, 69 n. 113, 70 n. 118, 71 n. 122, 72 nn. 124 and 126, 74 n. 132, 77 n. 145, 78 n. 147, 79 n. 149, 213
Galter, Hannes D.   180 n. 36, 187 n. 82
Garelli, Paul   2 n. 3, 209 n. 9
Garsiel, Moshe   12 n. 8, 147 n. 79
Gaspa, Salvatore   159 n. 34, 160 n. 37
George, A. R.   25 n. 81, 26 n. 86, 167 n. 74, 217
Gichon, Mordechai   202 n. 164
Gillmann, Nicolas   192 n. 119
Gitin, Seymour   64 n. 96, 65 n. 97, 75 n. 138, 88 n. 183
Goetze, Albrecht   104 n. 71
Goldberg, Jeremy   85 n. 171, 86 n. 177
Goldman, Hetty   104 n. 71
Gonçalves, Francolino C.   7 n. 25
Grabbe, Lester L.   7 n. 25, 53 n. 48, 69 n. 113, 70 n. 118, 72 n. 127, 73 n. 130, 74 n. 133, 82 n. 160, 84 n. 166, 213
Grayson, Albert Kirk   4 n. 10, 6 n. 22, 7, 14 n. 20, 30 n. 5, 45 n. 9, 46 n. 17, 47 nn. 18–19, 71 n. 123, 85 n. 172, 90 n. 5, 93 n. 23, 109 n. 7, 110 n. 11, 111 nn. 13–14, 112 nn. 20 and 22–23, 113 n. 26, 114 nn. 29 and 33, 115 n. 37, 116 n. 42, 121 nn. 63–64, 122, 123 n. 68, 126 nn. 86–87, 127, 134 n. 6, 137 nn. 24–28, 140 n. 44, 141 nn. 50 and 52, 146 n. 74, 149 n. 89, 152 n. 99, 162 n. 48, 167 n. 71, 183 n. 49, 184 n. 61, 211–12, 216–17
Hardin, James W.   74 n. 131
Harper, Prudence   200 n. 155
Heidel, Alexandra   105 n. 78
Herzog, Chaim   202 n. 164
Hirschberg, Hans   147 n. 81
Holm, Tawny L.   5 n. 14
Honor, Leo L.   7 n. 25
Horn, Siegfried H.   85 n. 171
Hornung, Erik   66 n. 101
Howgego, Christopher   158 n. 26
Hunger, Hermann   13 n. 12, 29 n. 1, 212
Hutchinson, Richard Wyatt   6 n. 18
Huxley, Margaret   186 n. 75, 191 n. 110
Ivantchik, Askold I.   32 n. 15, 146 n. 76, 212
Jacobsen, Thorkild   7 n. 27, 121 n. 64, 197 n. 143
Jacoby, Felix   93 n. 23, 103 n. 65
Jacquet, Antoine   164 n. 54
Jasink, Anna M.   100 n. 56
Jean, Cynthia   163 n. 50
Jeffers, Joshua   98 n. 47, 99 n. 48, 176 n. 18, 215
Joannès, Francis   29 n. 3, 33 n. 16, 45 n. 13, 46 n. 16, 92 n. 18, 120 n. 59, 136 n. 22, 159 n. 34, 166 n. 68, 178 n. 29, 182 n. 46, 201 n. 161, 209 n. 9
Kahn, Dan'el   66 n. 101, 67 n. 105, 86 n. 175, 87 n. 179, 213
Kalimi, Isaac   1 n. 1, 5 n. 14, 7 n. 25, 8 n. 28, 43 n. 3, 67 n. 105, 68 n. 110, 73 n. 129, 211, 213
Kamil, Ahmed   13 n. 14
Kataja, Laura   xi, 13 n. 9
Katzenstein, H. Jacob   53 n. 48, 59 n. 77
Kennedy, D.A.   45 n. 10, 135 n. 13
Kertai, David   13 n. 13, 16 n. 34, 182 n. 47, 188 nn. 85–86, 212
Kessler, Karlheinz   33 n. 17
Killebrew, Ann E.   53 n. 47, 76 n. 141, 101 n. 56, 214
King, L.W.   6, 175
Knapp, Andrew   138 n. 33, 148 n. 82
Knauf, Ernst Axel   72 n. 127, 84 n. 166
Knorr, Wilbur R.   199 n. 152
Kofoed, Jenns Bruun   70 n. 115
König, Friedrich Wilhelm   110 n. 12, 149 n. 88
Kravitz, Kathryn F.   38 n. 48
Kupper, Jean-Robert   120 n. 59
Kwasman, Theodore   xi, 139
Laato, Antii   4 n. 9, 20 n. 60, 70 n. 114, 84 n. 170, 93 n. 22, 212
Labat, René   144 nn. 63 and 66, 169 n. 85

INDEX OF MODERN AUTHORS

Lackenbacher, Sylvie   176 n. 15
Lambert, Wilfred G.   160 n. 36, 167 n. 74, 170 n. 88
Landsberger, Benno   41 n. 67, 43 n. 3, 121 n. 64, 144 n. 65, 145 n. 70, 147 nn. 81–82, 150 n. 93, 213
Lanfranchi, Giovanni Battista   3 n. 8, 16 n. 32, 49 nn. 24 and 26, 52 n. 43, 96 n. 38, 105 n. 76, 206 n. 2, 213, 215–16
Larsen, Mogens Trolle   84 n. 166, 145 n. 68, 158 n. 25
Layard, Austen Henry   5 n. 16, 6 n. 20, 57 n. 65, 178 n. 27
Leichty, Erle   145 n. 67, 216
Lemaire, André   209 n. 9
Le Rider, Georges   158 n. 26
Leroux, Magdel   80 n. 152
Levine, Baruch A.   83 n. 161
Levine, Louis D.   45 n. 11, 49 n. 27, 50 nn. 29–30, 52 n. 44, 90 n. 8, 92 n. 16, 93 n. 22, 108 n. 1, 110 n. 11, 112 nn. 22–23, 114 nn. 31 and 33, 116 n. 41, 122 nn. 65 and 67, 125 nn. 82–83, 130 n. 100, 137 n. 28, 180 n. 36, 213
Lewis, Theodore J.   22 n. 67
Lewy, Hildegard   141 n. 52, 145 n. 69
Lie, Arthur Gotfred   174 n. 5
Lindenberger, J. M.   4 n. 14
Lipiński, Edward   147 n. 78, 158 n. 29, 159 nn. 32–33
Liverani, Mario   6 n. 21, 27 n. 91, 49 n. 27, 65 n. 100, 119 n. 58, 185 nn. 66 and 68, 212
Livingstone, A.   168 n. 77
Liwak, Rüdiger   70 n. 117
Lloyd, Seton   7 n. 27, 197 n. 143
Luckenbill, Daniel David   2 n. 5, 6, 7 n. 24, 47 n. 20, 49 n. 28, 56 n. 64, 58 nn. 75–76, 71 n. 119, 76 n. 139, 95 n. 28, 113 n. 27, 122 n. 67, 126 n. 85, 156 n. 16, 158 n. 27, 183 n. 51, 184 nn. 59–60, 202 n. 164, 211
Lumsden, Stephen   193 n. 120, 194 nn. 123–24 and 127, 195 n. 129, 218
Lundström, Steven   188 n. 89
Luukko, Mikko   xi
Macadam, M. F. L.   69 n. 113
MacGinnis, John   182 n. 45
Machinist, Peter   46 n. 16, 78 n. 147, 169 nn. 82–83, 217
Madhloom, T.   6 n. 18, 202 n. 164
Magee, Peter   198 n. 149
Magen, Ursula   162 n. 40, 169 n. 81
Maila-Afeiche, Anne-Marie   20 n. 55
Malbran-Labat, Florence   110 n. 12
Manitius, Walther   156 n. 18
Marcus, D.   63 n. 89
Marti, Lionel   23 n. 71, 26 n. 88, 76 n. 142, 126 n. 84, 163 n. 49, 196 n. 134, 212
Mattila, Raija   xii
Matty, Nazek Khalid   7 n. 25, 69 n. 113, 70 n. 118, 74 n. 134, 75 n. 135, 76 n. 141, 77 n. 145, 80 nn. 153 and 155, 81 n. 158, 214
Maul, Stefan Mario   186 n. 71
Mayer, Walter   47 n. 18, 53 n. 48, 75 n. 136, 76 n. 139, 81 n. 156, 83 n. 163, 103 n. 65, 121 n. 64
McCormick, Clifford Mark   175 n. 11, 176 n. 15, 177 nn. 19 and 21, 190 n. 105, 191 nn. 107 and 110, 192 nn. 118–19, 208 n. 7, 218
Meissner, Bruno   2 n. 5, 6, 7 n. 24
Melville, Sarah C.   xii, 13 n. 13, 14 n. 18, 15 n. 30, 16 n. 34, 138, 142, 165, 212
Micale, Maria Gabriella   157 nn. 21 and 23–24, 217
Michalowski, Piotr   167 n. 74
Miglus, Peter A.   154 n. 6, 174 n. 7, 188 nn. 85–86 and 89, 218
Millard, Alan   xi
Moinard, Victoire   130 n. 102, 150 n. 94
Moorey, Peter Roger Stuart   192 n. 117
Morandi Bonacossi, Daniele   16 n. 32, 179 n. 30, 185 n. 67
Moreno García, Juan Carlos   160 n. 34, 217
Morrow, William   180 n. 40, 218
Moulherat, Christophe   201 n. 161

Muhly, James D. 192 n. 117
Musil, Alois 123 n. 70, 124 n. 74
Na'aman, Nadav 56 n. 62, 61 n. 83, 65 n. 96, 72 n. 127, 76 n. 141, 152 n. 102, 213–14
Nadali, Davide 50 n. 34, 51 n. 37, 76 n. 142, 157 nn. 21 and 23–24, 181 n. 42, 214, 217, 219
Naveh, Joseph 65 n. 97
Neate, Geoffrey 111 n. 15
Nougayrol, Jean 165 n. 63
Novák, Mirko 182 n. 48, 219
Novotny, Jamie x, 3 n. 5, 7, 71 n. 119, 211
Oded, Bustenay 20 n. 60, 155 n. 7
Oegema, Gerbern S. 5 n. 14
Oleson, John Peter 159 n. 31, 199 nn. 150–53, 200, 154 nn. 156–58, 218
Olmstead, Albert Ten Eyck 153 n. 1, 160 n. 37
Onasch, Hans-Ulrich 17 n. 46, 67 n. 107
Oppenheim, A. Leo 157 n. 25, 158 n. 25
Ornan, Tallay 12 n. 5, 212
Otzen, Benedikt 84 n. 166
Parker, Bradley J. 3 n. 8, 34 n. 27, 36 n. 35, 96 n. 36, 97 n. 42, 212, 215
Parpola, Simo x–xi, 4 n. 11, 15 n. 25, 18 n. 47, 29 n. 3, 30 n. 7, 41 n. 67, 43 n. 3, 47 n. 22, 88 n. 183, 96 n. 38, 105 n. 78, 111 n. 18, 114 n. 32, 131 n. 1, 139 n. 36, 140 n. 46, 142 n. 60, 144 n. 63, 147 nn. 80–81, 148 n. 84, 149, 150 n. 93, 161 n. 39, 164 nn. 55–56, 164 n. 58, 165 n. 59, 166 n. 68, 170 n. 86, 181 n. 42, 209 n. 9, 213, 216–17
Parrot, André 165 n. 63
Paterson, Archibald 7 n. 26
Payraudeau, Frédéric 66 n. 101, 67 n. 104
Pečirková, Jana 87 n. 182, 152 n. 101, 153 n. 2, 154 n. 4, 169 n. 84, 217
Pedde, Friedhelm 188 n. 86
Petit, Lucas P. 179 n. 30

Pickworth, Diana 179 n. 29
Polinger Foster, Karen 182 n. 47, 185 n. 67, 219
Ponchia, Simonetta 16 n. 32, 161 n. 38, 217
Pongratz-Leisten, Beate 168 n. 77, 187 n. 80
Pope, Jeremy 67 n. 105
Porten, Bezalel 87 n. 178
Postgate, John Nicholas xi, 2 n. 3, 22 n. 68, 55 n. 55, 155 n. 11, 156 nn. 15 and 18, 158 n. 25, 182 n. 45, 217, 219
Powell, Marvin A. 158 n. 29
Prinsloo, Gert T. M. 70 n. 116, 214
Radner, Karen x, 16 n. 32, 33 n. 17, 52 nn. 43 and 45, 67 n. 107, 94 n. 27, 96 n. 37, 98 n. 46, 154 n. 6, 158 n. 25, 162 n. 48, 163 n. 49, 185 n. 69, 214–16, 218
Rassam, Hormuzd 5, 6 n. 18
Rawlinson, George 85 n. 172
Rawlinson, Henry Cresswicke 5
Reade, Julian E. 26 n. 89, 44 n. 6, 49 n. 27, 114 n. 33, 126 n. 85, 134 n. 3, 153 n. 2, 162 n. 42, 165, 169 n. 81, 177 n. 19, 179 n. 31, 180 n. 36, 182 nn. 45 and 49, 183 n. 50, 192 n. 119, 195 n. 129, 198 n. 147, 219
Redford, Donald B. 66 n. 101, 85 n. 172, 87 n. 180
Reuther, Oskar 129 n. 98
Reynolds, Frances xi
Richardson, Seth 1 n. 1, 5 n. 14, 7 n. 7, 8 n. 28, 43 n. 3, 68 n. 110, 73 n. 129, 211, 213
Rivaroli, Martha 193 n. 120, 194 n. 125, 219
Rost, Paul 2 n. 5, 6, 7 n. 24
Roth, Martha 18 n. 49, 145 n. 67, 174 n. 3, 216, 219
Röthlin, Gail A. 80 n. 152
Ruby, J. 162 n. 48, 217
Russell, G. L. 2 n. 5, 6
Russell, John Malcolm 5 n. 17, 6 nn. 18–19, 7 nn. 24 and 26, 11 n. 2,

INDEX OF MODERN AUTHORS

20 n. 56, 50 n. 35, 57 n. 65, 69 n. 113, 74 nn. 132–34, 98 n. 45, 174 n. 4, 175, 176 nn. 15 and 17, 178 nn. 26–27 and 29, 179 nn. 30 and 33–34, 180 nn. 37 and 41, 181 nn. 42 and 44, 182 nn. 46–47, 191 n. 108, 192 n. 119, 194 n. 127, 211–12, 219
Sader, Hélène 58 n. 72
Safar, Fuad 198 n. 148
Saggs, Henry William Frederick 55 n. 55, 158 n. 28, 202 n. 166
Salonen, Erkki 202 n. 166
Salvini, Mirjo 32 n. 15
Sanlaville, Paul 92 n. 18
Sano, Katsuji 4 n. 9
Saporetti, Claudio 7 n. 25
Schaudig, Hanspeter 4 n. 11, 149 n. 90, 150 n. 91, 216
Schmidtke, Friedrich 147 n. 81, 148 n. 83
Schroeder, Otto 186 n. 75
Scurlock, Jo Ann 121 n. 64
Sence, Guillaume 75 n. 136
Shea, William H. 85 nn. 171 and 173, 86 n. 174
Sivan, Gabriel A. 78 n. 147, 214
Smelik, Klaas A. D. 79 n. 149
Smith, C. Wayne 201 n. 161
Smith, George 5 n. 6
Smith, Sidney 157 n. 25
Snell, Daniel C. 16 n. 34, 158 n. 25
Sommerfeld, Walter 166 n. 68
Spalinger, Anthony 66 n. 101, 70 n. 117
Stern, Ephraim ix
Strachey, Lytton 1 n. 1
Streck, Maximilian 147 n. 80
Stronach, David 147 n. 80
Svärd, Saana xii, 16 n. 37, 156 n. 14, 218
Tadmor, Hayim 2 n. 3, 3 n. 8, 20 n. 57, 21 n. 63, 41 n. 67, 43 n. 3, 61 n. 83, 63 n. 89, 64 n. 93, 70 n. 114, 100 n. 53, 150 n. 93, 153 n. 3, 154 n. 4, 165 n. 61, 171 n. 91, 194 n. 127, 212–14
Tallqvist, Knut Leonard 147 n. 82
Talon, Françoise 200 n. 155
Tammuz, Oded 147 nn. 81–82, 148 n. 85, 149 n. 86, 217
Thomas, Felix 14 n. 17
Turner, Geoffrey 7 n. 26, 11 n. 1, 12 n. 5, 74 n. 133, 174 n. 4, 178 n. 27, 211
Uehlinger, Christophe 74 n. 133
Ulmer, Rivka 5 n. 14
Ungnad, Arthur 178 n. 26
Ur, Jason 195 nn. 131–32, 196 nn. 135–36 and 140, 219
Ussishkin, David 7 n. 25, 65 n. 96, 73 nn. 129–30, 74 n. 133, 75 n. 137, 77 n. 143, 83 n. 163, 214
Vallat, François 110 n. 12, 115 n. 35
Van Buylaere, Gretta xi
Van De Mieroop, Marc 7 n. 28, 21 n. 65, 22 n. 66, 93 n. 22, 111 n. 17, 120 n. 58, 126 n. 84, 150 n. 93, 216
Van Der Brugge, Caroline 61 n. 85, 64 n. 95, 67, 68 n. 109, 71 n. 121, 214
Van Leeuwen, Cornelis 82 n. 160
Vargyas, Peter 159 nn. 30 and 34, 218
Vaughn, Andrew G. 53 n. 47, 76 n. 141, 214
Veenhof, Klaas R. 29 n. 3, 117 n. 47, 213
Verbruggte, Gerald P. 103 n. 65
Verheyden, Joseph 1 n. 1, 5 n. 14
Villard, Pierre 163 n. 49, 218
Von Soden, Wolfram vii, 71 n. 123, 121 n. 64, 144 n. 65, 147 nn. 81–82
Wäfler, Markus 74 n. 132
Walker, C. B. F. 17 n. 41, 139 n. 38, 189 n. 94
Watanabe, Kazuko x, 39 n. 57
Waters, Matthew William xii, 117
Weidner, Ernst Friedrich 158 n. 26
Weissert, Elnathan 13 n. 52, 130 n. 101, 216
Wertime, Theodore A. 192 n. 117
Whiting, Robert M. xi, 105 n. 76, 161 n. 39, 181 n. 42, 215
Wickerstam, John M. 103 n. 65
Wilkinson, Tony J. 195 n. 129

Winter, Irène J.   12 n. 5, 173 n. 3, 190
   n. 103, 208 n. 6, 212, 219
Yamada, Shigeo   x
Younger, K. Lawson   52 n. 47, 214
Yurco, Frank J.   66 n. 101, 86 n. 175
Zamazalová, Silvie   67 n. 106
Zawadski, Stefan   80 n. 153, 147 n. 78,
   149 n. 88, 161 n. 39, 217
Zevit, Ziony   75 n. 138, 78 n. 146
Zilberg, Peter   83 n. 164, 214

Index of Personal Names

Abdi-liti, king of Arwad (ca. 701) 60
Abdimilkot, king of Sidon (ca. 677) 59
Abdimilkuti. *See* Abdimilkot
Abibaal, king of Samsimuruna (688–681) 138
Abydenus, Greek historian (second century CE) 103, 149
Adad-shumu-usur, exorcist from Nineveh, son of Nabû-zuqup-kênu 163
Adapu, first of the seven mythical antideluvian sages 19
Adinu, nephew (son of a sister) of Merodach-baladan 48
Adrammelek, son of Sennacherib according to the Bible 148
Adremelos. *See* Urdu-Mullissu
Ahat-Abisha, daughter of Sargon and wife of Ambaris 15, 33, 37
Ahaz, king of Judah (ca. 735–719) 14
Ahî-Mîti, king of Ashdod, brother of Azuri 32, 61
Ahiqar, high official at the court of Sennacherib and Esarhaddon 4, 5 n. 14
Alexander III the Great, king of Macedonia (336–323) 8
Alexander Polyhistor, Roman historian (first century BCE) 103
Ambaris, king of Tabal/Bit Purutash, son of Hullî 15, 33–34
Andromachos, name given by Josephus to the murderer of Sennacherib 149
Apkallatu. *See* Te'elhunu
Aplaya, palace herald of the crown prince 162
Aplaya, "third man" of the crown prince Urdu-Mullissu 139
Aplaya, exorcist from Nineveh 163
Arad-Ninlil. *See* Ardi
Archimedes, Greek mathematician from Syracuse (ca. 285–212) 159 n. 31, 199 n. 150, 199 nn. 152–53, 200 n. 54, 200 nn. 6–8, 209, 218
Ardi, supposed son of Sennacherib 148
Ardumuzan. *See* Urdu-Mullissu
Argishti II, king of Urartu (713–679) 33–35
Ariazâ, co-ruler or crown prince of Kumme 34
Ariye, king of Kumme 34–36
Ashpa-bara, king of Ellipi xv, 51, 205
Ashurbanipal, king of Assyria (668–627) 2, 12 n. 6, 13, 16, 30, 41 n. 66, 57, 123, 134, 138–40, 142, 146, 163–64, 166, 188–89, 200
Ashur-bêlu-usur, governor of Katmuhi, eponym in 695 104
Ashur-etellu-ilâni-mukîn-apli. *See* Esarhaddon
Ashur-gimilli-tirri, treasurer of the crown prince 162
Ashur-ilî-muballissu, (second-eldest?) son of Sennacherib 17
Ashur-nâdin-shumi, king of Babylon (700–694), oldest son of Sennacherib xv–xvi, 91, 93, 106, 111, 114, 136, 138–39, 155, 188, 205–6
Ashurnasirpal II, king of Assyria (883–859) 12, 21, 49, 187, 201

Ashur-rêsûwa, royal delegate of Kumme, reporting on Urartian activities 35–37

Ashur-shumu-ushabshi, son of Sennacherib 17, 184

Atalia, wife of Sargon II 13–14, 83 n. 162

Aya-râmu, king of Edom 60

Azekah. *See* Hezekiah

Azuri, king of Ashdod, deposed by Sargon shortly before 711 32

Balassû, exorcist of Nineveh under the reigns of Sennacherib and Esarhaddon 163

Banîtu, queen of Assyria, possibly the same as Iabâ 14, 136

Banûnu, cohort commander of the queen 156

Basqânu, brother of Iatie, queen of the Arabs 48

Bazia, crown prince of Ukku 97

Bêl-êmurrani, commander of the right, eponym in 686 156

Bêl-ibni, king of Babylon (703–700) xv, 48 n. 23, 88, 90 n. 8, 91, 93, 154–55, 205, 215

Belibos. *See* Bêl-ibni

Bêl-ushezib, Babylonian astrologer, exorcist from Nineveh 163

Berossus, Babylonian priest (end of fourth century BCE) 4, 15 n. 24, 47 n. 18, 93, 103 nn. 65–66, 148–49, 149 n. 86

Bûdi-il, king of Ammon 60

Cleopatra (VII), queen of Egypt (69–30 BCE) 8

Dadâ, exorcist from Nineveh under the reigns of Sennacherib and Esarhaddon 144

Daltâ. *See* Taltâ

David, king of Israel and Judah (ca. 1010–970) 55, 79

Elulaios. *See* Lulî

Erîba-Marduk, Chaldean chief, king of Babylonia (769–761) 45

Esarhaddon, king of Assyria (680–669) x–xi, xvi, 2, 4, 6 n. 22, 13, 15 n. 25, 16–17, 18 n. 47, 30, 41, 58–59, 87, 111 n. 18, 123–24, 128–29, 133 n. 1, 134–37, 139–43, 143 n. 60, 144–45, 145 n. 67, 146–47, 147 n. 81, 148–52, 154, 162–64, 167, 206, 209, 216

Eusebius of Caesarea, Greek historian (fourth century CE) 103

Gabbu-ana-Ashur, high official, possibly palace herald under Sargon II 36

Gahal, family name of Nergal-ushezib, king of Babylonia 112

Gidgiddânu, individual working in Khorsabad 39

Gurdî, Tabalian ruler of Kulummu xvi, 105–106, 205

Gurdî, ruler of Til-Garimmu and Urdutu on the border of Tabal 104–106

Hallushu. *See* Hallutash-inshushinak I

Hallutash-inshushinak I, king of Elam (699–693) 110–11, 113–14, 116

Hazail, leader (king) of the Arabs under the reigns of Sennacherib and Esarhaddon 123–24

Herodotus, Greek historian (fifth century) 4, 5 n. 14, 69 n. 113, 82 nn. 159–60, 124 n. 81, 201 n. 162

Hezekiah, king of Judah (719–699) 61 n. 85, 86 n. 177

Hiram II, king of Tyre (ca. 739–730) 55

Hullî, king of Tabal/Bit-Purutash 34

Humban-haltash I, king of Elam (689–681) 123, 137

Humban-haltash II, king of Elam (681–675) 137

Humban-menânu, king of Elam (692–689) 115–18, 120–21, 123, 137, 150

Humban-nimena. *See* Humban-menânu

Humban-undasha, commander of the Elamite army 118

Humban-untash. *See* Humban-undasha

Hunnî, teacher of Sennacherib 14, 18

Iabâ, Assyrian queen, wife of Tiglath-pileser III 14

INDEX OF PERSONAL NAMES

Iatie, queen of the Arabs 48
Ilu-isse'a, governor of Damascus, eponym in 694 139
Isaiah, biblical prophet 22 n. 67, 32, 70 n. 118, 77–78, 79 n. 149, 81, 149–50, 215
Ishtarhundu. *See* Shutruk-nahhunte II
Ittobaal, king of Sidon (ca. 701) 58–61, 78
Jonah, biblical prophet 182 n. 46, 194 n. 124
Josephus, Jewish historian (first century CE) 5 n. 14, 53 n. 50, 55 n. 58, 56 n. 61, 69 n. 113, 77, 149 n. 87
Kaqqadanu, Urartian commander-in-chief 37
Karib-il, king of Saba 138
Kirûa, city ruler of Illubru xv, 101–102, 106
Kudur-nahhunte, king of Elam (693–692) 113–16, 166
Kutur-nahhunte. *See* Kudur-nahhunte
Lulî, king of Tyre (ca. 728–695) xv, 53, 56, 57 n. 66, 58–60, 84, 88
Maniye, king of Ukku under the reign of Sennacherib and possibly earlier xv, 96–99, 205
Man-ki-Harran, majordomo of the crown prince 162
Mannu-kî-assâr-lê'i, cohort commander of the queen 156
Marduk-apla-iddina II. *See* Merodach-baladan II
Marduk-balâssu-iqbi, king of Babylonia (ca. 818–813) 46
Marduk-nâdin-ahhê, king of Akkad 127
Marduk-nâdin-ahhê, king of Babylon (1099–1082) 128
Marduk-rêmânni, governor of Kalhu 71
Marduk-zâkir-shumi I, king of Babylonia (854–819) 46
Marduk-zâkir-shumi II, king of Babylonia (704) 45

Mattan II, king of Tyre (ca. 729) 56
Menahem, king of Samsimuruna 60
Menander of Ephesus, Greek author (second century BCE) 4
Merodach-baladan II, king of Babylon (721–710, 704 or 703) 45 n. 13, 46–48, 53, 72, 88, 90 n. 8, 91–92, 108, 120, 135–36, 205
Midas, king of Mushku/Phrygia (ca. 738–695) 34, 101
Minuhimmu. *See* Menahem
Mitinti, king of Ashdod 60–61, 63, 78
Mitûnu, governor of Isâna, eponym in 700 90
Murshili I, Hittite king (ca. 1595) 166
Mushezib-Marduk, king of Babylonia (692–689) 91, 108, 112–13, 115–18, 120, 123, 126–27
Mutallu, king of Kummuhu 33
Nabonidus, king of Babylonia (555–539) 129, 149–50, 150 n. 91
Nabopolassar, king of Babylonia (625–605) 129
Nabû-bêl-shumâti, official in charge of the city of Hararatu 48
Nabû-dênî-epush, governor of Nineveh, eponym in 704 44
Nabû-dur-ilishu, priest from Tarsus 104
Nabû-etir-napshati, official from Nimrud 39
Nabû-lê'i, majordomo of Ahat-Abi-sha 33, 37
Nabû-lê'i, governor of the province of Birtu, eponym in 702 37, 50, 52
Nabû-mukîn-zêri, chief of the Chaldean tribe of Bît-Amukâni, king of Babylonia (731–729) 46
Nabû-nâsir, king of Babylon (747–734) 46
Nabû-riba-ahhe, subordinate of the crown prince, from Nineveh 31
Nabû-sharru-usur, governor of Marash/Marqasi, eponym in 682 145, 148, 156

Nabû-sharru-usur, "third man" of the queen 156
Nabû-sharru-usur. *See* Sharezer
Nabû-shuma-ishkun, son of Merodach-baladan II 120, 148
Nabû-shuma-ukîn II, rebellious candidate to the throne of Babylon (732) 46
Nabû-zêr-kitti-lîshir, governor of the Sealand, son of Merodach-baladan 135–36, 138
Nabû-zêru-lêshir, son of Nabû-zuqup-kênu, scribe 163
Nabû-zuqup-kênu, scribe from Nimrud 163, 174
Naqi'a, wife of Sennacherib xii, 15–17, 26, 141 n. 52, 141–43, 145 n. 69, 151–52, 165 n. 63, 206
Nergal-shumu-ibni, son of Sennacherib, possibly crown prince of Babylonia 17, 140 n. 43
Nergal-ushezib, king of Babylonia (693) 112, 116
Nero, Roman emperor (37–68 CE) 8
Nibê, king of Ellipi 51
Nicolaus of Damascus, Greek historian from Damascus (ca. 64 CE) 149
Nikkal-iddin, governor of Ur 136–37
Padî, king of Ekron 60, 64–65, 65 n. 97, 68, 72, 78
Ptolemies, Greek kings of Egypt, successors of Alexander III 200
Pulû. *See* Tiglath-pileser III
Qurdi-ashur-lâmur, Assyrian official, possibly settled at Ushu 55
Rabsaris, probably the chief eunuch 77
Rabshakeh, probably the chief cupbearer 72, 77–78, 78 n. 147, 214
Rahianu, king of Damascus (ca. 750–732) 76
Raimâ, mother of Sennacherib 14–15
Rezin. *See* Rahianu
Rûkibtu, king of Ashkelon 63
Rusâ I, king of Urartu (730–714) 34, 37–38

Sama', horse raiser of the crown prince 140
Samsî-Addu. *See* Shamshi Adad I
Sargon II, king of Assyria (722–705) x–xi, 1–2, 2 n. 4, 4, 8 n. 29, 9 n. 32, 12–14, 14 n. 17, 15 n. 27, 16, 18 n. 48, 19–20, 20 n. 57, 22, 29–30, 30 n. 4, 31–32, 32 nn. 11 13 15, 33 nn. 17 22, 34 nn. 24 26, 35 n. 31, 36 n. 34, 37 nn. 42–43, 38 n. 48, 39 n. 58, 40–41, 41 n. 67, 42–43, 43 nn. 2 3, 44 n. 6, 45 n. 12, 46–47, 47 nn. 18 22, 48 n. 23, 49 n. 26, 50 n. 32, 51 n. 39, 52 n. 45, 53 n. 48, 55–56, 56 n. 62, 57, 61 nn. 83 85, 63 n. 86, 66 nn. 101 103, 71 n. 120, 72, 83–84, 85 n. 171, 86–88, 90 n. 8, 93 n. 22, 96–97, 97 n. 39, 99, 101 n. 57, 102, 103 n. 69, 104 n. 74, 105 n. 80, 106, 111 n. 17, 114, 133 n. 1, 138, 142 n. 54, 147, 150 n. 93, 153–55, 156 n. 11, 160–61, 161 n. 38, 162 n. 41, 163, 165, 169 n. 85, 173 n. 3, 174 nn. 5 8, 177 n. 23, 189, 202 n. 166, 203–204, 204 n. 1, 205, 206 n. 2, 209, 211–13, 215–16
Sargon of Akkad/Agade, king of Assyria (ca. 2335–2279) 2 n. 4
Seleukaros, name given by Josephus to the murderer of Sennacherib 149
Se'madi, village manager of the crown prince Esarhaddon 140
Semiramis, legendary queen of Assyria and Babylonia 149
Shabaka, pharaoh (ca. 720–707/6) 66 n. 101, 86 n. 175
Shabatka, pharaoh (accession year, ca. 707/6) 66
Shadditu, daughter of Sennacherib and sister of Esarhaddon 17
Shagarakti-Shuriash, Kassite king who reigned over Babylonia (1245–1233) 134
Shalmaneser III, king of Assyria (858–824) 46, 52, 157, 171
Shalmaneser V, king of Assyria (726–722) x, 14, 18–19, 29, 46, 156 n. 11

Shamash-ibni, chief (king) of Bît-Dakkûri   137
Shamash-sharru-usur, chief eunuch of the crown prince   162
Shamash-shumu-ukîn, king of Babylonia (667–648)   13, 111, 140
Shamshi-Adad I, king of Ekallâtum (ca. 1807–1776)   167
Shamshi-Adad V, king of Assyria (823–811)   46
Sharezer, son of Sennacherib (Nabû-sharru-usur) according to the Bible   17
Sharru-lû-dâri, king of Ashkelon, son of Rûkibtu   63, 155
Sharru-lû-dâri, military official active in the Urartian border   36
Shilta, ghost king of Tyre   56 n. 62
Shulmu-bêli, cavalryman under the command of Sharru-lû-dâri   36
Shulmu-bêli, deputy of the palace herald Gabbu-ana-Ashur   36
Shulmu-bêli, governor of Talmusu, eponym in 696   100
Shulmu-sharri, governor of Halziatbar, eponym in 698
Shusanqu, Egyptian, possibly husband of Shadditu   17
Shutruk-nahhunte II, king of Elam (717–699)   47, 51, 111
Shûzubu. *See* Mushezib-Marduk
Shûzubu. *See* Nergal-ushezib
Sidqâ, king of Ashkelon   53, 60–61, 63–64, 70, 155
Sillâ, Assyrian official   148
Silli-Bêl, king of Gaza   61, 78
Sin-sharru-ishkun, king of Assyria (ca. 627–612)   13
Solomon, king of Israel and Judah (ca. 970–931)   55
Tab-shar-Ashur, chief treasurer, governor of the Mashennu province, eponym in 717   39
Taharqa, pharaoh (689–664)   66–67, 67 n. 104, 85–87, 87 n. 180
Taltâ, king of Ellipi (737–713)   51

Tartan, probably the commander-in-chief   77
Tashmêtu-sharrat, wife of Sennacherib   15, 17, 26, 165, 181
Te'elhunu, queen of the Arabs   123–24
Tiglath-pileser I, king of Assyria (1114–1076)   127, 187
Tiglath-pileser III, king of Assyria (744–727)   x–xi, 2 n. 3, 14, 18, 22, 29, 46, 49, 51, 55–56, 66, 76 n. 142, 105
Tûâiu, individual working in Khorsabad   39
Tuba'lu. *See* Ittobaal
Tukultî-Ninurta I, king of Assyria (1243–1207)   134, 166, 171
Ubaru, governor of Babylon   129
Ullusunu, Mannean ruler   83
Ulûlâyu. *See* Shalmaneser V
Urdu-Mullissu, son of Sennacherib   148–49
Uru-milki I, king of Byblos (ca. 701)   60
Urzana, king of Musasir   36, 51
Yakinlu, king of Arwad (ca. 670–660)   57
Yamani, king of Ashdod   32, 61
Zakûtu. *See* Naqi'a

www.ingramcontent.com/pod-product-compliance
Lightning Source LLC
Chambersburg PA
CBHW021701230426
43668CB00008B/693